Introduction
to Digital Libraries

Introduction to Digital Libraries

G G Chowdhury

Sudatta Chowdhury

facet publishing

Published by
Facet Publishing
7 Ridgmount Street
London WC1E 7AE

Facet Publishing (formerly Library Association Publishing) is wholly owned by CILIP: the Chartered Institute of Library and Information Professionals.

First published 2003

British Library Cataloguing in Publication Data

A catalogue record for this book is available from the British Library.

ISBN 1-85604-465-3

Typeset from author's disk in 11/14pt Elegant Garamond and Humanist 521 by Facet Publishing.
Printed and made in Great Britain by MPG Books Ltd, Bodmin, Cornwall.

To

Reetee, Reek, Reevu, Ritun and Oli

Contents

Preface

Recent developments in information and communication technologies, particularly the world wide web, coupled with the increasing availability of research funds in the UK, USA and other parts of the world, have given birth to a number of digital libraries. While many of these have been developed in the course of research projects, a growing number of universities, national libraries, professional associations, etc., are also investing in building digital libraries. The development of digital libraries is bringing about significant change in the creation, access, use and management of information.

Digital library research and development activities around the globe have brought together experts from many different fields. Many new digital library courses are now being offered at universities, both in library and information science and in computer science programmes. The major objective of these courses should be to provide a holistic view of digital library issues and challenges, with a correct balance between theoretical and practical knowledge. Students of digital library courses, as well as novice researchers in the field, need to know about the underlying technology, i.e., the infrastructure and technological issues; the challenges of creation (by digitization or acquisition), organization and retrieval of various types of information; the user and service implications; as well as the various social, economic and political issues. The dream of successful digital libraries leading to a global digital environment can only be fulfilled when we have people adequately trained to design, build and manage them.

Purpose

This book aims to provide a comprehensive view of digital libraries. Design, development and management of digital libraries involve a number of skills ranging from ICT (information and communication technology) to library and information management skills. The issues involved in the design and management of digital libraries range from purely technical matters of design and architecture, digitization, storage and retrieval of digital objects and so forth, to information processing, retrieval, and service-related questions. A large number of research projects have been undertaken, or are currently under way, to resolve these and a host of other issues. Digital libraries are also bringing about significant changes to the information and library profession, resulting in the need for information professionals to acquire a number of new and improved skills. This book aims to cover all these issues, and uses appropriate examples from the currently available digital library and research projects to illustrate them.

Audience

The book is primarily intended for students researching digital libraries as part of information and library science, as well as computer science, courses. However, it will also help practising professionals who need to know about recent developments in the field of digital libraries, and digital library researchers who want to become more familiar with the latest research issues and related research projects. Examples have been drawn from digital libraries and research projects from around the world, and the book is appropriate for readers across the globe.

Sources

In order to illustrate the text, we have included screenshots of selected digital library products and services. Requests were made to the concerned parties for permission to reprint screenshots of their web pages. Fortunately, most gave permission on time, and in this section we have acknowledged them. Whilst every effort has been made to obtain permission, please contact the publisher if there is any query.

Figures 7.1, 7.2 and 7.3: Reprinted with kind permission of the Director of the Centre for Digital Library Research, University of Strathclyde, on behalf of the BUBL Information Service.

Figures 7.4 and 7.5: Source: www.unige.ch/biblio/ses/cyberdewey.html.

Figures 7.6, 7.7, 7.8 and 7.9: Reprinted with kind permission of INFOMINE, The Regents of the University of California.

Figures 7.10 and 7.11: Reprinted with kind permission of Internet Scout Project.

Figures 7.14 and 7.15: Reprinted with kind permission of SOSIG, a service of the RDN.

Figure 7.19: Reprinted with kind permission of the Renardus project and service (www.renardus.org).

Figure 8.2: Source: www.acm.org.

Figure 8.3: Materials related to the THOMAS digital library of the US Library of Congress are in the public domain.

Figures 8.4 and 8.5: Reprinted with kind permission of California Digital Library, the Regents of the University of California.

Figures 8.6, 8.7, 8.11, 8.12 and 8.13: Reprinted with kind permission of VT ETD, an initiative of the Digital Library and Archives of the University Libraries at Virginia Tech.

Figures 8.8 and 8.10: Reprinted with kind permission of NCSTRL.

Figure 8.9: Hyperbolic Tree, now called Star Tree, image reprinted with kind permission of Inxight Software, Inc.

Acknowledgements

We would like to express our sincere thanks to all the publishers and institutions who have given us permission to use the screenshots of their products and services as examples in this book. We would like to thank the people at Facet Publishing, London, without whose constant support and help this book would not have seen the light of the day. Thanks to our parents and relatives, who have always encouraged us to accomplish this task. Finally, we would like to thank our two charming sons, Avirup and Anubhav who have always been our sources of inspiration. They have been very considerate and co-operative through the whole process.

G. G. Chowdhury and Sudatta Chowdhury

Chapter 1

Digital libraries: definition and characteristics

Outline

Digital libraries have been defined differently by researchers and practitioners. Two major categories of definitions are available, one focusing on the access and retrieval of digital content and the other focusing on the collection, organization and service aspects of digital libraries. Definitions that fall into the first category come mainly from researchers who are computer scientists and engineers, while those in the second category come mainly from library and information professionals. This chapter looks at several definitions of digital libraries and discusses their major characteristics. It then looks at the potential benefits of building digital libraries. Finally an outline of the book is presented with brief information on the purpose and content of each chapter.

Introduction

Recent developments in information and communication technologies, especially the internet and the web, have brought significant changes in the ways we generate, distribute, access and use information. For centuries we have been used to printed information sources; publishers have played a key role in the generation of printed information while distributors, booksellers and especially libraries have played a key role in the distribution of information. For hundreds of years we have been used to using printed information sources – either by purchasing them, or by using them through libraries. The situation began to alter about four decades ago with the introduction of computers in information handling, and there has been a dramatic change over the past few years.

The first use of computers in information management opened the door to new ways of accessing and using information, making it possible to create and access electronic indexes to collections, electronic databases of journal articles, conference papers, and so on. This was a new era and, in addition to using the printed information resources, people could access electronic databases of information resources created locally and accessible remotely. Over the years, remote online information search services became a regular part of our information-seeking and information use patterns. These services did not replace libraries of printed material, but enhanced information access and use by exploiting information and communication technologies. Subsequently libraries began to convert their card catalogues to the electronic catalogue databases which eventually became the online public access catalogues (OPACs), providing local as well as remote access.

Another major change in the process of the storage, retrieval and dissemination of information was brought by the invention of CD-ROMs. Major databases began to appear on the new medium, facilitating distribution and access. Users could access electronic information sources – bibliographic as well as non-bibliographic databases – at their own end, in libraries, offices, and so on. Although CD-ROM databases became an obvious competitor of online search services, they did not replace them. As a result end-users had more choices for access to information – publishers continued to publish printed as well as electronic information resources, on CD-ROM and/or in the form of electronic databases for local and remote access. Dictionaries, encyclopedias and many other information sources began to appear in more than one format – print as well as electronic. In most cases, people either had to buy information sources or go to libraries to use them, either for free or upon payment of a fee. This situation continued till the appearance of the internet and especially the web. Within a span of ten years or so, the web has made a tremendous impact on all aspects of our life, especially in matters related to the generation, distribution and use of information.

One of the most important contributions of web technology has been the creation of digital libraries, which allow users to access digital information resources from virtually anywhere in the world. Recent developments in information and communication technologies, including the web, and the availability of research funding have led to the development of digital library research projects, many of which have resulted in working digital libraries.

Rapid developments in the field of digital libraries all over the world have given rise to a large number of publications appearing in different forms. *Communications of the ACM* (Association of Computing Machinery) has brought out three special issues on digital libraries (38/4, 1995; 41/4, 1998 and 41/5, 2001), as has the *Journal of the American Society for Information Science* (44/8, 1993; 51/3, 2000 and 51/4, 2000). *Information Processing and Management* (35/3, 1999) and the *Journal of Visual Communication and Image Representation* (7/1, 1996) have had one special issue each. In addition, thousands of articles and reports have appeared in different media – in e-journals like *D-Lib Magazine* and *Ariadne*, in various ACM journals, library and information journals, at conferences (e.g. the ACM and Joint ACM/IEEE-CS Conferences on Digital Libraries, the European Digital Library Conference and the International Asian Digital Library Conference), in workshops, and on various project, institutional and personal web pages. The extent of digital library research has been reviewed recently in an ARIST chapter (Fox and Urs, 2002).

What are digital libraries? How do they differ from online databases and search services? Will they replace print libraries? What impact will they have on people and society? Many such questions are obvious and occur to people every time they come across the concept of digital libraries. While these are general matters, there are many technical issues as well. For example, what sort of technological infrastructure will be needed to make the dream of digital libraries a reality – that every person in the world will have instant access to the information that he/she needs in digital form with minimum effort and costs? There are other issues too. What will happen to the multi-million-dollar publishing industry? What will happen to the existing print resources? Can we preserve all the existing as well as newly generated information in digital form? How can we control access to the digital resources? Who owns them, and how can ownership be asserted? And so on.

This book aims to address various issues related to digital libraries. It begins with a general introduction to the concept. By analysing various definitions of digital libraries, this book tries to identify their major characteristics, which may be used to decide how they differ from print libraries or electronic databases. It also identifies the various issues related to the development, management and use of digital libraries. There are many technical and social issues involved, and some of these issues are discussed with reference to the current state of research aimed at resolving some of the underlying problems. A look at the current state of research in digital libraries in the world shows a number of promising advances as well as gaps. The book highlights some of both.

What is a digital library?

Several definitions of digital libraries are available in the literature. Many of these definitions were formulated in the course of digital library research projects. Consequently they have been influenced by the people involved in the projects, their understanding of the concept of libraries vis-à-vis electronic databases, and also by the nature of the research project. Borgman (1999; 2000b, Chapter 2) analyses a number of definitions of digital libraries and concludes that there are two major classes: (1) those coming from digital library researchers – who in the US context are mostly computer scientists and engineers – and (2) those coming from library and information professionals. According to Borgman (1999, 239):

> The research community's definitions serve to identify and focus attention on research problems and to expand the community of interest around those problems. The library community's definitions focus on practical challenges involved in transforming library institutions and services.

In the following sections we shall review some definitions with a view to understanding the connotation of digital libraries.

Emphasis on digital content

Borgman (2000b, 40) suggests that the first research-oriented definition of digital libraries appeared in 1992 when the phrase 'electronic libraries' was used for what is now called digital libraries. Incidentally, that definition was given by Borgman herself (Borgman, 1993) and was included in a report by Fox also in 1993. Since then many definitions of digital libraries (variously called digital libraries, electronic libraries and virtual libraries) have appeared in the literature. While reviewing these definitions, Borgman (1999) notes that 'in general, researchers (who primarily come from a computer science and/or engineering background) focus on digital libraries as content collected on behalf of user communities, while librarians focus on digital libraries as institutions or services'.

So two different schools of thought, one emphasizing the 'enabling technologies' and the other the 'service aspects' of digital libraries, may be noted in the literature. The articles appearing in two special issues of the *Journal of the American Society for Information Science* (2000a; 2000b) provide excellent accounts of digital library research, especially in the USA, but none focus on digital library services *per se*. Chen in his editorial (2000) emphasizes the access to information and suggests the various methods, tools and techniques that facilitate improved access to information in digital libraries.

Emphasis on services

However, Marchionini and Fox (1999) in their editorial in the special issue of *Information Processing and Management* (1999) on digital libraries state that 'Digital library work occurs in the context of a complex design space shaped by four dimensions: community, technology, services and content.' They further suggest that:

- The community dimension of digital libraries reflects social, political, legal and cultural issues.
- Technology serves as the engine moving the digital library field, including technical progress in computing, networking, and more specifically information storage and retrieval, multimedia, interface design, and so on.
- Services form the central focus of digital libraries and future digital libraries should facilitate digital reference services, real-time question answering, on-demand help, information literacy and user involvement mechanisms.
- Content represents all possible kinds of form and genre of information, printed as well as digital.

The fact that digital libraries should not be regarded only as a point of access to digital information was emphasized by the definition of digital libraries given by Borgman as early as 1992 when she asserted that a digital library (then defined as electronic library) is a combination of: '(1) a service; (2) an architecture; (3) a set of information resources, databases of text, numbers, graphics, sound, video, etc. and (4) a set of tools and capabilities to locate, retrieve and utilize the information resources available' (Borgman, 2000b, 41). The Stanford digital library research team defined a digital library as a co-ordinated collection of services that are based on collections of materials, some of which may not be directly under the control of the organization providing a service in which they play a role (Reich and Winograd, 1995). The latter part of this definition reflects an important characteristic of digital libraries.

The definition of digital libraries provided by Arms points towards the management aspects of digital collections and services. According to Arms (2000b, 2), a digital library is a 'managed collection of information, with associated services, where the information is stored in digital formats and accessible over a network'. The definition provided by Oppenheim and Smithson, on the other hand, lays emphasis on digital technologies. According to them, a 'digital library is an information service in which all the information resources are available in computer processable form and the functions of acquisition, storage, preservation, retrieval, access and display are carried out through the use of digital technologies' (Oppenheim and Smithson, 1999, 97).

The consensus opinion from a Delphi study conducted by Kochtanek and Hein (1999) suggests that an array of expertise is required to collect, organize and deliver digital information, and the primary role of librarians in digital library development will be an extension of what has been going on for decades. The fact that digital libraries have a major role to play in society has been emphasized in the definition given by Borgman: 'Digital libraries encompass two complementary ideas, one emphasizing that they extend and enhance existing information storage and retrieval systems, incorporating digital data and metadata in any form; the other emphasizing that the design, policy, and practice should reflect the social context in which they exist' (Borgman, 1997).

Perhaps the most comprehensive definition of a digital library, which emphasizes both the technical and service aspects, came up in the course of the 1994 IEEE CAIA Workshop on Intelligent Access to On-line Digital Libraries (Gladney et al., 1994):

> A digital library is an assemblage of digital computing, storage, and communications machinery together with the content and software needed to reproduce, emulate, and extend the services provided by conventional libraries based on paper and other material means of collecting, cataloging, finding, and disseminating information. A full service digital library must accomplish all essential services of traditional libraries and also exploit the well-known advantages of digital storage, searching, and communication.

Hybrid libraries

Although the term digital library is used widely in the literature, a new term, 'hybrid library', appeared in the course of digital library research in the UK. A hybrid library has been defined as a library where digital and printed information resources co-exist and are brought together in an integrated information service accessible locally as well as remotely (HyLife, 2002a). A number of researchers believe that for the foreseeable future we shall live in the world of hybrid libraries that will integrate traditional libraries with the emerging digital ones (for example, Oppenheim and Smithson, 1999; Pinfield et al., 1998; Rusbridge, 1998). Pinfield et al. (1998) comment that the hybrid library is on the continuum between the conventional and digital library, where electronic and paper-based information sources are used alongside each other. Rusbridge (1998) suggests that a hybrid library brings a range of technologies from different sources together, and integrates systems and services in both the electronic and print environments. He further argues that 'the name hybrid library is intended to reflect the transitional state of the library, which today can neither be fully print nor fully digital'.

From the above definitions, it may be noted that digital libraries are meant to deal with digital materials, whereas hybrid libraries deal with both printed and digital materials. However, this distinction is not always maintained in practice. Many digital libraries, for example the California Digital Library at the University of California and iGEMS, the digital library at Nanyang Technological University in Singapore, deal with both traditional and digital information resources, though they are called digital libraries and not hybrid ones. In this book we have chosen to use the term digital libraries to denote both digital and hybrid libraries. However, in some cases the term hybrid library has been used specifically to indicate that the issues, tools and techniques under discussion appeared and/or developed in the course of the hybrid library projects in the UK.

Characteristics of digital libraries

Historically, libraries have been described as the 'storehouses of knowledge'. The famous Five Laws of Library Science of Ranganathan (1931) were the first source to give a user- and service-centred view of libraries. The five laws are:

1   Books are for use.
2   Every reader his book.
3   Every book its reader.
4   Save the time of the reader.
5   A library is a growing organism.

These laws, although apparently very simple, describe the philosophy of libraries by emphasizing the collection, service and users. Several researchers have analysed the philosophy of librarianship, and of late many (for example Brophy, 2000; Clayton and Gorman, 2001) have attempted to study the implications of these philosophies on the modern-day library.

The above definitions reveal the various characteristics of digital libraries; they also to some extent define their role and functions, and differentiate them from traditional libraries. Many researchers have discussed the specific characteristics of digital libraries (for example Arms, 2000b, 4; Chowdhury and Chowdhury, 1999; Oppenheim and Smithson, 1999). The major characteristics may be described as follows.

- Digital libraries may contain a variety of digital information resources ranging from text to image, audio and video.
- Digital libraries largely reduce the need for the physical space required for building and maintaining traditional libraries.
- Digital library users may be distributed anywhere in the world, and in some cases several different levels of services have to be designed to meet the needs of local as well as remote users.
- Unlike in traditional libraries, digital library users may build their own personal collection(s) by using the facilities provided by digital libraries, for example in the HeadLine hybrid library and in iGEMS, the digital library of Nanyang Technological University, Singapore (both discussed later in this book), users can build their own digital collection in their personal workspace for future use.
- Digital libraries provide access to various types of information resources that may reside on different servers around the globe, and hence infrastructure, interoperability (discussed in Chapter 4) and so on, are very critical issues in digital library development and management.
- Several users can use the same information resource at the same time, which is not possible in a traditional library.
- Digital libraries have brought a paradigm shift not only in the use of information (from print to digital), but also in the concept of ownership. Most digital libraries provide access to materials that they do not own; some of this may be available for free and some provided upon payment of a fee.
- Libraries have for many years used collection development policies as excellent filtering mechanisms. Library staff do not collect all the materials potentially available; rather, they select only that portion considered most suitable for their target users. Collection development policies have largely been guided by the principle of 'the best book for the right user at the right time'. This role will be even more crucial in the digital world, since there the problem is not availability of information but 'information overload', and therefore digital libraries should use appropriate mechanisms for filtering out what is unwanted.

- In order to fulfil the dream of building a truly global information infra-structure, digital libraries should be able to handle multilingual information resources.
- Digital libraries presuppose the absence of human intermediaries, and hence appropriate mechanisms should be put in place to support users with all the different levels of IT, subject and linguistic skills.
- Digital libraries should allow for better searching and retrieval facilities.
- Digital information can be viewed and used by different people according to their individual needs.
- Digital libraries break time, space and language barriers. Ideally, users from anywhere in the world should be able to use a digital library at any time and possibly in any language.

The impact of digital libraries

Building and managing digital libraries involves huge intellectual and financial resources. Hundreds of millions of pounds have already been spent on digital library research and development activities throughout the world. In the USA, over US$68 million have been awarded for digital library research: over US$24 million was awarded in 1994 as part of the first Digital Library Initiative (DLI 1), and about US$44 million has been allocated for the second phase (DLI 2) (Fox, 1999; Griffin, 1999). Research on digital libraries in the UK has largely been funded by the Electronic Libraries (eLib) programme. Rusbridge (2001) mentions that the three phases of eLib had a cost in excess of £20 million. In addition, many digital library projects have been funded by libraries, institutions and universities, the costs of which are not included in the figures shown here. A large number of digital library projects have also been undertaken in Europe and in other parts of the world (Lesk, 1999a, 1999b; see also Chapter 3 for details).

If such a huge amount is spent on research, one can imagine how big the budget required to build fully fledged digital libraries will be. Many researchers (for example, Bishop, 1999) believe that we have yet to see how digital libraries are going to support the full life cycle of information from document identification, to reviewing and filtering, to reading, and finally to the application of the information in the work or in problem solving, which subsequently gives birth to new information.

So, why should we build digital libraries, and how are they going to help us in different walks of life? Arms (2000b, 4) provides a simple answer to this question: 'Digital libraries are being built with the belief that they will facilitate better delivery of information than was possible in the past.' Digital libraries are bringing a paradigm shift in the creation, distribution, management and use of information. While authors and publishers are now focusing more and more on digital publications, digital libraries through improved access and management of these resources are facilitating the consumption, creation and sharing of knowledge in different sectors of human society. Arms (2000b, 4–7) lists a number of benefits of having digital libraries. An extended list of the potential benefits is given below. A closer look at these points will help us justify the resources required for building and managing digital libraries.

A digital library brings information to the user

As mentioned above, digital libraries can be used from anywhere, and users can access and retrieve information, provided appropriate access management mechanisms are in place, from anywhere in the world. Hence, one can say that instead of users going to the library for information, digital libraries bring the information to users in real-time (when they need it).

Improved searching and manipulation of information

Digital libraries facilitate improved access to information by providing various sophisticated search and retrieval facilities. Details of the information retrieval facilities provided by the currently available digital libraries are discussed in Chapter 9. There have been significant improvements in the end-user search facilities provided by electronic database search services and web search engines (Arms, 2000a).

Improved facilities for information sharing

Digital libraries provide improved facilities for information sharing among users. Many companies, institutions and research groups are using the resources of the internet and digital libraries to share information among members by notification, file sharing and co-operative document preparation and use. Digital libraries greatly facilitate these activities.

Timely access to information

Digital libraries help users get up-to-date information. The usual time lag between the creation of information and its access in a traditional library setting is significant. This time lag is usually reduced by digital libraries with the help of the web and digital publishing, and quick inclusion of digital information in the digital library's collection and services. The improved search and retrieval features of digital libraries also allow users to search for, and use, information on a particular timescale, for example information published within a particular period. The hypertext features also allow inquisitive users to navigate among sources to discover the origin and growth of a new concept within a discipline. Digital libraries will help users view the same information in a number of ways by using various software and/or visualization techniques.

Improved use of information

Digital libraries break the barriers of time, space, language and culture, thus improving the use of information. Information generated in other parts of the world, in a different language, or from a different culture, can easily reach users. Improved research in information retrieval and user interfaces may also allow us to present or repackage the same information differently as appropriate for different categories of users – for example children, adults, professionals or managers. This will eventually lead to an improved knowledge management environment (discussed in detail in Chapter 15).

Improved collaboration

Research at the University of California at Berkeley shows that digital libraries facilitate improved collaboration among users (Wilensky, 2000). Many researchers (for example, Borgman, 2000a; Wilensky, 2000) comment that such improved collaboration will have a profound impact on the scholarly information life cycle – the process by which researchers and scholars create, use and disseminate information.

Reduction of the digital divide

While the recent developments in information and communication technologies, especially the internet, have reduced the distance between people in the world, there still exists a big gap between nations and people in terms of infrastructure, facilities and resources. This increasing gap is called the digital divide. The Organization for Economic Co-operation and Development (OECD; www.oecd.org) defines digital divide as the gap between individuals, households, businesses and geographic areas at different socio-economic levels with regard to (1) their opportunities to access information and communication technologies and (2) their use of the internet for a wide variety of activities. Ross

Shimmon, the Secretary General of the International Federation of Library Associations and Institutions (IFLA) comments that the digital divide is one of the biggest issues facing the world today (Shimmon, 2001a). Digital libraries, by breaking the barriers of distance, time, language and culture, can play a significant role in reducing the digital divide. This is discussed in detail in Chapter 12.

The structure of this book

Libraries have always been classified into different groups, for example by the community of users, or parent body, that they serve – academic library (school or university library), public library, research library or business library; the type of materials that they handle – music library, patent library or map library; or by the age of user groups that they cater for – adults' library, children's library or youth library. The digital library is a new addition to this list of categories. However, from the definition and characteristics of digital libraries discussed in Chapter 1, we can see that digital libraries are somewhat different from the other categories. They may deal with any or all of the different types of materials, or they may be designed to serve all or any specific group of users, or a specific type of institution, and so on. Another characteristic feature is that they are virtual – digital libraries do not need to have massive buildings, a large visible collection of materials or a group of people working in them. The nature and characteristics of some selected digital libraries from around the world are discussed in Chapter 2. These discussions are intended to give an overall understanding of existing digital libraries.

As discussed earlier in this chapter, a tremendous amount of research activity has gone into the tasks of building digital libraries, and many large and small research projects are currently in progress in different parts of the world. The characteristics of some major digital library research projects in the USA, UK, Europe and other parts of the world are discussed in Chapter 3.

Digital libraries overcome the barriers of geographical distance, language and culture. In a true global digital library environment, virtually anyone should be able to access and use a digital library from anywhere in the world. To make digital libraries this versatile is not easy. A number of issues are involved here, including architecture, interoperability and standards. Chapter 4 addresses these issues.

Building a collection in a digital library is a complex task. Recent developments in the internet and web have brought a revolution in the world of the publication, distribution and management of information resources. A digital library may contain information in any form and in any format – text, audio, video, multimedia, and so on – running on any software and hardware platform from anywhere in the world. Digital libraries, unlike traditional libraries, provide access to information resources that are owned by others. Thus, collection development and management tasks have become complex. Various issues of collection management in a digital library are discussed in Chapter 5.

A large part of a digital library will comprise information resources generated within the organization, for example theses and reports in a university, and documents, reports, and e-mail messages in a company or in a public sector office. Digitizing these collections and managing them as part of the digital library is a challenging task. A number of technical and management issues are involved, ranging from the conversion of the printed text to digital form, to the storage of the various files, their indexing, retrieval issues, and so on. This is the theme of Chapter 6.

Libraries have played an excellent role in organizing information resources. Tools and techniques for the cataloguing and classification of library resources were developed long ago, and they have been used successfully. As a result, in big libraries like the Library of Congress, one can locate a particular item from among millions. Subsequently, with the appearance of various non-print media such as audio and video cassettes, films and compact discs, improvements have been made in cataloguing techniques in order to help libraries handle these materials. One of the burning questions for digital library managers is whether traditional tools and techniques can be used in managing digital resources and, if so, how best this can be done. Several researchers have been trying to develop appropriate tools and techniques for organizing digital library resources. Chapter 7 addresses these issues.

Many digital libraries have been built specifically to benefit local as well as remote users. For example, the Networked Digital Library of Theses and Dissertations (NDLTD), at Virginia Tech., USA (www.theses.org) is available to anyone for access to electronic theses of a number of universities in the USA and in other parts of the world; the Networked Computer Science Technical Reference Library (NCSTRL; www.ncstrl.org) is a digital library in the USA comprising computer science resources that are accessible to users from anywhere in the world. There are many such examples. Users of these digital libraries may come with varying degrees of IT and linguistic skills, varying subject backgrounds, and varying information needs. Some digital libraries on the other hand are designed for a defined set of users, such as the California Digital Library, or a homogenous group of users, such as the ACM digital library. In every case, user interfaces form an important part of any digital library. The issues of digital library users, their information needs and the consequences of these needs for the design of user interfaces are discussed in Chapter 8.

One of the objectives of a digital library is to allow users to search and retrieve the required information as easily as possible. Again, the basic tenet of a digital library is that there will be no human intermediary in the information search and retrieval process. This means that the user interface and the search and retrieval mechanisms should be so simple that every member of the user community can use the facilities easily. Building such a hassle-free information retrieval system, which is capable of handling multilingual and multimedia information coming from virtually anywhere, and developed using any hardware and software, is a great challenge. Chapter 9 addresses these information retrieval issues.

In addition to serving their users, libraries have traditionally played another major role in society: preserving knowledge. The major libraries in the world have invested huge resources in the preservation of their resources. However, with digital libraries there will be a major shift – ownership of information will be replaced by access rights. Hence libraries will no longer be directly responsible for the preservation of information resources. There is another problem, especially with web information resources. Since many digital resources frequently change their content, presentation and location, mechanisms need to be developed for digital libraries to keep track of these changes and of different versions of the same resources. Digital archiving, preservation and related issues are discussed in Chapter 10.

It is often said that a library is not judged by its buildings, collections or people, but by its services. This is even truer for digital libraries since their overall objective is to provide improved information services. For many years libraries have been providing valuable reference and information services to their users. With the advent of the web the concept of reference and information services has changed significantly. Several free and fee-based information services are now available through the web. So, what will the role of digital libraries be in the context of reference and information services? How will manual and traditional online reference services (current awareness and selective dissemination of information) take shape in digital libraries? These issues are addressed in Chapter 11.

Libraries have always played a significant role in society, and digital libraries, with the promise of breaking the barriers of geographical distance, language and culture, have a potentially even more significant social role. Digital libraries will not only change our reading and information use habits, they are also going to bring major changes in the economic models of information generation, distribution and management functions. Consequently there are many related social, economic and legal issues, including privacy and security, and so on. These issues are discussed in Chapter 12.

The evaluation of library and information systems and services has always been difficult. It has become even more so in the case of digital libraries, as additional factors are involved. It is necessary to take into account such aspects as: contents, services, infrastructure, information retrieval, user interfaces and networking. Digital library research and development is at a very early stage so very few detailed evaluation studies have been conducted so far. Nevertheless, several researchers have addressed various issues related to digital library evaluation. Chapter 13 discusses these.

One of the major characteristics of digital libraries is that they reduce the direct involvement of human intermediaries in the process of information access by end-users. Nevertheless, in order to build and manage effective and efficient digital libraries, library and information professionals need to be more versatile. They need to acquire a number of technical as well as information skills. The role of library and information professionals in the age of digital libraries is the theme of Chapter 14.

A tremendous amount of research and development activity has gone into the study of digital libraries. Many issues have been addressed and problems have been partly or fully resolved. Researchers from a variety of disciplines, such as library and information science, computer science and engineering, and social sciences and humanities, are working closely together to look into the myriad of unresolved issues. Chapter 15 discusses the trends of digital library research and development.

Chapter 2
Features of some digital libraries

Outline

A large number of digital libraries have been developed throughout the world over the past few years. Many of these have been born in the course of digital library research and development activities. They differ in terms of such matters as their nature and characteristics, content and facilities. This chapter provides a brief overview of some selected digital libraries from around the globe. Through these discussions, this chapter aims to provide an idea of the variety of digital library available today in different parts of the world.

Introduction

Interest in digital libraries, both scholarly and professional, grew very rapidly in the 1990s. However, the basic notion of digital libraries differed according to the contexts, approaches, emphasis, practices and views of the researchers. For example, early digital library developments in the USA took place mainly in the course of research led primarily by the computer science community that concentrated on designing and developing technologies for various digital library systems, developing interfaces, improving search facilities, and so on; later the research also focused on digital library collections, users and services as well (Fox and Urs, 2002). However, in the UK, the picture was different from the beginning. The library and information science community took the initiative and thus digital library research mainly focused on enhancing the information collection and services.

Nevertheless, as a result of digital library research in the USA, UK, Europe and in other parts of the world, a number of digital libraries have been established during the past ten or so years. These digital libraries differ in terms of their objectives, content, facilities, and so on. In this chapter we shall briefly discuss the features of some digital libraries chosen from around the globe.

Digital libraries: types

Digital libraries can be grouped in different ways. They can be classified by origin, such as digital libraries developed in the USA as part of DLI 1 and DLI 2 (the Digital Library Initiatives), digital libraries developed in the course of the eLib (Electronic Libraries) programme in the UK, digital libraries built by individual institutions, digital libraries that are part of national libraries, digital libraries that are part of universities; or by period, by country of origin, and so on. For our discussions in this chapter we have grouped the chosen digital libraries as follows:

- early digital libraries, e.g. ELINOR, Gutenberg
- digital libraries of institutional publications, e.g. ACM, IEL
- digital library developments at national libraries, e.g. the British Library, Library of Congress (THOMAS), Digital Library of Canada
- digital libraries at universities, e.g. Berkeley Digital Library SunSITE, Bodleian Library Digital Library Projects, California Digital Library, DIG-ILIB, iGEMS and SETIS
- digital libraries of special materials, e.g. Alexandria, Informedia, Grainger Engineering Library
- digital libraries as research projects, e.g. GDL, NCSTRL, NDLTD
- digital libraries as hybrid library projects, e.g., HeadLine.

Brief information on 20 digital libraries is provided in this chapter and detailed discussions of their specific characteristics, such as information organization, information retrieval and user interfaces, are provided in the later chapters in this book.

Table 2.1 presents some general information about the chosen digital libraries, namely the parent organization or institution hosting the digital library, type of digital library, nature and type of information.

Table 2.1 *Basic information on selected digital libraries*

Name	ELINOR
Type of digital library	Early digital library
Main organization	De Montfort University
Nature	Early digital library providing network access to electronic materials within a university campus
Type of information	Scanned images of books, journals, course materials, multimedia learning packages, etc.
Name	Gutenberg
Type of digital library	Early digital library
Main organization	University of Illinois
Nature	Digital library of early texts in literature
Type of information	Full texts of documents mainly on literature
Name	ACM Portal: the ACM digital library
Type of digital library	Digital library of institutional publications
Main organization	ACM
Nature	Digital library of institutional publications
Type of information	ACM publications including journals, magazines, conferences, etc.
Name	IEL Online
Type of digital library	Digital library of institutional publications
Main organization	IEEE
Nature	Digital library of institutional publications
Type of information	IEEE publications including journals, conference papers, technical reports and standards, etc.
Name	The British Library's digital library programme
Type of digital library	Digital library as part of a national library
Main organization	The British Library
Nature	Digital collection of a national library
Type of information	Text, moving and still images on various subjects
Name	THOMAS
Type of digital library	Digital library as part of a national library
Main organization	Library of Congress
Nature	Digital library of a specific collection of a national library
Type of information	Full texts of legislative and Congressional records, proceedings, etc.
Name	Digital Library of Canada
Type of digital library	Digital library as part of a national library
Main organization	National Library of Canada

continued

Table 2.1 *continued*

Nature	Digital library of specific collections of a national library
Type of information	Music – from encyclopedia of music to music collections on gramophone records, history – text and images, literature – texts and manuscripts including children's literature
Name	Bodleian Library Digital Library Projects
Type of digital library	Digital library at a university
Main organization	Oxford University
Nature	Digital library of images, manuscripts and early journals
Type of information	A number of collections of images, manuscripts and early journals
Name	California Digital Library
Type of digital library	Digital library at a university
Main organization	University of California
Nature	Hybrid library
Type of information	From OPACs to electronic databases, e-journals and internet resources
Name	DIGILIB
Type of digital library	Digital library at a university
Main organization	University of Queensland
Nature	Digital library of images
Type of information	Architectural image database
Name	iGEMS
Type of digital library	Digital library at a university
Main organization	Nanyang Technological University, Singapore
Nature	Hybrid library
Type of information	From OPACs to electronic databases, e-journals, local digital library resources and internet resources
Name	SETIS
Type of digital library	Digital library at a university
Main organization	University of Sydney
Nature	Digital library of humanities databases and theses
Type of information	Full-text databases of Australian studies resources, manuscripts, theses, etc.
Name	Berkeley Digital Library SunSITE
Type of digital library	Digital library developed in the course of the US Digital Library Initiatives
Main organization	University of California at Berkeley

continued

Table 2.1 *continued*

Nature	Digital library of text and images
Type of information	A variety of text and image collections
Name	Alexandria Digital Library
Type of digital library	Digital library developed in the course of the US Digital Library Initiatives
Main organization	University of California at Santa Barbara
Nature	Digital library of spatial information
Type of information	Spatial information – text, maps and other geographical information
Name	Informedia Digital Video Library
Type of digital library	Digital library developed in the course of the US Digital Library Initiatives
Main organization	Carnegie Mellon University, USA
Nature	Multimedia digital library
Type of information	Digital video
Name	Grainger Engineering Library Information Center
Type of digital library	Digital library developed in the course of the US Digital Library Initiatives
Main organization	University of Illinois at Urbana-Champaign
Nature	Digital library of engineering resources
Type of information	Full text of books, journal articles, reports, etc., on different branches of engineering
Name	Greenstone Digital Library
Type of digital library	Digital library originated as a research project
Main organization	Greenstone Digital Library, University of Waikato, New Zealand
Nature	Digital library of different types of information resources
Type of information	Collections of text, manuscripts and images on various subjects, and music
Name	NCSTRL
Type of digital library	Digital library originated as a research project
Main organization	Cornell University
Nature	Digital library of computer science literature
Type of information	Full text of books, journal articles, reports, theses, etc., on computer science literature
Name	NDLTD
Type of digital library	Digital library originated as a research project
Main organization	Virginia Tech, USA

continued

Table 2.1 *continued*

Nature	Digital library of theses and dissertations
Type of information	Full text of theses and dissertations submitted at various US and international universities
Name	HeadLine
Type of digital library	Hybrid library as part of the eLib Phase 3 programme
Main organization	London School of Economics
Nature	Hybrid library with provisions for personal information environment (PIE)
Type of information	e-journals, locally digitized materials, secondary sources (e.g. BIDS, IBSS, ECONLit, SOSIG, Biz/Ed), local course-related materials (e.g. reading lists, exam papers), catalogues, commercial intermediaries (e.g. subscription agent services, FT Profile), real-time data services (e.g. newswires, financial markets data) financial datasets and government information

Brief descriptions of selected digital libraries

A brief description of each chosen digital library is provided in the following sections.

Early digital libraries

ELINOR

ELINOR (Electronic Library Information Online Retrieval) was the first electronic library project in the UK, starting in 1992 and continuing until April 1996, and was funded by De Montfort University, the British Library and IBM UK (Ramsden et al., 1998). The project started with the objective of building an electronic library system that could be directly accessed by students and staff via Window-based PCs and workstations. It was a two-phase project: the first phase (March 1992–May 1994) focused on the technical issues of delivering scanned images of books, journals, course materials, multimedia learning packages, and so on; and the second phase (June 1994–April 1996) aimed to develop better copyright management, and the user and modelling aspects of the electronic library.

A prototype web interface was developed for general users, and a prototype electronic library user interface (ELVIS) was developed for those who were visually impaired. Initially, the subject coverage of the system was limited to the business and computing needs of the pilot undergraduate course. However, the coverage was later extended to the high-demand core texts such as reading lists provided by academic staff for the other courses taught in the University. Users browsed, viewed, searched and printed electronic collections of high-use (copyright) materials, examination papers and other university documents. Full-text searching and hierarchical browsing were possible in this system. Natural language queries and fuzzy searching were also available.

Gutenberg (http://gutenberg.hwg.org/)

Project Gutenberg started in 1971 at the Materials Research Lab at the University of Illinois. The main objective of the project was to provide easy access for the general public to the humanities literature available in electronic format. It is one of the oldest digital libraries, with a collection of electronic texts mainly on literature, which is grouped as: light literature and heavy literature, and references. Electronic texts are stored in ASCII format so that they can be read and searched using most of the hardware and software in use all over the world. The digital library can be searched with a simple search program.

Digital libraries of institutional publications

ACM Portal: the ACM Digital Library (www.portal.acm.org/)

The ACM (Association of Computing Machinery) digital library provides access to:

- over 69,000 full-text articles from ACM journals, magazines and conference proceedings
- tables of contents with nearly 23,000 citations from articles published in ACM journals and magazines from 1954 onwards
- tables of contents with more than 48,000 citations from articles published in over 990 volumes of conference proceedings since 1985.

Selected works published by affiliated organizations are also available. Members of the Association and registered users can access the digital library through the ACM digital library portal website. Users can search and browse the digital library by magazines, transactions, proceedings, journals, newsletters, affiliated organizations and by special interest groups (SIGs). The search engine has some unique search features, which are discussed in Chapter 9.

IEL Online (www.ieee.org/products/onlinepubs/iel/iel.html)

The IEEE/IEE Electronic Library (IEL) is a digital library of publications from the Institute of Electrical and Electronic Engineers (IEEE) and the Institution of Electrical Engineers (IEE). IEL provides access in one single source to almost a third of the world's current electrical engineering and computer science literature comprising:

- more than 750,000 documents from over 12,000 publications, including journals, conference proceedings and IEEE Standards
- more than two million full-page documents, including all original charts, graphs, diagrams, photographs and illustrative material
- more than 25,000 new pages per month
- full-text archives of IEEE and IEE publications from 1988 to the present
- unlimited access to a subset of the INSPEC bibliographic and abstract database.

Members of the Institute and Institution and registered users can search and browse the entire collection through a simple search interface.

Digital library developments at national libraries

The British Library's digital library programme

The British Library's Research and Innovation Centre is leading the Library's digital library programme, which entails establishing a number of digital information services based on the content of the British Library's collections including text, images, sound and a combination of these. 'The British Library on the web' contains information about the Library, the collections and about its services. The Treasures section of the British Library website includes information on a selection of the major literary treasures in the British Library's collections. Two items that are available in their entirety over the web are the Magna Carta and the Gutenberg Bible. The Library has many other unique and important items in digital form from early manuscripts to sound recordings.

THOMAS (http://thomas.loc.gov/)

THOMAS, a digital library of the Library of Congress established in January 1995, is a comprehensive library of federal legislative information. THOMAS currently offers the following databases:

- *House Floor This Week*. For the current week (when the House is in session), the date and time of the House session is listed, along with bills that are expected to be passed under suspension of the rules or expected to receive floor action. The file is updated throughout the week when the House is in session.
- *House Floor Now*. For the current legislative day, floor actions occurring in the House are listed in reverse chronological order.
- *Quick Search of Text of Bills*. Searches text of legislation for current Congress by word, phrase or bill number.
- Legislation:
  - *Bill Summary and Status*. Information about bills and amendments.
  - *Bill Text*. Searchable by word, phrase and number.
  - *Public Laws by Law Number*: Summary and status records for each bill that became public law, listed by law number and in bill number sequence.
  - *House Roll Call Votes*
  - *Senate Roll Call Votes*
- *Congressional Record*:
  - *Most Recent Issue*
  - *Congressional Record Text*. Searchable by word or phrase, by Member of Congress and/or date or date range.
  - *Congressional Record Index*
  - *Days-in-Session Calendars*
- Committee information:
  - *Committee Reports*. Searchable by word or phrase, report number, bill number, committee; searches can be limited by type of report (House, Senate, Conference, Joint).
  - *Committee Home Pages*. Browsable links to House and Senate Committee home pages residing on House and Senate servers.
  - *House Committees*. Browsable links to House servers with information on (1) schedules and oversight plans for each of the House committees, and (2) selected hearing transcripts from some of the House committees. Because each committee provides its own hearing schedules, there is no common format.
  - *Senate Committees*. Browsable links to Senate servers with information on Senate hearing schedules.

In addition, the THOMAS home page provides the following links of interest to the legislative searcher including:

- Frequently Asked Questions
- House and Senate Directories
- Congressional Internet Services
- Library of Congress Web Links
- The Legislative Process:
  — House: How Our Laws Are Made
  — Senate: Enactment of a Law
- Summary of Congressional Activity
- Historical Documents
- US Congressional Documents and Debates: 1774–1873.

Each collection can be browsed or searched separately by appropriate criteria.

Digital Library of Canada (www.nlc-bnc.ca/index-e/html)

The National Library of Canada (NLC), under its digital library programme, has built the Digital Library of Canada, which provides access to digital libraries of music, history and literature. Users can select any specific digital library from the main NLC web page that will lead the user to the specific digital library's page showing the list of resources accessible under each collection. Users can select any particular resource and the corresponding search/browse screen appears. In addition to text, specific search options for images and music are also provided.

Digital libraries at universities

Bodleian Library Digital Library Projects (www.bodley.ox.ac.uk/)

A number of digital collections have been built under the Bodleian Library Digital Library Projects umbrella:

- the John Johnson Collection of Printed Ephemera
- images of manuscripts arranged by century and country of origin
- early manuscripts at Oxford University: over 80 early manuscripts now in institutions associated with the University of Oxford
- the Bodleian Library/Toyota City Imaging Project

- the Internet Library of Early Journals: a digital collection of 18th- and 19th-century journals
- the Broadside Ballads Project: holdings of over 30,000 ballads ranging from the 16th to the 20th century
- Oxford examination papers online
- the Todhunter Allen Collection of maps and county atlases.

Each collection can be browsed separately.

California Digital Library (www.cdlib.org/about/overview/)

The California Digital Library (CDL) was founded in 1997 at the University of California. It provides access to the following digital resources:

- the Online Archive of California (OAC): a digital information resource that facilitates and provides access to materials such as manuscripts, photographs and works of art held in libraries, museums, archives and other institutions across California
- Counting California: government data and statistics about California
- the Melvyl® Catalog: records for materials (books, archives, audiovisual materials, computer files, video recordings, dissertations, government documents, maps, music scores and recordings) in the libraries of the nine UC campuses with over 10 million unique titles representing over 15 million holdings
- the California Periodicals database containing periodicals, newspapers, annuals, some monographic series, and other ongoing publications owned by more than 550 California libraries
- electronic journals: thousands of e-journals from major scholarly publishers and information providers
- abstracting and indexing databases: abstracts and indexes to tens of thousands of journals for scholarly research, instruction and reference
- specialized and reference resources: such as the Web of Science, government data and *Encyclopedia Britannica* online.

Users can select a particular collection for searching and/or browsing. The SearchLight option allows users to conduct a cross-database search in specific collections. Details of the user interfaces and information retrieval features of CDL appear in Chapters 8 and 9.

DIGILIB (www.architect.uq.edu.au/digilib/)

DIGILIB is an initiative of the Department of Architecture and the University Library, University of Queensland, Australia, providing easy access to a collection of architectural images of Queensland historic buildings including a wide range of domestic, public, mining and agricultural buildings. A simple search interface allows users to enter search keywords or phrases, and searches can be limited by selecting a specific collection, a specific format of image (for example sheet images) and a sort criteria. The advanced search interface allows users to conduct complex searches by selecting various options from drop-down boxes, such as town name, building type (e.g. agricultural, commercial, educational), features (e.g. arches, circular), structure (e.g. concrete, steel, timber) and context (e.g. cliffs, cloud, grass).

iGEMS (http://gemsweb.ntu.edu.sg/iGems/)

iGEMS (i-Gateway to Educational and Media Services) was launched as GEMS in April 1999. It is an internet-based university portal that provides essential information on Nanyang Technological University, Singapore (NTU).

A number of digital library services are available through iGEMS, such as:

- consolidated search, which allows users to select a number of data sources including subscribed databases, the NTU web pages, public folders, OPAC and NTU publications
- access to library resources online, viz. audiovisual, online CD-ROMs and databases, e-journals, multimedia resources, full-text NTU publications such as theses, applied research projects, final-year projects, the OPAC and subject guides to authorized users
- access to EdveNTUre, the campus online learning platform maintained by the Centre for Educational Development, to authorized users
- personalized information services on such topics as campus news and events, conferences, seminars and talks, short courses and recent library acquisitions and resources, and an AV programme listing, new title alerts from publishers, event calendar, and so on
- selective dissemination of information (SDI) services that include new title alerts, new preview resources from the library, conference announcements, resources from other institutions or organizations.

SETIS (http://setis.library.usyd.edu.au/ozlit/)

The Scholarly Electronic Text and Image Service (SETIS) was formed in 1995 at the University of Sydney Library. It provides access to a large number of networked and in-house full-text databases, primarily humanities texts. SETIS also provides access to digital theses. The Australian studies resources comprise a number of collections such as:

- the Australian Federation Full Text Database
- Australian Literary and Historical Texts
- Australian Literature Articles from the AustLit Database
- the John Anderson Papers at the University of Sydney
- Joseph Henry Maiden's Botanical Works
- Journals of Inland Exploration
- R. W. Parson's Australian Taxation Law
- the Henry Lawson Manuscripts.

The 'browse all texts' option allows users to browse the collection by author, title or subject. Alternatively, users can conduct a search by keywords or phrase. A search can be limited by field (e.g. title, author), collection, etc. The 'digital theses' option links to locally stored theses available in PDF (portable document format), as well as to the national distributed database.

Berkeley Digital Library SunSITE (www.cdlib.org/about/overview/)

The objective of this project was to develop tools and technologies to support models of the scholarly information life cycle in a distributed, continuous and self-publishing mode. A large variety of digital information resources are now accessible through this digital library, such as:

- the Advanced Papyrological Information System (APIS): the largest US collection of papyri from a single site
- the American Heritage Project: collections documenting American history and culture
- the Anthropology Emeritus Lecture Series – UC Berkeley: biographical and bibliographical selections featuring the UC Berkeley Anthropology Faculty
- Association of Research Libraries (ARL) @ SunSITE: a collection of digital-library-related documents from ARL

- Bridging the Bay: Bridging the Campus: a collaborative exhibit documenting the design and politics of San Francisco Bay Area bridges
- California Heritage: a collection of thousands of photographs relating to the history of California
- Catalonian Manuscripts
- Current Cites: the complete collection of this annotated monthly bibliography of selected articles, books and electronic documents on information technology
- Days of Cal: a virtual tour through the history of the University of California, Berkeley
- Digital Scriptorium: a joint project of the Bancroft Library (UC Berkeley) and the Rare Book and Manuscript Library of Columbia University to digitize and make available on the world wide web the two universities' medieval and early Renaissance manuscript holdings
- Electronic Reserves at UC Berkeley: online course readings for UC Berkeley classes
- the Emma Goldman Papers: selected documents and photographs relating to Emma Goldman's life and work as well as indexes to thousands of other documents and photographs available in collections aroound the world
- the Free Speech Movement: a co-operative project between the Bancroft Library and the FSM-A; funding provided by Stephen M. Silberstein
- Government Documents Round Table
- the Jack London Collection: materials that reflect on the life and influence of one of turn-of-the-century America's most enduring authors
- The Last Jews of Libya: a site chronicling some of the last Jews remaining in Libya, by photographs, writings and the spoken word
- Literature @ SunSITE: a collection of literature, largely US authors at the moment
- Making PCR (Polymerase Chain Reaction): a collection of documents relating to the history of the discovery of PCR
- Mapping the Icelandic Genome
- NCSTRL: Networked Computer Science Technical Reports Library
- Online Archive of California
- the Online Medieval and Classical Library: a collection of medieval and classical texts
- Oral Histories Online: oral histories from the UC Berkeley Regional Oral History Office.

Users can search the Berkeley Digital Library SunSITE though a simple search interface where the user is expected to enter a word or a phrase. The user can also select a particular collection for more detailed searching and/or browsing.

Digital libraries of special materials

Alexandria Digital Library (www.alexandria.ucsb.edu/frames1.html)

The Alexandria Digital Library (ADL) was designed in 1995 to provide access to a large range of maps and images to text and multimedia using spatially indexed information. The major objectives of ADL were:

- research on issues critical for the construction of distributed digital libraries of geospatially referenced, multimedia materials
- the development of technologies necessary to support such a library
- the design, construction and evaluation of test-bed systems based on research and development results
- the resolution of organizational and technological issues underlying the transition from test-bed system to operational digital library.

ADL has a collection of geographically referenced materials in earth and social sciences such as maps, images and texts and datasets in multimedia form. The datasets include the following:

- metadata and basic data
  — AVHRR imagery
  — digital elevation models (DEMs)
  — digital raster graphics (DRGs)
  — scanned aerial photographs
  — Landsat™
  — Seismic datasets and technical reports
  — Sierra Nevada Ecologic Project datasets
  — Mojave Ecologic Project datasets
- metadata only
  — gazetteers
  — Geodex
  — GeoRef

— Mojave bibliography
— PEGASUS map records.

ADL can be browsed and searched through the Map Browser interface (http://webclient.alexandria.ucsb.edu/), as well as through the ADL Gazetteer Server (http://fat-albert.alexandria.ucsb.edu:8827/gazetteer/). Interesting search and retrieval features of ADL are discussed in Chapters 8 and 9.

Informedia Digital Video Library (www.informedia.cs.cmu.edu/)

The Informedia project at Carnegie Mellon University has pioneered new approaches for automated video and audio indexing, navigation, visualization, search and retrieval. The Multilingual Informedia project developed automated systems and tools to enable multilingual and multimedia information capture, search, retrieval, summarization and reuse. The second phase of the project, Informedia-II, deals with video information summarization and visualization.

Grainger Engineering Library Information Center (www.library.uiuc.edu/grainger/)

This digital library of engineering information at the University of Illinois at Urbana-Champaign has a variety of collections including:

- article databases, such as Compendex, INSPEC, Current Contents, NTIS and the Applied Science and Technology database
- Grainger databases, such as multiple local databases, multimedia database, new books database and the reference collection
- electronic journals, such as ACM journals, IEEE journals, and full-text journals in physics, computer science and civil engineering
- special resources, such as patents, standards and technical reports
- web resources.

Each collection has a specific search interface that can be used to search the collection.

Digital libraries as research projects

Greenstone Digital Library (www.nzdl.org/cgi-bin/library)

The Greenstone Digital Library (GDL, formerly the New Zealand Digital

Library) aims to develop the underlying technology for digital libraries and make it available to the public. GDL provides access to a number of collections ranging from Computer Science to Human Computer Interactions, a Frequently Asked Questions archive, Humanity Development Library, Indigenous Peoples, Youth Oral History Collection and Music – audio and video collections. Users can choose a specific collection that has a specific search and browse screen attached to it. Interesting search and retrieval features of GDL are discussed in Chapters 8 and 9.

NCSTRL (www.ncstrl.org/)

NCSTRL (Networked Computer Science Technical Reference Library) is a digital library of computer science research reports and papers made available for non-commercial use from a number of participating institutions and archives. Most of the NCSTRL institutions are universities that grant PhDs in computer science or engineering, with some industrial or government research laboratories. The objective of NCSTRL was to develop a distributed technical reports library containing a collection of technical reports relating to computer science from the institutions or organizations offering PhD programmes in computer science or engineering in different parts of the world. NCSTRL covers computer science technical reports from computer science departments and industrial and government research laboratories from different parts of the world, and its collection is available from the servers of the participating institutions from anywhere and to anybody in the world. Author, year and institution can be searched using the browse index facility, or keywords can be searched for under abstract and title. From the search results users can link to full-text documents subject to the authors' terms and conditions.

NDLTD (www.ndltd.org)

NDLTD (Networked Digital Library of Theses and Dissertations) was designed to build a digital library of theses and dissertations by Masters and doctoral students from various universities in the USA and around the globe. It started at Virginia Tech, USA. Subsequently many institutions in the USA and overseas joined this programme to form a federation. Users accessing the NDLTD website can search theses and dissertations in Virginia Tech, or can conduct a federated search to retrieve information on theses and dissertations from all the participating institutions. The Virginia Tech Digital library of electronic theses and dissertations (ETD) covers theses and dissertations in various disciplines submitted by the students of the University. In addition to theses and dissertations the Virginia Tech ETD has electronic journals, VT Spectrum and WDBJ7 script archives. Details of the search and retrieval features of ETD appear later in this book (Chapters 8 and 9).

Digital libraries built as part of the UK hybrid library projects

HeadLine (www.headline.ac.uk)

HeadLine (Hybrid Electronic Access and Delivery in the Library Networked Environment) was one of the hybrid library projects funded under Phase 3 of the Electronic Libraries (eLib) programme of the UK higher education Joint Information Systems Committee (JISC). The project aimed to develop and implement a working model of the hybrid library in an academic environment by providing facilities for personalized access to library resources regardless of physical form via a common web interface. A wide range of search options is available. Users can browse through the subject page created by the system, through the institutional resource page – the entire collection – or through the personal subject page, called the personal information environment (PIE). The PIE is the main feature of this digital library. When a user logs in for the first time the system automatically creates an information page on the subject of interest to the user. The necessary information is gathered from the user's log-in screen. The subject page gives information on the subject and allows user to customize the page to create their personal information page.

Summary

These brief discussions of selected digital libraries show that different types of digital libraries have been developed over the past few years. Some are designed to provide access to digital resources in one or more specific types of documents or in specific subject fields, for example NDLTD and NCSTRL. Other digital libraries were built in the course of experiments in developing enabling technologies for providing access to special type of materials, for example ADL and Informedia. Some digital libraries discussed above are perfect examples of hybrid libraries, for example CDL and iGEMS. HeadLine and iGEMS give examples of how a personal work environment can be created and supported for every user through the digital library interface. Overall this chapter shows the variety of digital libraries currently available – some accessible through membership and/or registration, while many others are available freely. Such features as their collection organization, user interfaces and information retrieval will be discussed in detail in the relevant chapters later in the book.

Chapter 3
Digital library research

Outline

Tremendous amounts of research effort have been devoted to studying different issues and problems of digital libraries. This chapter provides an outline of digital library research efforts in the USA, UK, Europe and in other parts of the world. Overall the aim of this chapter is to provide an overview of digital library research around the globe. Specific issues and the findings of some related research projects appear in other chapters.

Introduction

A great amount of work has been carried out on digital library research and development worldwide over the past decade. Digital library research in the USA has been spearheaded by the Digital Library Initiative, and in the UK by the Electronic Libraries programme (eLib). Similar research initiatives have also taken place in Europe and in other parts of the world.

Early research in digital libraries focused on technology and content rather than on people or communities (Marchionini, 1998). However, the situation has changed over time. Researchers have subsequently recognized the impact of digital libraries on organizations and societies, and vice versa, as legitimate areas of research (Muir, 20001a). Digital library research is scattered across a wide range of disciplines and published sources. Literature on digital library research may be grouped under eight thematic clusters (Bawden and Rowlands, 1999; Rowlands and Bawden, 1999): human factors, organizational factors, library management, future studies and scenarios, information law and policy, systems factors, knowledge organization and discovery, and impacts on the information transfer chain.

It would be impossible to provide information about all the research activities that have taken place so far. However, an attempt has been made here to provide an overview of digital library research around the globe.

UK

In the UK, the main umbrella digital library research and development programme has been eLib, which has concentrated mainly on the higher education sector (Pinfield, 2001a). It was in the 1990s that it became clear that electronic information would play a major role within higher education, but how the medium change would occur and what the main impact would be on libraries was not obvious (Whitelaw and Joy, 2000a, 2000b). The two main concerns were increasing costs and the growth in student numbers for higher education libraries. These issues were linked in the Follett report, which was published in December 1993. This was the report of the Joint Funding Councils' Libraries Review Group, which was chaired by Sir Brian Follett (JISC, 2000). This Group reviewed libraries and related provisions in the higher education sector in the UK, and was commissioned jointly by the four UK higher education funding bodies: the Higher Education Funding Council for England, Scottish Higher Education Funding Council, Higher Education Funding Council for Wales and Department of Education for Northern Ireland. eLib was the result of the recommendations in Chapter 7 of the report.

The programme started in 1995 with a funding of £15 million over three years, aiming to transform the use and storage of knowledge in higher education institutions (*eLib: Electronic Libraries programme*, n.d.). It was managed by the Joint Information Systems Committee on Electronic Information, through the JISC committee which was set up initially to take forward the Follett recommendations, the Follett Implementation Group for Information Technology, FIGIT (Rusbridge, 1995).

The eLib programme had three phases: Phases 1 and 2, a successful £15 million initiative over a period of three years (1995–97), sought to implement the IT recommendations from the Follett report by addressing the issue of changes within higher education libraries, whereas in Phase 3 £4.1 million was spent over three years in order to consolidate this work in a practical context and to extend Phase 1 and 2 benefits by helping to achieve 'practical mass' in key areas (Whitelaw and Joy, 2000b, 2001).

eLib 1 and eLib 2

The first two phases of eLib funded 59 projects (Rusbridge, 1998). The first phase was divided into seven programme areas, while the second mostly covered areas perceived as weaknesses in the first phase. An important overall aim was the inclusion of a wide range of stakeholders. eLib used mature technologies within a managed framework, covering a limited number of key development areas. Those in Phase 1 were (Whitelaw and Joy, 2000a):

- electronic document delivery
- electronic storage of books and journals (digitization)
- electronic journals
- on-demand publishing and the electronic book
- awareness and training
- navigational tools (access to network resources)
- supporting studies.

And in Phase 2:

- pre-prints
- quality assurance
- electronic short loans
- images.

Table 3.1 shows the achievements of the different eLib programmes areas in Phases 1 and 2 (Whitelaw and Joy, 2000a).

Table 3.1 *Achievements of eLib Phases 1 and 2*

Programme area	Total costs	No. of projects	Achievements
Electronic document delivery	£2,285,000	5	• Self-sustaining services established. • Important developments made in library co-operation. • Commercial products have also emerged.

continued

Table 3.1 *continued*

Programme area	Total costs	No. of projects	Achievements
Electronic storage of books and journals (digitization)	£500,000	2	• Different models explored issues such as copyright and total costs. • Lessons used to develop a more centralized approach.
Electronic journals	£2,905,000	12	• A variety of different approaches tested and important lessons learned, particularly user profiles. • Large number of publishers engaged. • Platforms developed which have supported National Electronic Site Licence Initiative (NESLI).
On-demand publishing and the electronic book .	£1,775,000	7	• Broad scope, tackling major issues of teaching and learning • Student users found to be very enthusiastic. • Progress made with both academic conservatism and copyright. • Work developed through the eLib Phase 3 HERON project.
Awareness and training	£2,530,000	7	• Improved staff skills and awareness. • Continuing services with good reviews from users com-munities. • Direct impact on library culture and development potential.
Navigational tools (access to network resources)	£1,920,000	9	• Services improved search quality, saving staff and students' time • Services now being developed as national services

continued

Table 3.1 *continued*

Programme area	Total costs	No. of projects	Achievements
			• Contributions to Distributed National Electronic Resources (DNER) and the Resource Discovery Network (RDN)
Supporting studies	£510,000	3	• Successful in rationalizing ongoing developments. • Essential role in synthesizing lessons from earlier eLib activities. • Highly influential in determining course for eLib Phase 3.
Pre-prints	£655,000	5	• Important lessons learnt from Phase 2 tackling specific gaps identified in the initial set of projects.
Quality assurance	£105,000	1	
Electronic short loans	£650,000	5	
Images	£1,030,000	3	
Total	**£14,865,000**	**59**	**Average project costs approximately £250,000**

The following points summarize the results of Phases 1 and 2 (Whitelaw and Joy, 2000b).

- eLib covered a number of issues involved in the development of the electronic libraries.
- A number of services have been established as a result of eLib projects, some of which are self-sustaining.
- eLib directly engaged 175 organizations in the higher education, publishing and commercial supply communities. Some of the lessons learned by these communities have already been taken up by eLib Phase 3.
- Within the higher education organizations involved, eLib has improved awareness and practical experience of the opportunities offered by electronic resources, which will allow them to adapt more effectively to rapid changes in technologies and evolving user expectations.
- Considerable developments in library co-operation have been achieved.
- eLib has raised the profile of libraries within the higher education sector and has given greater confidence to those responsible for investing in

information and communication technologies within the library system.

- eLib has achieved a high level of impact within the higher education library community and has promoted changes in its culture related to the application of electronic techniques, preparing libraries for a more project-based funding balance and combining the R & D culture with library operations.
- In some areas, such as electronic journals, the impact of eLib has been mainly limited to the higher education sector, although some valuable information on user requirements has been gained by publishers.
- eLib has not made major cost savings or directly reduced pressure on library space.
- Management of the programme has been effective and efficient and therefore the number of project failures linked to poor project management has been small.
- Two important underlying activities have been the formative evaluation work of the Tavistock Institute and eLib supporting studies which have played an important role in formulating Phase 3.
- eLib has received considerable national and international acclaim and has been used as a programme model in a number of countries.

eLib 3

Phase 3 of eLib started in 1998 with the aim of bringing developments together and building on the previous successful work with 12 projects (Whitelaw and Joy, 2001). It had four components (eLib, 1998; JISC, 2000):

- hybrid libraries
- large-scale resource discovery, or clumps
- preservation
- turning early projects into services.

Twenty-one organizations were involved in Phase 3 through clumps projects, which had not been involved previously. Table 3.2 shows the major programme areas of Phase 3. Table 3.3 shows their major achievements (Whitelaw and Joy, 2001).

Table 3.2 *Programme areas of eLib Phase 3*

Programme areas	No. of projects	Project name	Major topic focus
Hybrid libraries	5	Agora (http://hosted.ukoln.ac.uk/agora/) BUILDER (http://builder.bham.ac.uk/main.asp) HeadLine (www.headline.ac.uk/) HyLife (http://hylife.unn.ac.uk/) MALIBU (www.kcl.ac.uk/humanities/cch/malibu/index.htm)	These projects are focused on the higher education sector dealing with common problems like • authentication • user profiles • interface design • management of digitization • interconnection of databases • staff development.
Clumps	4	Co-operative Academic Information Retrieval Network for Scotland (CAIRNS) (http://cairns.lib.gla.ac.uk/) M25 Link (www.m25lib.ac.uk/M25link/) RIDING (www.shef.ac.uk/~riding/) Music Libraries Online (www.musiconline.ac.uk/)	Though these projects covered different geographical areas and subjects, they explored the possibility of virtual union catalogues using standards like Z39.50.
Preservation	1	CURL Exemplars in Digital Archives (CEDARS) (www.leeds.ac.uk/cedars/)	This project concentrated on developing guidelines for preserving different types of materials, policies for collection management, and recommendations for standards and techniques.
The turning of early projects into services	2	Higher Education Resources On-Demand (HERON) (www.heron.ac.uk/) Electronic Publishing Resource Service (EPRESS) (www.epress.ac.uk/)	HERON offers a national service to the UK academic community for copyright clearance, digitization and delivery of book extracts and journal articles. EPRESS provides tools, knowledge and information to help people publish electronic journals.

Table 3.3 *Achievements of eLib Phase 3*

Programme areas	Total costs	Achievements
Hybrid libraries	£2,188,147	• Contributed significantly to the knowledge of how hybrid libraries work in practice and their impact on various communities. • Working models were established by all five projects with positive evaluation. Wide range of content and functionality was covered. • Enough diversity to allow the community to compare and contrast the approaches. • Clear evidence of institutional embedding. • Some functionality built into commercial products. • Influence on the design of DNER. • Forward links to Managed Learning Environment (MLE) activities.
Clumps	£977,863	• Four working clumps established. • Made valuable progress on Z39.50 issues. • Important work on organizational aspects such as collection-level descriptions and access policies. • Directly developed library co-operation. • Evidence of effective exit strategies in that two major clumps which represent a substantial fraction of UK higher education have continued their work with self-funding.
Preservation	£370,000	• Tackled an important and difficult area of work. • Made recommendations in the areas addressed. • Provided a framework in the key area of cost models. • Provided higher education input to the broader debate on legal deposits of electronic materials. • High-profile project with a high level of external interest.
The turning of early projects into services	£586,000	• Maintains the development of the on-demand publishing work. • Many higher education copyright clearances are now coming via HERON. • HERON is addressing one of the critical issues in library provision – improving access to recommended study materials. • EPRESS has succeeded in developing a framework for the production of electronic journals.

Centres for research on digital libraries in the UK

The Centre for Digital Library Research (CDLR) was established in summer 1999 at the University of Strathclyde, managed jointly by the University's Directorate of Information Strategy and Department of Information Science (presently Department of Computer and Information Sciences) (Centre for Digital Library Research, 2000). The CDLR brings together long-standing research interests in the digital information area ranging from information policy and information retrieval to document storage technologies and standards. A list of projects can be accessed through the CDLR's website (http://cdlr.strath.ac.uk/). Some CDLR projects are briefly discussed below.

ASPECT (http://cdlr.strath.ac.uk/projects/projects-aspect.html)

Access to Scottish Parliamentary Election Candidate Materials 1999 was funded by the University of Strathclyde's Directorate of Information Strategy to create a digital archive of the ephemera – leaflets, flyers, postcards, newsletters – produced by candidates and political parties for the first Scottish parliamentary election in May 1999. The archive is based on the collection of election ephemera held by the Andersonian Library at the University of Strathclyde. ASPECT includes transcriptions of the text of many of the leaflets and supplementary information on electoral constituencies and regions, political parties, the electoral process and the results of the election.

BUBL (http://cdlr.strath.ac.uk/projects/projects-bubl.html)

BUBL is an internet-based information service, which was established in 1990 as Bulletin Board for Libraries for the UK higher education community. It is currently operating from the University of Strathclyde. It also provides a specialist service to librarians and information specialists. Its major services include BUBL LINK/5:15 (an internet resource catalogue), BUBL Journals, BUBL UK, BUBL News, BUBL Search, BUBL Mail, BUBL Internet Archive and Acqlink.

COPAC/CLUMPS (http://cdlr.strath.ac.uk/projects/projects-copacclumps.html)

COPAC/CLUMPS, built on the expertise acquired in recent years in the area of union catalogues (both physical and virtual), has the overall aim of reaching conclusions about the feasibility of interlinking between virtual and physical union catalogues, and of identifying technical and organizational issues.

EBONI (http://cdlr.strath.ac.uk/projects/projects-eboni.html)

EBONI (Electronic Books ON-screen Interface) developed a set of recommendations for publishing educational works on the web which reflect the needs of academics and a diversifying population of students throughout the UK. One of the major objectives of the project was to determine the most effective way of representing information in electronic books, aiming to maximize usability and information intake by users.

GDL (http://cdlr.strath.ac.uk/projects/projects-gdl.html)

GDL (Glasgow Digital Library) aims to establish a virtual co-library of the majority of public institutions in Glasgow. The main aim is to create an environment for digital resources to support teaching, learning and research at all levels in the city by bringing together materials currently separated by ownership and physical location.

HILT (http://cdlr.strath.ac.uk/projects/projects-hilt.html)

HILT (HIgh-Level Thesaurus) can be considered as an extension of the SCONE (see below) and CAIRNS projects in terms of the mapping and use of the Conspectus subject scheme. The initial purpose of the project, which has now moved on to a second phase, was to focus on the problem of cross-searching and browsing by subject across a range of communities, services and resource types.

HILT Phase 2 (http://cdlr.strath.ac.uk/projects/projects-hilt2.html)

HILT Phase 2 is focusing on terminology and thesauri requirements at the collection level as well as retrieval level. The project aims to determine the detailed requirements, costs and benefits to further education and higher education users focusing primarily on collection-level needs.

INSPIRAL (http://cdlr.strath.ac.uk/projects/projects-inspiral.html)

INSPIRAL (INveStigating Portals for Information Resources And Learning) puts its emphasis on the identification and critical analysis of issues like institutional and end-user perspectives rather than on technical issues around linking virtual learning environments (VLEs) and digital libraries.

SCONE (http://cdlr.strath.ac.uk/projects/projects-scone.html)

The SCONE (Scottish COllections Network Extension) project aims to aid researchers by extending the collaborative collection management work carried out within the framework of the Scottish Confederation of University and Research Libraries (SCURL). Broadly it also aims at investigating effective models for building and sustaining a co-ordinated Scotland-wide distributed national resource that would be conveniently accessible to researchers via the CAIRNS distributed catalogue, the Research Collections Online-based dynamic clumping service, and SCURL inter-access policies. The project also aims to provide online information and other facilities to assist library staff in jointly handling collaborative collection management processes in order to get the best out of limited national resources.

USA

In the United States, digital libraries were designated a 'national challenge application area' under the High Performance Computing Communications (HPCC) initiative, and a key component of the National Information Infrastructure (Borgman, 2000a). The Digital Library Initiative (DLI) is a major US research and development initiative. The Digital Library Initiative 1 ran over the period of 1994 to 1998 and Initiative 2 is now underway for the period 1999–2004. In addition an international digital libraries programme was announced in 1998 by the National Science Foundation (NSF).

DLI research covers three areas (Borgman, 2000b):

- the capturing of data and metadata of all kinds (text, images, sound, speech, etc.), and categorizing and organizing them
- advanced software and algorithm for browsing, searching, filtering, abstracting, summarizing and combining large volumes of data, imagery and all kinds of information
- the use of distributed networked databases.

DLI 1 mainly focused on research done by researchers with technical backgrounds, principally in computer and information sciences, whereas DLI 2 has expanded the scope of research by including researchers of different disciplines (Lesk, 1999a).

Compared with those of DLI 1, DLI 2 projects include far more concern for the social, behavioural and economic aspects of digital libraries, and include research areas encompassing a broader range of academic disciplines, reflecting most of the issues raised in the definition from the Social Aspects of Digital Libraries Workshop sponsored by the National Science Foundation. The call for research divided the main research focus into human-centred research, content- and collection-based research and systems-centred research. Other topics addressed are testbeds and applications (Borgman, 2000b).

Digital Library Initiative 1 (DLI 1)

DLI 1 was a $24 million programme funded by the NSF, the Defense Advanced Research Projects Agency (DARPA) and National Aeronautics and Space Administration (NASA) for a five-year period (1994–98) (Digital Library Initiatives, 2002; Fox, 1999; Griffin, 1999). The funding was split evenly among six DLI 1 teams: the University of California at Berkeley's Digital Library project, the University of California at Santa Barbara's Alexandria project, Carnegie Mellon University's Informedia Digital Video Library project, the University of Illinois at Urbana-Champaign's Digital Library project, the University of Michigan's Digital Library project and Stanford University's Digital Library project (see Table 3.4). The main goal was to advance the methods used to collect, store and organize information in a variety of electronic forms, and make it available for searching, retrieval and processing via communication networks in user-friendly ways (Chen, 1999).

Table 3.4 DLI 1 projects

Project	Environmental Planning and Geographic Information Systems
University	University of California, Berkeley
URL	http://elib.cs.berkeley.edu/
Major focus	To develop tools and testbeds of datasets pertaining to the environment, including environment documents and reports, image collections, maps, sensor data and other collections.
Project	The Alexandria Project: Spatially Referenced Map Information
University	University of California, Santa Barbara
URL	www.alexandria.ucsb.edu/adl.html
Major focus	To research issues critical for the construction of distributed digital libraries of geospatially referenced, multimedia materials.
Project	Informedia Digital Video Library
University	Carnegie Mellon University
URL	www.informedia.cs.cmu.edu/
Major focus	To develop new technologies for data storage, search and retrieval, and for embedding them in a video library system for use in education, training, sports and entertainment.

continued

Table 3.4 *continued*

Project	Federating Repositories of Scientific Literature
University	University of Illinois at Urbana-Champaign
URL	http://dli.grainger.uiuc.edu/
Major focus	To build a collection of full-text journal articles from physics, engineering and computer science and to make them available over the web.
Project	Intelligent Agents for Information Location
University	University of Michigan
URL	www.si.umich.edu/UMDL/ intro.html
Major focus	To research the creation, operation and use of large-scale, continually evolving digital libraries.
Project	Interoperation Mechanisms among Heterogeneous Services
University	Stanford University
URL	www-diglib.stanford.edu/diglib/pub/userinfo.html
Major focus	To design and implement the infrastructure and services needed for collaboratively creating, disseminating, sharing and managing information in a digital library context.

Digital Library Initiative 2 (DLI 2)

DLI 2 is an interagency programme sponsored by the NSF, DARPA, the National Library of Medicine (NLM), Library of Congress (LC), National Endowment for the Humanities (NEH), NASA and the Federal Bureau of Investigation (FBI) in partnership with the Institute of Museum and Library Services (IMLS), Smithsonian Institution (SI) and National Archives and Records Administration (NARA) for a period of six years (1999–2004) (Borgman, 2000b, 34). Around US$44 million was awarded in funding (Fox, 1999; Griffin, 1999; Lesk, 1999a, 1999b).

DLI 2 consists of three major components (Griffin, 1999):

- research, testbeds and applications (www.nsf.gov/cgi-bin/getpub?nsf9863)
- undergraduate emphasis (www.nsf.gov/cgi-bin/getpub?nsf9863 plus updates at www.dli2.nsf.gov/under.html)
- international digital libraries collaborative research (www.dli2.nsf.gov/intl.html).

The DLI 2 projects cover a wide range of subjects and media (Digital Library Initiatives, 2002). Examples of the subjects covered include anthropological models and images at the University of Texas, patient care at Columbia University, literary manuscripts at the University of Kentucky and folk literature at the University of California, Davis. New kinds of media are also dealt with, for example recordings of the human voice at Michigan State University, music at Johns Hopkins University, political and economic data at Harvard University. Also studied are a combination of software and data at the University of South Carolina, video materials at Carnegie Mellon University, images at several places including the University of California, Santa Barbara, and Stanford University, and textual materials as a part of nearly all projects. Several projects, including those at the University of California, Berkeley, and Tufts University, combine several kinds of media. These projects also involve new technology, for example mapping and imaging information together with text at the Tufts University project and new ways of digitizing literary manuscripts at the University of Kentucky. New technological areas are also being explored, such as interoperability and security issues at Cornell University and Stanford University, automatic classification at the University of Arizona, information filtering at the University of Indiana, data provenance at the University of Pennsylvania, and new summarization methods in the medical area of patient care information at Columbia University (Lesk, 1999a). Table 3.5 provides a brief overview of the DLI 2 projects and Table 3.6 lists those that have an undergraduate emphasis.

Table 3.5 *DLI 2 projects*

Project title	A Patient Care Digital Library: personalized search and summarization over multimedia information
University	Columbia University
URL	www.cs.columbia.edu/diglib/PERSIVAL/
Major focus	To provide personalized access to a distributed patient care digital library by developing a system called PERSIVAL (PErsonalized Retrieval and Summarization of Image, Video And Language resources).
Project title	Informedia-II: auto summarization and visualization over multiple video documents and libraries
University	Carnegie Mellon University
URL	www.informedia.cs.cmu.edu/dli2/
Major focus	To continue the pursuit of search and discovery in the video medium with a view to transforming the paradigm for accessing digital video libraries through meaningful, changeable overviews of video document sets, multimodal queries and adaptive summarizations of very large amounts of video from heterogeneous distributed sources.
Project title	Simplifying Interactive Layout and Video Editing and Re-use
University	Carnegie Mellon University

continued

Table 3.5 *continued*

URL	www-2.cs.cmu.edu/~silver/
Major focus	To create a comprehensive Intelligent Video Editor that will allow people without special training to author interesting compositions using digital video.
Project title	The Alexandria Digital Earth Prototype (ADEPT)
University	University of California at Santa Barbara
URL	www.alexandria.ucsb.edu/adept/overview.pdf
Major focus	To develop digital library environments and services that will support access to, and use of, heterogeneous digital information distributed across the internet on the basis of georeference as well as other criteria.
Project title	A Multi-media Digital Library of Folk Literature
University	University of California at Davis
URL	http://philo.ucdavis.edu/SEFARAD/projdesc/projdesc.html
Major focus	Conversion of materials to a multimedia digital corpus so that these materials can be made more widely available, with increased access and analytic capabilities.
Project title	Cuneiform Digital Library Initiative (CDLI)
University	University of California at Los Angeles
URL	http://cdli.ucla.edu/
Major focus	To represent the efforts of an international group of Assyriologists, museum curators and historians of science to make available through the internet the form and content of cuneiform tablets dating from the beginning of writing, c. 3200 BC, until the end of the third millennium BC.
Project title	Re-inventing Scholarly Information Dissemination and Use
University	University of California at Berkeley
URL	http://elib.cs.berkeley.edu/
Major focus	To develop tools and technologies that support highly improved models of information dissemination and access.
Project title	Image Filtering for Secure Distribution of Medical Information
University	Stanford University
URL	www-db.stanford.edu/pub/gio/TIHI/TID.html
Major focus	To provide image filtering capabilities to complement other means of checking the contents of documents.
Project title	Stanford Interlib Technologies
University	Stanford University
URL	www-diglib.stanford.edu/diglib/

continued

Table 3.5 *continued*

Major focus	To develop base technologies to overcome critical barriers to effective digital libraries including heterogeneity of information and services, lack of powerful filtering mechanisms, insufficient availability of interfaces and tools; and lack of a solid economic infrastructure.
Project title	The Stanford Encyclopedia of Philosophy
University	Stanford University
URL	http://plato.stanford.edu/
Major focus	To design a dynamic reference work in which each entry is maintained and kept up to date by an expert or group of experts in the field.
Project title	A Digital Library of Vertebrate Morphology, using high-resolution X-ray CT
University	University of Texas at Austin
URL	www.ctlab.geo.utexas.edu/dmg/
Major focus	To develop an intensive application of high-resolution X-ray Computed Tomography scanning (X-ray CT) to the study of the vertebrate skeleton.
Project title	A Software and Data Library for Experiments, Simulations and Archiving
University	University of South Carolina
URL	http://weblab.badm.sc.edu/
Major focus	To build, maintain and evaluate for experiments, simulations and archiving primarily for the social and economic sciences a software and data library that will serve as a 'Web-Lab Library' and multi-functional knowledge centre.
Project title	Virtual Data Center Project: an operational social science digital data library
University	Harvard University
URL	http://thedata.org/
Major focus	To develop a Virtual Data Center (VDC) to manage and share numerical social science data for teaching and research purposes across multiple institutions.
Project title	Founding a National Gallery of the Spoken Word
University	Michigan State University
URL	www.ngsw.org/
Major focus	To preserve spoken word collections that span the 20th century and to make these and other historically significant voice recordings freely available and easily accessible via the internet.

continued

Table 3.5 *continued*

Project title	Project Prism at Cornell University: information integrity in digital libraries
University	Cornell University
URL	www.prism.cornell.edu/
Major focus	To investigate and develop working prototypes of a digital library architecture with particular attention to supporting integrity issues.
Project title	A Digital Library for the Humanities
University	Tufts University
URL	www.perseus.tufts.edu/
Major focus	To access a wide range of source materials for the humanities.
Project title	Digital Workflow Management: Lester S. Levy Collection of Sheet Music, Phase Two
University	Johns Hopkins University
URL	http://levysheetmusic.mse.jhu.edu/
Major focus	To enhance the use and usability of the library's sheet music and similar collections located elsewhere.
Project title	The Digital Atheneum: new techniques for restoring, searching and editing humanities collections
University	University of Kentucky
URL	www.digitalatheneum.org/
Major focus	To develop new digital libraries for scholars in the humanities with state-of-the-art techniques for restoring, searching and editing.
Project title	Data Provenance
University	University of Pennsylvania
URL	http://db.cis.upenn.edu/Research/provenance.html
Major focus	To address issues associated with data provenance.
Project title	High-Performance Digital Library Classification Systems: From Information Retrieval to Knowledge Management
University	University of Arizona
URL	http://ai.bpa.arizona.edu/go/dl/
Major focus	To develop the necessary techniques to generate classification systems automatically from large domain-specific textual collections and to unify them with manually created classification systems to assist in effective digital library retrieval and analysis.
Project title	Automatic Reference Librarians for the World Wide Web
University	University of Washington
URL	www.cs.washington.edu/research/diglib

continued

Table 3.5 *continued*

Major focus	To create software agents that possess reference intelligence – a limited understanding of complex technical topics, but a very sophisticated understanding of how and where to find high-quality information on the web.
Project title	Creating the Digital Music Library
University	Indiana University
URL	http://dml.indiana.edu/
Major focus	To provide users with access to a collection of music in several formats from a range of musical styles and types.
Project title	A Distributed Information Filtering System for Digital Libraries
University	Indiana University Indianapolis/Bloomington
URL	http://sifter.indiana.edu/
Major focus	To design and develop a distributed intelligent information distribution and filtering system that provides personalized information services to the user.
Project title	Digital Library for Human Movement
University	University of Illinois, Chicago
URL	http://arik.eecs.uic.edu/cgi-bin/vdsearch.cgi
Major focus	To develop a video database for a digital library of human actions/ activities.
Project title	Shuhai Wenyuan Classical Chinese Digital Database and Interactive Internet Worktable
University	University of Hawaii at Mamoa
URL	http://shuhai.hawaii.edu/
Major focus	To provide an innovative Interactive Internet Worktable to facilitate the reading and understanding of ancient Chinese philosophy.
Project title	Tracking Footprints through an Information Space: leveraging the document selections of expert problem solvers
University	Oregon Health and Science University
URL	www.cse.ogi.edu/dot/research/footprints/
Major focus	To help expert problem solvers find needed information in a large, complex information space.
Project title	Word Spotting: indexing handwritten manuscripts
University	University of Massachusetts, Amherst
URL	http://clir.cs.umass.edu/research/wordspotting/
Major focus	To research and develop techniques for indexing handwritten historical manuscripts.

Table 3.6 *DLI 2 projects with undergraduate emphasis*

Project title	Using the National Engineering Education Delivery System as the Foundation for Building a Test-Bed Digital Library for Science, Mathematics, Engineering and Technology Education
Institution	University of California at Berkeley
URL	www.needs.org/
Major focus	To develop a testbed digital library for science, mathematics, engineering and technology education (SMETE) that would provide courseware, cataloguing, indexing, searching and downloading to the science and mathematics communities.
Project title	Columbia Earthscape: a model for a sustainable online educational resource in earth sciences
Institution	Columbia University
URL	https://wwwc.cc.columbia.edu/sec/dlc/ earthscape/
Major focus	To develop a model for an online resource on the global environment.
Project title	Research on a Digital Library for Graphics and Visualization Education
Institution	Georgia State University
URL	http://asec.cs.gsu.edu/asecdl-nsf-dli2/
Major focus	To enhance the usability and flexibility of the digital library and to address some of the needs of its community.
Project title	Planning Grant for the Use of Digital Libraries in Undergraduate Learning in Science
Institution	Old Dominion University
URL	http://dlib.cs.odu/edu/
Major focus	To develop a set of prototype tools, processes and an environment to provide preliminary answers to a set of questions that underlie the design and implementation of a digital library for science, mathematics and engineering education.
Project title	iLumina: a Digital Library of Reusable Science and Math Resources for Undergraduate Education
Institution	University of North Carolina, Wilmington
URL	http://turing.csc.uncwil.edu/ilumina/homePage.xml
Major focus	To provide a digital library of shareable undergraduate teaching materials for science, mathematics, technology and engineering; was primarily created by and contributed to by faculty for use in undergraduate classes and labs.
Project title	Digital Libraries for Children: computational tools that support children as researchers
Institution	University of Maryland

continued

Table 3.6 *continued*

URL	www.cs.umd.edu/hcil/kiddesign/
Major focus	To develop visual interfaces to help young children in querying, searching, browsing and organizing multimedia information.
Project title	The JOMA Applet Project: applet support for the undergraduate mathematics curriculum
Institution	Swarthmore College
URL	http://mathforum.org/joma_applet/
Major focus	To produce a digital library of interactive web-based mathematics instructional material for the undergraduate mathematics curriculum.
Project title	Virtual Skeletons in Three Dimensions: the digital library as a platform for studying web-anatomical form and function
Institution	University of Texas at Austin
URL	www.eskeletons.org/
Major focus	To create a library of anatomical forms and to design an interface that will provide an interactive framework for investigation by users.

Centres for research on digital libraries in the USA

Many centres for digital library research have been set up in the USA over the past few years. Features of some such research centres are briefly discussed below:

Center for Intelligent Information Retrieval (http://ciir.cs.umass.edu/)

The Center for Intelligent Information Retrieval (CIIR) is one of the leading information retrieval research laboratories in the world and develops tools that provide effective and efficient access to large distributed digital libraries. The website states that 'CIIR accomplishments include significant research advances in the areas of distributed information retrieval, information filtering, topic detection, multimedia indexing and retrieval, document image processing, terabyte collections, data mining, summarization, resource discovery, interfaces and visualization, and cross-lingual information retrieval.'

Center for the Study of Digital Libraries (http://csdl.tamu.edu/)

The Center for the Study of Digital Libraries (CSDL) was established in 1995 to provide a focal point for digital library research and technology for the State of Texas. Its mission is to foster pioneering research on the theory and application of digital libraries and to create flexible and efficient new technologies for their use.

Center for Electronic Texts in the Humanities (www.ceth.rutgers.edu/)

The Center for Electronic Texts in the Humanities (CETH) was established in

1991 as a joint project of Rutgers and Princeton Universities. It provides a national focus for the development of electronic text applications for scholarship and teaching. CETH concentrates on applications of SGML in order to help scholars create electronic texts in conformance with emerging standards, and to develop means of effective dissemination and the use of electronic texts for teaching and scholarship.

Center for Research on Information Access
(www.cs.columbia.edu/~klavans/cria.html)
The Center for Research on Information Access (CRIA) was established in early 1995 to act as a vehicle for linking different projects on the Columbia campus involved in developing and using digital technology, and thus to establish visibility for Columbia University as a leader in digital libraries.

Electronic Text Center at the University of Virginia
(http://etext.lib.virginia.edu/)
The Electronic Text Center (ETC) at the University of Virginia Library was established in 1992 to build and maintain an internet-accessible collection of SGML texts and images, and to build and maintain user communities adept at the creation and use of these materials.

Harvard Information Infrastructure Project
(http://ksgwww.harvard.edu/iip/)
The Harvard Information Infrastructure Project (HIIP), established in 1989, provides an interdisciplinary forum for addressing a wide range of emerging policy issues relating to information infrastructure, its development, use and growth, with particular reference to electronic commerce, the internet, and governance, economic and policy issues.

Rutgers Center for Information Management, Integration, and Connectivity
(http://cimic3.rutgers.edu/)
The Center for Information Management, Integration, and Connectivity (CIMIC) at Rutgers University is engaged in applied scientific research on issues related to digital libraries and e-commerce. It fosters a multi-disciplinary research programme that brings together researchers from such diverse fields as computer information systems, computer science, environmental science, healthcare, marketing, finance and economics, and industrial engineering.

Joint NSF/JISC international digital library projects

International digital library research programmes are intended to contribute to the fundamental knowledge required to create information systems that can operate in multiple languages, formats, media, and social and organizational contexts. The main objective of the joint initiatives is to avoid duplication of effort, prevent the development of fragmented digital systems, and encourage the productive interchange of scientific knowledge and scholarly data around the world (National Science Foundation, n.d.).

With a view to addressing some of the research challenges associated with creating international digital libraries, the NSF in the USA issued a call for proposals in October 1998 for multi-country, multi-team projects involving at least one research team in the USA and one in another country. JISC was the first to join the NSF in this endeavour and issued a matching call. JISC committed £500,000 per year for three years to fund new development work in this programme (Wiseman, Rusbridge and Griffin, 1999). Table 3.7 provides brief information on six projects that were recommended for funding over a three-year project term (JISC, 2001; Wiseman, Rusbridge and Griffin, 1999).

Table 3.7 *NSF/JISC funded projects*

Project title	Cross-Domain Resource Discovery: integrated discovery and use of textual, numeric and spatial data
Universities	University of California at Berkeley/Special Collections and Archives, University of Liverpool
URL	http://cheshire.berkley.edu (USA) http://sca.lib.liv.ac.uk/cheshire (UK)
Major focus	To enable cross-domain searching in a multi-database environment. To produce an advanced online information retrieval system ('Cheshire') that will facilitate searching on the internet across collections of original materials, printed books, records, archives, manuscripts and museum objects, statistical databases, full-text, geospatial and multimedia data resources.
Project title	CAMiLEON: Creative Archiving at Michigan and Leeds: Emulating the Old on the New
Universities	University of Michigan/The University of Leeds in association with the existing CEDARS Project (CURL Exemplars in Digital ARchives)
URL	www.si.umich.edu/CAMILEON
Major focus	To evaluate the publicly available emulators to assess their suitability for long-term preservation. The project will also develop and test a suite of

continued

Table 3.7 *continued*

	emulation tools, evaluate the costs and benefits of emulation as a preservation strategy for complex multimedia documents and objects, and develop models for collection management decisions about how much effort and resources to invest in the replication of digital objects.
Project title	Online Music Recognition and Searching (OMRAS)
Universities	The Center for Intelligent Information Retrieval at the University of Massachusetts/King's College, London
URL	www.omras.org
Major focus	To provide efficient and user-friendly content-based searching and retrieval of musical information from online databases stored in a variety of formats ranging from encoded score files to digital audio.
Project title	The Open Citation Project: reference linking for open archives
Universities	Cornell University/Southampton University/Los Alamos National Laboratory
URL	http://opcit.eprints.org/
Major focus	To hyperlink each of the over 100,000 papers in Los Alamos's unique online Physics Archive to every other paper in the archive that it cites; and to extend this work to link references in papers held in other freely accessible archives that conform with the proposal for Open Archives.
Project title	The IMesh Toolkit: an architecture and toolkit for distributed subject gateways
Universities	The Internet Scout Project at the University of Wisconsin-Madison/ UKOLN (UK Office for Library and Information Networking) at the University of Bath/the ILRT (Institute for Learning and Research Technology) at the University of Bristol
URL	www.ukoln.ac.uk/metadata/imesh-toolkit/
Major focus	To advance the system framework within which subject gateways and related services operate by defining an architecture that specifies individual components and how they communicate.
Project title	HARMONY: metadata for resource discovery of multimedia digital objects
Universities	Cornell University/the ILRT at the University of Bristol/the Australian Distributed Systems Technology Centre (DSTC)
URL	www.ilrt.bris.ac.uk/discovery/harmony
Major focus	To devise a framework to deal with the challenge of describing networked collections of highly complex and mixed-media digital objects and to allow experts of multiple communities to define overlapping descriptive vocabularies for annotating multimedia content.

Canada

Canadian Initiative on Digital Libraries (www.nlc-bnc.ca/cidl/)

The Canadian Initiative on Digital Libraries (CIDL), an alliance of more than 50 Canadian libraries that recognize the growing importance of digital information, was founded in 1997.

It was established to promote, co-ordinate and facilitate the development of Canadian digital collections and services in order to optimize national interoperability and long-term access to Canadian digital library resources. Specific objectives of this initiative include the following (www.nlc-bnc.ca/cidl/cidldese.htm#objs):

- the formulation and implementation of strategies towards increased communication, awareness and education on digital library matters
- the identification and promulgation of digital library standards and best practices
- the exploration of licensing agreement issues
- the exploration of methods to better co-ordinate efforts among institutions and to avoid duplication in the development of digital resources
- the resolution of digital library issues that are particularly Canadian in context, such as bilingualism
- the preparation of guidelines for the application of present copyright legislation and the development of position statements with respect to intellectual property in a digital environment
- the establishment of relations with other stakeholders involved in the information chain from creation to archiving: creators and publishers, industry suppliers (software, hardware and telecommunications), users, archives, museums and cultural agencies, and government agencies at the federal, provincial, regional and municipal levels
- the raising of the profile of Canadian digital library activities, both within Canada and internationally.

Europe

DELOS Network of Excellence on Digital Libraries (http://delos-noe.iei.pi.cnr.it/)

The DELOS Network of Excellence on Digital Libraries is an instrument to promote digital library research and development in Europe. Its objectives are to:

- contribute towards improving the effectiveness of European research in this emerging domain
- provide a forum where researchers, practitioners and representatives of interested application communities and industries can exchange ideas and experiences
- train young researchers in the field of digital libraries
- contribute towards defining a European Union research policy in the digital library domain
- co-operate with ongoing standardization activities in relevant digital library fields
- facilitate take-up of DL technologies in all interested application communities
- create a forum where the results of EU-funded digital library projects can be presented and where common problems can be discussed and areas of co-operation identified
- promote co-operation between European and national digital library initiatives
- promote international co-operation in the digital library research domain.

In addition to the DELOS programme, digital library research in Europe is supported by various initiatives, including national libraries and information systems in each European country. Examples include: NORDINFO (Nordic Council for Scientific Information) at www.nordinfo.helsinki.fi/nordinfo/index.htm; DEF (Denmark's Electronic Research Library) at www.deflink.dk/eng/default.asp; FinELib (the National Electronic Library of Finland) at www.lib.helsinki.fi/finelib/english/index.html and MEDLIB (internet-based Virtual Library Network for the Mediterranean Region) at www.unesco.org/webworld/mediter/medlib.htm.

Digital library projects funded by the European Union

A number of digital library research programmes have been funded under the Fourth and Fifth Framework Programmes of the European Union. Some of these projects are described below.

Fifth Framework Programme, 1998–2002

Digital Heritage and Cultural Content (DIGICULT) (www.cordis.lu/ist/ka3/digicult/)

DIGICULT is one of the five main areas for research and technological development under Multimedia Content and Tools – Key Action 3 of the Information Society Technologies (IST) programme of the European Commission. It is aimed at expanding the contribution of libraries, museums and archives to the emerging culture economy, including economic, scientific and technological development.

There are three research priorities:

- ensuring integrated access to collections and materials held in libraries, museums and archives
- improving the operational efficiency of large-scale content holdings by means of powerful interfacing and management techniques
- preserving and accessing multimedia content of various types, including electronic materials and surrogates of physical objects.

A list of some IST RTD (Research and Technological Development) projects in the cultural heritage area is given below.

An Advanced Lightweight Architecture for Accessing Scientific Collections (ARION) (http://dlforum.external.forth.gr:8080/)

ARION aims to provide a new generation of digital library services through the retrieval of digital scientific information that resides within research and consultancy organizations. ARION advances the findings of previous studies in this area and consolidates the work of international interoperability standards development.

Access to Scientific Space Heritage (ASH) (www.ashproject.org/)

The ASH project aims to create a virtual control room to simulate space missions and astronomy exploration, allowing groups of the public to experience basic physical laws and principles, the complexity of exploring space and the excitement of discoveries.

Cross-Language Evaluation Forum (CLEF) (http://clef.iei.pi.cnr.it:2002/)

The CLEF project supports global digital library applications by (1) providing an infrastructure for the testing and evaluation of information retrieval systems using European languages in both monolingual and cross-language contexts, and (2) creating test-suites of reusable data which can be employed by system developers for benchmarking purposes.

Collaboratory for Annotation, Indexing and Retrieval of Digitized Historical Archive Material (COLLATE) (www.collate.de/index.htm)

COLLATE aims to develop a web-based collaboratory for archives, researchers and end-users working with digitized cultural material.

CYCLADES – An Open Collaborative Virtual Archive Environment (http://galileo.iei.pi.cnr.it/cyclades/)

CYCLADES aims to develop advanced mediator technologies and services to support scholars interacting with large interdisciplinary e-print archives.

MIND – Resource Selection and Data Fusion for Multimedia International Digital Libraries (www.mind.cs.strath.ac.uk/)

MIND aims to design models and build a set of tools and associated testbeds for improving the effectiveness of resource selection, multimedia information access and retrieval and fusion of the retrieved data.

MUMIS – Multimedia Indexing and Searching Environment (http://parlevink.cs.utwente.nl/projects/mumis/)

MUMIS will develop basic technology for the automatic indexing of multimedia programme material, in the following stages:

1   Use data from different media sources (documents, radio and television programmes) to build a specialized set of lexica and an ontology for the selected domain (soccer).
2   Digitize non-text data and apply speech recognition techniques to extract text.
3   Develop information extraction techniques and apply them to the texts to extract significant text elements (such as the names of players in a team, goals scored) and use these to build annotations.
4   Build a novel type of merging tool, to combine the event descriptions

generated from different data sources, and from sources in different languages (Dutch, English and German).

5 Store the merged event descriptions (the domain ontology) in a central database, with relevant metadata.

6 Develop a user interface (in Dutch, English, German and Swedish) to enable professional users to query the database, by selecting from menus of event descriptions, metadata, and so on, and to view video fragments retrieved to satisfy the query.

Renardus – Academic Subject Gateway Service Europe (www.renardus.org)

Renardus aims to develop a subject gateway of selected, high-quality internet resources of cultural and scientific information across Europe to support teaching, learning and research in higher education in Europe. Renardus provides integrated search and browse access to records from individual participating subject gateway services.

SCHEMAS – Forum for Metadata Schema Implementers (www.schemas-forum.org/)

SCHEMAS aims to provide a training platform for metadata schema designers involved in projects under the IST programme and national initiatives in Europe. The main objectives are to guide and educate metadata schema implementers about the status and proper use of new and emerging metadata standards, and to promote good-practice guidelines for adapting multiple standards or metadata modules for local use in customized schemas.

SCHOLNET – Developing a Digital Library Testbed to Support Networked Scholarly Communities (www.ercim.org/scholnet/)

SCHOLNET aims to develop a digital library infrastructure to support communication and collaboration within networked scholarly communities. The digital library will provide library services in addition to support for non-textual data types, hypermedia annotation, cross-language search and retrieval, and personalized information dissemination. This testbed will be used to demonstrate how an enhanced digital library can enable members of a networked scholarly community to learn from, contribute to, and collectively build upon the community's discipline-oriented digital collections.

Fourth Framework Programme, 1990–98

Some library projects funded under the Telematics for Libraries Programme are discussed below; the complete list can be accessed through the Telematics for Libraries website (www.cordis.lu/libraries/en/projects.html).

CASA – A Cooperative Archive of Serials and Articles (http://decsite.cib.unibo.it:1999/)

The aim is to create a serials authority list based on the ISSN system, allowing users to search distributed catalogues of national serials holdings and to locate serials, while offering national union catalogues and ISSN agencies the possibility of exchanging and revising bibliographic serials data in co-operation with the ISSN international centre.

EULER – European Libraries and Electronic Resources in Mathematical Sciences (www.emis.de/projects/EULER/)

EULER's aim is to provide strictly user-oriented, integrated, network-based access to mathematical publications. The EULER service intends to offer a 'one-stop shopping site' for users of information about mathematics.

ONE II – OPAC Network in Europe – II. (www.one-2.org/)

One I was a collaborative project involving 15 organizations in eight European countries, funded by the European Commission's Libraries Programme in 1997 to provide library users with better ways to access library OPACs and national catalogues. ONE II extends the results of ONE I by implementing more services and integrating advanced Z39.50 retrieval. The project will produce common software, adding facilities for interlibrary loan, electronic document delivery and distributed shared cataloguing capabilities. Users will include professional cataloguers, researchers, museums and library patrons.

Australia

Australian libraries at the federal, state and university levels, together with commercial and research organizations, are supporting a diverse set of digital library projects. Ianella (1996) reviewed 18 such projects:

- *Australian Cooperative Digitisation Project 1840–45*. A digital library of Australian serials and fiction of the seminal period 1840–45.
- *Australian Museums On Line*. A project that aims to provide access to the

vast cultural resources of Australian museums via the internet.

- *DIGILIB: Queensland Country Towns Image Project*. A collaborative project between the University of Queensland's Architecture Department and Library.
- *The Documentary Images Project*. A digital library of images of works of art including water-colours, paintings, drawings, prints and photographs at the National Library of Australia.
- *Electronic Journal Project*. The project involves the University Library, the Unit of Medical Informatics and the UNESCO-supported International Centre for Engineering Education (USICEE), in the Faculty of Engineering at Monash University.
- *Electronic Reserve Project*. Electronic library at the Berwick campus of Monash University.
- *Hume Image Collection Project*. The Hume collection at the University of Queensland consists of rare photographic prints that capture the life of the Humes, a leading Queensland pastoral family, between 1870 and 1890. This collection is a primary research resource, the originals of which are largely inaccessible because of fragility.
- *Indian Ocean Rim Region Virtual Library Project*. A co-operative project jointly developed by Edith Cowan and Murdoch University Libraries, the Centre for Development Studies at Edith Cowan University and the Inter-University Consortium for Development Studies Western Australia (comprising Edith Cowan University, Murdoch University, Curtin University of Technology and the University of Western Australia). The project focuses on social development, including health issues, in the Indian Ocean Rim region.
- *The Information Storage and Retrieval Project*. The project aims to develop a set of tools for data structure and presentation for the Parliamentary Library, including the use of a common data access/retrieval mechanism to access various databases and the provision of gateways to general external data stores.
- *LISWEB Project*. A project of Curtin University that provides clients with information about library services, tells them what the library can do for them, and offers easy access to quality sources of scholarly information.
- *Multimedia Source Project*. A project at the State Library of Victoria providing online access to digitized content from the library's unique collections of paintings, drawings, postcards, maps, rare books, theatre posters, oral history tapes and other items ranging from 1803 to the present day.

- *NSW Parliaments Newspaper Clippings and Press Releases Imaging Project.* A digital library of the New South Wales Parliamentary Library's newspaper clipping collection.
- *Preserving Oral History Recordings Project.* A digital library of the oral history collections of the National Library of Australia.
- *REDD: An Electronic Document Delivery Project.* An electronic document delivery system developed by the University of Queensland, Queensland University of Technology and Griffith University libraries to meet the need for a fast, inexpensive and accessible electronic document delivery infrastructure for Australia.
- *The Resource Discovery Project.* A project at the Distributed Systems Technology Centre with the goal of investigating issues to do with locating and retrieving information in a digital library environment.
- *Scholarly Electronic Text and Image Service (SETIS).* Located in and operated by Sydney University Library, SETIS aims to exploit the latest developments in ICT for students and scholars, particularly within the arts and humanities.
- *UNILINC projects.* Electronic journal projects run by a non-profit cooperative of higher education and related libraries in Australia.
- *WORLD 1.* The National Library of Australia's service developed by the National Document and Information Service (NDIS) project in partnership with the National Library of New Zealand.

New Zealand

Greenstone Digital Library (www.nzdl.org/cgi-bin/library)

The New Zealand digital library project, presently called the Greenstone Digital Library, is a research programme at the University of Waikato that aims to develop the underlying technology for digital libraries and make it available publicly so that others can use it to create their own collections. The site provides several document collections, including historical material, humanitarian and development information, computer science technical reports and bibliographies, and literary works and magazines, and can be accessed through the searching and browsing interfaces provided by the Greenstone Digital Library software. Details of GDL appear in many chapters in this book (see, for example, Chapters 7, 8 and 9).

Summary

As we have seen, tremendous amounts of research effort and money have been devoted to digital library research throughout the world over the past decade. While digital library research in the USA has been spearheaded by the Digital Library Initiatives, in the UK by the eLib programme, in Europe by EU Fourth and Fifth Framework funding and the DELOS programme, many more projects have been undertaken in these countries, and indeed throughout the world, which have been funded by individual institutions such as universities, national libraries and laboratories, companies and professional associations.

While most of the early research in the USA focused on building enabling technologies, the scope of digital library research has been broadened significantly under the DLI 2 programme to include various other issues related to the development and management of digital libraries such as user issues, economic and legal issues, and various social issues including the impact of digital libraries on different walks of life.

Compared with the US scenario, digital library research in the UK has been more practitioner based, involving more library and information science departments and practising professionals. Critical reviews of digital library research under the three phases of the eLib programme have been made by Rusbridge (1998, 2001) and Pinfield (2001a).

Different issues and problems have been addressed by the researchers and many solutions have been proposed, while some issues and problems are still being investigated. Detailed discussions of each area, problem and solution is not possible within the scope of only one book. However, some relevant research in each area of digital libraries is mentioned elsewhere in the relevant chapters.

Chapter 4
Digital library design

Outline

This chapter addresses the major issues of digital library design with particular reference to interoperability and integration. It shows that several standards must be used in order to achieve interoperability. It highlights some digital library design approaches proposed by researchers in the USA and UK. Digital library design also involves a number of softer issues, especially those relating to the user and usability. A number of these are discussed in this chapter. Finally some important standards that are required for digital library design and development are mentioned. This chapter will thus give readers a basic understanding of digital library design issues and the various approaches taken by researchers.

Introduction

Providing access to a variety of information resources residing on a variety of computer systems in different parts of the world to a number of users of differing nature and with different needs is a major challenge for digital library designers. Digital libraries, especially hybrid libraries, aim to work as the 'one-stop shop' for all kinds of information resources. This means that there are a number of complex issues related to integration and seamlessness.

Figure 4.1 shows the basic design of a digital library. It shows that users of a digital library may have access to a range of information resources. There are two basic modes of getting access to these resources. The first is when users go through a custom-built interface that allows them to select a particular type of resource and opens the corresponding search interface. Some digital libraries follow this model. A typical example is the Greenstone Digital Library, which

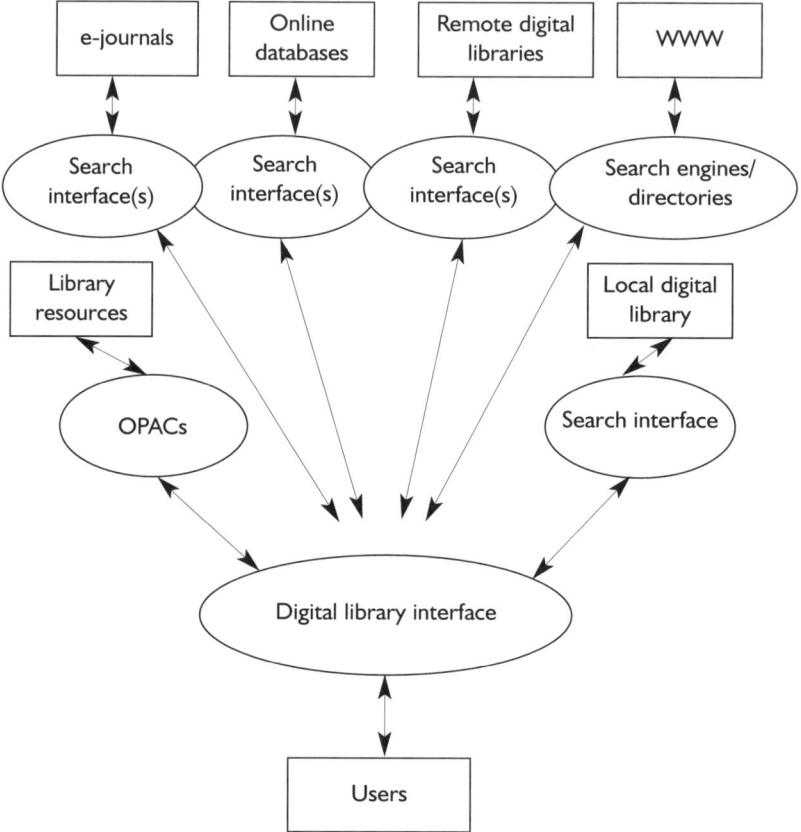

Fig. 4.1 *Conceptual design of a digital library*

allows users to select a particular type of resource or collection, and then opens the interface of the corresponding resource, enabling the user to browse or search. The major problem of this model is that the user has to search or browse each collection separately.

Alternatively, some digital library interfaces offer the facility to search and retrieve results from several selected resources or collections at the same time with a single query. This is definitely a better approach from the users' perspective. The SearchLight option in the California Digital Library is a typical example of this. However, technologically this approach is more challenging, and a number of technical issues need to be considered in order to build this model.

In both the approaches mentioned above, users need to select one or more resource types and have to formulate one or more queries in order to conduct a search. However, selection of a suitable resource type may be a difficult task for many users, particularly if the area of study is unknown. These issues are discussed further in Chapters 8 and 9.

User-centred digital library models

The importance of users in the context of digital libraries is discussed in Chapter 8. In this section we shall only discuss some user-related issues that influence various technical design considerations. Borgman (2000b, 123) comments that while deciding the design features of a digital library, we should consider who is going to use the services, how and why. Marchionini and Komlodi (1998) review literature on user interfaces, particularly in a digital library environment, and suggest the need for a task-based digital library. Michelle and Wang (2000) discuss a user-centred interface for information exploration in a heterogeneous digital library. Tennant (1999) identifies several skills, including user interface design skills, needed to create and manage digital library collections and services. Zhao (1998) discusses the concept of a personal digital library (PDL) that acts as a front end to other electronic library systems and manages the user's information needs. The main focus of the system is providing adaptive contents whereby users have their own personal and personalized databases. Barry and Barbara (1999) also discuss the creation of personal digital libraries. Hill et al. (2000) discuss the use of the results of user evaluation studies in the evolution of the design features of the Alexandria Digital Library.

Many digital library researchers have proposed user-centred approaches that introduce a layer between the users and the digital library interface (shown in Figure 4.1) and do some automatic filtering or tailoring with a view to producing better results. The North Carolina State University (NCSU) Library developed MyLibrary@NCState (2001), which is a portal application to the Library's information resources. The interface allows user profiling to build a dynamic, customized gateway to both general and discipline-specific resources. MyLibrary (Cohen et al., 2000) is a Cornell University Library initiative to provide personalized library services to their students, faculty and staff on the basis of a focus group study to gauge library users.

HeadLine (Gambles, 2000, 2001) is one of the eLib programme's Phase 3 projects, developing a hybrid library system called the HeadLine personal information environment (PIE). The personal information environment presents users with pages of resources relevant to their courses and/or department. PIE users are also provided with an 'All resources' page that contains all the resources accessible through their library. Users can create their own lists of resources on their own pages. The HeadLine hybrid library model stores information about library users such as their department and course. This information is used to present information resources that are relevant to the user's subject area or course. Users themselves can create and customize their own PIE pages, building their own collections of resources that they can share with other PIE users, such as researchers in the same field or students taking the same course (Gambles, 2001).

Meyyappan, Chowdhury and Foo (2001a, 2001b, 2001c) propose a user-centred model of a digital library. This model proposes a digital work environment (DWE) that provides access to a digital library as well as intranet resources through a customized user interface. The DWE organizes the information resources on the basis of their relevance to the user tasks. This model may be useful for building a knowledge management environment (discussed in Chapter 15). Figure 4.2 shows an outline of the DWE model.

Design issues

The major problems of digital library design are caused by differences in the computer systems, file structures, formats, information organization and retrieval features of the various information systems or collections that are accessible through a digital library. While the web has emerged as the prime means of delivering information in digital and hybrid libraries, behind the web interface the integration of systems for seamless access depends on the use of agreed standards, implemented in agreed ways (HyLife, 2002a). Arms (2000b, 207) suggests that an ideal approach would be to develop only one set of standards and ask all the digital libraries and other stakeholders, such as information creators and service providers, to follow them strictly. However, this approach is not only difficult to implement for practical and political reasons, but may not be desirable, either, since forcing everyone to follow only one set of standards may close the door to innovation. Nevertheless, in order to attain interoperability, we need to develop acceptable standards for formats, protocols and security, and agreements on semantics; building, testing and adopting such standards would be a very costly affair (Arms, 2000b, 208).

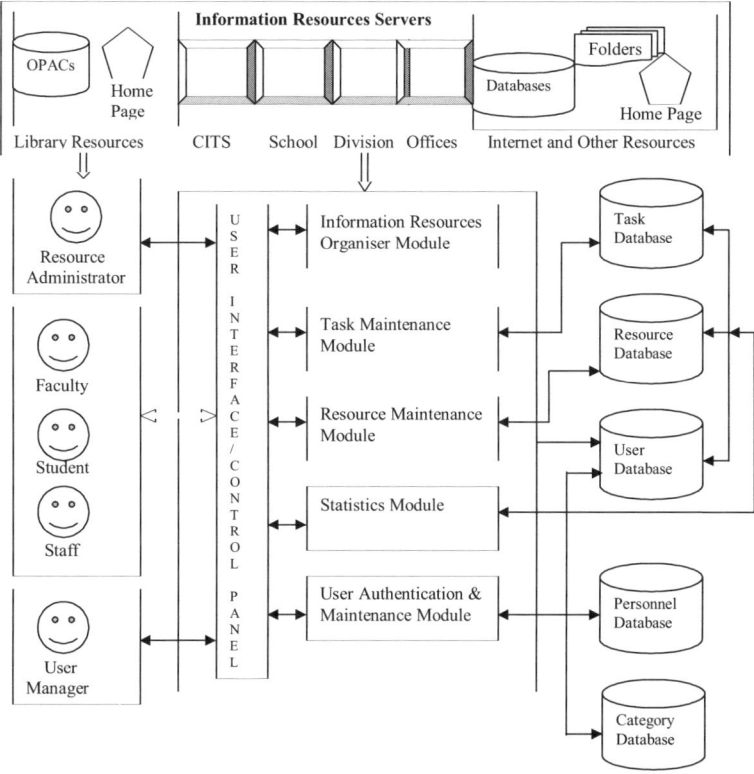

Fig. 4.2   *The DWE model (Meyyappan, Chowdhury and Foo, 2001c)*

Scaleability and sustainability

Scaleability and sustainability are the two most important issues for the design of large-scale operational digital libraries. Most digital library experiments do not scale up for a number of reasons, such as:

- The software can support only small applications.
- The hardware and network specifications do not match the operational requirements.
- The operational overheads increase significantly.
- The human and financial requirements increase drastically.
- An unexpected difference in the performance level is noticed, or unexpected incidents in terms of functionality and performance are noted.

- Certain operations or routines are too complex for large-scale implement-
  ations.

The issue of scaleability has an impact on the sustainability of digital libraries. Sustainability means the long-term survival of a service, its ability to remain responsive to the users, and its adaptability to internal and external challenges. Several factors affect sustainability, such as continued financial, managerial and technical support, the restructuring of staffing in terms of roles and responsibilities, and continued evolution to keep pace with the changing environments and technologies as well as users.

Interoperability

One of the major problems facing digital libraries is the issue of interoperability – how to get a wide variety of computing systems to work together and/or to talk to one another (Arms, 2000b, 69). Interoperability in a digital library environment is difficult to attain. There are different types of interoperability, such as systems interoperability, software interoperability or portability, semantic interoperability, linguistic interoperability, and so on. Different methods must be adopted to achieve each one of these, for instance (Arms, 2000b, 70–2; HyLife, 2002b) using:

- common user interfaces
- uniform naming and identification systems
- standard formats for information resources
- standard metadata formats
- standard network protocols
- standard information retrieval protocols
- standard measures for authentication and security, and so on.

Libraries have faced the problems of interoperability since computers were first used to create catalogues. Consequently, they have built and adopted standards for the exchange of bibliographic data. ISO 2709 (International Organization for Standardization, 1996) is an international standard that specifies the requirements for a generalized machine format for holding any type of bibliographic record. This standard does not define the content of individual records or the meanings assigned to tags, indicators or identifiers. It only prescribes a generalized structure which can be used to transmit, between data processing systems, records describing all forms of material capable of bibliographic description

(Chowdhury, 1999, 29). While ISO 2709 prescribes the generalized structure of bibliographic records, libraries have followed another de facto standard format for encoding data: MARC (Machine-Readable Cataloguing). MARC is a system of allocating labels to each part of a catalogue record which, once assigned, enable the record to be handled by computer. The original MARC format was developed in the USA (by the Library of Congress) in 1965–66, and since then a number of varieties have appeared (Chowdhury, 1999, 32). USMARC, UKMARC and other national MARC formats have some differences in content designations, although all are meant for the representation of bibliographic items.

The differences in data contents in these formats mean that editing is required before records can be exchanged. One solution to the incompatibility was to develop an international (Universal) MARC (*UNIMARC manual*, 1994) format which would accept records created in any MARC format; the idea being that records in one MARC format could be converted first into UNIMARC and then another MARC format. This would require each national agency to write only two programs – one to convert to UNIMARC and another to convert from UNIMARC – instead of having to write a separate program for each MARC format. UNIMARC was brought out by IFLA in 1977.

In 1984 UNESCO developed the Common Communication Format (CCF), which is also a switching format like UNIMARC. A second edition of CCF was published in 1988 and subsequently it was decided that its scope would be extended to incorporate provisions for data elements for recording factual information that are used most often for referral purposes. As a result, the third edition of CCF, published in 1992, has been divided into two volumes: CCF/B for holding bibliographic information and CCF/F for factual information (Simmons and Hopkinson, 1992).

Design principles

Kahn and Wilensky (1995) describe the basic infrastructure for a digital library which is 'open in its architecture and which supports a large and extensible class of distributed digital information services'. This architecture has been the subject of a series of useful discussions from which the following eight general principles have emerged (Arms, 1995). These may be considered as the guiding principles for the design of digital libraries.

1   *The technical framework exists within a legal and social framework.* The essence of this principle is that digital libraries form part of the social,

economic and legal framework of human society. Digital libraries are bringing major changes in the ways people create, distribute and use information. Hence, in order to facilitate the design and development of digital libraries, changes must be made in the economic and legal framework of society in order to protect the rights and benefits of every stakeholder in the chain of information generation and use.

2   *Understanding of digital library concepts needs standard terminology.* Since people from many different disciplines are involved in the design, development and management of digital libraries, standard terminologies must be developed and used by all concerned. This will facilitate collaboration and hence pave the way for the development of a global digital library system.

3   *The underlying architecture should be separate from the content stored in the library.* There should be an underlying architecture that applies to all types of digital materials. This will help in the identification of materials. However, specific measures are to be taken to handle the formats, protocols and rights management necessary for each specific type of material, such as music, video, databases and software. Arms (1995) suggests that separating general functions from those specific to the type of content 'encourages different markets to emerge and allows a legal framework in which storage, transmission and delivery of digital objects is separate from activities to create and manage the intellectual content'.

4   *Names and identifiers are the basic building blocks for the digital library.* Every digital object should have a unique name or identifier that should remain valid for a very long period.

5   *Digital library objects are more than collections of bits.* A digital item may have one or more type of content, for instance text and image or video. The object description should contain information about this content. It should also contain some other metadata that characterize the particular object, including the intellectual property information and rights and access methods. The kind of metadata to be stored depends on the nature of the object as well as the nature and characteristics of the users and the purpose for which it will be used, and so on.

6   *A digital library object should not be tied to a particular technology.* One of the major benefits of a digital library is that different users can view and use the same information differently, if necessary. It is important that digital objects should be stored in such a way that they are tied to a particular hardware or

software as little as possible. This will allow flexibility at the user's end to receive, view and use the information in a chosen way.

7   *Repositories must look after the information they hold*. Repositories will have to store information on content as well as additional information on rights and access methods. It is also necessary that the repository provides the necessary security to ensure that only valid operations are carried out on the digital objects.

8   *Users want intellectual works, not digital objects*. A flexible digital library architecture should support abstraction of data to suit the needs of specific types of users. Individual digital objects should be stored in such a way that they may be assembled to build a coherent whole object, as and when necessary.

Digital library models

Designing a computer-mediated system that can be used easily and effectively by laypeople is an extremely difficult task. The Computer Science and Telecommunications Board of the USA (1997) recommends that computer-mediated systems should be easy to understand and learn, tolerant of errors, flexible, adaptable, appropriate and effective for a given task, powerful, efficient, inexpensive, portable, compatible, intelligent, supportive of social and group interactions, trustworthy, information centred and pleasant to use. The Board further recommends (1998) that the following approaches be taken for designing systems that are intended for large user populations:

- Involve representative users in substantive design and evaluation activities regularly.
- Expand the repertoire of research methods to be more inclusive and innovative.
- Consider ways to minimize the separation of design and evaluation from implementation and use.
- Consider the prospect of research-based principles for design.

The challenges of designing digital library architectures and systems may be described as follows:

- to provide access to diverse information sources from a variety of computer systems

- to hide the complexities of distributed information processing and retrieval
- to accommodate the different models of user information behaviour.

Although the physical proximity or collocation of resources is irrelevant to networked information systems, attributes of the traditional library such as organization, specialization and selection have been shown, in many instances, to be necessary for effective resource discovery and use (Lagoze and Fielding, 1998). Over the past few years researchers have proposed, and experimented with, various digital library models. The Cornell Digital Library Research Group has been investigating the various technologies and means of deployment of distributed digital libraries. This work is based on three major principles: open architecture, federation (management by aggregation) and distribution (the libraries are distributed). Researchers in the UK have also been experimenting with various hybrid library models. Some of these models are discussed in the following sections.

Dienst and NCSTRL

Over the past few years the Digital Library Research Group at Cornell University has been engaged in developing appropriate models for distributed digital libraries based on three principles: open architecture, federation and distribution (Davis and Lagoze, 2000; Lagoze and Fielding, 1998). The initial result of this work is Dienst (Lagoze et al., 1995), which is the technical foundation for the Networked Computer Science Technical Research Library (NCSTRL) discussed in Chapter 2. The Dienst architecture specifies four core digital library services (Davis and Lagoze, 2000):

- *user interface services*, which provide gateways to information obtained from other services
- *repository services*, which store and provide access to documents
- *index services*, which provide search capabilities: queries are accepted and matching items returned
- *collection services*, which define the components, services and documents of the digital library collection, and thereby make it possible for the user interface services to interact with them.

A central component to the Dienst architecture is the document model that provides three important abstractions (Lagoze et al., 1995):

- *unique document names*: a location-independent, unique identifier called docid
- *multiple document formats* such as ASCII, PS and TIFF
- *document decompositions*: physical and logical decompositions of a document.

Interoperability among Dienst servers provides the user with a single logical document collection, even though the actual collection is distributed across multiple servers. This is accomplished by interaction between a set of Dienst servers at three functional levels: server registration (for locating the indexing and repository site for a specific publisher identified through the docid), distributed searching, and distributed document access.

The NCSTRL collection provides access to several thousand computer science research reports from over 150 institutions. The discovery of documents and giving access to them involve the interoperation of several servers communicating via the Dienst protocol. The NCSTRL collection is logically and administratively divided into publishing authorities, each having control over the addition and administration of documents in its own sub-collection repositories. The metadata fields (title, author, abstract, and so on) for each document in these repositories are indexed by one or more index servers. The metadata is accessed through the Dienst protocol requests to the respective repository. The Dienst protocol requests defined for the collection service give access to the following information (Lagoze and Fielding, 1998):

- the list of publishing authorities that are part of the collection
- the network location: the address and port of the Dienst index servers that store indexing information
- meta information about each index server
- the correspondence of index servers to repository servers.

Initially, the Dienst architecture and NCSTRL had many limitations, some of which were identified and overcome through continual research. For example, to overcome the delay in response time, regional index servers were set up and queries are sent to them instead of sending them to all the index servers (Davis and Lagoze, 2000).

CRADDL

Cornell Reference Architecture for Distributed Digital Libraries (CRADDL) is a component-or service-based digital library architecture. It defines the following five basic services (Lagoze and Fielding, 1998):

- the *repository service*, which provides the mechanisms for the deposit and storage of, and access to, digital objects
- the *naming service*, which identifies digital objects by unique names, URNs, then registered with the naming service
- the *index service*, which provides the mechanism for discovery of digital objects via query
- the *collection service*, which provides the mechanisms for the aggregation of access to sets of digital objects and services into meaningful collections
- *user interface services* or *gateways*, which provide human-centred entry points to the functionality of the digital library.

Of these five services, only the user interface is accessed directly by a human. The design of the user interface gateway can be customized for a specific community using mechanisms such as language, help facilities and graphical aids. The user interface provides users with access to one or more collections through interaction with the collection services corresponding to those collections. Figure 4.3 provides an outline of the CRADDL design.

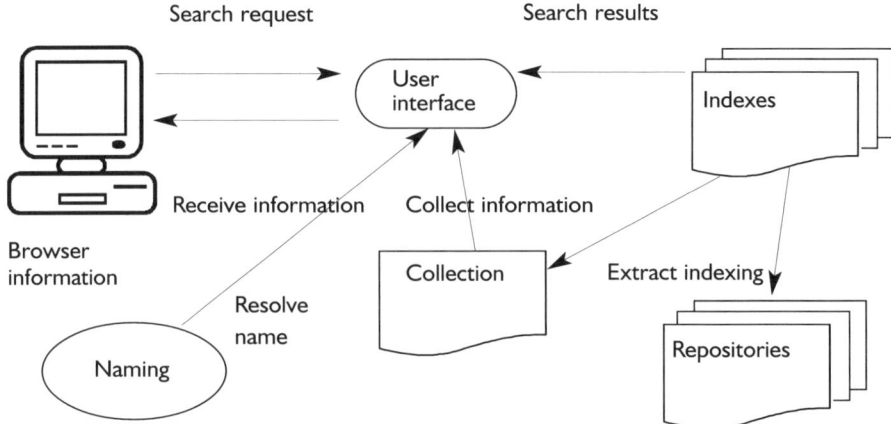

Fig. 4.3 *Interaction among the digital library services in CRADDL*

NSDL

The National Science Digital Library (NSDL) is a broad programme funded by the National Science Foundation (NSF) Division of Undergraduate Education. Its objective is to build a digital library for education in science, mathematics, engineering and technology. The NSF is funding a number of projects, each making its own contribution to the library, with a total annual budget of about US$24 million (Arms et al., 2002). Many of these projects are building collections while others are developing services. The challenge for an integrated design is to ensure that the NSDL is a single coherent library, not simply a set of unrelated activities. In order to achieve interoperability, three sets of agreements are necessary (Arms et al., 2002):

- *technical agreements* to decide on formats, protocols, security systems, etc., so that messages can be exchanged
- *content agreements* to decide on the data and metadata, including semantic agreements on the interpretation of the information
- *organizational agreements* to decide on the ground rules for access, preservation of collections and services, payment, authentication, etc.

The researchers for the NSDL design team identified three levels of interoperability:

- *Federation*. This requires the formation of a federation, the participants in which follow an agreed set of standards and technologies. This provides the strongest form of interoperability, but places the greatest burden on participants for developing and following an agreed set of standards, technologies and tools.
- *Harvesting*. The participants agree to make small efforts to enable some basic shared services, without being required to adopt a complete set of agreements as in a federation.
- *Gathering*. This is the approach taken by web search engines. The basic idea is that even if the various organizations do not co-operate in any formal manner, a base level of interoperability can be achieved by gathering openly accessible information using a web crawler.

Metadata from all the collections is stored in the repository and made available to providers of NSDL services. The following observations of the NSDL research team provide useful insight into the digital library design alternatives (Arms et al., 2002):

- Tightly knit federations often rely on distributed computing to provide services such as searching; the search is broadcast automatically, or the user selects the specific sites to search.
- Federated services decline in responsiveness and reliability as the number of independent servers grows.
- In a digital library environment, where every system does not support the same query formats and protocols, the metadata repository approach of NSDL may be appropriate.

Metadata harvesting

Metadata harvesting is now an important design approach whereby each digital library makes metadata about its collections available in a simple exchange format which can be harvested by service providers and built into services such as information discovery or reference linking. The Open Archives Initiative (OAI; www.openarchives.org/) is based around this concept (Lagoze and Van de Sompel, 2001a, 2001b). Open archives are data repositories that allow remote access using a simple and well-defined publicly available protocol (Suleman and Fox, 2001).

Federated digital library design and NDLTD

Some digital libraries work as a federation with some mutually agreed standards and technology that provide for interoperability at lower costs. The term federated digital library, according to Arms (2000b, 214), describes 'a group of organizations, working together formally or informally, that agree to support a set of common services and standards, thus providing interoperability among their members'. As opposed to the federated search system, metasearch systems allow users to search across a range of diverse systems. However, adoption of such a metasearch system in a digital library environment may lead to a number of problems, for example (Fox and Powell, 1998):

- The system needs to know the characteristics of each search site – the content as well as the search system.
- It has to select the sites to search at every instance.
- It has to distribute the query to each site's software.

- It has to overcome the barriers of language and software to achieve good search results.
- It has to map the search options on each site's search software.
- Upon receiving the results, the meta search system has to deal with the problems of links, duplications, etc.
- The metasearch engine has to integrate the results obtained from the various sites which may be ranked differently.
- It has to resolve the problems caused by the differences in response rates.
- It has to distribute the total workload appropriately.

To resolve these problems, the research team for NDLTD, the digital library of theses and dissertations of masters and doctoral students from various universities in the USA and around the globe (see Chapter 2) adopted a federated design approach. To avoid the work and negotiation involved in adding protocol support to diverse search systems, the team created an intermediate application that mediates search requests, and has access to descriptions of the search engines' user interfaces, the types of queries supported, and the operators that define and qualify those queries (Fox and Powell, 1998). The team also defined the Searchable Database Markup Language (SearchDB-ML), an application of the eXtensible Markup Language (XML), for describing a search site. Initially the model was tested on five sites using different software: two sites used OpenText, one used Dienst, another used HyperWave and the fifth used a Perl-based search script (search.pl). All could easily be described with SearchDB-ML Lite, and the Federated Searcher application was able to support cross-language retrieval, for instance to submit queries in English to the German site and request translations (Fox and Powell, 1998). The federated search system distributes a query to multiple sites and then gathers the result pages into a cache for browsing; results are not merged (Fox et al., 2001b).

Continual research efforts by the NDLTD team have given rise to a mechanism for the creation of, and access to, a union catalogue of theses and dissertations of participating institutions from around the globe. Of late the NDLTD team has developed a new metadata standard, based on Dublin Core (discussed in Chapter 7), and a related project for name authority control. The standard is called ETDMS, which stands for Electronic Thesis and Dissertation Metadata Standard (Fox et al., 2001a). This standard is used by partner sites to export their metadata using the Metadata Harvesting Protocol of the Open Archives Initiative. The goal of this protocol is 'to supply and promote an application-independent interoperability framework that can be used by a variety of communities who are engaged in publishing content on the Web' (Lagoze and Van de Sompel, 2001a, 2001b). By making the theses metadata available in ETDMS format, the participating institutions make the theses accessible at a central portal. The portal is maintained by VTLS (www.vtls.com), using their Virtua system, which provides a web interface to the ETD Union Catalog. The Virtua NDLTD portal provides users with a simple interface to search and browse the merged collection of theses and dissertations. After the users have identified relevant theses, they can follow the links provided to go directly to the items in their source archives (Fox et al., 2001b).

The iLumina model

McClelland et al. (2002) discuss the experiences and lessons learned by iLumina after importing IMS metadata, a set of rich metadata that can be used to map simpler metadata like the Dublin Core. iLumina is a digital library of undergraduate teaching materials for science, mathematics, technology and engineering (SMETE) education, now being developed by Eduprise, the University of North Carolina at Wilmington (UNCW), Georgia State University, Grand Valley State and Virginia Tech. The model is based on a simple, high-level view of the interaction of metadata entities which illustrates the logical separation of data providers and service providers to distinguish between the different roles in handling metadata. Some of the functionality of iLumina is built on the expectation that data will be present in certain fields to drive the browse functionality; the browse page provides views of the metadata based on media type and learning resource type (McClelland et al., 2002).

Hybrid library models

Hybrid library models are based on the concept of information landscapes. The term information landscape relates to how information resources are presented to users to enable them to make sense of the rapidly changing information environment (HyLife, 2002d). From the perspectives of end-users, the seamless cross-searching of relevant services provided by the information landscape in a hybrid library environment greatly improves the opportunities for finding the desired information. Brophy (2000) proposes a generic model for hybrid libraries. The central point of this model is the IAU (Information Access and Use) process and it links the user communities with the information sources.

One of the major roles of a library has been to select the most appropriate information sources from the world of information. Thus, in a digital library environment, one of the major tasks of information professionals will be to select the most appropriate information resources and also, as in traditional libraries, to store the metadata for every information resource. According to Brophy's model, digital libraries should also be engaged in the preservation function and preservation activities should include the information as well as the metadata. On the user front, the model should include the user interface and detailed information about the users. User advice and training are also important parts of this model.

Pinfield (2001b) suggests that the fundamental challenge of digital libraries is integration – bringing the different components of the library together as a coherent whole. He refers to some interesting studies addressing the problem of integration under the hybrid library projects in the third phase of the eLib programme in the UK. Both the RIDING and Agora projects in the UK were designed to investigate the importance of collection-level descriptions, especially metadata, in achieving interoperability among diverse digital resources. While the RIDING project focused on building a mechanism for collecting and storing metadata information about various digital collections, the Agora project focused on investigating the use of this metadata for facilitating access to, and organization of, hybrid library resources (Brack, Palmer and Robinson, 2000).

One of the important questions related to digital library design is the relationship between the OPAC and the other elements of the digital library (Pinfield, 2001b). Many libraries have developed their websites to be used as the gateways to information resources available to users. Most websites of university libraries (which are good examples of hybrid libraries), for example, contain direct links to e-journals, online databases, and selected, and often categorized, web resources. Many libraries have developed databases behind their website to provide access to these kinds of sources (for example, Gardner and Pinfield, 2001). In such cases the library website can be used as a search tool in its own right.

MODELS Information Architecture (MIA)

MODELS (Moving to Distributed Environments for Library Services; www. ukoln.ac.uk/dlis/models/) is a UK Office for Library and Information Networking (UKOLN) initiative supported by eLib and the British Library. It was set up to address the need for conceptual models, technical standards and generic services to be provided to the users of a hybrid library from heterogeneous information resources. MODELS worked through a number of workshops and addressed issues like article discovery and request, metadata for network information objects, national resource discovery and integrating access to resources across multiple domains (HyLife, 2002d). One of the most significant achievements of MODELS was the articulation of MIA (MODELS Information Architecture).

MIA has provided the conceptual underpinning for many hybrid library developments such as Agora and the DNER (HyLife, 2002d). MIA describes a hybrid library environment as (Russell, Gardner and Miller, 1999):

> one where an appropriate range of heterogeneous information services is presented to the user in a consistent and integrated way via a single interface. It may include local and/or remote distributed services, both print and electronic. The environment will provide some or all of the following functions: discovery, location, request, delivery and use, regardless of the domain in which objects are held. Domains may include e.g. libraries, archives, museums, government. There may be dynamic configuration to reflect an individual user's interests (or a group's interests). The environment will depend on open systems and standard protocols.

MIA proposes five layers of architecture for a digital library (*MODELS*, n.d.):

- The *Presenter*, which is responsible for presenting information to, and accepting input from, the user.
- The *Co-ordinator*, which provides an application layer on top of the Mediator. It is responsible for the application logic including user profiles. When a search request is received from the Presenter, the Co-ordinator manipulates the request according to the user's profile and the current session. Again, when the result is returned similar contextualization may occur which may include removing resources that have already been seen within the current session.
- The *Mediator*, which is responsible for understanding the meaning of the services – such as search, locate, request and deliver – that may be requested by the Co-ordinator. The Mediator receives requests from the Co-ordinator and determines which service providers can satisfy the request.
- The *Communicator*, which is responsible for communicating with external services, by shielding the Mediator from details such as communication protocols and service locations. The Communicator provides a gateway between the Mediator and Provider based on a network service profile

associated with each service. The network service profile provides details of the location, protocol, query and response formats and metadata vocabularies that are required in order to access a service.

- The *Provider*, which contains the external services accessed by the system. The layer includes the 'primary' services for which the system exists to provide access, for example library catalogues, abstracting services and subject gateways. The provider layer also includes 'secondary' services that the system must access in order to provide primary services, for example schema registries, authentication services and user profile directories.

Agora hybrid library management system

Agora, the eLib Phase 3 hybrid library project led by the University of East Anglia, with other partners including UKOLN, Fretwell-Downing Informatics and CERLIM (the Centre for Research in Library and Information Management at Manchester Metropolitan University), is based on concepts that emerged from the MODELS project (*MODELS*, n.d.). The central part of the Agora framework is a layer of 'broker' services or a 'middleware' which shields the user from the complex and repetitive processes involved in interacting with individual services. Agora is based on Fretwell-Downing's VDX software, which is also the basis of the RIDING project (Brack, Palmer and Robinson, 2000).

An integral part of Agora's organization is the concept of information landscapes. The construction of these forms an important part of the user-centred focus of Agora's design (*Agora*, n.d.). In order to provide information landscaping, it is necessary to match information about users against the collection-level descriptions – the information about resources.

The collection-level descriptions in the Agora project have been created using the same schema as RIDING, a consortium of libraries which provides improved access to resources through the RIDING Gateway (www.riding.ac.uk/):

- RIDING Gateway: a web service enabling simultaneous access to multiple library catalogues
- RIDING Plus: a reciprocal access and borrowing scheme for researchers in Yorkshire, Humberside and the North East.

The purpose of the RIDING collection-level description (CLD) schema was to provide a standard description of any type of collection – not only books but also all other library materials, such as artworks, sculpture, living material, digital or physical items. Participating libraries are provided with the CLD schema which they can use to complete CLDs describing their own collections and library catalogues. There were 58 CLDs in the first release of the Agora hybrid library management system (HLMS), and these include catalogues (library and internet), gateways, commercial databases and other mixed media (Brack, Palmer and Robinson, 2000). The CLDs are critical to the Agora concept of the HLMS in that these can be used to provide a guide to the aggregation of resources into 'landscapes' and as a guide to the resources themselves.

The DNER

The Distributed National Electronic Resource (DNER) is a managed environment for accessing quality-assured information resources on the internet including journals, monographs, textbooks, abstracts, manuscripts, maps, music scores, still images, geospatial images and numeric data, as well as moving picture and sound collections. The main objective of the DNER is to stimulate the use of high-quality digital resources within all areas of the higher and further education community, by (JISC, 1999):

- developing services that will enable users to identify the information they need and to access it easily in a consistent manner
- facilitating access and contributing to other public resource networks, thus enabling the creation of a unified resource base that will support the operation of a learning society throughout the UK
- facilitating access to resources at national level through purchase and leasing arrangements to achieve best value for the higher and further education community
- playing a leading role in the creation of an environment to stimulate developments at local, regional and national levels throughout the UK and beyond.

The DNER aims to make extensive use of gateways and portals – some based on subjects or disciplines and services, and others developed locally or regionally. The idea is that each gateway should provide access to the full range of resources and should offer a range of different ways of presenting them to the user.

Digital library standards

Digital libraries need to follow a number of standards in order to achieve the objectives of interoperability and integration among the various resources and information systems. Arms (2000b, 209) suggests that the development and adoption of appropriate standards for digital libraries is an expensive affair. He divides the currently available digital library standards for information handling into three categories in terms of the functionality and cost of adoption:

- standards that have moderate functionality and low cost of acceptance, such as the web standards HTTP (Hypertext Transfer Protocol), HTML (Hypertext Markup language) and URL (Uniform Resource Locator)
- standards that have greater functionality but are expensive to adopt, such as SGML (Standard Generalized Markup Language, discussed in Chapter 7) and Z39.50 (discussed in Chapter 9)
- standards with substantial functionality and moderate cost of acceptance, such as Dublin Core and XML (discussed in Chapter 7).

Dempsey et al. (1998) propose the following list of standards for use in the eLib projects:

Standards for the user interface

Common web browsers are recommended.

Standards for data handling and interchange

The following are recommended:

- *for graphics formats*: JPEG, TIFF, GIF, PNG, Group 4 fax, CGM
- *for page description*: PostScript Level 2, PDF
- *for structured documents*: SGML, HTML, XML
- *for moving images/3-D*: MPEG, AVI, GIF89A, QuickTime, RealVideo, VivoActive, VRML
- *for audio formats*: AU, MP3, WAV, RAM/RM, MIDI/MODs.

Some of these formats are discussed in Chapter 6.

Standards for metadata

The following are recommended:

- *for resource description*: Dublin Core, WHOIS++ templates, US-MARC, TEI headers, other community- or domain-specific approaches

- *for resource identification*: URN, PURL, DOI, SICI.

Various metadata formats are discussed in Chapter 7.

Standards for security, authentication and payment services

Many new standards are emerging for the internet and specifically for e-commerce applications which may be used in digital library applications. For details on security and authentication, see Chapter 12.

Summary

Digital libraries are designed to work in a distributed environment. They provide access to a diverse set of information resources located on different computer systems at different locations. A number of technical as well as softer issues are involved in design considerations. Technical considerations include issues of interoperability and integration. Different models have been proposed by digital library researchers for achieving interoperability among diverse systems. Some researchers have proposed the federated search approach, which aims to use a small set of simple and mutually agreed standards and technologies.

Recent research findings reveal that the traditional library approaches to collection development are useful in the design of digital libraries. The Digital Library Research Group at Cornell University has built models around collection-level descriptions, and similar approaches have been taken by researchers in the UK in the course of the MIA and Agora projects. Realizing that purely distributed search and retrieval leads to problems in a distributed digital library environment, researchers have proposed two alternatives: the regional repository model that allows users to search on a regional index, as in the case of the NCSTRL model, and the union catalogue model that allows users to search a central repository for searching and locating a particular resource, as available in the NDLTD union catalogue of theses and dissertations. A number of researchers have also advocated user-centred approaches where the information organization and access are controlled by the user requirements, rather than the system ones.

Digital libraries need to adhere to a number of standards for various activities. This chapter lists some important standards that may be useful at different levels of digital library design and development. Details of some of these standards and formats appear in other chapters.

Chapter 5
Collection management

Outline
Collection management in digital libraries involves a number of activities – from selection to preservation and archiving. This chapter discusses the key issues involved and identifies the main points that may be used as a checklist for selection of digital information resources. Measures for managing specific collections like e-journals, e-books and online databases are also discussed.

Introduction

As discussed in Chapter 2, a digital library may contain information of any type, available in any format. Some digital libraries deal with only one type of material, for example NDLTD only deals with theses and dissertations, while NCSTRL deals with theses, reports and papers on computer science, and the Greenstone Digital Library deals with different types of materials – text, images and music – covering different subjects. Hybrid libraries contain digital as well as traditional library materials – printed sources, as well as documents available on CD-ROM and online databases and internet resources. Many items in a digital and/or a hybrid library are born digital while others are digitized from their analogue version. In today's world many information resources, especially journals, are available both in analogue and digital versions.

Although collection development has remained one of the most important activities in the library world, of late the term 'collection management' is used more frequently in the literature. While some authors use the terms interchangeably, others argue that the term collection management is more inclusive of the various activities involved in the process of building and managing a library's collections. Jenkins and Morley (1999) comment that collection management goes beyond the policy of acquisition to the policies of storage, preservation and weeding. Clayton and Gorman (2001) argue that collection management may be driven in part by collection development needs, but collection management involves many more activities, and in effect collection development is a subset of collection management. Collection development involves the formulation of a systematic general plan for the creation of a library collection that will meet the need of that library's clients, whereas collection management involves the systematic management of the planning, composition, funding, evaluation and use of a library's collection (Clayton and Gorman, 2001).

Collection management is a major area of activity in traditional libraries and is even more challenging in the current digital and/or hybrid library world. Recent developments in ICT have brought significant changes in the publishing industry, thereby making a tremendous impact on the library world. Individuals and institutions can now publish their information on the web, making it accessible freely or upon the payment of a fee. Many traditional publishers, especially the journal and conference publishers, make their products available both in print and digital form, and many new publishers are now producing materials only in digital form. The notion of access and ownership has also changed in the digital world. In contrast with the printed world, digital materials are not owned by libraries; libraries provide access to them – usually for a certain period of time under certain access conditions. In the printed world there is only one common model – libraries pay for each copy of an item, and can keep and use it as long as they want to. Various alternative economic models are available in the digital world – in some cases libraries can get a licence for unlimited access to a digital item for a certain period of time (for a year, say), or in others can enter into a pay-per-use arrangement for digital items. Many issues are associated with access, such as user authentication and access control. Since users may access information from anywhere, libraries, and especially publishers and service providers, want to keep track of how the information is used – who uses it, how often, for how long, and so on.

This chapter addresses various issues of collection management in a digital library environment. Major issues are discussed with reference to some specific types of digital information resources – e-journals, e-books and databases.

The process of collection management

Libraries are charged with the responsibility of applying judgements to determine what to select, organize, preserve and provide for access to the user community (Borgman, 2000b, 106). Collection management in a digital library, or more specifically in a hybrid library, has to follow the policies and practices followed in traditional collection development processes used for printed materials while keeping in view the issues and complexities that are specifically related to digital materials. A host of technical, economic, user and usability issues are related to collection management in digital libraries. While discussing the collection management projects at Macquarie University in Australia, McLean (2000) mentions that the issues of authentication, authorization and access management are the basic building blocks for collection management in a digital library. However, the selection of materials remains the most important part of a collection management programme.

Selection of materials

The collection development process aims to select only those materials that are deemed to be useful and relevant for the users of a library. For many years this process has been carefully performed in libraries of printed materials by experienced staff who have a good understanding of the institution's characteristics and goals, and also of the users, their nature and requirements. Several standard tools, ranging from national bibliographies to publishers' catalogues and book reviews, have been used side by side with user and publisher recommendations. Librarians have always attempted to make the best use of their budget by selecting the most appropriate information resources.

In the digital world, the selection of materials is an extremely difficult task, since there is neither a single catalogue of all the different varieties of digital information resource, nor are there tools equivalent to the national bibliographies or union catalogues. Many digital library services are now trying to build a union catalogue of specific types of digital information resource, for example NDLTD is creating a union catalogue of digital dissertations and theses, but union catalogues for each kind of digital information resource do not exist.

The identification process for digital resources can be time-consuming and laborious (Jones, 1999). Library managers often employ specific members of staff to scan the web regularly using various web search tools to discover new and relevant digital materials. They also have to depend on one or more vendors for access to specific types of resource, such as e-journals or e-books.

Digital information resources are tied to the technology to such an extent that the content cannot be used at all without the appropriate software and hardware. Hence information other than the content and source is necessary for each electronic information resource to help in the process of selection. Libraries may need to buy, and make necessary arrangements to preserve, the content as well as the technology. Thus a host of issues, such as digital preservation and technology preservation or migration, are associated with the process of collection development in a digital library. Digital archiving and preservation issues are discussed in Chapter 10, while various other activities associated with collection development are discussed in the following sections in this chapter.

Selection criteria

Detailed guidelines for the selection of library materials have been provided by Spiller (2000), while some simple guidelines have been recommended by Clayton and Gorman (2001). According to Clayton and Gorman (2001, 89) a selection policy should take the following points into account:

- the authority of creators – authors, publishers, etc.
- scope – the breadth and depth of coverage
- treatment and level – suitability for the intended audience
- arrangement – organization of content
- format – accessibility and searchability, readability, portability, durability, etc.
- special features – what makes an item different from similar products.

Such traditional selection criteria, based on the nature and characteristics of the parent organization, the user community as well as the subject matter, apply equally to the selection of digital information resources. However, various other criteria have to be considered for digital resources, such as content and format of the resource, technology requirements, access and user interfaces, licensing and preservation. Since digital information resources abound in number, and there are many agencies and vendors that provide access to them under different terms and conditions, it is very important that each resource is evaluated before making a selection. Many guidelines for the selection of electronic information resource are now available; see, for example, Chowdhury and Chowdhury, 2001a; HEIR alliance, 1995; Smith, 2002; UC Berkeley Library, 2001.

Clayton and Gorman (2001, 93–4) draw together a number of criteria for the selection of digital information resources. In fact, they have proposed two sets of criteria, one for the selection of CD-ROMs and online resources, and another for the selection of internet resources. Major factors to be considered for the selection of digital information resources include the following:

- content, quality, currency, etc.
- hardware, software and network requirements
- the version of the product – network or standalone version (for CD-ROM products)
- the number of concurrent users allowed
- access control – through password, proxy server authorization, etc.
- price and licensing and copyright agreements
- database features, the retrieval engine and the user interface(s)
- ease of use and user training/efforts required
- archiving procedures.

A number of issues are related to the content of digital resource, such as the quality and completeness of the data and images, coverage, accuracy, and authority of the producer. Some digital information resources are replicas of their printed counterparts while others are available only in digital form. Digital information resources that are available from different vendors may often vary in terms of content and coverage. For example, some vendors only provide access to abstracts while others provide access to the full text; in some cases a collection is divided into different years, or blocks of years, and one can select a range. Libraries may also have to decide whether to go for the electronic version of a product only, or for both the printed and the electronic version.

User interfaces and information retrieval features are very important aspects of any electronic information resource. The interface should be appropriate to the information resource as well as the target users. Some products have more than one interface, to suit the needs of different types of users, or users with different information retrieval skills. Details of the user interfaces and inform-ation retrieval features of various digital information products and services appear in Chapters 8 and 9. From the perspective of collection management, it is important to know whether a particular information product has to be used with, and only with, the interface that comes with the product. This poses a restriction on users, since every time they change a product, they will come across a different interface. However, to overcome this problem, many companies, for example Ingenta and Ovid Online, provide one search interface for a range of products. Similarly, many digital libraries provide users with only one interface to search a range of products, while others come with a different interface for each. Examples of these appear in Chapters 8 and 9.

The selection of information resources is also influenced by the equipment required for their use. This is particularly true for resources that appear on CD-ROM. The most common concern is whether the CD-ROM can run on a network or must be restricted to a standalone computer. Collection development is also influenced by a digital library's design. As discussed in Chapter 4, the design architecture has an influence on how the digital library provides access to the different types of digital information resources that are available locally as well as on remote computers.

Another issue related to selection is the archiving and preservation of the information resources. Many libraries and institutions are now involved in procedures and policies for the archiving and preservation of scholarly publications (for details see Chapter 10). However, internet resources, especially websites, also contain a tremendous amount of valuable information, and these information resources are not always preserved by their creators. As a result, these digital information resources often get lost, and it is extremely difficult to see the changes that have taken place in any given website in terms of its content, design and other features. The Internet Archive (www.archive.org/) is an exemplary effort in this regard. Founded in 1996, the Archive has built a collection of over 100 terabytes of text and moving images, comprising over 40 terabytes of text, 1000 movies, and television output. Users can get access to the archives of any website through the Internet Archive. The major challenges of building and managing the Internet Archive collection included issues of scale, funding, law, and access (Kahle, Prelinger and Jackson, 2001).

Collection development models

Traditionally libraries have received a sum of money for building their collection which they have distributed among various units, branches or subjects for acquiring information resources that are thought to be the most useful for their users. Over the years, and especially when the budget began to shrink while user requirements began to increase, library managers have adopted various measures for effective collection development. Roberts (2001) discusses six different collection development models that show a gradual shift from the traditional to digital library collection development programmes:

1   *Model A, Continuation.* This is based on traditional collection funding, with electronic resources treated as quasi-bibliographic (e.g. as serial subscriptions).
2   *Model B, Continuation with development of value-added markets.* In this model, revenue-generating commercial activity is allowed but usually only to the point of cost recovery. Standards are set to maintain core collections and core access, and protect certain user groups.
3   *Model C, Converged services.* In this model progressive moves towards substantial electronic resources are considered. The entire collection development process is refocused on cost saving, cost efficiency and concentration on user benefit.
4   *Model D, Hybrid library.* In this model electronic resources are identified and built up, with investment in technology platforms. Distributed resources are managed collectively, especially for areas of high demand. This model also involves appropriate intellectual property and licensing agreements in order to maximize access to information.
5   *Model E, Advanced hybrid library–information services.* This is an extension of Model D, with increased emphasis on digital information and digital surrogates, and improved access to digital information.
6   *Model F, Model E with content provision and repackaging.* In this model libraries use technology-based access to distributed resources with the objective of offering customized products to the user. While maintaining a base level of service for meeting the needs of frequently demanded information, this model particularly focuses on meeting the individual needs of each customer.

While reviewing the trends in collection management and information services, Roberts (2001) predicts that public institutions may actually shadow the current private publisher–producer model, repackaging information and providing customer-centred services and products of their own, and the conventional publisher monopolies will be challenged by independent citizen publishers who will benefit from cheap access to the web.

Electronic journals

Electronic journals form a large part of the collection of a digital library. Collection management related to e-journals involves a number of issues, such as technology requirements, access regulations, access mechanisms – via publisher or aggregator – and cataloguing to make the library patrons aware of the e-journals. Several authors discuss these issues; see, for example, Clayton and Gorman, 2001; Hudson and Windsor, 1998; Luther, 1998; Machovec, 1997; Porteous, 1997; Schoonbaert, 1998 .

Access to electronic journals is provided either by publishers themselves or aggregators. Most e-journal publishers provide access to their journals from their websites (Lee and Morris, 2000). Usually if a library subscribes to the print version of a journal, access to its electronic version is available either at no cost or for a small additional fee; the price of the online-only version may be slightly lower than the cost of the print version. In order to save the time and hassle of negotiating and dealing with each and every individual publisher of e-journals, libraries mostly choose to work with one or more of the aggregators who gather the journals of several publishers under one interface and search system. These services organize e-journal access and administer passwords, table of content services, usage statistics and archiving (Lee and Morris, 2000). Luther (1998) and Machovec (1997) list the major publishers and aggregators with details of their products, formats used, special features and collaborations with other online products. Schoonbaert (1998) provides a list of URLs for publishers and aggregators, such as Blackwell's Electronic Journal Navigator, Swetsnet, Ebsco Online, and so on.

Some international societies and associations have developed their own digital libraries through which users can get access to all of their publications; the most prominent examples are the ACM digital library and IEL (the digital library of the IEE and IEEE). These services are available to the members of the society or association, or through subscription. However, over the years several high-quality, productive free scholarly electronic journals have appeared. Fosmire and Yu (2000) conducted a survey of 1209 scholarly e-journals and noted that 213 (18%) were free, and each free e-journal contained a reasonable number of good articles.

Access to e-journals is an important issue, and several models are now available. In some cases, users need to use a password to get access to a particular journal or service from an aggregator; in other cases, the service may be accessed from anywhere within a particular network; in yet another model the service automatically recognizes authorized users through the IP address of the computer that they are using.

One of the major differences, from the collection management perspective, between a print and an online collection is that, in the case of the former, the library owns the printed journals and can do anything with them, while in the case of the latter, the access rights may remain valid only as long as the subscription is renewed. This is a major point that makes e-journals different from their printed counterparts. Printed journals, once subscribed to, are owned by a library, and therefore even if a library discontinues the subscription to a particular journal at any point in time, users can still get access to the previous issues held in the library. However, in the case of e-journals, a subscribing library is only given access rights to one or more issues, while the material is owned by someone else – the publisher or the aggregator, say. In such a situation, if the library discontinues the subscription, then it may lose the right to access the past issues for which it was a bona fide subscriber.

Thus, a digital library collection management programme should take into account several issues, such as who owns the back issues, how to get access to them, what happens if the subscription is discontinued, and so on. JSTOR (www.jstor.org) is a service that can solve the problem of access to back issues of journals in the digital library world. The major goals of JSTOR are to build a reliable and comprehensive archive of important scholarly journal literature, and improve access to these journals. Libraries can join JSTOR by paying fees, and this can provide their users with access to JSTOR's electronic journal collections. Usually a participating institution pays two types of fee: (1) a one-time archive capital fee (ACF), which initiates access rights to information in a specific collection archive, and (2) an annual access fee (AAF), to help cover the recurring costs of updating and maintaining the archive into the future.

Electronic books

Electronic books are not as new as digital libraries. They appeared long ago, for example reference books on CD-ROM (for details see Chowdhury and Chowdhury, 2001a). However, of late two different types of e-books have appeared – one that needs special equipment to be read and another that can be read online.

Reference books

Many reference books are now available on CD-ROM and/or online and can be accessed through payment. Many reference books are also available online at no cost. Chapter 14 lists a number of sites that provide such free access.

While there are several advantages of having online access to reference sources, a major question is what happens when the subscription is discontinued. As in the case of e-journals, access to editions that were previously subscribed to may be blocked when the subscription to a specific reference source is cancelled. Thus the collection management staff should make sure who owns the back issues, and what happens if the subscription is discontinued.

Since reference sources can be used by all types of users – from experts to novice users, students to professionals – the selection procedure should take a number of issues into consideration. Chowdhury and Chowdhury (2001a) discuss the criteria for selection and evaluation of electronic reference sources with particular reference to those that are available on CD-ROM or through online search services.

e-books

Although electronic books have existed for quite some time – online (accessible through information search services, like Dialog), on CD-ROM and more recently now on the web – many electronic books are produced that can be used only with specific readers. There are a number of advantages of these e-books, for example (Chowdhury and Chowdhury, 2001b):

- They are cheaper than their printed equivalents.
- They can be delivered instantly.
- They are portable with e-book reading machines or laptops on which one can carry 100 books at a time.
- They are searchable.
- They are easy to use since users can use the hyperlinks and cut and paste text to use specific sections in another work.
- They do not deteriorate over time, as happens in the case of printed books with poor-quality paper and printing.
- Users can view images, graphics and multimedia.

Examples of e-book readers include the following:

- Microsoft Reader
- RCA eBook

- Adobe Acrobat eBook Reader
- Mobipocket reader
- Gemstar eBooks
- Softbook Reader.

Each e-book reader provides a list of books that are available for purchase and can be read using it. Chowdhury and Chowdhury (2001b) compare the features of three e-book readers: Microsoft Reader, RCA eBook reader and Adobe Acrobat eBook reader.

EBONI (Electronic Books On-Screen Interface), a research project at the University of Strathclyde, was designed to evaluate different approaches to the design of learning and teaching resources on the web, and to identify the techniques and styles that are most appropriate in enabling users to retrieve, quickly and easily, the information they require. This research came up with a number of issues and guidelines for the design and evaluation of e-books (for example, Landoni, Wilson and Gibb, 2000a, 2000b, 2001; R. Wilson, 2001, 2002; Wilson and Landoni, 2001). The e-book task force for the University of California digital library identified the following eight elements that are important to the evaluation of academic e-book use: content, software and hardware standards and protocols, digital rights management, access, archiving, privacy, the market and pricing, and enhancements and ideal e-book features (Connaway, 2001).

netLibrary (www.netlibrary.com)

Although electronic books are available in many forms from many sources, a significant change in the world of electronic books has been made by netLibrary, a division of OCLC Online Computer Library Center. It was founded in August 1998 and is located in Boulder, Colorado. netLibrary has come up with a model for e-books that is different from the other e-book models discussed earlier in this chapter and is an alternative to the print library model. Under their model, books are produced in digital form, and libraries are encouraged to let their users access the digital books through membership of netLibrary.

netLibrary offers access to the full text of a large number of reference, scholarly and professional books. With netLibrary, librarians can purchase collections of e-books on any subject. The users of the library can then search, retrieve and read those books online. The collection features thousands of titles from leading publishers such as ABC-CLIO, Cambridge University Press, John Wiley and Sons, Inc., Oxford University Press, Palgrave and Routledge. The

Title Select service allows librarians to search the netLibrary e-book catalogue to view complete collections. Users of each member library are asked to register for the first time and then they can select one or more e-books for their current or future use.

Questia (www.questia.com)

Questia is a service that provides online access to a large collection of books and journal articles in the humanities and social sciences. In addition to providing facilities for searching and reading documents online, it offers a range of search, note-taking and writing tools for users. It targets subscription at individual users as opposed to netLibrary, which provides access through libraries. Individual users can subscribe to Questia by one of the two following means:

- for a monthly subscription of US$19.95 a month
- for an annual subscription of US$119.95.

Users have access to over 70,000 titles (over 45,000 books and over 25,000 articles) covering various humanities and social science subjects including history, philosophy, economics, political science, literature, education, psychology and sociology.

ebrary (www.ebrary.com)

ebrary, founded in February, 1999 in Mountain View, California, offers libraries and other institutions access to more than 7500 books from over 115 commercial and academic publishers. Libraries can also use ebrary to archive and distribute their own reserves and special collections online. There are two payment models for print or copy transactions:

- 'All you can eat': libraries can pay a flat rate and provide patrons with unlimited print or copy transactions.
- Patrons pay: libraries can choose to have users set up their own accounts with ebrary and pay for their own print or copy transactions. The average cost per transaction is 15 to 50 US cents per page.

ebrary has a specific reader that can be downloaded from the site. With the ebrary reader, users can perform full-text searches within a specific document or search the full text of all available documents in the ebrary repository. Users can also search by author, title, publisher or subject. Libraries need to pay an annual licence fee for the ebrary service based on the number of users and library type.

Databases and services

A large proportion of a digital, especially hybrid, library's collection comprises online databases that can be accessed directly through the creator, for example through the PubMed service of the US National Library of Medicine, or through online search services like Dialog, Lexis-Nexis, Ovid Online, and so on. Each service allows users to search one or more databases and read the abstract or full text of the documents. Each has a specific set of terms and conditions for access. Details of selected online search services, including payment mechanisms, have been discussed in the literature (for example, Chowdhury and Chowdhury, 2001a).

In addition to the traditional online search services, a number of new services are now available and are frequently used by libraries for providing access to digital information resources. For example, since its launch in May 1998, Ingenta (www.ingenta.com) has become a leading information service provider that supplies access to a large number of digital documents from a variety of publishers. According to the Ingenta website, 'More than 8,000 academic, research and corporate libraries, institutions and consortia, from around the world, currently rely on Ingenta for managed access to academic and professional content.' Another organization, Factiva (www.factiva.com), a Dow Jones and Reuters company, provides access to digital information resources including Dow Jones and Reuters Newswires and the *Wall Street Journal*. It is one of the most prominent sources of business information comprising nearly 8000 sources from 118 countries in 22 languages.

Summary

Collection management in digital and hybrid libraries is an extremely important activity. It encompasses a number of tasks, from formulating a selection policy to managing access to information resources, and making decisions about the retention and preservation of information resources. Proper collection management in digital libraries is influenced by a number of stakeholders in the information world, such as librarians, publishers, subscription agents, database hosts and information service aggregators.

An appropriate selection methodology acts as an excellent filtering mechanism whereby the massive collection of available information resources is sieved and selected to meet the information needs of the user population. Complex technological and economic measures are also integral parts of the collection management process. Digital library managers need to assess and select the most appropriate business model available from the vendors for providing users with access to digital information resources. Complex technological issues governing access control, payment mechanisms, and so on are also involved.

In addition to managing the collection that is paid for, digital library collection management programmes should also build mechanisms for managing those information resources that are available without charge on the internet and yet are very useful for their users. Burnett and Seuring (2001) discuss how libraries are now integrating free internet resources into their descriptions of information.

The digital library world is going through major changes caused by research, innovation and developments in ICT. Collection management will continue to be a complex process, and digital library managers need to make complex decisions about providing access to various digital information sources – e-journals, databases, e-books, and so on. A number of new reference and information services are now available through the internet. Chapter 11 discusses some of these services. Since many reference and information services are now available for free through the internet, it is now important for digital library managers to decide whether it is worth spending a large amount of money on building and maintaining a collection of reference sources which are by nature expensive to acquire and update. There are some risks, too – the sustainability of the free reference and information services is not ensured and, as discussed in Chapter 11, their quality is not always high. Nevertheless, these developments have forced library managers to think carefully about the management of digital reference collections and services. Chowdhury (2002b) comments that this is a time when digital library researchers and managers should think of the best ways and means to make optimum use of the technology and of the experience and expertise of human intermediaries in improving digital libraries from mere access centres to information service providers.

Chapter 6
Digitization

Outline

A digital library may contain materials that are born digital, such as e-journals and e-books, or may contain materials that were originally produced in another form but subsequently digitized. The process of digitizing materials involves a number of considerations and this chapter discusses the major steps in carrying out a digitization project. It discusses various technical issues, such as hardware and software, file formats and file compression, and then the various post processing requirements for making the digitized files accessible to end-users. Finally the chapter oultines various cost factors associated with a digitization project. Thus this chapter will provide readers with an understanding of the whole digitization process, together with various technical, economic and other issues it raises.

Introduction

Although a large proportion of a digital library's collection comprises materials that are born digital, such as e-journals, internet resources, databases, and so on, there are many resources that are not originally created in digital form, but are digitized in order to include them in a digital library's collection. Digitization is the conversion of an analogue signal or code into a digital signal or code (Lee, 2001, 3). Though the process of digitization forms an important part of building a digital library, it is not an entirely new phenomenom. Many libraries and information systems have long been engaged in digitizing some of their printed materials, for example newspapers, and the entire process, from digitization to indexing, storage and retrieval, used to be called document management. However, digitization has become a major area of activity and research in digital libraries, and many big digitization projects have been undertaken over the past few years.

In order to meet the needs of distributed digital libraries, digitization projects need to consider several standards for text and multimedia file formats, as well as their indexing, storage and so on. In this chapter we discuss the basic process of digitization, then look at various file formats, and finally at the essential features of some digitization projects as part of the digital library development process. Many recent publications describe the process of digitization in detail (for example, Beagrie, 2000; Beagrie and Greenstein, 1998; Hampson, 2001; Lee, 2001; Pan and Higgins, 2001; Reid, 2000; Tanner, 2001). There are many websites that also provide detailed guidelines for digitization. In the UK, HEDS (the Higher Education Digitization Service; http://heds.herts.ac.uk/), funded by JISC, provides advice on, and guidelines for, digitization. TASI (the Technical Advisory Service for Images) is another JISC-funded service designed to advise and support the academic community on digitization. The TASI website provides specific guidelines and standards for each step of a digitization project (TASI, 2001a, 2001b, 2001c, 2001d). Many other websites also provide detailed descriptions of specific digitization projects (for example, the Research Libraries Group website (www.rlg.ac.uk); Harvard University Resources on Digitization (Harvard University, 2002); Department of Special Collections (n.d.), University of California at Santa Barbara (UCSB). The VADS (Visual Arts Data Service) website provides a set of guidelines for good practice in the creation, management and use of electronic resources in the visual arts (VADS, 2001).

The major steps of a digitization project are discussed in this chapter, and appropriate references are provided for further studies. The process of digitization actually involves two major sets of activities: (1) the process of digital conversion whereby source materials are converted into digital form, and (2) the processing of digitized information, which involves several activities related to the storage, organization, processing and retrieval of digitized information.

Issues related to a digitization project

The two most obvious benefits of digitization are improved access and preservation. Items, once digitized, can be used by many people from different places simultaneously at any point in time. Unlike printed or analogue collections (such as papers, photographs, paintings, and audio and video cassettes) digitized collections are not damaged by heavy and frequent usage, which helps in the preservation of information.

While there are these obvious benefits of digitization, there are some problems too. The most obvious problem relates to the quality. While digitizing, we may lose some important aspects of the original document. The other problem relates to access management. Proper mechanisms need to be put in place to determine the authenticity of materials, as well as to control unauthorized access and use. These issues are discussed in Chapters 10 and 12. The process of digitization also involves huge cost. In addition to paying for equipment and the digitization process, there are many other types of costs, for example staff salaries, and those associated with various related activities before and after digitization, such as movement of physical items, copyright clearance, creation of records and indexes, and so on.

Descriptions of the various stages of a digitization project have been provided in a number of guidelines (for example, the TASI, HEDS and VADS guidelines). Descriptions of some recent digitization projects are also available in the literature (for example, Hamson, 2001; Pan and Higgins, 2001; Tanner, 2001). Lee (2001, 8 and 153) describes the life cycle of a digitization project.

The process of digitization

As Figure 6.1 shows, there are basically three major phases of a digitization project. The main activities involved in the first phase relate to the preparation for digitization, and the actual process of digitizing materials. Once a source material has been digitized the second phase begins, which is concerned with the processing required to make the digitized materials easily accessible to users. This involves a number of editorial and processing activities such as cataloguing, indexing and compression. End-users can use the digitized materials only when the digitized materials are properly processed. There are other issues too, which come in the third phase; they relate to the preservation and maintenance of the digitized collections and services. Activities involved in the first phase are discussed in this chapter while preservation and related issues are discussed in Chapter 10.

A digitization project may start in response to an external request and/or availability of funding, or as part of an institutional plan for digitizing one or more specific collections. The first kind is called reactive digitization and the second proactive digitization (Lee, 2001, 11). Whatever the reason for a digitization process's origin, the first step is the selection of materials to be digitized. Although the process of selection is influenced by a number of factors, for example the objective of the project, the target users, the available resources, time,

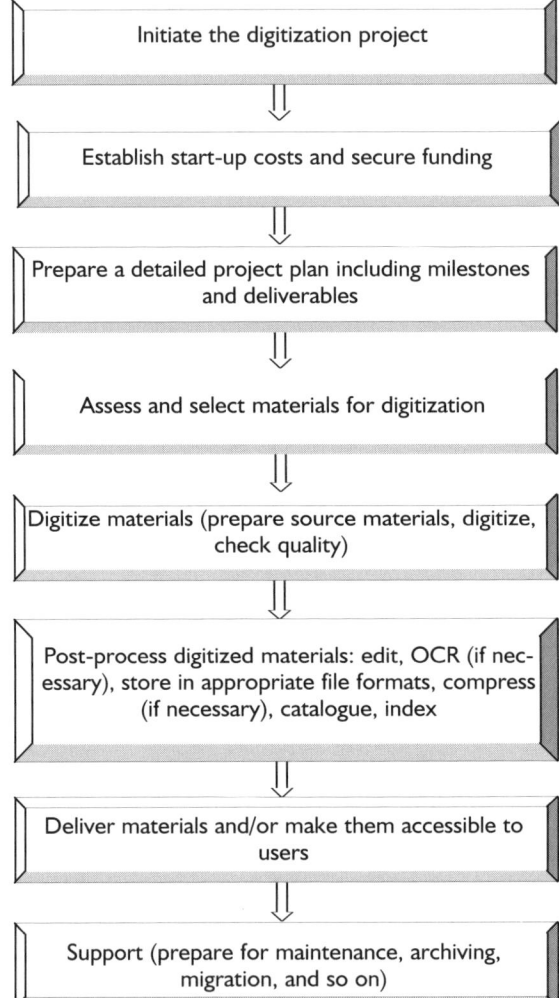

Fig. 6.1 *Steps involved in digitization*

and so on, the process should draw up clear guidelines for selection (and rejection) of materials. A number of considerations are involved. The Technical Advisory Service for Images website (TASI, 2001d) includes a set of guidelines for this purpose:

- Get the copyright situation clear.
- Get adequate information about the image to ensure retrieval from a database.

- Find out the various image modalities that are available in the collection.
- Determine whether it is technically feasible to capture the information.
- Determine who will use the images and how.

Items selected for digitization may be of different types, for example they may be printed materials, drawings, photographs, paintings, manuscripts, rare book materials, and museum objects or relics. Different types of materials may require different digitization approaches and also different hardware, software, technology and skills. The physical condition and vulnerability of the source materials are also very important factors. At the beginning of any digitization project, it is very important to know the various attributes of the source documents, such as their size, condition, text characteristics, tone and whether they include illustrations (Chapman and Kenney, 1996). If the source documents are bound then it is necessary to know whether the documents can be stripped from the binding (Hamson, 2001).

The Harvard University Library Digitization Initiative (n.d.) provides the following guidelines for digitization of images and text materials:

- Determine whether page images, full text, or both need to be produced to meet project requirements.
- Assess source materials and plan appropriate preparation, transfer, handling and disposition procedures.
- Create *archival* versions of page images and/or full text for long-term storage and production of *deliverables* as needed.
- Create *deliverables* for distribution as page images and/or full text.
- Control costs and workflow.

Similar guidelines have also been prepared by other libraries or library federations; see, for example, the guidelines prepared by the Research Libraries Group and Digital Library Federation (Colet, 2000). A number of issues are related to the size and format of materials, especially the handling of framed images and oversized materials. Colet (2000) provides a list of questions to be considered when digitizing mounted images.

- Can the item be removed easily and safely from its mount or mat for capture? If not, can the image of the item be captured while it is attached to the mount or mat?

- If the items need to be removed, who should be involved and at what level – conservators, framing personnel, or material preparers?
- Should an original mount be treated as part of the item, and should it be included in the scan?
- What type of physical adjustments are to be made if the original item needs to remain as it is and what type of complications may be involved for scanning or imaging?

For digitizing oversized materials, the following points are to be considered (Colet, 2000):

- type of digital capture device (equipment and techniques) needed for the oversized materials
- type of scanning judgements necessary to accommodate the critical features such as density and type size
- file compression issues for storage and dissemination
- mechanisms for access to the materials by end-users, such as whether they can enlarge the size of the digital material to match the original size.

Technical issues

A number of technical issues such as hardware, software and image file compression are critical to a successful digitization project. These issues are discussed in the following sections.

Hardware and software issues

The selection of hardware and software for a digitization project depends on many factors. The primary selection criterion for the hardware is governed by the type of source materials that need to be digitized. Scanners are the most commonly used devices for capturing digital images. Different types of scanners are available, such as flatbed, drum, film, network and hand scanners. Four major factors need to be considered when selecting an appropriate scanner: optical resolution, bit depth (optical density or OD), scan area and scan time. Each factor has an impact on the quality of the final digital image. The other type of commonly used device for digitization is the digital camera. They may come in different shapes and sizes and can produce images of different qualities.

Software may be used for different purposes in the process of digitization. After an image has been created, software may be required to edit or post-process the image, for example to adjust the tone or colour. Software may also be required for other purposes, such as the creation of a text file from an image file containing only text, or text with graphics. The processing of the digitized items may entail other software uses, for example for cataloguing and indexing, conversion into a chosen file format or compression.

Selecting an imaging application is an important decision. TASI guidelines list the following factors to be taken into consideration (TASI, 2001c):

- cost of the application, as well as of any training or familiarization time
- hardware requirements, including memory, processor, display and hard disk space
- operating system and the need for interoperability (suitability for cross-platform operation)
- capabilities: in addition to the manipulation of the images, the software may need to perform other tasks, such as file import and/or export, colour management, screen/printer/scanner calibration, and large file handling.

Compression

Bitmap files (see below) can become very large for high-resolution images. Compression is one way of reducing file sizes. There are two types of file compression: lossless and lossy compression.

Lossless compression uses algorithms that, typically, encode repeating elements or patterns within an image. For example, stretches of pixels that share the same colour are taken and stored in just two bytes – one for the colour and the other for the number of adjacent pixels. An important property of lossless compression is that when the file is decompressed the image is restored to its original condition.

The compression ratios of lossless compressions are not very high, typically around 2:1. Lossy compression techniques produce much higher compression ratios, sometimes in excess of 100:1. The down side of this is that there is a significant reduction in image quality, the degree of image degradation depending on the image content and the amount of compression applied.

File formats

Various file formats for texts and images are available. A number of sources describe file formats (for example Lee, 2001, Chapter 3; Lesk, 1997, Chapter 4), and many such sources are available on the internet (for example, *JISC Multi-*

media File Formats Database; Zhang, 1999). Some of the common file formats are discussed below. Different factors affect the choice of format at each stage of the digitization process, such as:

• *Acquisition.* This is the first and most important step. It is important to maintain the highest fidelity to the original.
• *Archival storage.* There must be a standard format that will be readable in the future. The ability to hold associated metadata may be useful.
• *Editing.* Proprietary formats may be useful to support any editing of information.
• *Delivery.* Factors to be taken into account include destination device (screen, printer) and its capabilities, delivery method, file size and network bandwidth, and format support at destination.

A general rule of thumb is that a chosen format should minimize data loss as far as practicable.

Text file formats

Broadly speaking, there are only two types of text file formats: ASCII and binary. ASCII files are text files that one can read from a DOS editor or any word-processor. ASCII text files usually have an extension such as .doc or .txt. Binary files contain non-ASCII characters, and if they are displayed on the screen a set of strange symbols can be seen. While ASCII files are basically text files, binary file formats may be used for compressed files, text, software, games, pictures, foreign languages, music and movies.

Another type of text file is the postscript file. Postscript is a page description language developed by Adobe Systems in 1985. Postscript (PS) language is used to describe page settings and to tell a printer what to print. PS files cannot be read on the screen without a postscript viewer.

General file formats

PDF (Portable Documents Format) is a very common file format used in many digital documents. With the PDF format, one can get all media – colour, graphics, fonts, and format. Adobe Acrobat reader software is needed to read a PDF file.

Another very common file format used in the web and digital libraries is the HTML file format. An HTML file may comprise text as well as non-text materials such as graphics, images and multimedia information. HTML files (for details, see Chapter 7) can be read by any web browser and also by software like MSWord.

Image file formats

A number of image file formats are now available, each having its own characteristics. Selection of an appropriate image file format should be governed by a number of factors, such as the file size, number of colours, resolution, and so on.

Colet (2000) provides the following formula for calculating the file size of images:

> Pixel dimensions *times* number of channels = file size
> *Example*: 4,300 × 5,300 pixels × 3 channels = 68,370,000 bytes = approximately 69 Mb
>
> *OR*
>
> Dimensions (in inches) *times* resolution per inch *times* number of channels = file size
> *Example*: 8 inches by 10 inches at 300 ppi, 3 channels:
> 8 × 300 × 10 × 300 × 3 = approximately 22 Mb

ppi (pixels per inch) is a measure of on-screen resolution. The most common screen resolution is 72 ppi, though high-end monitors can display 84–200 ppi.

Channels control the colour of the images. Single channels are required for grey-scale or monochromatic images as well as for the reduced colour palette used by the web. A full-colour picture on the monitor requires three channels: red, green and blue (RGB), whereas an offset reproduction requires four channels: cyan, magenta, yellow and black (CMYK). While archival files are usually stored in RGB, copies of the archival files are converted to CMYK by printers for reproduction.

Vector and raster images

Vector images consist of a series of objects – lines, ellipses, polygons, and so on – and each object has a number of properties associated with it such as position, line thickness, line colour and line style (TASI, 2001b). Technical illustrations, floor plans, maps, diagrams and charts are typical examples of images suitable to be captured in this way. The major advantages of this format are as follows:

- Objects can be edited independently.
- Files tend to be small.
- Images can be scaled or resized without loss of resolution.
- Image resolution is independent of the output device.

Raster or bit-mapped images are made up of a matrix of pixels (picture elements). Each pixel contains the digital colour information sampled from its corresponding position in the original artwork. A 24-bit (16 million colours or true colour) image uses 3 bytes (8 bits for green, 8 for blue, 8 for red) to describe the colour of each pixel (TASI, 2001b). Since information about every individual pixel is stored in them, bit-mapped image file sizes tend to be large. The main advantages of bit-mapped or raster images are (TASI, 2001b) as follows:

- Each pixel can be edited individually.
- A high degree of photorealism can be obtained.

BMP

BMP or bitmap file format is available in almost all Windows-based graphics applications. It is the native graphics format for both OS/2 and Windows, and is good for reading and writing small images. BMP supports very simple compression, hence file sizes can be large, thereby making the files unsuitable for storage and/or exchange.

GIF

GIF (Graphic Interchange Format), developed by CompuServe, is a device-independent method of storing pictures. GIF images can store 8 bits/pixel (256 or fewer colours), and are suitable for images with only a few distinct colours, line drawings and simple cartoons.

JPEG

JPEG (Joint Photographic Experts Group) format stores full-colour information: 24 bits/pixel (16 million colours). It works well with photographs, naturalistic scenes and similar materials. The files are much smaller than GIF files and hence are suitable for sending through the internet. It is used commonly for encoding digitized photographs.

PCX

PCX is a raster file originally available on the PC. PageMaker, Photoshop and QuarkXPress (Mac) support the PCX file format. It is very suitable for cartoon-type computer graphics

PNG

Portable Network Graphics (PNG) was created to overcome some copyright problems with GIF formats and now supersedes GIF. PNG files can have *trillions* of colours in a single image and are much smaller than GIF files. It provides for lossless compression and can contain searchable information about content, history and authorship. The height and width of the images can be scaled automatically to fit the browser window.

TGA

TARGA or TGA is common for high-resolution video images. TGA format has many variations and supports several types of compression. It also supports grey scale, colour and colour maps.

TIFF

TIFF (Tagged Image File Format) is a multi-purpose raster file format developed by Aldus and Microsoft with an objective of providing a basis for importing scanned images into desktop publishing packages. It supports large photographic images, multi-image files, and a variety of different compression methods. There are many versions and types of compression for the TIFF file format.

VRML

VRML (Virtual Reality Modeling Language) is used for 3-D models. Its graphics format is based on Silicon Graphics Open Inventor. In order to use VRML, one needs a VRML browser.

Sound and music file formats

Different file formats are used for storing sound and music files. Some common ones are discussed below.

WAV, SND, VOC and AIFF

WAV is Wave Form Audio File Format. A WAV file has the extension .wav. It supports a variety of bit resolutions, sample rates, and channels of audio. This format is very popular on PC platforms, and is widely used in professional programs that process digital audio waveforms. WAV files are huge data files and thus take much disk space.

SND is another file format for storing sound data files. It has the extension .snd.

Creative Voice (VOC) is a format for sound blaster VOC files.

Audio Interchange File Format (AIFF) is a file format for storing digital audio (waveform) data. It supports a variety of bit resolutions, sample rates and channels of audio. This format is very popular on Apple platforms, and is again widely used in professional programs that process digital audio waveforms.

MIDI

MIDI (Music Instrument Digital Interface) is a standard for transmitting musical information between electronic instruments and computers. A MIDI file has the extension .mid or .midi. The quality of music is very good and the size of a MIDI file is small.

MP3

MP3 stands for Moving Picture Expert Group, Audio Layer3. It is an audio file format and allows for compression; thus high-quality audio may be contained in small files.

Movie file formats

Digital movie files are multimedia files. Movies are made up of a series of still images played in sequence, and each image is called a frame. Movie files are huge files that take a lot of disk space. Different file formats are used for digital video.

MPEG

The MPEG (Moving Pictures Expert Group) is a group of people that meet under the auspices of the International Standards Organization (ISO) to generate standards for digital video (sequences of images in time) and audio compression. Members of this group come from many companies and institutions worldwide and they continually improve the standard, giving birth to different versions of MPEG such as MPEG-1, MPEG-2, MPEG-3, MPEG-4, and so on. MPEG deals with three issues: video, audio and system (the combination of the two into one stream). The most common file extension is .mpg. Other MPEG file extensions are .mp2 for MPEG-2 audio; .mps for MPEG system and .mpa for MPEG audio.

QuickTime

QuickTime is an ISO standard for digital media. It was originally created by Apple Computers but can now be played on PCs too. It brings audio, animation, video and interactive capabilities to PCs. QuickTime movies have the file extensions .qt & .mov.

AVI

AVI is a video format for MS Windows. More and more .avi files are becoming available on the internet. Windows uses Media Player to play .avi files; .avi files can be converted to .mov files.

Post-processing

The scanned files need some processing in order to make them suitable for access through a network. The processing may involve a number of activities, such as:

- conversion to a suitable file format with or without compression
- the creation of an index using metadata and/or the full content
- the creation of an interface for searching and/or browsing the materials.

File conversion and compression

The selection of a suitable file format for storage of scanned documents should take into account the nature and volume of data, the nature and needs of the potential users, and the mode of access and delivery. PDF (Portable Document Format) is a suitable file format for storage as well as delivery of scanned files, especially if the file contains text as well as graphics, charts and images. PDF files are small enough for delivery over the internet and this is a very common file format for material such as books and articles. In the Builder digitization project (digitization of English Midlands history), the average size of a PDF file consisting of 20 pages of text and images was 1 Mb whereas a PDF file with the same number of pages of course text (a course text digitization project) was 500 kb (Hamson, 2001). However, in order to be able to read PDF files, users need to have specific software, such as the Adobe Acrobat Reader, which is available freely from the Adobe site (www.adobe.com/products/acrobat/readstep2.html). Often scanned files are indexed before they are converted to PDF files. However, some information retrieval software can index PDF files.

For images, file conversion and compression is often a very critical decision, since image files are usually large, and quality may be affected by the conversion. Often different versions of each image file are kept – one very small compressed file called the thumbnail version, which is used for browsing and searching, and one standard version, which is used for retrieval and display purposes.

Access to digitized information

Access to digitized information can be provided in a number of ways. The most common approaches adopted in digital libraries are searching and browsing. In browsing mode, users can glance through a list or hierarchy for the required digitized information resource. The categories or the hierarchy may be based on certain keys, such as authors or titles, or it may be based on subject classification approaches (see Chapters 7 and 9). Searching may be based on the words or content of the digitized resources. This may be enabled by indexing the full texts of the digitized materials or indexing according to some metadata structure, such as author, title or descriptor. Selection of an appropriate metadata scheme depends on a number of factors as discussed in Chapter 7.

Content-based retrieval is the most common, and yet often the most difficult, approach to information retrieval. Librarians have long used subject heading lists and thesauri for assigning the content descriptors to materials (see Chapter 9 for further details). For images, content-based image retrieval (CBIR) techniques may be the best for searching images by content. However, CBIR is a relatively expensive process, hence often images are described by textual notes that are used for (text-based) searching and retrieval of images. So far as the metadata format is concerned, the nature of the image file, for example whether it is a photograph, painting or artwork, will dictate the various categories to be employed. Lee (2001, 110) suggests that the following metadata may be useful to describe image files:

- name or unique identifier
- date of creation
- name of creator
- mode – bi-tonal, grey, etc.

- resolution
- file type
- highlight – post-processing technique
- shadow – post-processing technique
- gamma setting
- height
- width
- size
- original used
- contrast, curve, levels, brightness
- scanner used
- compression.

Various other metadata formats have been proposed for specific types of digitized materials. See, for example, the VADS (2001) guidelines for metadata for materials on digital visual arts.

Costs of digitization

Any digitization project involves considerable costs. Several studies report on the costing of digitization projects (for example, HEDS, n.d.(a); Lee, 2001, Chapter 4; Puglia, 1999; Tanner, 2001; Tanner and Smith, 1999. Hamson (2001) reports on the following two major lessons learnt in the course of three digitization projects that were part of the Builder hybrid library project:

- Scanning is only one stage in the complex workflow of a digitization project.
- Costs need to be monitored closely as they can grow quickly as a result of the intensive use of staff resources involved in different phases of the digitization project.

Lee (2001, 93) identifies four major factors that influence the cost of a digitization project. They are the nature of the source item, throughput, preparation and technical requirements. Lee also (2001, Chapter 4) provides a ready reckoner that may be quite useful for managers and project planners in calculating the estimated costs of a digitization project. A detailed list of the various cost heads for digitization has been provided in the HEDS guideline, as follows.

- *Preparation time cost.* This relates to the time it takes to get the originals ready for scanning, which may involve, for instance, work on the originals, inventories, packaging and movement.
- *Handling cost.* This relates to the costs intrinsic to the handling of the medium of the originals. It is obvious that large items such as maps, and fragile materials like glass or paintings, will require more time and effort in handling the original onto the scan mechanism than will, for example, modern monographs.
- *Automated processing cost.* This relates to the extent to which the process can be automated, whether the physical transition of originals through a scanning process or the conversion of data to machine-readable form. The more human intervention is required, the more expensive the process will be.
- *Skills/experience cost.* This relates to the experience and skills required for the job. For example, the scanning of bound volume materials requires more skills than are required for loose sheet scanning. Again, for post-processing operations, the creation of complex metadata requires experienced and knowledgeable persons.
- *Optimization cost.* This relates to the activities required to improve the quality of the scanned items, which may include cropping, de-skewing or colour matching, or other manipulations such as checking and verifying against other sources or enabling better layout of end presentation.
- *Resource cost.* This relates to the costs of equipment, set up, software, etc.
- *Quality assurance (QA) cost.* This relates to the costs of quality assurance. For example, the cost of QA for colour or photographic data will generally be higher than for black and white.
- *File size cost.* If the original source is large and requires a high resolution output, then the resultant file will be big. The larger the file the higher the cost of storage media, movement of data and its management.

A quick look at these cost factors reveals that the cost of scanning or digitization is small compared with the overall preparation, handling, equipment and human costs. The more person hours are required to complete a task, the higher the staff costs. Some staff costs are hidden and are often difficult to calculate, for example the time required for planning and preparation, benchmarking, specification, quality assurance and editing. Tanner (2001) comments that the costs of digitization can vary and good feasibility and pilot studies are essential to gain proper metrics of cost.

Summary

The conversion of analogue sources into a digital form and their appropriate storage and processing form an important part of building a digital library. Digitization is a complex process requiring managerial and technical skills. Proper planning and management help in keeping the cost down, and they also lead to the successful completion of a digitization project. Digitization may be carried out in-house or outsourced. In either case, the activities and costs related to the actual digitization are much less than the overall costs of a digitization project.

Various technical issues need to be considered in a digitization project ranging from hardware to software and standards for file formats, file compression and post-processing. Content-based retrieval may be achieved by full-text indexing of text materials, and by content-based image retrieval. However, they are expensive methods of retrieval compared with metadata-based searching and browsing. Selection of a metadata format depends on the nature of the documents as well as the nature and needs of the users.

Chapter 7
Information organization

Outline

Libraries have used a number of tools for organizing their information resources, including classification schemes, catalogue codes, bibliographic formats and vocabulary control tools. Many researchers have also used these tools for organizing web information resources. This chapter discusses some such projects. Researchers noted that traditional cataloguing tools were inadequate for the creation of metadata for digital information resources to support resource discovery and information access. Hence new metadata standards had to be developed. This chapter also discusses the concept of metadata in the context of information access and resource discovery, and briefly discusses the features of selected metadata standards. It then discusses markup languages, which were designed to encode sections of electronic documents in order to enable computers to process the text automatically. The basics of markup languages like SGML, HTML and XML are discussed and the chapter ends with a brief account of current research projects on digital information resources. Overall, this chapter will help readers understand the concept of information organization in digital libraries vis-à-vis the relevant tools and standards.

Introduction

Organizing information resources to provide easy access to a collection has been the major task of libraries for several decades. Two different sets of measures are taken. First, a method of *bibliographic classification* is used to organize the physical items (books, journals, CD-ROMs, audio, video) and so on, systematically on the library shelves. Bibliographic classification schemes such as Dewey Decimal Classification (DDC), Universal Decimal Classification (UDC) and Library of Congress Classification (LCC) are used to assign a specific class number to every item according to its subject matter or content. Items are then arranged on the shelves in order of their class numbers. This method puts materials on a related subject together so that users looking for items on a specific subject can go to the appropriate section of the library and find all the related materials close together. This is a very useful method to facilitate browsing of a library's collection.

However, classification schemes use an artificial notation comprising numbers and/or alphabets and punctuation marks to denote a subject. It is not always possible for users to know what the notation would be for a given subject they are looking for. To make this easier libraries use a system of subject indexing that allows users to browse an alphabetical list of subject names, each pointing to a specific notation. Users looking for materials on a specific subject or topic can browse the alphabetical index first, and once the chosen subject/topic is found, follow the pointer (the class number) to the specific location on the shelves for retrieving the items.

Thus classification and indexing systems, taken together, help librarians organize information resources for easy access. Several researchers have taken similar approaches to organizing internet information resources. We shall discuss some such studies later in this chapter. The process, however, is resource intensive and to some extent subjective, since each item needs to be classified and indexed manually based on the content of the item as perceived by the classifier the indexer.

While bibliographic classification helps libraries organize information resources physically on the shelves, *cataloguing* helps libraries tell users about their collection. Simply speaking, cataloguing is a technique that is used in libraries to create a brief record for every document in a library to enable easy access. Information on a catalogue record is usually divided into eight sections (Chowdhury, 1999, 65):

- Area 1: title; other title information & statement of responsibility; subsequent statements of responsibility
- Area 2: edition
- Area 3: type of material or publication
- Area 4: publication, distribution, etc.
- Area 5: physical description

- Area 6: series
- Area 7: notes
- Area 8: standard number and terms of availability.

Once catalogue records are created, they are organized in alphabetic order and/or in a classified sequence. Early library catalogues were prepared on 5 × 3 in. cards which were organized alphabetically to enable users to search a library's collection by author's name, title, subject, and so on. Computerized catalogues (online public access catalogues or OPACs) allow users to browse or search the catalogue records online by various keys such as author, title or subject. Although OPACs were initially designed to provide access to the local library's collections, present-day OPACs provide access to other collections too (those that belong to other library and non-library organizations) (Taylor, 1999, 7).

Producers of bibliographic databases, of abstracts and/or of full text do not fully catalogue and classify every item, but they use specific indexing techniques to facilitate access. In most cases, these systems create one or more indexes with information extracted from several fields – author, title, journal or conference title, and so on. The index also contains keywords and/or descriptors, either assigned by the indexer, or derived from the title, abstract and/or full text of the documents. Thus, these systems allow users to search for terms or phrases in one or more fields in the database.

Digital libraries, or more specifically hybrid libraries, provide access to the traditional library resources – printed books, journals, and so on – as well as electronic databases available online or on CD-ROM. In addition, they provide access to digital collections – those that are created specifically for the digital libraries and also those that are available on the web. Proper organization of these resources is necessary in order to facilitate easy access and retrieval. While traditional cataloguing and classification tools have been used by many researchers in organizing information resources on the internet and the web, many new tools and techniques have also been developed in the recent past for organizing these materials.

This chapter discusses these new tools, techniques and approaches to organizing digital information. It first briefly looks at some projects and services that have used the traditional classification and cataloguing/indexing techniques for organizing digital resources. It then discusses several metadata standards and markup languages that have been developed specifically to handle digital information resources. The chapter then looks at the current practice followed in some digital libraries for organizing information to facilitate better access. Finally, some recent studies and projects in this area are mentioned.

Problems of information organization in digital libraries

As discussed in Chapters 2 and 5, digital libraries provide access to different types of information resources which may be organized in varying ways by their producers or access providers. It is a challenge for a given digital library to build and/or adopt a simple and yet effective method for organizing information.

Some researchers argue that the traditional classification schemes may not be required in digital libraries (Jones, 2002), though others don't agree (for example, E. Hunter, 2002; Pollitt, 2002). As discussed later in this chapter, many research projects have shown that the traditional classification schemes are useful for organizing web information resources according to the disciplines and specific subjects and topics within a discipline. Users find it comparatively easy to get information from such organized resource structures. However, digital libraries deal with many new and nascent subjects, and existing classification schemes may not be suitable for detailed classification of them. However, many projects have extended the existing classes of bibliographic classification schemes to accommodate new subjects and topics.

Traditional catalogue codes and bibliographic formats – such as AACR (Anglo-American Cataloguing Rules) and MARC (Machine-Readable Cataloguing) – are not useful for digital resources because catalogue systems and MARC formats do not have provisions for describing different types of digital information resources, especially web pages. Moreover, it is practically impossible to catalogue each and every digital information resource manually. Separate standards have had to be developed for recording metadata information for digital, especially web, information resources.

While metadata standards help us to create metadata for digital documents, they cannot be used to denote the content of the particular section of a digital document. Markup languages, especially SGML (Standard Generalized Markup Language, discussed later in this chapter), were developed to mark specific sections of electronic documents by using precise tags, so that the content of a particular section of a document can be extracted and/or processed by identifying this set of tags. Different types of markup language are now available in order to facilitate content-based access, and for the processing and representation of digital information resources.

Classification of digital information

While many web directories and subject gateways provide access to the categorized information resources on the web, many researchers have also used library classification schemes and subject indexing tools for organizing such resources. Some typical examples of the use of classification schemes and subject heading lists in the organization of web information resources are discussed below.

BUBL LINK (www.bubl.ac.uk/link/)

BUBL Link provides access to a catalogue of over 11,000 selected internet resources, catalogued according to DDC, on all academic subjects. Users can search the catalogue by selecting a Dewey class, for example, '300 Social Sciences', or by selecting a term or phrase from the alphabetical index. The subject terms used in BUBL LINK/5:15 were originally based on LCSH (Library of Congress Subject Headings) but have been heavily customized and expanded to suit the content of the service. If the users opt to search the catalogue by Dewey class, they get a page that lists the main classes of DDC. Then they may select a particular class, which will in turn lead to a subclass, sub-subclass and so on. Finally users can select a specific topic. Figure 7.1 shows the classified list of items about digital libraries, and Figure 7.2 shows the results of a search on a specific topic. Alternatively, instead of going through the classified list, the user can go through the alphabetical index. Figure 7.3 shows the section of the BUBL Link index on digital libraries. Thus users can get access to digital resources by a classified list or through an alphabetical list of subjects.

CyberDewey (www.anthus.com/CyberDewey/CyberDewey.html)

CyberDewey is another example of the use of DDC in organizing digital information resources. It started as an individual effort, by David Mundie in 1995, in organizing internet information resources by using DDC. Here users can select a specific Dewey class (see Figure 7.4) or can select a term or phrase from the alphabetical index (Figure 7.5). Selection of a Dewey class takes users to the specific subdivisions of the class with items listed against each subclass. Users can select a specific subclass or topic to get access to the listed digital information resource. Instead of using a Dewey class, the user can choose to go through the alphabetical index. It may be noted that the corresponding Dewey class number appears against each entry in the index. Here users may select any particular topic, which will lead them to a classified list of topics, the same place they could reach through selecting a Dewey class.

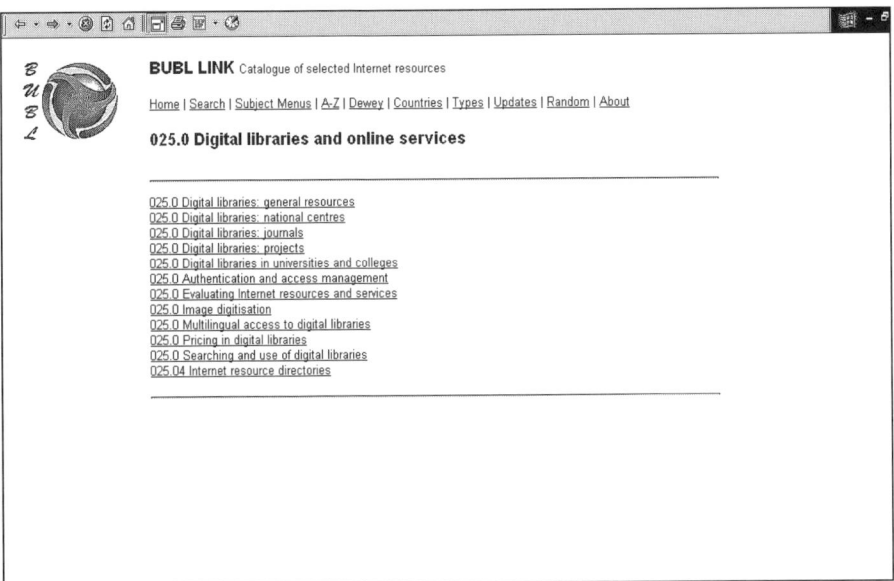

Fig. 7.1   *Classified items on the topic 'digital libraries' in BUBL Link*

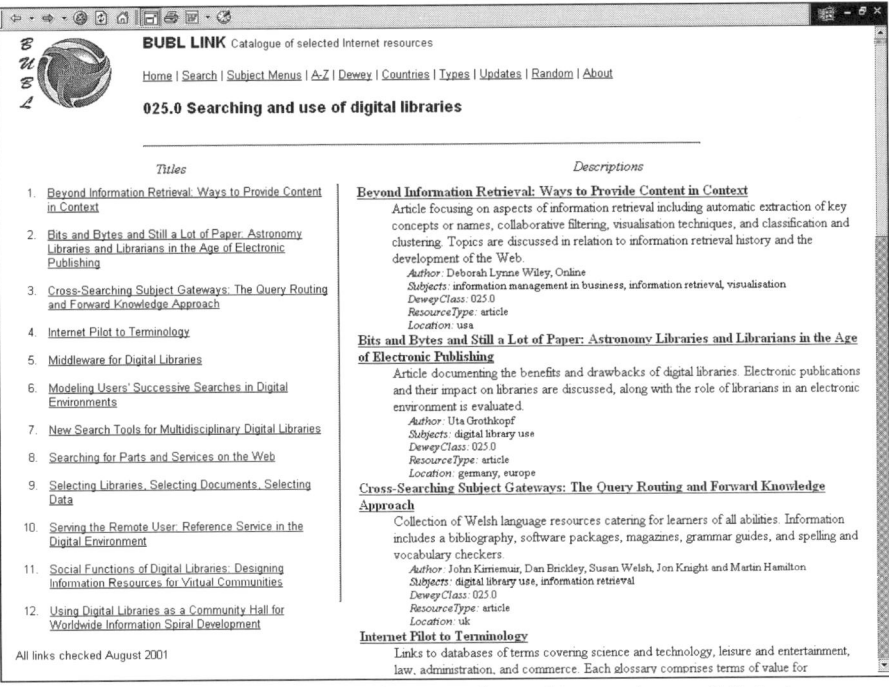

Fig. 7.2   *BUBL Link output on the topic 'searching and use of digital libraries'*

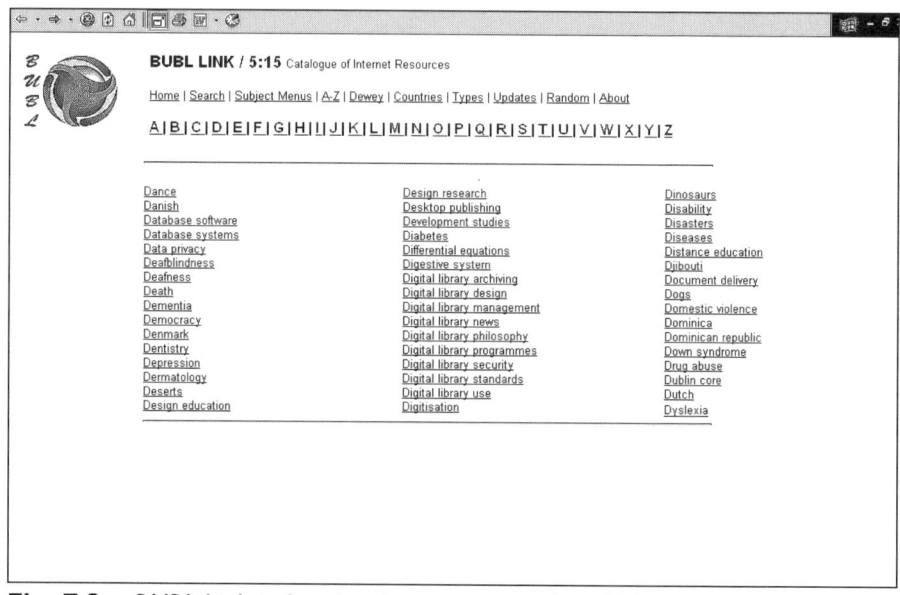

Fig. 7.3 *BUBL Link index showing entries on digital libraries*

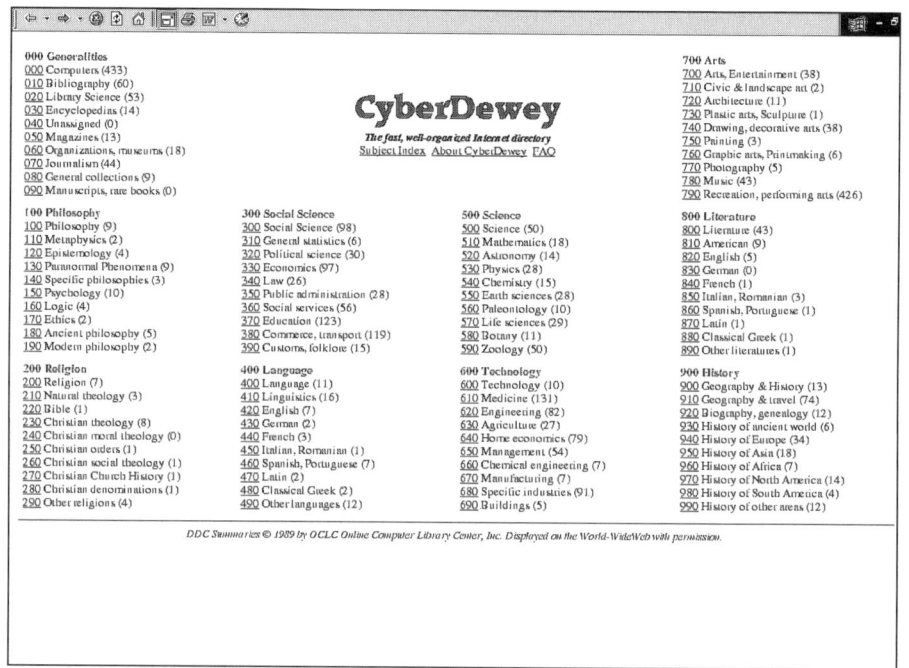

Fig. 7.4 *CyberDewey*

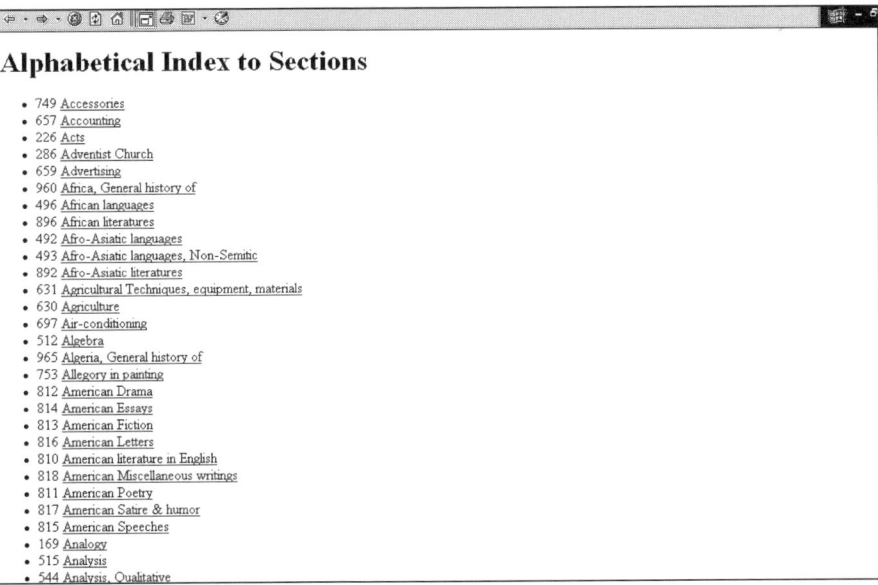

Fig. 7.5   *The CyberDewey alphabetical index*

SCORPION (http://orc.rsch.oclc.org:6109/)

Scorpion is a project of the OCLC Office of Research which explores the indexing and cataloguing of internet resources. Its objective was to build tools for automatic subject recognition by combining library science and information retrieval techniques. It began as a research project with a view to (Shafer, 1997):

- building tools to perform automatic subject assignment
- building tools to reduce the cost of human cataloguing
- having a better understanding of what cataloguing concepts can be automated
- furthering the use and enhancement of Dewey Decimal Classification
- finding means for improved retrieval.

Scorpion assigns subject codes to a document, and the document can then be treated as a query against a DDC database using ranked retrieval. The results of the search can then be treated as the subjects of the document (Shafer, 1997).

CyberStacks (www.public.iastate.edu/~CYBERSTACKS/)

CyberStacks[sm] is a centralized, integrated and unified collection of selected digital resources categorized using the Library of Congress Classification scheme.

Using an abridged Library of Congress call number, Cyberstacks[sm] allows users to browse through virtual library stacks containing monographic or serial works, files, databases or search services to identify potentially relevant information resources. Resources are categorized first within a broad classification (see Figure 7.6), then within narrower subclasses (see Figure 7.7), and resources are listed under a specific class (see Figure 7.8).

INFOMINE (http://infomine.ucr.edu)

INFOMINE is a service providing access to several thousand web resources comprising databases, electronic journals, guides to the internet for most disciplines, textbooks and conference proceedings. It began in January 1994 as a project of the Library of the University of California, Riverside (Mitchell and Mooney, 1996). INFOMINE uses Library of Congress Subject Headings for indexing the information resources. Users can simply select a discipline and enter the search terms or phrases to conduct a search. The catalogue can also be browsed by author, title, keyword and subject. If the option for browsing by subject is chosen, users are taken to an alphabetical list of subjects created by LCSH. Figure 7.9 shows the alphabetical index of resources in physical sciences, engineering, computing and mathematics.

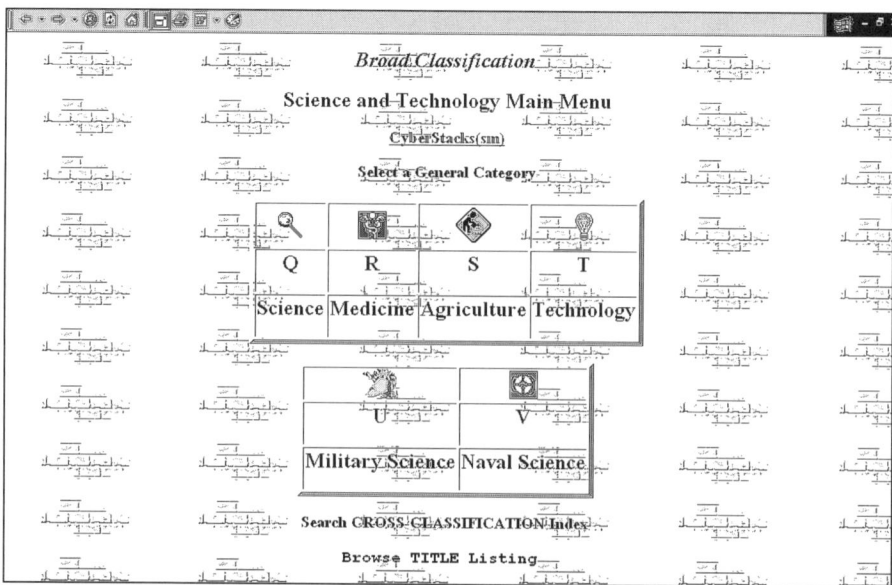

Fig. 7.6 *CyberStacks broad classification*

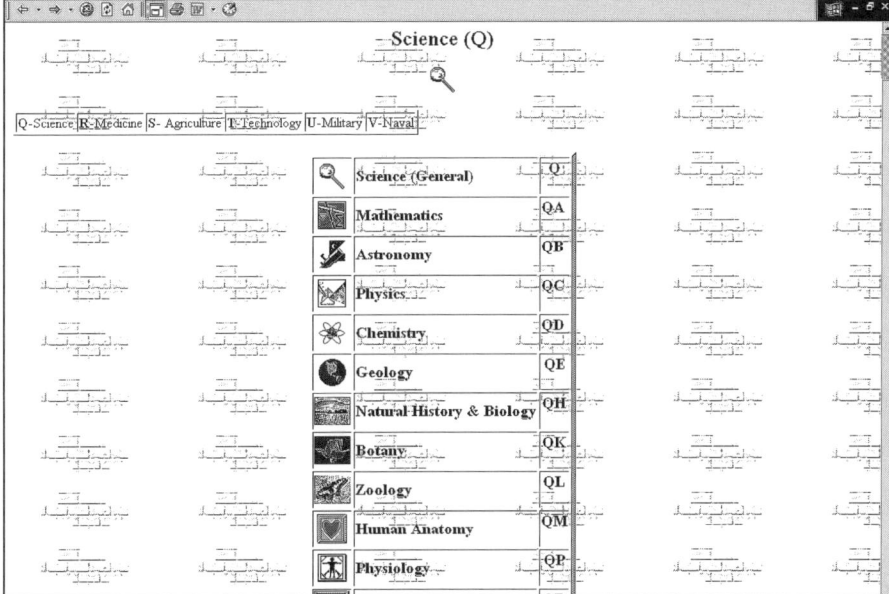

Fig. 7.7   *CyberStacks subclasses*

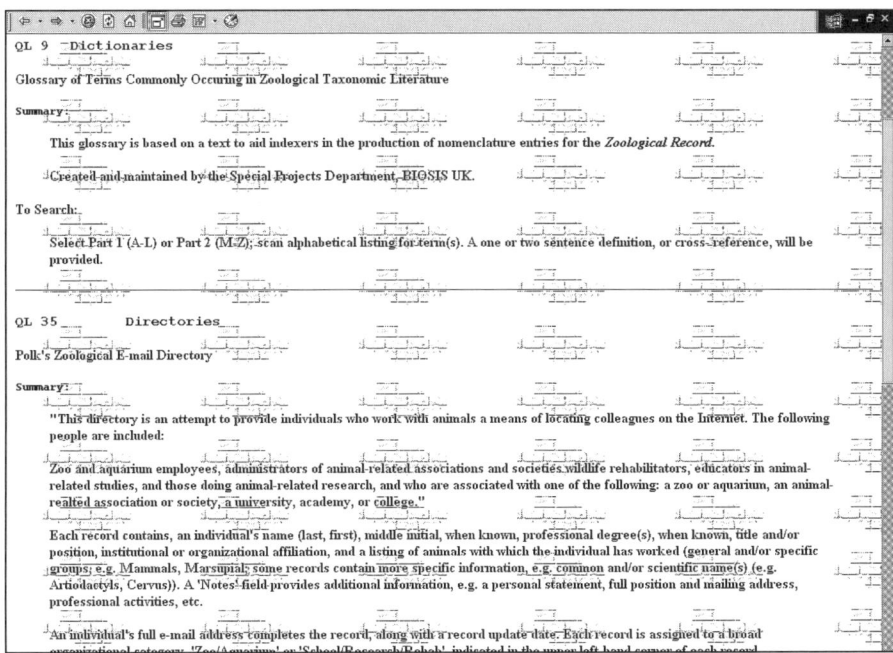

Fig. 7.8   *Specific items listed under the CyberStacks specific classes*

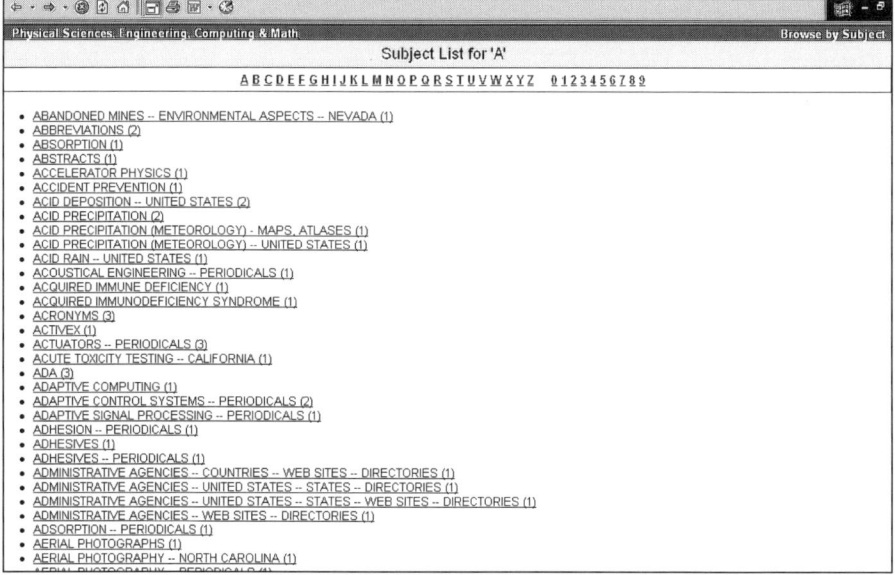

Fig. 7.9   *INFOMINE index*

Scout Report
(www.ilrt.bris.ac.uk/mirrors/scout/addserv/signpost/help.html#01)

The Scout Report Signpost was a US National Science Foundation-funded research project from 1996 to 2000. The primary goal was to demonstrate that internet resources could be catalogued, classified and arranged using existing controlled vocabularies and taxonomies such as LCC and LCSH, in concert with the Dublin Core metadata standard (discussed later in this chapter). The project ended in 2000 and the materials are now available in the Scout Report Archives, which is a searchable and browsable database containing 12,711 critical annotations of selected internet sites and mailing lists. Here users can conduct a search or can browse the database by using LCSH (see Figure 7.10). Figure 7.11 shows the index page listing the index entries according to LCSH. Users may select any heading to display the corresponding items on the screen.

EELS and EEVL (http://eels.lub.lu.se and www.eevl.ac.uk)

EELS (Engineering E-Library, Sweden) is a gateway for quality-assessed engineering information resources on the internet. The main part of EELS is structured according to the EI (Engineering Information) subject classification scheme. Users can conduct a search or browse for engineering information resources according to the various EI class numbers, as shown in Figure 7.12.

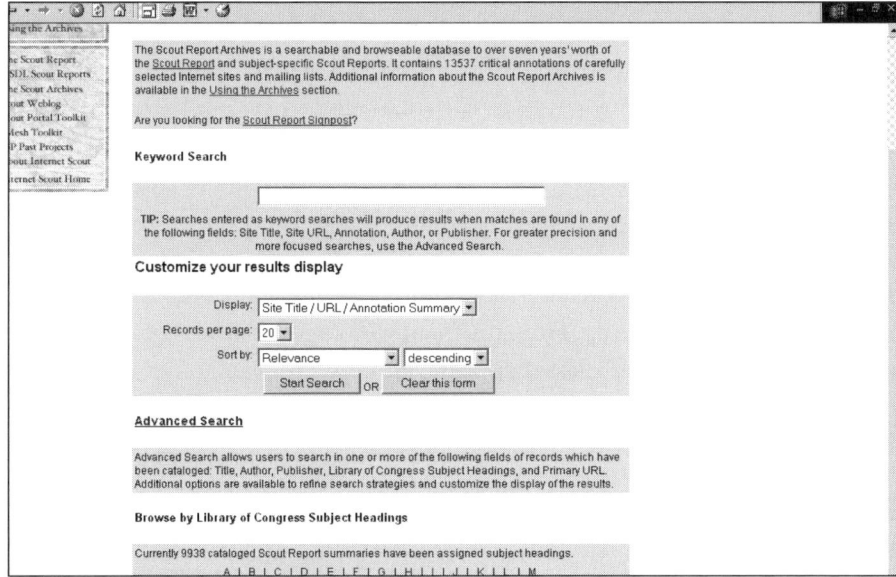

Fig. 7.10 *Scout Report Archives interface*

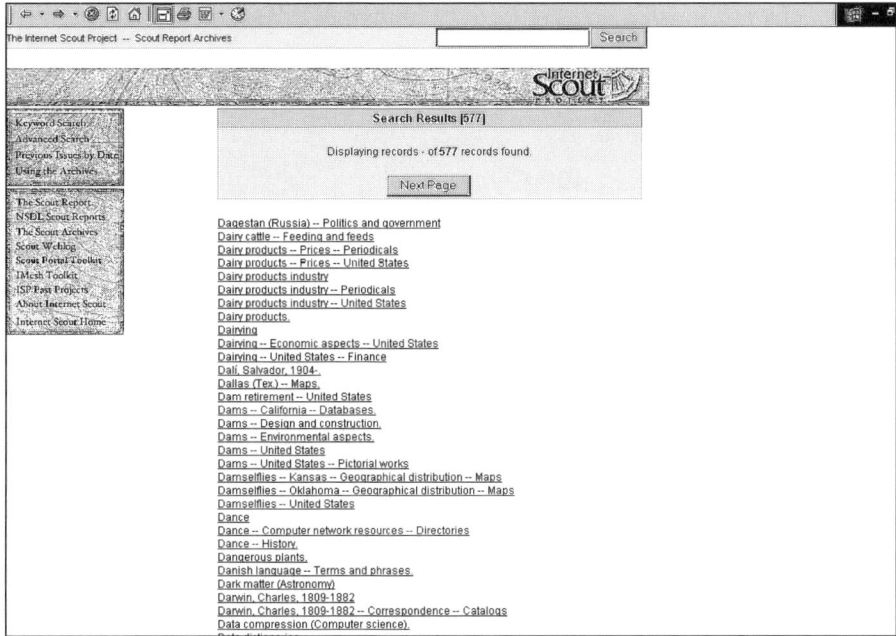

Fig. 7.11 *Scout Report Archives index*

The user can select any class, move down the hierarchy, and finally get a list of items belonging to a specific class. Recently EELS has been discontinued as a manually indexed subject gateway, to be replaced by a new service consisting of automatically harvested records in the field of engineering.

Another engineering subject gateway, EEVL (Enhanced and Evaluated Virtual Library) also uses the EI classification scheme. It is created and run by a team of information specialists from a number of universities and institutions in the UK to provide access to digital information in the areas of engineering, mathematics and computing. From the main web page of EEVL users can select a subject; then a list of subclasses appears, and the user can go down the hierarchy and finally get a list of items on a specific class or topic. Figure 7.13 shows the subclasses of engineering.

SOSIG (www.sosig.ac.uk)

SOSIG, the Social Science Information Gateway, is an internet service that provides access to selected, high-quality internet information for students, academics, researchers and practitioners in the social sciences, business and law. SOSIG uses the Humanities and Social Science Electronic Thesaurus (HASSET) (Schwartz, 2001, 98). Figure 7.14 shows SOSIG's home page, which

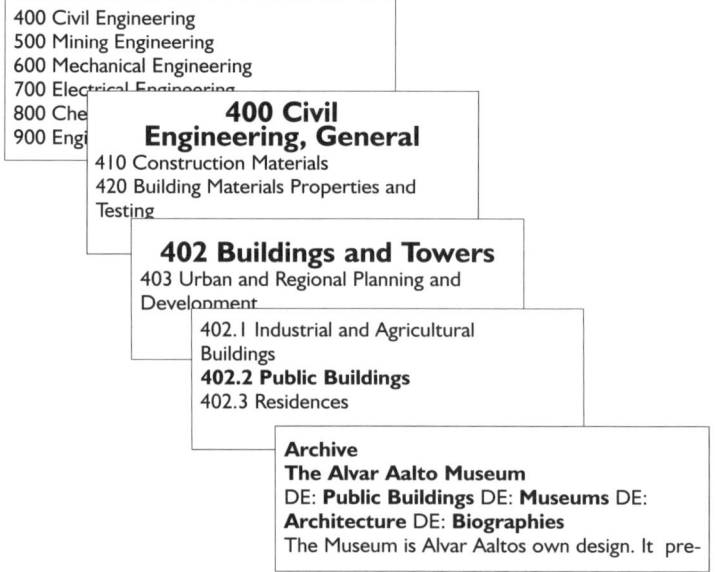

Fig. 7.12 *Browse categories in EELS*

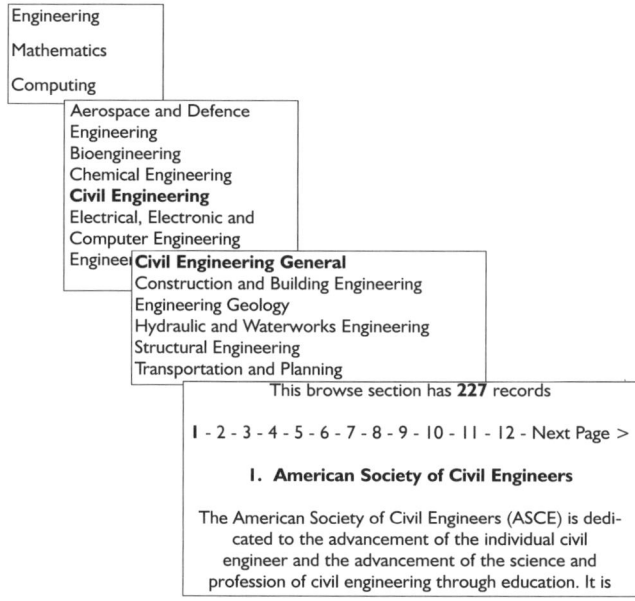

Fig. 7.13 *Browse categories in EEVL*

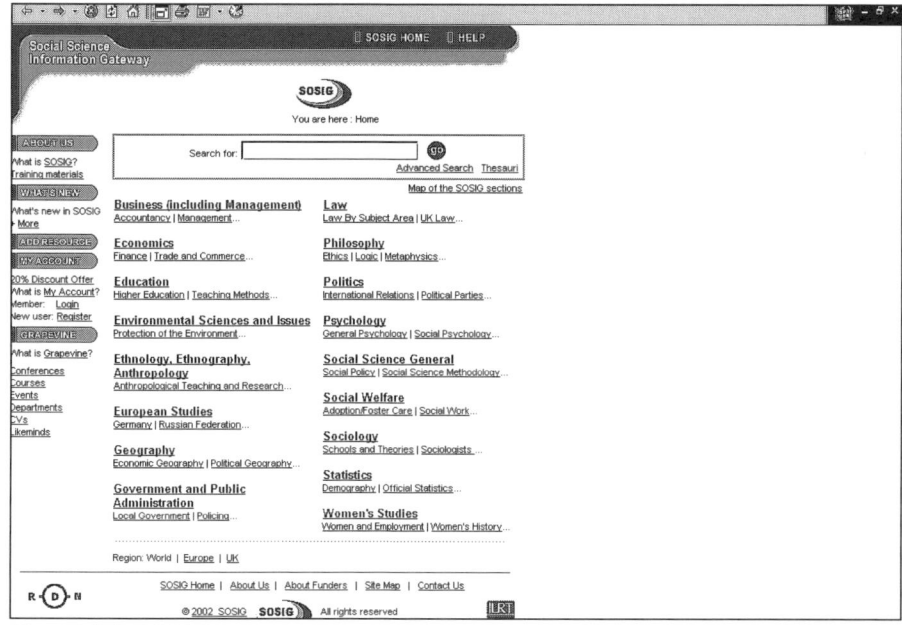

Fig. 7.14 *SOSIG home page*

allows users to select a subject category to browse. Users can conduct a simple or an advanced search for materials on the SOSIG catalogue. They can also choose a thesaurus for selection of search terms. Three thesauri are available: general social science; government, politics and anthropology; and social work and welfare. A search for the term 'economics' in the general social science thesaurus is shown in Figure 7.15. The user can select a particular term by clicking on it, which then brings up the relevant thesaurus entry, or can select an item as a search term by checking the corresponding box and clicking on the search button.

As well as searching the whole SOSIG catalogue, users can select an option to restrict their search to a subject section of SOSIG. Selection of a broad subject category will lead the users to the corresponding sub-categories, and so on down the hierarchy. At each stage, a list of items corresponding to the currently chosen category will be displayed. In addition there is also an option for browsing a specific collection. Here the user has first to select a region – world, Europe or UK – and then a SOSIG subject heading(s) to get information on the topic filtered by region.

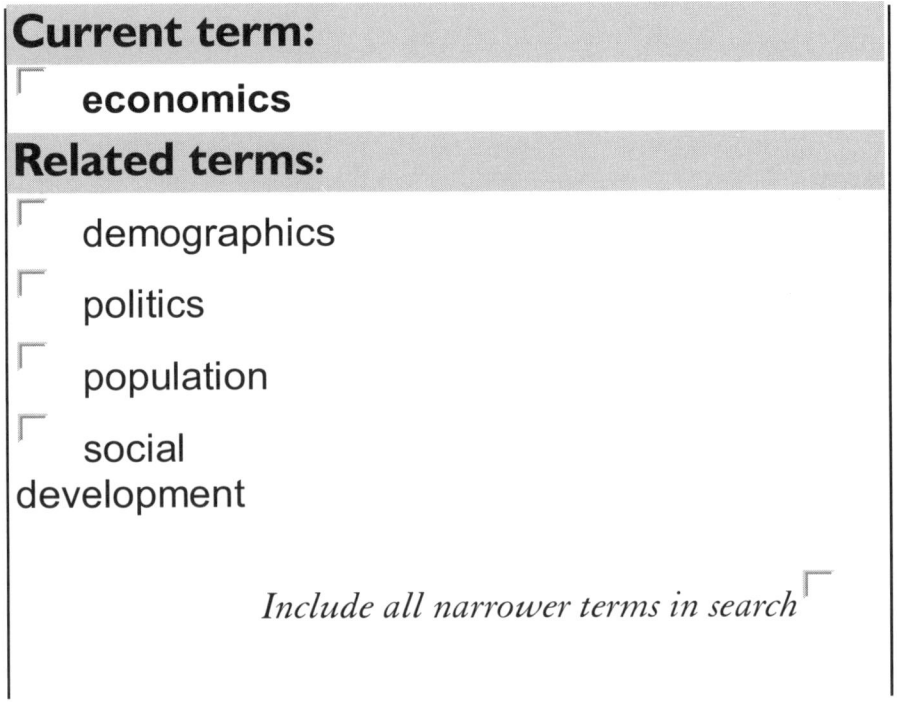

Current term:

⌐ **economics**

Related terms:

⌐ demographics

⌐ politics

⌐ population

⌐ social development

Include all narrower terms in search ⌐

Fig. 7.15 *Thesaurus terms in the general social science thesaurus in SOSIG*

BIOME (www.biome.ac.uk)

BIOME offers access to a searchable catalogue of internet sites and resources covering the health and life sciences. Users can choose to search BIOME for internet resources in the field of the health and life sciences, or can choose one of the five subject-specific gateways: OMNI, VetGate, BioResearch, NATURAL and AgriFor. In addition to searching, users can also browse the BIOME database by keyword or classification scheme.

Since each gateway uses slightly different indexing and classification tools, the user first has to select one, and can then start browsing. There are two methods of browsing: by keyword and by classification scheme. All records in BIOME are indexed using keywords from one of several thesauri. Users can browse AgriFor and VetGate using terms from the CAB thesaurus; BioResearch, OMNI and NMAP using MeSH keywords; and NMAP using the Royal College of Nursing (RCN) thesaurus. As well as being able to browse resources using keywords, it is also possible to browse by classification scheme. Users can browse VetGate using the Library of Congress classification scheme, AgriFor using DDC, and OMNI and BioResearch using the National Library of Medicine (NLM) classification scheme.

Figure 7.16 shows the options that a user gets for browsing the collection using the OMNI gateway – browse by NLM subject headings, or browse by MeSH2000 headings. Both are alphabetical lists. The user in Figure 7.16 has chosen to browse by subject headings. Selection of any heading from either list takes the user to the items indexed by the chosen heading.

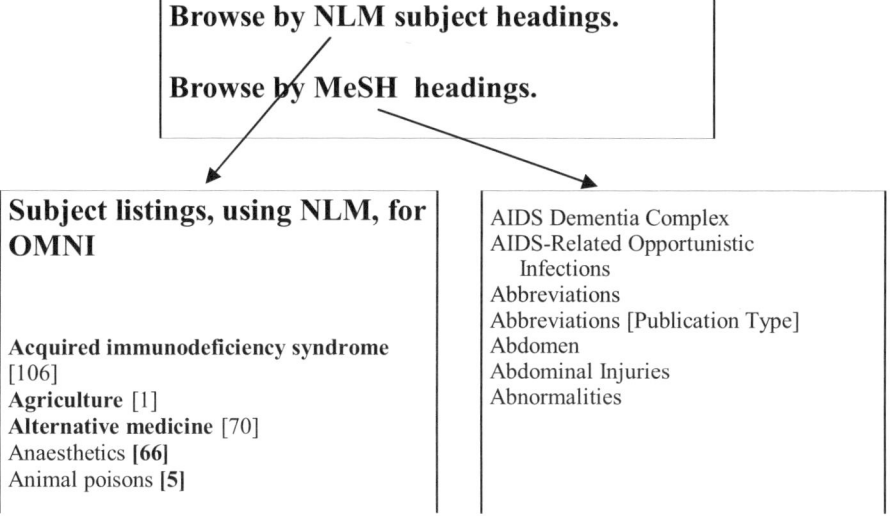

Browse by NLM subject headings.

Browse by MeSH headings.

Subject listings, using NLM, for OMNI

Acquired immunodeficiency syndrome [106]
Agriculture [1]
Alternative medicine [70]
Anaesthetics **[66]**
Animal poisons **[5]**

AIDS Dementia Complex
AIDS-Related Opportunistic
    Infections
Abbreviations
Abbreviations [Publication Type]
Abdomen
Abdominal Injuries
Abnormalities

Fig. 7.16 *Browse options in OMNI*

Information organization in selected digital libraries

In the previous sections we have seen some interesting projects and services that use traditional library classification tools and techniques for organizing web information resources. While formal classification is not commonly used for organizing information items in digital libraries, many of these libraries use some form of organization to facilitate access. In the following sections we shall see how information has been organized in some digital libraries.

California Digital Library (www.cdlib.org)

California Digital Library has minimal organization. Here the user can select a specific collection, for example, the Melvyl Catalogue, and then conduct a search. Alternatively, the user can select the SearchLight option, which allows cross-database searching in one or more collections. Then users can select a specific collection, like science and engineering, or a specific class within a broad group, like physical science or engineering. In any case, the items are not classified; instead, the collection is partitioned according to disciplines or broad classes.

ACM Portal: the ACM digital library (http://portal.ac.org)

ACM Portal allows users to select a specific collection, for example, journals or conferences, to browse. The items are classified according to the ACM Computing Classification System (CCS). In the advanced search mode, users can search by these descriptors. For example, a search for the notation '.d2' would retrieve information on software engineering.

THOMAS and American Memory (http://thomas.loc.gov/ and http://memory.loc.gov/)

THOMAS, the digital library of legislative information of the Library of Congress, classifies legal documents under broad categories, such as legislation, congressional records and committee information, and also under specific subgroups, such as bills, public laws, committee reports, and so on. Users can select a specific category to get access to the legal information resources.

American Memory is a gateway to over 7 million materials relating to the history and culture of the USA. Among other features, the site allows users to browse the collection by subject headings, LCSH (Library of Congress Subject Headings) and TGM (Thesaurus of Graphic Materials) terms having been applied to the collections. One starts from a page giving ranges of headings (see

Figure 7.17). Each range is hyperlinked to the pages listing the individual alphabetical headings, which in turn take the user to the specific items in the collection on the chosen heading. The entire collection is divided into several broad topics, which are derived from the Dewey Decimal and Library of Congress Classification schemes.

From	Abolitionists—United States.	to	City and town life—New York (State)—New York.
From	Cityscape photographs—1890–1970.	to	Indians of North America—Northwest, Pacific.
From	Indians of North America—West (U.S.)—History—Photographs.	to	Ohio—Race relations.
From	Omaha Indians—Music.	to	Spanish-American War, 1898.
From	Sports—United States—History.	to	Yiddish drama—20th century.

Fig. 7.17 *Browsing American Memory collections by subject headings*

Cataloguing and metadata

Different measures are currently taken for informing users about the materials accessible through a given digital or hybrid library. In many cases users are pointed to separate lists or web pages providing information about various digital collections, such as online databases, electronic journals and internet resources. However, all these resources are selected and entered manually on the lists or web pages by library staff. Having a centralized catalogue of all the digital resources available on the web would greatly reduce the burdens of individual digital or hybrid libraries, because staff could then simply download the catalogue entries, as libraries do for printed information materials. However, there are many problems with cataloguing digital information resources. First of all, digital, especially internet, resources are so numerous and they increase so rapidly that it is practically impossible for human cataloguers to cope with each and every one. Second, the characteristics of digital information resources demand that a different standard be followed for each major type of document. The bibliographic formats, like the MARC family, and the catalogue codes, like AACR2, are not adequate for representing all the useful characteristics of digital resources. Various metadata standards have been developed over the past few years for representing different types of digital information resources.

Schwartz (2001, 9) mentions that the term metadata, previously used primarily in the field of database management, began to appear in LIS literature in the mid-1990s. However, within a very short period metadata became very popular and an important area of research concentration, giving rise to several hundred publications, including an ARIST chapter in 1998 (Vellucci, 1998). Lange and Winkler (1997) trace the history of the term metadata back to the 1960s, but note that it began to appear more frequently in DBMS literature in the 1980s. Vellucci (1998) notes that the term transcends boundaries among various stakeholders in the internet arena, and provides a common vocabulary to describe a variety of data structures. Simply speaking, metadata is data about data, but this definition does not say much about its purpose. Better definitions of metadata include the following:

- 'Data which describes attributes of a resource' (Dempsey and Heery, 1997)
- 'Meaningful data describing another discrete data object' (Gill, 1998, 9)
- 'Data associated with objects which relieves their potential users of having to have full advance knowledge of their existence or characteristics' (Dempsey and Heery, 1998, 149).

Metadata supports a variety of operations and its users may be human beings or computer programs. The primary functions of metadata are to facilitate the identification, location, retrieval, manipulation and use of digital objects in a networked environment (Vellucci, 1998).

Libraries have long been used to creating catalogue records, a kind of metadata, of their collections, and these records have been used by library users as well as librarians for a variety of purposes, including the searching and retrieval of records. Such metadata produced by libraries consist of some item-specific information, as well as headings, that have associated rules for further processing, such as the creation of headings, rules for filing and about their relationship with other records. In today's world, however, while the term metadata does not exclude non-electronic data, it is applied most often to data in electronic form (Vellucci, 1998).

The growth of internet and digital libraries has led to an increased awareness of the need for metadata for diverse categories of items to be available in digital form. Various subject experts have developed, or are engaged in developing, metadata formats for materials in specific domains and formats, for example internet resources, museum objects and archival records. Weibel, Iannella and Cathro (1997) comment that there are two distinct schools of thought that influence the development of metadata standards:

- the minimalist camp, whose point of view reflects a strong commitment to the notion of simple metadata, for the sake of both its creation by authors and its use by tools
- the structuralist camp, whose members emphasize the greater flexibility of a formal means of extending or qualifying elements such that they can be made more useful for the needs of a particular community.

Dempsey and Heery (1998) have identified three groups of metadata:

- *Proprietary formats used by web indexing and search services*. Data is gathered by robot programs, and automatic records are created which are typically searched using the basic HTTP protocol with CGI (Common Gateway Interface) scripts.
- *Formats used for resource description*. Examples are Dublin Core and IAFA/WHOIS++ templates (ROADS templates). Services that use this type of format include OCLC's NetFirst and subject gateways created under the eLib programme. The metadata records may be created manually or automatically.
- *Formats used for location, analysis, evaluation, documentation, etc*. These formats are more complex and detailed, and require specialist knowledge to create and maintain. They may also be domain specific. Examples are MARC, FGDC (Federal Geographic Data Committee's content standard for digital geospatial metadata), TEI (Text Encoding Initiative) headers, EAD (Encoded Archival Description) (Pitti, 1999), and the ICPSR (Inter-University Consortium for Political and Social Research) initiative.

Gilliland-Swetland (1998) classifies metadata into five categories on the basis of their use:

- administrative metadata used in managing and administering information resources
- descriptive metadata used to describe or identify information resources
- preservation metadata related to the preservation management of information resources
- technical metadata related to how a system functions or metadata behave
- use metadata related to the level and types of use of information resources.

Metadata standards have been built in different subject areas by experts with different understandings of their domain and its information resources, users and use behaviour, and overall requirements for resource discovery and description. Some of these metadata formats, such as MARC and Dublin Core, are general in nature and can accommodate descriptive information about digital information resources of different types coming from different disciplines, while others, such as FGDC and EAD, are more specialized and apply to information in a specific discipline or domain (Vellucci, 1998).

Dublin Core

The Dublin Core Metadata Workshop Series began in 1995 with an invitational workshop that brought together librarians, digital library researchers, content experts, and text-markup experts to develop discovery standards for electronic resources. The first meeting took place in Dublin, Ohio; hence the standard's name. It is a 15-element set of descriptors intended to promote author-generated description of internet resources (see Table 7.1). The elements fall into three groups which roughly indicate the class or scope of information stored in them: (1) elements related mainly to the content of the resource, (2) elements related mainly to the resource when viewed as intellectual property, and (3) elements related mainly to the instantiation of the resource (Weibel, 1995; Weibel et al., 1998).

Table 7.1 *Dublin Core data elements*

Group	Element	Description
Content	Title	Name of the resource
	Subject	Topic describing the content of the resource
	Description	About the content of the resource
	Type	The nature or genre of the content of the resource
	Source	A reference to a resource from which the present resource is derived
	Relation	A reference to a related resource
	Coverage	The extent or scope of the content of the resource
Intellectual property	Creator	Who is primarily responsible for creating the content of the resource
	Publisher	Who is responsible for making the resource available
	Contributor	Who makes contributions to the content of the resource
	Rights	Information about rights held in and over the resource
Instantiation	Date	Date associated with the resource
	Format	The physical or digital manifestation of the resource
	Identifier	A unique reference to the resource within a given context
	Language	The language of the intellectual content of the resource

The Dublin Core Metadata Editor (*DCDot*, n.d.) is a service that retrieves a given web page and automatically generates Dublin Core metadata suitable for embedding in the <head>...</head> section of the page. In addition to instantly generating the DC tags for a given web page, the DCDot service also provides an editor for the users to edit the tags or add/edit the contents, which can then be re-submitted to create metadata. Figure 7.18 shows the DC metadata for a sample web page.

```
<link rel="schema DC" href="http://purl.org/dc">
<meta name="DC.Title" content="Gobinda Gopal Chowdhury">
<meta name="DC.Creator" content="Gobinda Chowdhury">
<meta name="DC.Subject" content="Gobinda Gopal Chowdhury; Department of Computer and
Information Sciences; University of Strathclyde">
<meta name="DC.Description" content="Personal web page">
<meta name="DC.Publisher" content="University of Strathclyde">
<meta name="DC.Contributor" content="Sudatta Chowdhury">
<meta name="DC.Date" content="31/01/2002">
<meta name="DC.Type" scheme="DCMIType" content="Text">
<meta name="DC.Format" content="text/html 110377 bytes">
<meta name="DC.Identifier" content= "http://www.cis.strath.ac.uk/people/gobinda">
<meta name="DC.Source" content="Personal files">
<meta name="DC.Language" content="English">
<meta name="DC.Relation" content="http://www.cis.strath.ac.uk; http://www.strath.ac.uk">
<meta name="DC.Coverage" content="Brief CV and Publications">
<meta name="DC.Rights" content="Gobinda Chowdhury">
```

Fig. 7.18 *DC metadata for a sample web page*

The Dublin Core standard has the following characteristics (Taylor, 1999, 89):

- The core set can be extended with further elements, as necessary, for a particular domain.
- All elements are optional.
- All elements are repeatable.
- Any element may be modified by a qualifier.

Other metadata standards

Several metadata standards have been developed over the past few years to deal with some specific types of digital material. Dempsey (1996) describes some metadata and resource discovery initiatives in the UK's Electronic Libraries programme (eLib) and within the European Union's Fourth Framework Programme for research and technological development. Dempsey and Heery (1997) provide an excellent review of several metadata standards, while Cromwell-Kessler (1998) maps several metadata standards to one another.

The Warwick Framework

Metadata systems differ in terms of content and structure (Cromwell-Kessler, 1998). Content may differ in terms of the rules that govern it and the language. Different metadata standards create an obvious problem of interoperability. Each metadata system may comprise diverse data elements functioning at different levels. A relatively simple way of integration may be to translate one system to another when necessary. UKOLN and OCLC jointly organized a conference in 1996 to examine various general metadata issues and Dublin Core metadata in particular. While there was a consensus among the participants that the concept of a simple metadata set is useful, there was a fundamental question as to whether the Dublin Core really qualifies as a standard that can be used for all types of digital documents. It was agreed that a higher-level context for the Dublin Core should be formulated to define how the Core can be combined with other sets of metadata in a manner that addresses the individual integrity, distinct audiences, and separate realms of responsibility of various distinct metadata sets. The meeting took place in Warwick, and gave rise to a new proposal, for a *container* architecture, known as the Warwick Framework (Dempsey and Weibel, 1996) – a mechanism for aggregating logically, and perhaps physically, distinct *packages* of metadata (Lagoze, 1996).

EAD

Encoded Archival Description (EAD) is a standard used internationally in an increasing number of archives and manuscript libraries to encode data describing corporate records and personal papers (Pitti, 1999). From its inception, EAD was based on SGML, and since the release of EAD version 1.0 in 1998 it has also been compliant with XML. The EAD DTD (document type definition) contains three high-level elements: the <eadheader>, <frontmatter> and <archdesc>. The <eadheader> is used to document the archival description or finding aid, while the <frontmatter> is used to supply publishing information such as a title page, and other prefatory text. The <archdesc> contains the archival description itself, and thus constitutes the core of the EAD (Pitti, 1999).

Digital content marking and manipulation

While metadata standards help us create a metadata record for a given item that may facilitate the discovery of digital documents, they do not help much in providing access to, and processing the content of, the records. For example, a metadata record of a journal article does not say where within the entire document the abstract begins and ends, how many tables or figures there are in the article, where they appear, and so on.

This is where markup languages come in. They supply the syntax for marking specific sections of items with standard codes that can be interpreted by computer programs and used to tell these programs what to do with the sections, for example how they should be presented (in bold, or in colour, say), or whether they should be extracted in order to store in a database for further processing (for example to create a title index). Several markup languages have been developed to serve different purposes. In this chapter we shall briefly discuss SGML (Standard Generalized Markup Language), HTML (HyperText Markup Language, the language of the world wide web), and XML (eXtensible Markup Language).

SGML

SGML was accepted as a standard in 1986 (ISO 8879, 1986). It was created to provide a set of rules to describe the structure of an electronic document so that it may be interchanged across various computer platforms. SGML also allows users to:

- link files together to form composite documents
- identify where illustrations are to be incorporated into text files
- create different versions of a document in a single file
- add editorial comments to a file
- provide information to supporting programs.

To allow the computer to do as much of the work as possible, SGML requires users to provide a model of the document being produced. This model, the DTD (see previous page), describes each element of the document and formally identifies the relationships between the various elements in the document.

SGML defines data in terms of elements and attributes. An element is a particular unit of an item, such as the title, abstract or section heading. An attribute gives particular information about an element. SGML provides tags and delimiters to mark up elements.

An SGML tag is a code element that appears as letters or words between a < (less than sign) and a > (greater than sign).

Example: <title>, <body>

To tell the computer program to 'end' doing what you just told it to start, a closing tag is supplied in the form of the opening tag preceded by a forward slash:

Example: </title>, </body>

Most tags come in matched 'start' and 'end' pairs, but this is not an absolute rule.

For example, the author of a text may be marked as <author>Gobinda G. Chowdhury </author>. The tags tell the computer program what to do with the content, in this case the author's name. SGML provides an extensive list of tags and supports many variations.

An SGML document consists of three parts (Schwartz, 2001, 30):

- the SGML declaration defining the document character set, name lengths for elements, and other basic parameters
- the document type definition (DTD)
- the document instance – the actual document.

SGML has been used widely in the publishing community, and has given rise to several applications, especially the TEI (Text Encoding Initiative), EAD (Encoded Archival Description) and XML (eXtensible Markup Language) (Schwartz, 2001, 30).

HTML

While SGML provides an extensive mechanism for marking electronic documents, it has some problems. The process of marking up a text with it is complex and resource intensive. A simpler markup language called HTML (Hypertext Markup Language) has been developed especially for preparing web documents. It contains a set of markup symbols or codes that are inserted in a file intended for display on a browser page. The HTML markup tells the web browser how to display a web page's content – text, images, and so on – for the user. Each individual element is encoded with an appropriate tag. Some tags come in pairs that indicate when a display effect is to begin and when it is to end. Use of HTML is formally recommended by the World Wide Web Consortium (W3C) and this is generally adhered to by the major browsers, Microsoft's Internet Explorer and Netscape's Navigator.

HTML tags are similar to those of SGML and, again, a closing tag is the opening tag preceded by a forward slash.

Any web page will contain the following tags at the start of the page:

- <HTML>: tells the web browser that this is the beginning of an HTML document.
- <HEAD>: tells that web browser that this is the header for the page.
- <TITLE>: tells the web browser that this is the title of the page.
- <BODY>: tells the web browser that this is the beginning of the web page content.

The simplicity of HTML has made it popular. However, there are many varieties, and software packages like Microsoft Frontpage use many non-standard codes, which make them proprietary formats. Several programs like Java and Perl have been designed to work with HTML for information processing on the web, but not every browser responds properly to these extended facilities (Deegan and Tanner, 2002b, 125).

Dynamic HTML

Many developers use Dynamic HTML, which is a combination of HTML, style sheets and scripting languages, to generate better web documents. W3C has developed XSL, a language for expressing style sheets (*The Extensible Stylesheet Language*, n.d.). The use of different style sheets and scripting languages creates a problem of interoperability since the style sheets and scripting languages may be tied to specific platforms. The Document Object Model (DOM) produced by W3C is a platform- and language-neutral interface that allows programs and scripts to access and update the content, structure and style of documents dynamically (*Document Object Model*, n.d.). The DOM makes it possible for programmers to write applications that would work properly on all browsers and servers and on all platforms. While programmers may need to use different programming languages, they do not need to change their programming model. The availability of the new standards – XML, RDF, XSL and DOM, removes several barriers that have long been problems for publishers and information service providers who wanted to provide the users with platform-independent access and processing of digital information (Chudnov, 1999).

XML

While SGML is too complex and resource intensive to encode in many circumstances, and also cannot be processed as it is by the web browsers, and HTML is too simple and only tells the browser how to present an element or how to link to another item, XML (eXtensible Markup Language) aims to offer the best of both worlds. XML is a set of rules for designing text formats that let users structure their data (W3C Communications Team, 2001). Development started in 1996 and use of XML has been a W3C recommendation since February 1998. The designers of XML simply took the best parts of SGML, guided by their experience with HTML, and produced something that is powerful and vastly more regular and simple to use.

XML is intended to allow computers to generate and read data, and to ensure that the data structure is unambiguous. It is extensible and platform independent, and it supports internationalization and localization. There is a significant difference between HTML and XML. While HTML specifies what each tag and attribute means, and often how the text between them should appear in a browser, XML uses the tags only to delimit pieces of data, and leaves the interpretation of the data completely to the application that reads it. Like HTML, XML files are text files that people shouldn't have to read, but may when the need arises. XML is a framework that allows users to write application-specific codes along with markup, so that the tags become meaningful in terms of data and content, making XML documents suitable for machine-processing. However, unlike HTML, XML is not fault tolerant, and a forgotten tag, or an attribute without quotes, makes an XML file unusable.

The XML family is a growing set of modules that offer a number of useful services to accomplish important and frequently demanded tasks, for example (W3C Communications Team, 2001):

- *XML 1.0* is the specification that defines the tags and attributes.
- *Xlink* describes a standard way to add hyperlinks to an XML file.
- *Xpointer* and *XFragments* are syntaxes for pointing to parts of an XML document. An XPointer is a bit like a URL, but instead of pointing to documents on the web, it points to pieces of data inside an XML file.
- *CSS*, the style sheet language, is applicable to XML, as it is to HTML.

- *XSL* is the advanced language for expressing style sheets. It is based on XSLT, a transformation language used for rearranging, adding and deleting tags and attributes.
- The *DOM* is a standard set of function calls for manipulating XML (and HTML) files from a programming language.
- *XML Schemas 1 and 2* help developers precisely define the structures of their own XML-based formats.

It is believed that XML will become a universal format, not only for business-to-business applications, but also for effective knowledge and information management (Baeza-Yates et al., 2002). It holds a number of promises for improved information access in digital libraries, for example (Luk et al., 2002):

- It produces a more precise search by providing additional information in each element.
- It enables a better integrated search from heterogeneous information sources.
- It provides for a powerful search paradigm using structural as well as content specifications.
- It facilitates information exchange to support collaborative research and learning.

Recent research projects

Metadata and markup languages have become the central focus of research for resource discovery and information access in digital libraries. Some recent and current projects are described below.

DESIRE (www.desire.org)

The DESIRE project, a collaboration between project partners working at ten institutions from four European countries – the Netherlands, Norway, Sweden and the UK – ran from July 1998 to June 2000 and focused on three main areas of activity: caching, resource discovery and directory services. One of the significant outcomes of DESIRE is the *Information Gateways handbook* (DESIRE, n.d.), which aims in particular to support the development of large-scale gateways in Europe to assist researchers looking for high-quality research information on the internet. By adopting standard practices, these gateways have the potential to form an international network that can be cross-searched by researchers across the continent. Another outcome of the project has been the development of a number of toolkits for resource discovery, cataloguing, and so on.

Imesh Toolkit (www.imesh.org/toolkit/)

The Imesh Toolkit project is a similar project in the USA, which began in September 1999 for a period of three years funded under the NSF/JISC International Digital Libraries Initiative. The project partners include the Internet Scout Project, UKOLN, Institute for Learning and Research Technology (ILRT), University of Bristol and Loughborough University. The major objectives of the project are to:

- develop a configurable, reusable and extensible toolkit for subject gateway providers
- consider issues of relevance in the distributed, international subject gateway environment.

Renardus (www.renardus.org)

Renardus, a pilot EU project, allows users to find internet resources selected by subject gateways from several European countries. A special feature of Renardus is the option to browse by subject through hierarchical trees of topics that subsequently lead the user to one or several related subcollections of the contributing subject gateways. It uses DDC for organizing web information resources. Users can browse the collection by subject or can use the advanced search screen to conduct searches. Figure 7.19 shows a visual representation of the various subject topics for navigation by users.

Resource Discovery Network (www.rdn.ac.uk)

Built on the experience gained by the eLib programme of building subject gateways (such as SOSIG and EEVL, discussed earlier in this chapter), the Resource Discovery Network (RDN) provides effective access to high quality internet resources for the learning, teaching and research community. Though the service is primarily aimed at internet users in further and higher education, in general it is of great value for personal and professional development. RDN resource descriptions are held in metadata records that conform to the RDN cataloguing guidelines (Cliff, 2002). Each subject gateway, as part of its service, provides the end-user with access to databases of descriptions of freely available, high-quality, web resources. Users with a specific subject in mind have to select

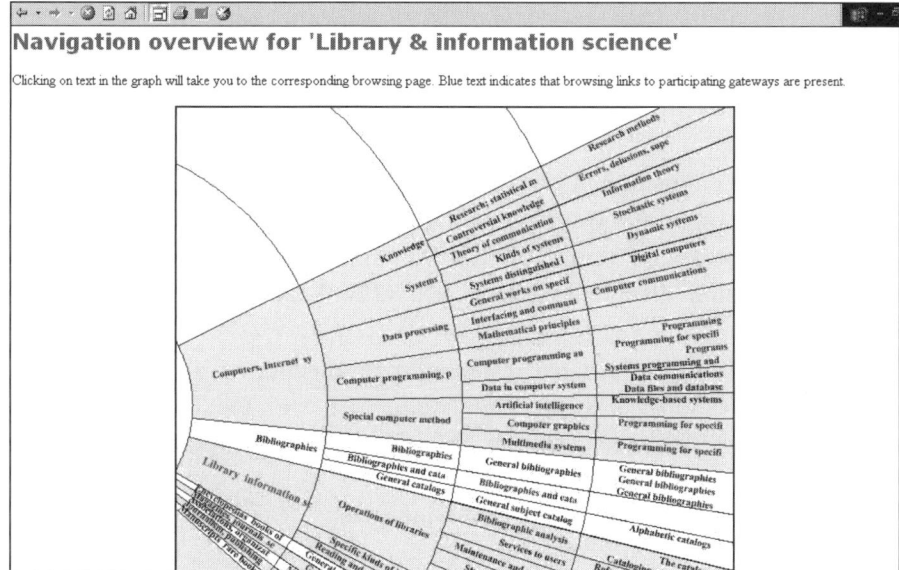

Fig. 7.19 *Visual representation of subject headings in Renardus*

a particular subject category from the RDN web page which will lead them to the specific gateway. Users with a query that is broad or may cover more than one category may try using the ResourceFinder option on the RDN web page.

Metadata principles and practicalities

Arguing that some convergence of encoding formats and commonly agreed semantics for metadata standards will be an absolute necessity, Duval et al. (2002) propose some principles and practicalities that form the bases of the work of the metadata communities. They define principles governing metadata standards as those concepts that are common to all domains of metadata and might inform the design of any metadata schema or application. These common principles are: the modularity namespace, extensibility, refinement and multilingualism. The practicalities are defined as the rules of thumb, and the infrastructure issues that emerge from bringing theory into practice, such as the application profiles, syntax and semantics, association models, identifying and naming metadata labels, metadata registries, completeness of description, mandatory vs optional elements, subjective and objective metadata, and automated generation of metadata (Duval et al., 2002).

iLumina (http://turing.csc.uncwil.edu/ilumina/homePage.xml)

McClelland et al. (2002) report on the experience and lessons learnt while importing metadata from various systems in the course of the iLumina project – a digital library of undergraduate teaching materials for science, mathematics, technology and engineering (SMETE) education being developed by Eduprise, the University of North Carolina at Wilmington, Georgia State University, Grand Valley State and Virginia Tech. The important lessons learnt through this project include the following (McClelland et al., 2002):

- Metadata from the original source may be incomplete and may contain errors that call for editing and validation.
- Developing specialized, custom vocabularies should be avoided because they may be confusing for others.
- The original XML should be maintained.

Resource Description Framework (www.w3.org/TR/REC-rdf-syntax/)

The Resource Description Framework (RDF), developed under the auspices of the World Wide Web Consortium (W3C) is an infrastructure that enables the encoding, exchange and reuse of structured metadata (Miller, 1998). It enables metadata interoperability through a mechanism that supports common conventions of semantics, syntax and structure. RDF does not stipulate semantics for each resource description community; it provides the facility for communities to define metadata elements as needed. XML is used in RDF as a common syntax for the exchange and processing of metadata. The structural constraints the RDF imposes to support the consistent encoding and exchange of standardized metadata provide for the interchangeability of separate packages of metadata defined by different resource description communities (Miller, 1998).

Summary

Providing access to information in digital libraries involves a number of complex issues. In this chapter some issues related to information organization are discussed, while those related to the user interfaces and information retrieval are covered in the next two chapters. While traditional libraries have long been used to using classification schemes for organizing physical documents, this has not been the case for digital libraries. As discussed in this chapter, some digital library gateways and projects have used bibliographic classification schemes, like DDC, UDC and LC, and vocabulary control tools, like LCSH and MeSH, for organizing digital resources. Some have also used these tools to facilitate information retrieval; see for example BUBL.

While it may not be possible to classify each and every item in a large digital library collection, a classificatory approach to organizing resources into related groups or classes may greatly enhance information access and can act as a simple filtering mechanism. The use of classification schemes and vocabulary control tools for facilitating information retrieval is an interesting area that needs further exploration. Many researchers believe that faceted classification schemes will be more suitable for organizing digital information resources (for example, Broughton and Lane, 2000; Ellis and Vasconcelos, 2000).

The creation of digital records that can be easily processed and manipulated in a digital library environment is a complex task, and traditional tools and standards are not adequate for the purpose. To meet this end, new metadata standards have been developed. While some of these standards provide a general schema for representing digital resources, many domain- and format-specific metadata standards have emerged. Metadata include both intrinsic data about the content of a record, as well as extrinsic data about its provenance, location, software requirements, etc. Some metadata can be generated automatically by computer programs while others call for manual coding. Overall, metadata provide mechanisms for the representation of documents, document-like objects and cumulative resources such as digital libraries (Borgman, 2000b, 80).

While metadata help us in resource discovery, markup languages specify the contents of the various sections of digital items. By combining the strengths of SGML and HTML, the new family of markup languages, the XML family, provides mechanisms for user-specific coding, thereby improving the semantic and syntactic processing of digital data. Indeed, the new set of standards, including XML, RDF, DOM and XSL, comprise revolutionary new tools for managing information in digital libraries.

Chapter 8
Information access and user interfaces

Outline

The central theme of this chapter is information access with particular reference to the user interfaces of digital libraries. It begins with a general discussion of information access and information-seeking models. It then examines the various stages of an information search process and user interface issues in the context of information seeking in a digital library environment. Sample digital library interfaces are shown to describe the various types of interfaces available to support the browsing, searching and display of digital information. Finally, the chapter mentions some areas of research into improvement of information access in digital libraries in order to support the creative activities of the end-users.

Introduction

One of the major objectives of a digital library is to provide improved access to information. In fact, as mentioned in Chapter 1, developing the enabling technologies to support improved access to digital information has been the primary goal of many digital library researchers. Digital library collections have several characteristic features that make information searching difficult. These collections are typically very large. They may involve many different kinds of objects, including all kinds of electronic publications – books, journals, conference proceedings, reports, images, audio, video and databases. Even within a single category, these objects may have widely different formats and internal structures. Furthermore, they have complex relationships with each other, and are required by different categories of user to meet different types of information needs.

Since digital libraries do not have any physical presence, users do not get a view of the collection and the contents as they do in a printed library. In fact, users of a digital library may not know much about its contents, and thus may find it difficult to formulate a query to get access to the required information. Users may not know how exhaustive the collection is in their area of interest or the size of the entire collection. Hence, it may become difficult for them to assess how exhaustive the retrieved information set at the end of a search is, and how precise the search results are. Determining how much information to show the users of a digital library is a major design choice in information access interfaces (Hearst, 1999).

Borgman (2000b, 79) comments that the concept of access to information has its roots in different areas such as library services, telecommunications policies, and so on. She defines access to information (Borgman, 2000b, 57) as connectivity to a computer network and to the available content, given that the technology is usable; the user has the requisite skills and knowledge; and the content is in usable and useful form. Thus, the three major factors influencing access to information are the technology, content, and above all the users.

In this chapter we discuss the basic issues of information access to digital libraries and the concept of user interfaces and interface design issues. A close look at the interfaces of some digital libraries reveals the different practices followed by designers to support the browsing, searching and display of digital information.

Information users

Theoretically speaking, a user of a digital library may be anyone living anywhere in the world. This is especially true for those digital libraries that aim to offer information access to a global audience, for example, the Networked Digital Library of Theses and Dissertations (NDLTD), the Networked Computer Science Technical Reference Library (NCSTRL) or the Greenstone Digital Library. Users of these digital libraries may vary in terms of their information need, characteristics, capabilities, and so on. Some digital libraries aim to cater for a rather homogeneous group of users though they may not be bound by any geographical boundary. Examples of such digital libraries include the Association of Computing Machinery (ACM) digital library and Institute of Electrical and Electronic Engineers (IEL) digital library. Yet there are other digital libraries that are designed specifically to support a defined group of users.

Most university digital libraries, for example the California Digital Library and HeadLine, belong to this category.

However, as Nicholas and Dobrowolski (2001) argue, the characteristics and role of users in a digital environment vary significantly from those in a traditional library environment. They propose a new term, 'information players', to replace the word users or end-users in order to reflect the changing nature of the users in a digital environment.

Users in a digital library environment need not only have adequate information literacy skills, but also some ICT skills to help them make optimum use of the digital environment. The SCONUL position paper (SCONUL, 1999) identified seven information skills that are considered necessary in a digital library environment:

- the ability to recognize a need for information
- the ability to distinguish ways in which the information need may be addressed
- the ability to construct appropriate information strategies
- the ability to locate and access appropriate information
- the ability to compare and evaluate information obtained from various sources
- the ability to organize, communicate and apply information in problem-solving tasks or in decision making
- the ability to synthesize and build upon existing information, and to contribute to the creation of new information.

Information needs

Information needs and how to provide access to information has remained a central theme of study among information and computer science researchers for many years. It is commonly agreed that the provision of information begins when a user has an information need. A significant amount of research on such matters as information needs and users' information-seeking behaviour has been conducted, and a large volume of literature has been produced over the past decades (for example, Bates, 1977, 1979, 1981, 1984; Belkin, Oddy and Brooks, 1982a, 1982b; Case, Borgman and Meadow, 1986; Dervin, 1977; Ellis, 1989; Kuhlthau, 1988a, 1988b; Marchionini and Komlodi, 1998; Spink et al., 2002a, 2002b, 2002c, 2002d; Wilson, T., 1981, 1994, 1999). Information need is a stage where the user senses that it may be useful to know something that they do not know at that particular point in time. Marchionini (1995, 6) comments that information seeking is a fundamental human process that is closely related to learning and problem solving. According to Borgman (2000b, 109) a need is a psychological construct, and it cannot be observed by a researcher, a librarian or an intelligent agent; only indicators or manifestations of needs can be observed.

The information needed by a user to accomplish a goal – to resolve a problem, to answer a specific question or to satisfy a curiosity – may be quick and brief factual data or exhaustive and detailed. Figure 8.1 shows a simple model of information access. Although it appears to be very basic, in essence several complex processes take place throughout. Some of these are technological and related to the information retrieval system, users interfaces, and so on. Other

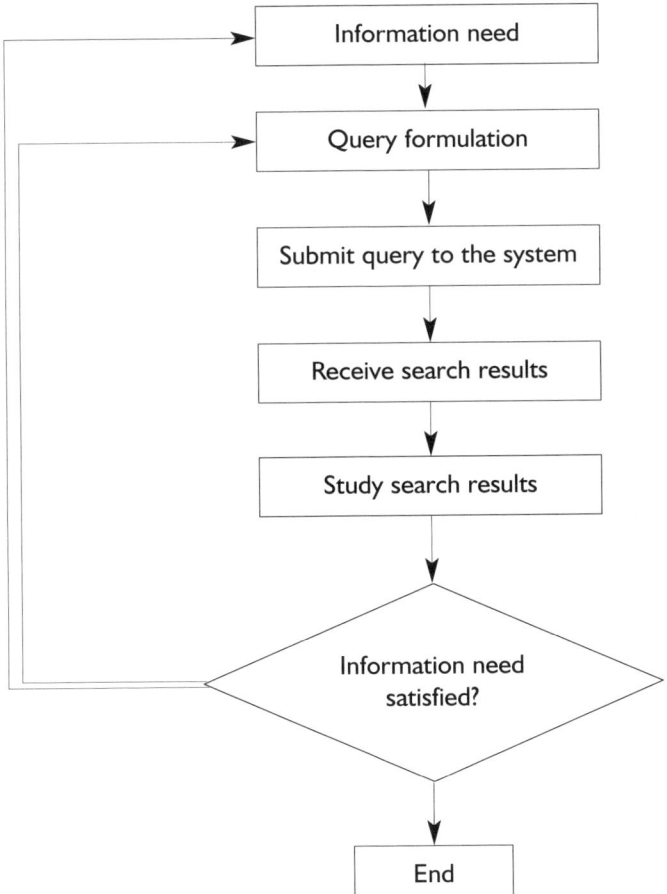

Fig. 8.1   *Basic information access model*

processes relate to the nature and characteristics of the content as well as the specific user. The process may take more or less time, and may become simple or complex depending on the nature of the users – their cognitive abilities and background, the specific nature of the information need, and so on.

Information seeking is an interactive process that depends on initiative on the part of the user, feedback from the information system, and the user's decisions about subsequent actions based on the feedback (Marchionini, 1995, 17). The user's initial information need may often change on receipt of some information. Hence, the information search process continues till the user gets the information required to satisfy the revised information need. Appropriate technology, such as a suitable information retrieval system and user interface, may facilitate the process, but is not the ultimate answer, because the process depends largely on an individual user and their information need, as well as the nature, volume and variety of the content.

Users often learn during the information search process. For example, they may come across some information that influences their information need. The user may also acquire new knowledge about the system, and thus be able to formulate queries more skillfully and appropriately to retrieve better output. The berry-picking model of information seeking proposed by Bates (1989) suggests that as a result of reading and learning from the information retrieved through the search process, users' information needs and the queries continually shift. The berry-picking model also suggests that the user's information needs are satisfied by a series of selections and bits of information found along the entire information search process, as opposed to the output of any particular search set. The ASK (Anomalous States of Knowledge) model proposed by Belkin and his associates (Belkin, 1980; Belkin, Oddy and Brooks, 1982a, 1982b) suggests that an information-seeking process begins with a problem, but initially that problem and the information needed to resolve it are not clearly understood. Hence, the information seekers need to go through an iterative process to articulate a search request, and the information system should support interactive searching.

The sense-making approach of Dervin (1977) posits that users go through different phases in making sense of the world. The first phase establishes the context for the information need, which she calls a situation. People find a gap between what they understand and what they need to know in order to make sense of the current situation. These gaps are manifested by the formulation of questions. The answers to these questions are then used to move to the next situation. Marchionini (1995, 29) comments that Dervin's model applies more to general human conditions than to information seeking, but the model has been adopted by researchers in information science and communications as a framework for studying the information-seeking process. Kuhlthau (1988a, 1988b; Kuhlthau et al., 1990) proposed a model of how students search for information as part of their writing process. The process involves seven stages: task initiation, topic selection, pre-focus exploration, focus formulation, information collection, search closure and the starting of writing.

Bates (2002) suggests that each layer in an information system interacts with every other design layer, and this cascade of interactions culminates in the interface, where all the prior interactions have either worked to produce effective information retrieval or to produce system elements that work at cross-purposes. She thus proposes a design model, called the Cascade Model, for operational information retrieval systems. The basic proposition of this model is that without the design of all the constituent layers of an information retrieval system being integrated, the resulting system is likely to be poor. There are four layers in this model:

- The first layer comprises the infrastructure – network, hardware, software and databases.
- The second layer comprises the information or content combined with the metadata structure.
- The third layer represents the information retrieval system – from information in searchable form to the interface design supported by the technical infrastructure.
- The fourth layer is the human part of the system, comprising user searching activities and user understanding and motivation.

Nicholas (1996) stresses the need for qualitative assessment of user needs. He identifies 11 major characteristics of information need: subject, level, quality, place of publication or origin, function, viewpoint, date, processing and packaging, nature, quality and speed of delivery. A number of interesting issues related to the information seeking and searching in digital libraries have been discussed in a DELOS workshop (Boehm, Croft and Schek, 2000).

The four-phase framework for information search

Information searching is a complex process. It involves a number of stages and at each stage a number of actions are taken and decisions made. The information retrieval system and the user interface may provide support in performing these actions and in making appropriate decisions. Shneiderman, Byrd and Croft (1997) divide the major activities in an information search process into four major phases: formulation, action, review of results, and refinement. They propose that this four-phase framework for interface design will provide a common structure and terminology for information searching while preserving the distinct features of individual digital library collections and search mechanisms (Shneiderman, Byrd and Croft, 1998).

Phase 1: Formulation

The formulation of a search is triggered by an information need, and several decisions are made regarding sources, fields, what to search for, and the search variants.

The selection of sources (collections and/or databases) is an important step in a search process. In a digital library environment, users may have access to many collections, and each collection may have one or more databases. Users need to have some idea about the nature and content of the collections and databases and use this to make a selection. Some digital library interfaces show a list of the available collections and allow users to select one particular collection; for example the Greenstone Digital Library allows users to select one particular collection to browse or search, and NDLTD allows users to search for the theses of a selected university or universities. In the case of the California Digital Library, users have many choices. For example, they may select a particular collection or use the Searchlight option to select by broad subject grouping like science and engineering, or social science and humanities. However, the selection of sources to search is not always an easy task, especially for new and novice users. Some systems provide support for this. In this case, users are asked to enter a search expression, and then the system searches across the databases and produces an output of best-matching databases instead of best-matching records. This gives the user an idea of the content of the collections and thus facilitates the selection of sources. In Dialog, for example, the DialIndex option allows users to search across a range of databases to get a list of those that best match their chosen search topic (Chowdhury and Chowdhury, 2001a, 141).

A search may be conducted against one or more selected fields in a database. A search on specific fields produces more specific search results than one on a complete record. However, it is sometimes difficult for the user to decide which field to search. This calls for a familiarity with the structure of the chosen database and also with the nature and content of the fields. Users may go to the help files, or to some other source, for example to the blue sheets (pages that contain information on a database including its content, coverage, structure and indexing) in the case of a Dialog database search. Some systems provide search interfaces (usually in the advanced search mode) with structured fields. For example, in the ACM digital library's advanced search interface, users can select a number of fields to which to restrict a search (see Figure 8.2). Similarly, in THOMAS (a digital library service of the Library of Congress), users can select a number of fields with which to conduct and/or restrict a search (see Figure 8.3) for Congressional records.

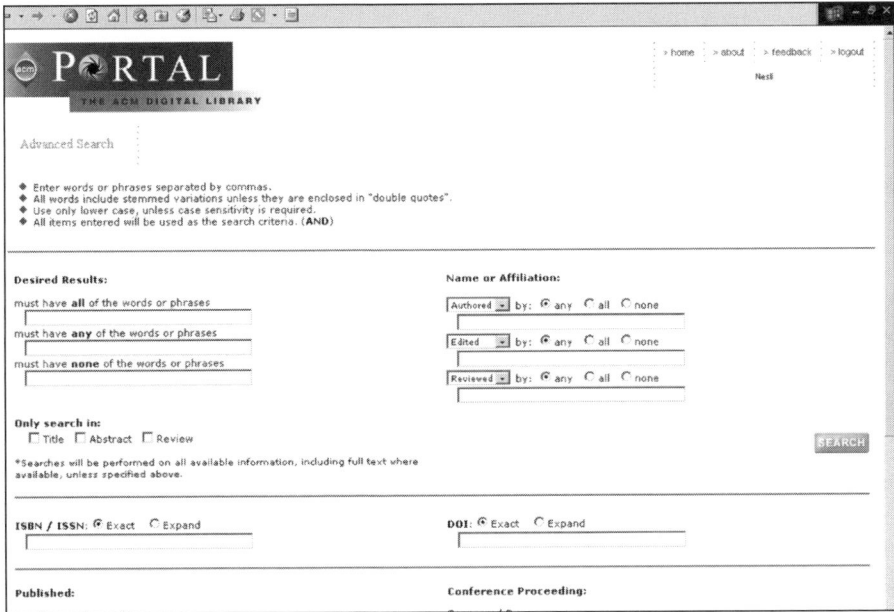

Fig. 8.2   *Advanced search interface of the ACM digital library*

A major challenge for users comes in writing the actual search statement. A search statement tells the system what to search for in the chosen database(s). Various techniques are available for specifying how the constituent search terms are to be looked for, for example by using appropriate search operators. The search operators are not always intuitive and are purely dependent on the chosen system. Users need to be familiar with the various operators and the conventions appropriate for the chosen search system. Examples of various search operators are provided in Chapter 9.

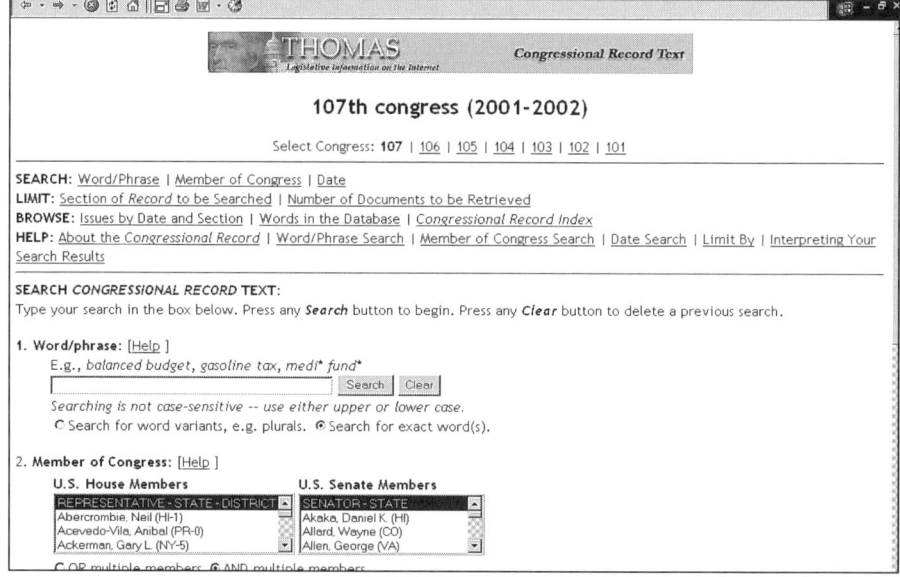

Fig. 8.3 *Search interface for text search in THOMAS*

A search term may be represented in a variety of ways. Users may want to choose a given search term or phrase that appears in the database records in a variety of ways, for example in singular plural forms, in various synonymous forms, with variant spellings, and so on. In such cases it can be very difficult for the user to decide which form or variant of a search term to use. The user interfaces of digital libraries often help by allowing for case sensitivity, stemming, phonetic variants, synonyms, abbreviations, broader and narrower terms, and stop words. Some of these issues are discussed in Chapter 9.

Phase 2: Action

Usually a search button needs to be pressed to conduct a search, although in some cases the user just needs to press <CR>. Once the search begins, the user is usually expected to wait till the search process end. Sometimes, this may take a long time and thus be frustrating. In some cases, the interface prompts the user that the search is being processed; it may also tell the user about the progress of the search (for example, Figure 8.4 shows the progress of a search in the California Digital Library search interface). A very appealing method of information searching is 'dynamic queries', a system where there is no search button and the result set is continuously displayed and updated as phases of the search are changed (Shneiderman, Byrd and Croft, 1997).

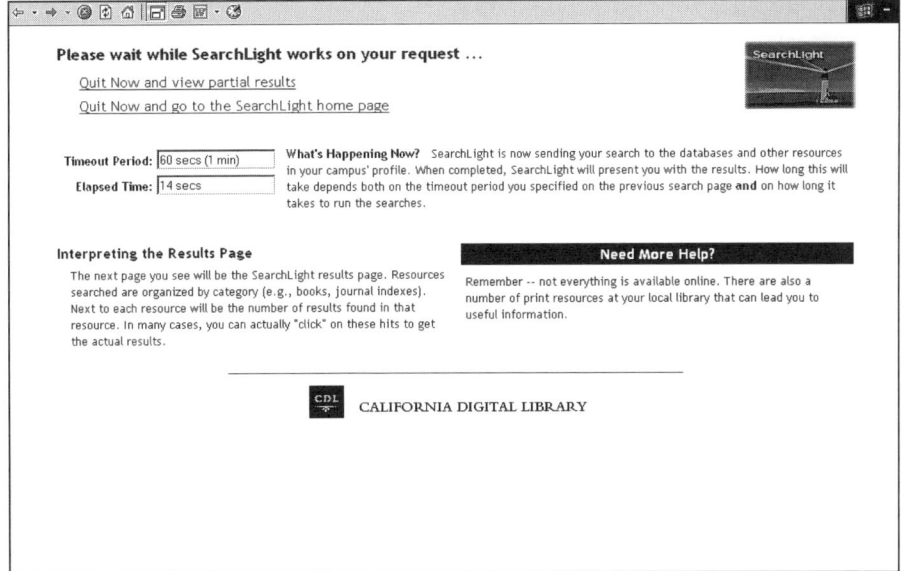

Fig. 8.4 *Progress of a search session in the California Digital Library*

Phase 3: Review of results

Information retrieval interfaces usually offer the user various choices for viewing results such as the size of display, display format and the order of the retrieved items (sorted by author, date, and so on). Some interfaces use different visualization techniques for the display of search results. Some interfaces also use helpful messages to explain the results, for example the degree of relevance. Some digital libraries, for example the California Digital Library, shows results from different collections separately (for example, Figure 8.5).

Phase 4: Refinement

Different search interfaces provide different facilities for modifying and refining queries. In some cases, users need to reformulate the search statement and conduct a new search, while in others users can refine a search and conduct a new search on the retrieved set. For example, in Dialog search, each search is automatically given a set number, and the user can specify any search set on which to conduct a refined search. Many digital library interfaces also support relevance feedback, a system where the user selects some retrieved output as relevant and the system conducts a new search based on the characteristics of the items identified as relevant (discussed further in Chapter 9).

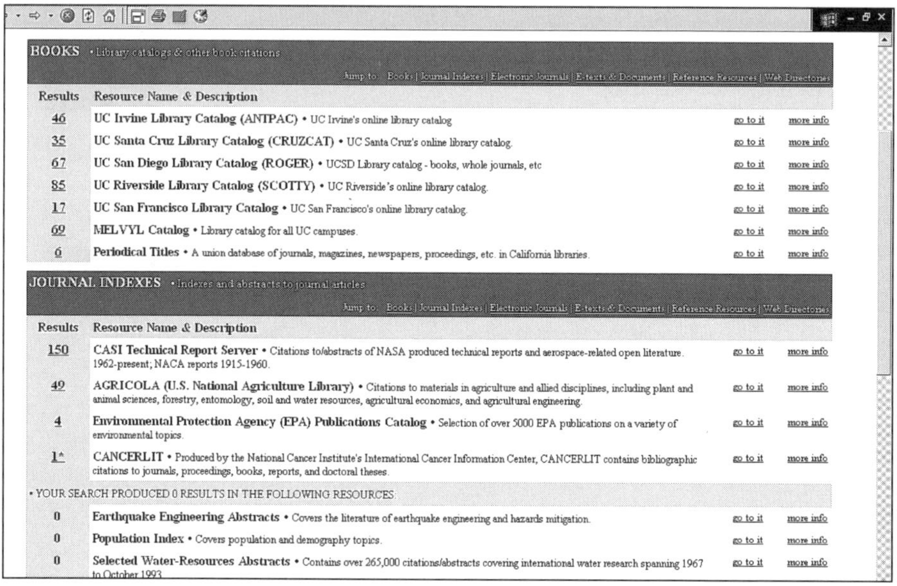

Fig. 8.5 *Results of a search in the California Digital Library showing output from various categories of sources*

Information seeking and user interfaces

User interfaces to information retrieval systems that support information-seeking processes have been widely discussed in the literature. Mitchell (1999) comments that the user interface is the means by which information is transferred between the user and the computer and vice versa. Mitchell further comments that well-designed user interfaces should allow users to find and use the information that the information system provides access to more efficiently. In fact a good user interface greatly enhances the quality of interactions with information systems.

Interface design encompasses what appears on the user's screen, how they view it, and how they manipulate it. Functional design specifies the functions that are offered to the user such as selecting parts of a digital object, searching a list or sorting retrieved output, obtaining help, and manipulating objects that appear on the screen. Almost all present-day PCs have a user interface that is based on the style derived at Xerox PARC and made popular on Apple Macs, and uses the metaphors of files and folders on a desktop (Arms, 2000b, 45).

Shneiderman, the guru of HCI (human–computer interaction) and user interface design, proposes a number of guiding principles for the design of user interfaces (Shneiderman, 1998b; Shneiderman, Byrd and Croft, 1997):

- Strive for consistency: terminology, layout, instructions, fonts and colour should be used consistently throughout the interface.
- Provide shortcuts for skilled users.
- Provide informative feedback: the system should provide users with appropriate feedback about the sources and what is being searched for.
- Design for closure: users should know when they have completed searching the entire collection or have viewed every item in a browse list.
- Permit reversal of actions: users should be able to undo or modify actions, for example they should be able to modify their queries, or should be able to go back to the previous state in a search session.
- Support user control: the user should be able to monitor the progress of a search and should be able to specify the parameters to control a search.
- Reduce short-term memory load: the system should keep track of some important actions performed by the users and should allow them to jump to a formerly performed action easily, for example to a former query or to a specific result set.
- Make error handling facilities simple: users should be able to rectify errors easily, and all error messages should be clear and specific.
- Provide plenty of space: a lot of room should be made available for entering text in search boxes.
- Provide alternative interfaces: separate interfaces should be available for expert and novice users.

Bates (2002) stresses that interface design is pivotal to the effective use of an information system, and that the application environment of information retrieval systems has its own distinctive needs and characteristics that need to be understood and addressed in design. Hearst (1999) comments that an interface designer must make decisions about how to arrange various kinds of information on the screen and how to structure the possible sequences of user-system interactions.

Marchionini (1992) provides a description of the essential features of interfaces to support end-user information seeking and suggests five information-seeking functions, namely problem definition, source selection, problem articulation, result examination and information extraction. He argues that much interface work has focused on problem articulation (including query formulation) and that the other functions need to be investigated in designing information-seeking interfaces. Marchionini and Komlodi (1998) discuss the evolution of interfaces and trace research and development in three areas, namely information seeking, interface design and computer technology. They provide a brief review of interfaces to online information retrieval systems as well as to online public access catalogues (OPACs). They also discuss the new generation of user interfaces influenced by the emergence of the web. They conclude that interface design has become more user-centred and that the trend is toward more mature interfaces that support a range of information-seeking strategies.

Savage-Knepshield and Belkin (1999) discuss the trends related to interface design challenges within the context of information retrieval interaction over the last three decades. They divide the period into three major eras, which they refer to simply as the early years, the middle years and the later years, and provide a description of the types of interfaces designed in each. Command language interfaces provided the main approach in the early years. In the middle years menu-driven and form-fill-in interfaces, which were more appropriate for novices and casual searchers, became the dominant interface type. In the later years, users and their information needs became the focus of the most complex interface design challenges. This period is characterized by use of the natural language and direct manipulation user interfaces. The authors note that the degree of interaction between the searcher and the IR system has dramatically increased but that much research is still required to meet the challenges in interface design for IR interaction.

Hearst (1999) discusses user interface support for the information-seeking process and describes the features of these interfaces that aid such processes as query formulation and specification, viewing results and interactive relevance feedback. She describes a number of graphical user interfaces that provide information seekers with a wide range of approaches to specify, view, analyse and evaluate queries and documents within the context of information retrieval systems. Interfaces that support the formulation of Boolean and natural language queries as well as those providing categorical and subject support are examples of those reviewed. Hearst points out that there is an increasing interest in taking the behaviour of individuals into account when designing interfaces.

User interfaces and visualization

Since human beings are highly attuned to images, and since visual representation facilitates rapid and easy communication, several visualization techniques have now been applied to the design of user interfaces. Various graphical representation and manipulation methods are used to represent information on the user screens though the visualization of textually represented information is challenging (Hearst, 1999).

Users of popular operating systems and common software packages use a number of visual tools and techniques for day-to-day operations. These include the icons, colour highlighting, windows and boxes, and so on. The most commonly used visualization techniques used in user interfaces for information access include the following (Hearst, 1999; Kakimoto and Kambayashi, 1999; Rao et al., 1995; Robertson, Card and Mackinlay, 1993):

- *Perspective wall*. This resembles a grey wall folded into three parts and provides a sort of a fish-eye view (a three-dimensional picture taken with a special lens called the fish-eye lens). The centre panel provides a detailed view, and the two wings provide a contextual view. It is suitable for information that has a linear structure.
- *Cone tree*. This provides a fish-eye view by displaying the nodes that are closer larger and more brightly than the ones that are further away. It is suitable for information that has a hierarchical structure.
- *Document lenses*. These are used to focus on one page in a document.
- *Hyperbolic tree browser*. This is used to show the hierarchical structure of a collection as a hyperbolic tree (there is an example in Figure 8.9).
- *Brushing and linking*. This involves connecting two or more views of the same data in such a way that a change to the representation of one view affects the representation of the other.
- *Panning and zooming*. This mimics the actions of a movie camera that can scan sideways across a scene, panning, and can move in for a close-up or back away to get a wider view, zooming.
- *Focus plus context*. One portion of the collection is made the focus of attention by making it larger while shrinking the surrounding objects that form the context.

User interfaces of digital libraries

Digital libraries vary in terms of design, objectives, characteristics, content and users. Consequently, many different types of digital library user interface can be found. While some of these user interfaces are simple, others are sophisticated in terms of design features as well as visualization techniques. In this section we shall brief discuss the user interfaces of some selected digital libraries and related services. The examples are by no means exhaustive, but give an idea of the various design techniques used in digital library interfaces for supporting various activities, such as query formulation, display of search results, and so on.

The digital library user interface is an exciting area of research, and researchers from various fields are now working in this area. The first International Workshop on Visual Interfaces to Digital Libraries was held at the first Joint ACM and IEEE conference on digital libraries in Roanoke, Virginia, on 28 June 2001. This one-day workshop drew an international audience of 37 researchers, practitioners and graduate students in the areas of information visualization, digital libraries, human–computer interaction, library and information science, computer science and geography. The primary aim of the workshop was to raise the awareness of several interconnected fields of research related to the design and use of visual interfaces to digital libraries, especially in information visualization, human–computer interaction and cognitive psychology (Börner, 2001).

The eighth DELOS Workshop on User Interfaces in Digital Libraries, held in Stockholm, Sweden, 21–23 October 1998, discussed the following issues: (Hansen, 1999; Hansen and Karlgren, 1999):

- information seeking and retrieval as embedded activities within digital libraries
- techniques and methods to analyse and evaluate different systems as well as different users, their behaviour, tasks and the ideas behind the systems developed
- interactions with information, such as texts and multimedia, and access to multilingual information in information-seeking activities
- alternative modalities for representations of information-seeking activities in digital libraries.

The major problem for designers of a digital library user interface is their lack of knowledge about the users, their infrastructure, needs and characteristics, since virtually anyone anywhere in the world can be a potential user. A good design must be effective in a range of computing environments. DLITE (the Digital Library Integrated Task Environment) is an example of a user interface model (developed at Stanford University as part of the Digital Library Initiative), which takes into account the tasks that the users of a digital library typically carry out (Cousins et al., 1997). It describes digital libraries in terms of four major components: documents, queries, collections and services. DLITE uses the InfoBus technology, which provides a unifying framework for bringing together services provided on the web as well as other traditional information retrieval services. Baldonado (2000) and associates (Baldonado and Winograd, 1996) describe the design and implementation of SenseMaker, an interface for information exploration across heterogeneous sources. The basic tenet of this approach is that a user's interests go through a process of development and that SenseMaker supports their context-driven evolution. SenseMaker allows users to first examine the current context and, secondly, progress from one context to the next.

Information access in digital libraries

The two basic modes of access to information in digital libraries are browsing and searching. Most digital libraries provide facilities for browsing as well as searching. In this chapter we shall take a look at the user interfaces of some digital libraries highlighting their features for supporting browsing, query formulation and display of search results.

A number of portals and subject gateways have been developed over the past few years to facilitate access to digital information. These gateways are not digital libraries per se; some prefer to call them virtual libraries since they provide organized and systematic access to the information resources on the web. Examples of such gateways include BUBL, EEVL, SOSIG, Biz/ed and BIOME. Chowdhury and Chowdhury (2001b, Chapter 5) provide useful discussions on the characteristics of these subject gateways.

Digital library interfaces and browsing

Digital library interfaces offer different types of browsing facilities. In this section we shall look at some such interfaces to get an idea of the different browsing options and features. Figure 8.6 and 8.7 show the browsing interfaces of the Virginia Tech ETD (Electronic Theses and Dissertations) digital library. When users open the VT ETD web page, they are offered the choice of either the search or the browse by author option. If the browsing option is chosen, a page appears which divides up the theses according to the letter of the alphabet with which their author's surname begins, gives a total number of theses for each letter, and offers a choice between them (Figure 8.6). This screen also tells the user which kind of access facilities are available for those theses. Once the user

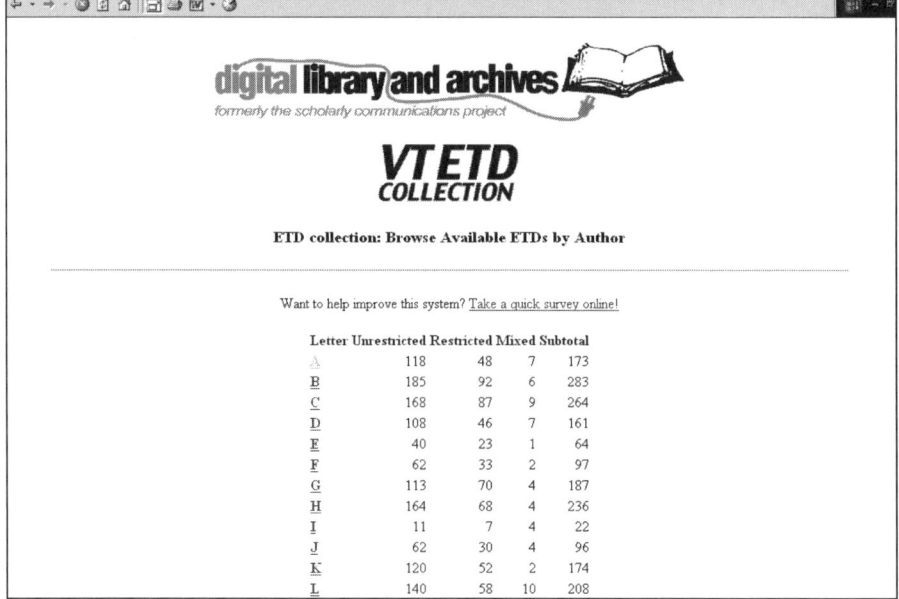

Fig. 8.6 *Virginia Tech ETD browse screen (1)*

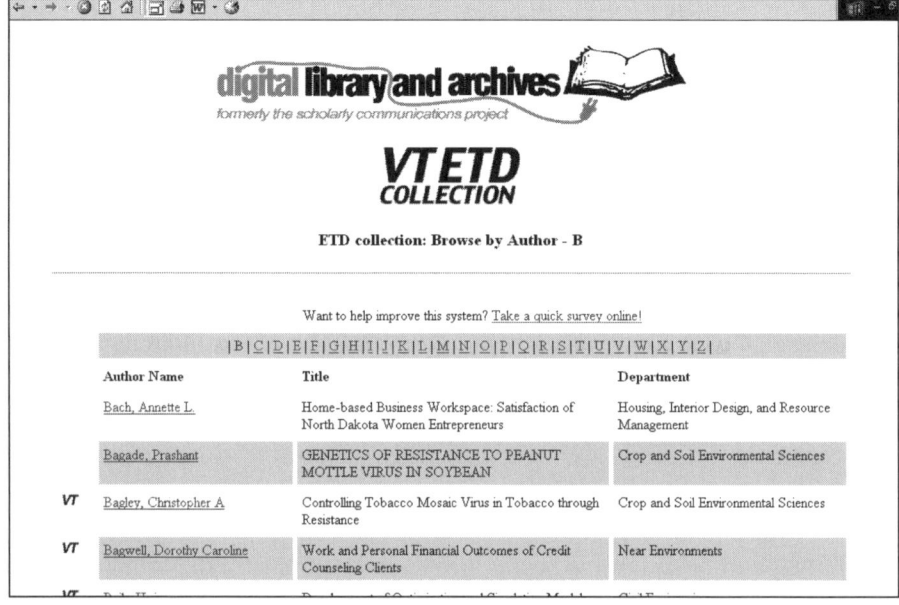

Fig. 8.7 *Virginia Tech ETD browse screen (2)*

chooses a specific letter of the alphabet, another screen (Figure 8.7) appears showing the actual titles available arranged alphabetically by author. The list also shows the name of the department. A click on the hyperlink on the author name takes the user to another page showing the metadata of the concerned dissertation, from where the user gets a link to the full text. The metadata page also shows the required download time for different types of access – through different types of modem, ISDN, and so on. Thus, a user has to follow four steps to get access to the full text, if available, of a thesis.

Figure 8.8 shows the browse screen of NCSTRL. Here, users can browse the documents by archives. The screen has two parts: the left part shows the list of archives and the total number of items available in each archive, and if the user selects any archive, the right window shows the list of documents available in it. A click on the title of a selected item takes the user to another screen which shows the abstract and other details, including a document identifier that takes the user to the full text of the item. The Universal Library, hosted by Carnegie Mellon University, provides a demonstration of a browsing screen using hyperbolic tree from Inxight Software (www.inxight.com). The various topics for each subject collection appear as nodes on the hyperbolic tree which take the user to the different parts of the collection (Figure 8.9).

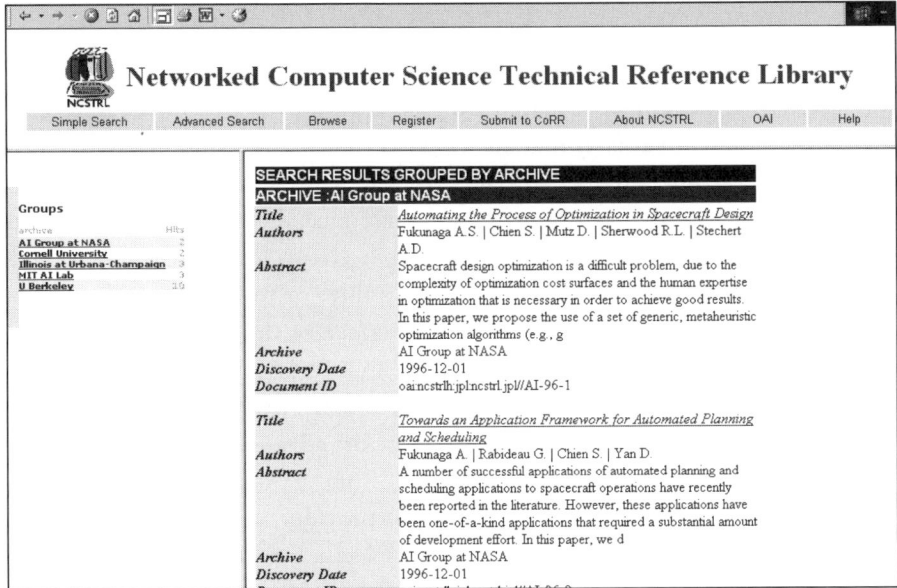

Fig. 8.8   *NCSTRL browse interface*

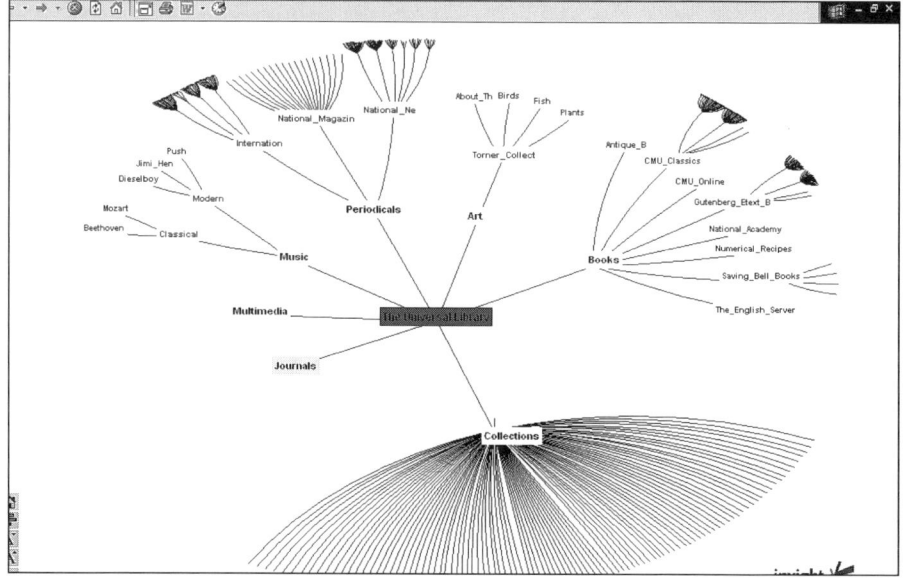

Fig. 8.9   *Universal Library browse interface*

Digital library interfaces and search and display

Digital library interfaces vary significantly in terms of the search features and facilities provided. They also differ significantly in terms of such matters as design, layout, conventions, fonts and colours. In this section, we shall look at the search interfaces of some selected digital libraries with a view to getting an idea of the different varieties that are available. These are by no means exhaustive, and indeed there are many more.

We shall begin with a very simple search interface, that of the NCSTRL digital library shown in Figure 8.10. This search screen allows users to enter a search or phrase, group the results by either archive or year, and sort the results by relevance or date. The simple search interface of the Virginia Tech ETD (Figure 8.11) provides a box for entering search term(s), and allows users to select one of the two collections. Here, users can also choose the advanced search option. Hence, even if users want to use the advanced search screen, they have to come first to the simple search screen from the main VT ETD page.

The advanced search screen (Figure 8.12) provides a number of options to formulate complex queries. Here users can select a field to search and specify whether the search terms should be treated as individual search terms or a phrase. They can also specify Boolean search conditions, but the conventions

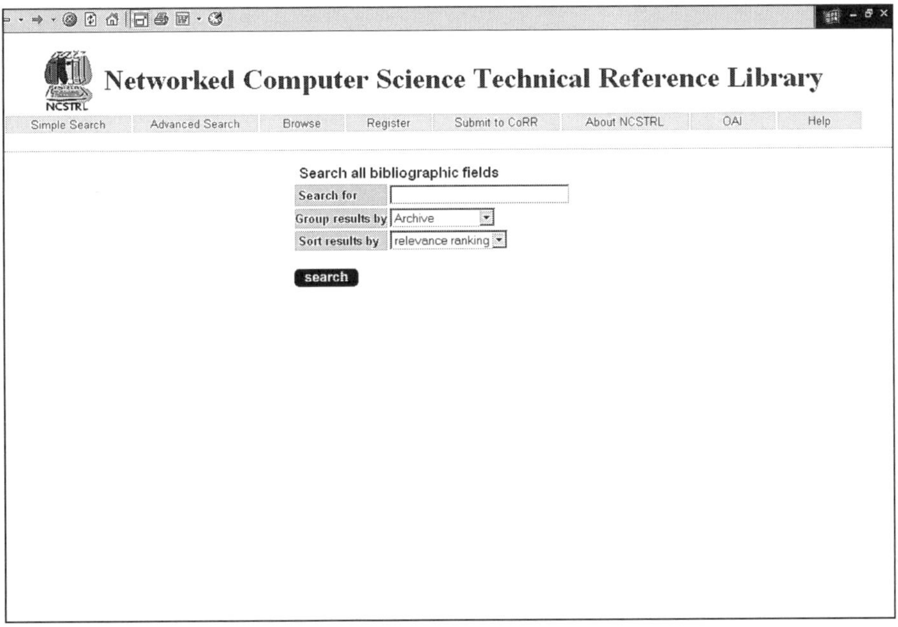

Fig. 8.10 *Simple search interface of NCSTRL*

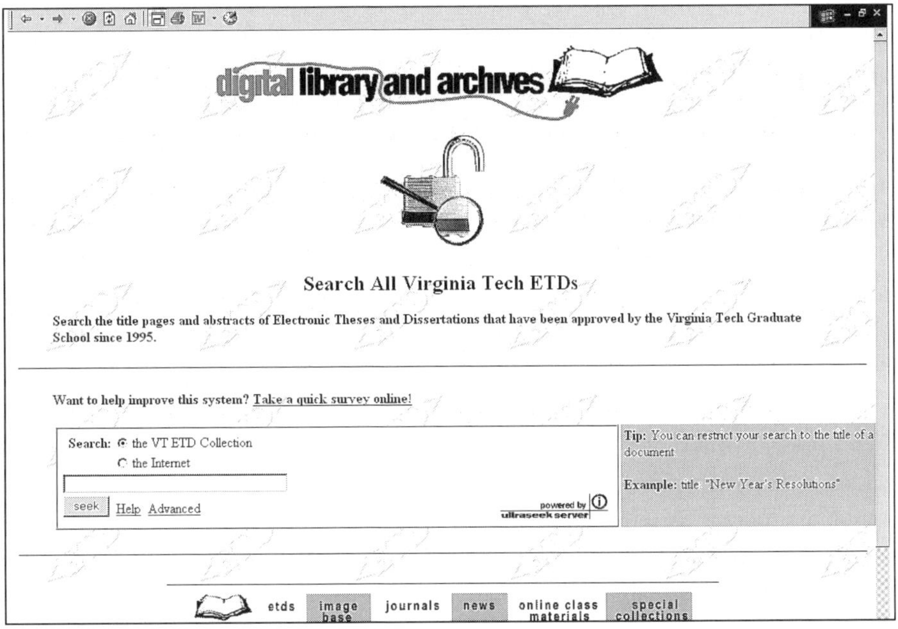

Fig. 8.11 *Simple search interface of VT ETD*

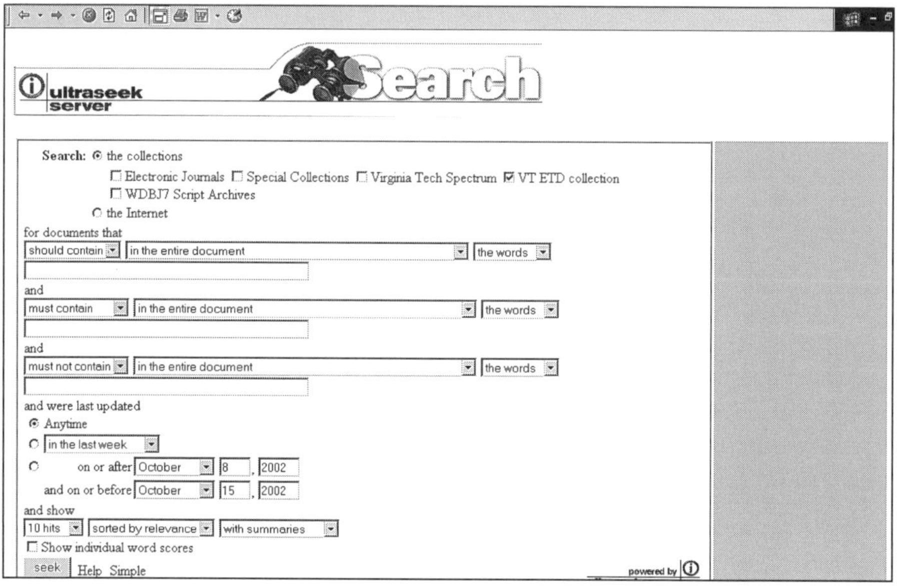

Fig. 8.12 *Advanced search interface of VT ETD*

are different here – 'should contain', 'must contain' and 'must not contain'. Users can also select display conditions, such as the number of hits per page, the criteria for sorting and presentation (with or without summaries). All these options can be chosen from one page.

However, when users conduct a search using the advanced search screen, the same search screen re-appears with the search results at the bottom. At times, it may be confusing for users, because unless they scroll down the screen they do not get any clue as to what has happened. However, once a search is conducted, they can select the option 'Search these results' to conduct a new search on the retrieved set, or can choose to 'search entire web'; if users do not choose either of these options, the ETD collection will be searched. Users also have to alter the display format by choosing 'hide summaries'.

If the user has used the simple search interface, then the results display interface appears differently – it is the same results display as for the advanced screen, but in this case it appears on top. Figure 8.13 shows the output of a search using the simple search interface of VT ETD. An interesting display screen appears in the California Digital Library interface where search results in each collection are shown separately (see Figure 8.5).

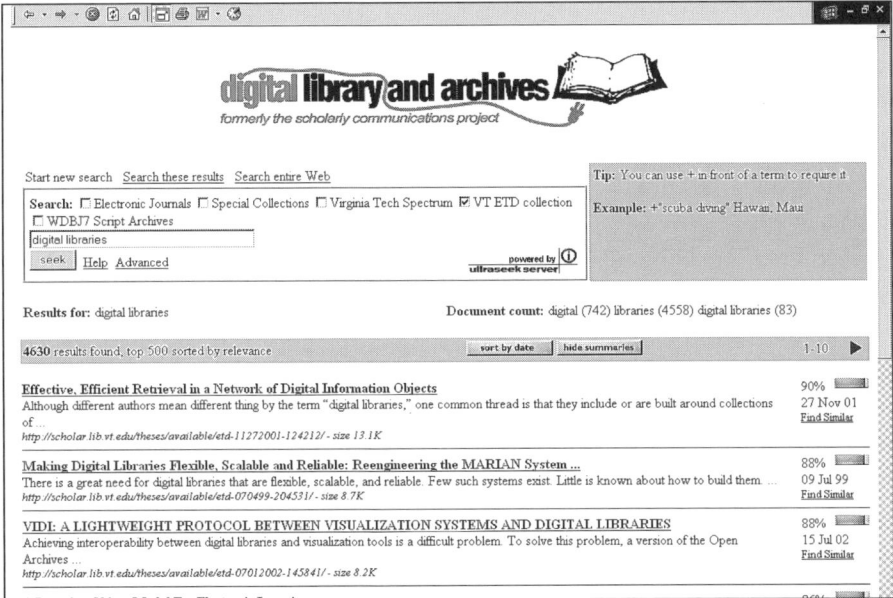

Fig. 8.13 *Search results from VT ETD*

User-centred digital libraries

While many of its users may be local, as in the case of a university library, a digital library by definition should provide global access both in terms of content and users. In other words, the users of a digital library may be located anywhere in the world. Since digital libraries are meant for end-users and eliminate the physical presence of human intermediaries, the only link between a digital library and its users is the user interface. Ideally speaking, therefore, the user interface of a digital library should be so simple and intuitive that it can be used easily and comfortably by anyone from anywhere at any time. This is practically an impossible proposition since a single interface cannot serve all the potential users, who may vary in terms of age, subject interests, profession, social and economic background, linguistic and cognitive abilities, and so on. Also the same interface cannot be suitable for all types of information content. Many digital library researchers have proposed user-centred design of digital libraries. Some of these user-centred models have been discussed in Chapter 4. Brophy (2001) argues that in the future libraries will need to keep detailed and accurate data about their users in order to provide personalized services. Such user information may include user activities, subject interests, display and reading preferences, and so on.

User-centred design digital library interfaces have been proposed by many researchers (Baldonado, 2000; Fox and Urs, 2002; Marchionini and Komlodi, 1998; Meyyappan, Chowdhury and Foo, 2001a, 2001b, 2001c; Sutcliffe, 1999 and Theng et al. 1999), and several researchers have proposed information access models to support creativity (for example, Ford, 1999; Shneiderman, 1998a, 1999).

Web browsers have significantly improved and standardized the features of user interfaces; thus it is now possible to have more uniform access to digital information. Before the emergence of web browsers, developers had to provide a separate interface for each type of computer and system. Now, the designers of digital libraries can to a large extent rely on the web browsers for a standard interface for the users, leaving aside the complexities of hardware and software variations, and can concentrate on how to organize the flow of information to the user (Arms, 2000b, 147).

Shneiderman (1998a, 1999) proposes the *genex framework*, which supports creativity through four phases:

- *Collect*. Learn from previous works stored in digital libraries.
- *Relate*. Consult with peers and mentors.
- *Create*. Explore, compose and evaluate possible solutions.
- *Donate*. Disseminate the results and contribute to the digital libraries.

He further describes eight activities that need powerful interfaces to support creative work. In other words, he proposes eight areas that need attention from researchers to make future digital libraries useful for creative work. These activities are (Shneiderman, 1999) as follows.

1   *Searching and browsing digital libraries*. Users should have more control over searching and browsing so that they can make use of their prior knowledge and retrieve information that supports their creative activities. Since searching is a part of the entire creative process, users should be able to save the search results into appropriate systems or software for future use, for example on a spreadsheet for further manipulation, as a file that can later be used for consultation with peers, or on a personal notebook for later referral.

2   *Consulting with peers*. Users may often consult their peers about new findings or research ideas. Information is collected at different stages in the consultation process. Different tools and techniques are also used for

consultation. This concerns the design and use of technologies for the interface design, since the appropriate balance of privacy with rights to, and ease of, access to information is very important.

3   *Visualizing data and processes.* Interfaces that support visualization of a digital library's contents are very useful and further work is necessary for the smooth integration of the technologies. For example, the interface should allow the user to view the results of a search using appropriate visualization tools that would help them select the most appropriate results. It should then be possible to export those results to appropriate packages, for example to a spreadsheet or to a database, and eventually to include the processed information in a report or presentation.

4   *Thinking by free association.* The association of ideas and using related concepts is a useful method of thinking and creativity. Thesauri are sometimes used in information retrieval systems to support the association of search terms. Various online tools are now available to associate concepts, for example IdeaFisher (www.ideafisher.com) and MindManager (www.mindman. com). Search interfaces should allow users to use these tools appropriately throughout the search process.

5   *Exploring solutions.* Digital libraries can help users make a decision by making use of the appropriate information and software. Various generic software packages allow users to explore solutions; one prominent example is the spreadsheet software that has 'what-if' tools to help users explore the various alternatives. Digital library interfaces should help users run a simulation, save the whole session, and/or send the session to someone for further discussion and exploration. The digital library interface should also allow users to store any successful sessions to help future researchers build on the best work.

6   *Composing artefacts and performances.* A number of software packages are available that allow users to compose artefacts and performances. Digital library interfaces should enable the integration of the results of a search with such interfaces, for example templates and macros for business operations, Adobe Photoshop Macros for redoing images, or music composition programmes in the case of music digital libraries to help users become more creative.

7   *Reviewing and replaying session histories.* Digital library users may like to replay previous sessions to get some new information, or to begin from there for a new search session. However, as Shneiderman (1999) comments,

success in this requires careful user interface and software design to ensure that the results are compact, comprehensible and useful.

8 *Disseminating results.* New information may be disseminated to different types of user. One possible group would be previous and current researchers in the field. Digital libraries should allow users to find workers in a field of study easily. Shneiderman (1999) recommends that digital libraries should be conceived of as digital library communities by the extensive use of online community software to turn every object into the focus of a discussion group.

Thus research and evaluation are necessary to build systems that can support users in all their activities related to creativity. Other researchers propose the need for further research in information access and user interfaces so that digital libraries can support (1) more collaborative activities (Nichols et al., 2000), (2) better access to digital video collections (Lee et al., 2000), (3) geographic and spatial information (Oliveira, Goncalves and Medeiros, 1999), and (4) complex interactions (Kovács et al., 2000). Abdulla, Liu and Fox (1998) suggest that comprehensive logs of digital library use should be kept for analysing user behaviour to provide insights for future developments in the mechanisms of information access and user interfaces.

Summary

In this chapter we have considered the basic process of information access. Information access and information seeking have been the major areas of research in information science for many years and consequently many theories and models have been proposed by researchers. We have discussed some basic models that are also applicable to a digital library environment.

Since digital libraries are designed for end-users without the involvement of intermediaries; the interface is the only gateway and tool that the user can use to get access to and retrieve required information. User interfaces and computer–human interactions have been major areas of research in the study of both computer science and information science. In this chapter we have discussed the basic issues of user interface design with particular reference to the interfaces for digital information access.

Information access also depends on the information retrieval systems used. Discussions on information retrieval system models, techniques and tools are included in Chapter 9. Although digital libraries are at an early stage of development, there have been some evaluation studies of them. Issues related to the evaluations, particularly on usability issues, appear in Chapter 13.

The development and proliferation of web browsers have largely standardized the design features of user interfaces, but digital libraries still vary significantly in terms of interface features. The examples given of user interfaces for supporting information browsing, searching and display in different digital libraries show some of the variations that exist. Advanced visualization techniques will greatly enhance access to, and display of, information in digital libraries.

In future digital library interfaces should integrate with a number of software packages and utility tools to increase the creativity of users.

Chapter 9
Information retrieval in digital libraries

Outline

This chapter describes the basic concepts of information retrieval including the various information retrieval models and search techniques. It outlines the information retrieval characteristics of various resources that are accessible through digital libraries, such as online public access catalogues, electronic journals, online databases and web search engines. The information retrieval features of selected digital libraries from around the world are then considered. Finally, the chapter discusses various problems and prospects of information retrieval in digital libraries and gives appropriate references to the ongoing research in this area. This chapter thus provides the reader with an overview of information retrieval features – covering both theoretical and practical aspects – of digital libraries, with references to related problems and ongoing research.

Introduction

The term information retrieval was coined over five decades ago to describe searching and retrieval from storage of information by subject specification. Although tremendous improvements have been made since then in terms of tools, techniques and applications, the basic principle of information retrieval has remained unchanged. Meadow, Boyce and Kraft (2000, 2) suggest that the main goal of information retrieval is to find desired information in a store of information or a database. Chowdhury (1999, 4) describes the basic functions of an information retrieval system through a simple diagram shown in Figure 9.1.

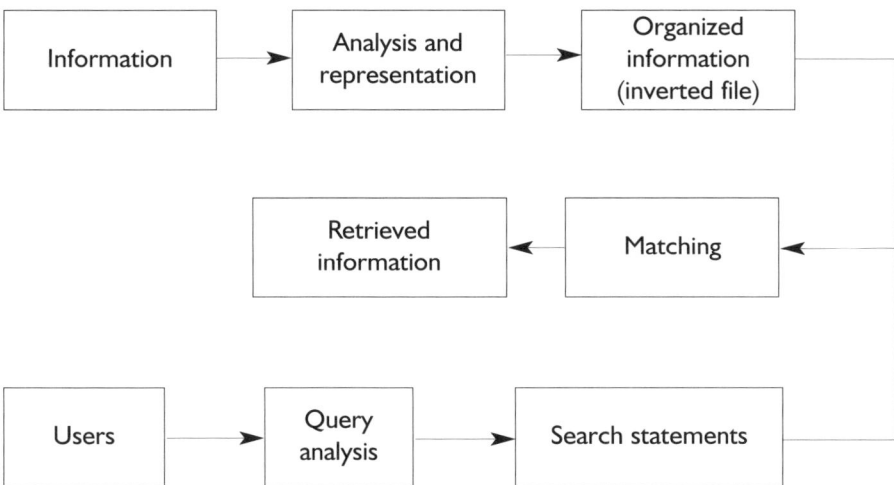

Fig. 9.1   *Broad outline of an information retrieval system*

As shown in Figure 9.1, the major functions of an information retrieval system can be divided into two categories: organization and retrieval of information. In the organization section, although the specific techniques vary from one information retrieval system to another, the basic task is to create an index (called the inverted index) of potential search terms (keywords and phrases). The index terms may be assigned by a human indexer or by an automatic process, or may be derived automatically from the document texts based on some selection criteria. An inverted index file, simply speaking, can be considered as a back-of-the-book index where search terms are arranged in a sequence; users use the index to locate a particular search term, and then follow the pointer to reach the main body of the text. Details of inverted file creation organization are available in a number of textbooks (for example, Chowdhury, 1999; Baeza-Yates and Ribeiro-Neto, 1999).

The retrieval process begins with a user query. A user with an information need interacts with the information retrieval system through the user interface and submits a query. A search query may contain a simple keyword or phrase, or may contain multiple keywords or phrases combined with search operators. The retrieval system matches each search term with the inverted index file and retrieves the matching items. Although this is the basic process in an information retrieval operation, the specifics of each of these activities may be complex depending on the retrieval system, or retrieval engine, as they are now called. A number of tools may also be used. For example, vocabulary control tools like thesauri, or machine translation tools, or both, may be used in the indexing or retrieval process.

Information retrieval models

The major objective of an information retrieval system is to retrieve information relevant to a user query. In effect, search terms from the user query are matched against index terms and items that contain the matching terms are retrieved. One of the major challenges of information retrieval is to create the index file. In theory each term in a document collection can be a candidate index term. However, information retrieval models have different techniques for selecting search terms for the index file, and different ways of matching the query terms and index terms to produce the search output. Three classical information retrieval models are:

- the Boolean or set theoretic model
- the vector-space model
- the probabilistic model.

All these models, in some way or other, match search terms with index terms to produce the search output. One of the major criticisms of them is that they look at individual search terms; they do not consider the search or index terms as part of a sentence or document. Alternative information retrieval models that use the linguistic features of documents and queries are called natural language processing (NLP) models.

All the information retrieval models have been discussed in detail in the literature (for example, Baeza-Yates and Ribeiro-Neto, 1999; Chowdhury, 1999; Harter and Hert, 1997; Korfhage, 1997; Meadow, Boyce and Kraft, 2000; Salton, 1989; Salton and McGill, 1983; Sparck Jones and Willett, 1997). In the following sections we shall briefly discuss the basic features of these models.

The Boolean search model

The Boolean search model is based on set theory and Boolean algebra. This model is very simple to implement. The basic idea is that a set of search terms is matched against a set of document index terms. Because of its inherent simplicity, the Boolean model has been adopted by almost all information retrieval systems. Multiple search terms in a query are combined according to Boolean logic: logical product (AND logic, for example computers and internet), logical sum (OR logic, for example computers or internet) and logical difference (NOT logic, for example computers not internet). Several examples of Boolean searches appear later in this chapter.

While the Boolean search model is very commonly used in information retrieval, it has some inherent problems. First, it is not always easy for users to understand the appropriate Boolean operators they must use to express their search requirements. Improper use of Boolean operators may result in too many or too few hits. Second, the Boolean model considers whether a search term is present or absent in an index file. As a result, it is difficult to assign weights or degrees of relevance to the retrieved items.

The vector-space model

The vector-space model aims to overcome the problem of the Boolean model using binary weights only. This model assigns non-binary weights to index terms in queries as well as in documents. This model computes the degree of similarity between each document in a collection and the query based on the weights of the terms. Thus, a ranked list of output can be produced with items that fully as well as partially match the query. There are many different ways of assigning weights to query and index terms, which have been discussed by Salton and McGill (1983) and Salton and Buckley (1988). The main advantages of the vector-space model are (Baeza-Yates and Ribeiro-Neto, 1999):

- The term weighting scheme improves the retrieval performance.
- It allows for partial matching.
- It generates a ranked list of output.

The major disadvantage of this model stems from the fact that it assumes that the index terms are mutually independent. This model also requires more computing power than the Boolean model. The vector-space model is now being applied to a number of search engines for web and digital libraries.

The probabilistic model

This model aims to deal with the problems of information retrieval within the framework of probability theory. Probabilistic models attempt to estimate the probability that an item will be relevant for a particular query. Several models based on probabilistic approaches have been proposed in the literature (for example, Maron and Kuhns, 1960; Rijsbergen, 1979; Robertson and Sparck Jones,

1976; Salton and McGill, 1983). Given a query 'q' and a document 'd' in a collection, the probabilistic model tries to estimate the probability that the user will find the document 'd' relevant. Maron and Kuhns proposed a model of information retrieval as early as 1960. They proposed that the likelihood that a document would be relevant to a user can be assessed by a calculation of probability, for each document in a collection, that a user submitting a particular query would judge that document relevant. The major problem of this approach is that one has to employ historical information to calculate the probability of relevance.

As opposed to the Maron and Kuhns approach, the model developed by Robertson and Sparck Jones (1976) proposes that the probability of relevance can be calculated not for a set of users employing a particular query term in relation to a given document, but for a given set of documents having a particular property in relation to a given user.

Vocabulary control

As shown in Figure 9.1, in an information retrieval system search terms are matched against document index terms and the matching items are retrieved. However, in order to match search terms with index terms, one must follow a vocabulary that is common to both. In other words, user requirements need to be translated and put to retrieval systems in the same language (using the same terms, for example) as was used to express the contents of the document records they cover. Lancaster (1986) suggests that the process of subject indexing involves two quite distinct intellectual steps: the conceptual analysis of the documents and the translation of the conceptual analysis into a particular vocabulary. The second step in any information retrieval environment involves the use of a controlled vocabulary, that is a limited set of terms that must be used to represent the subject matter of documents. Similarly, the process of preparing the search strategy also involves two stages: conceptual analysis and translation. The first step is an analysis of the request (submitted by the user) to determine what the user is really looking for; the second step is translation of the conceptual analysis to the vocabulary of the system. A number of vocabulary control tools have been designed over the years; they may differ in their structure and design features, but they all serve the same purpose in an information retrieval environment.

Thesauri, the most common type of vocabulary control tool used in information retrieval, appeared in the late 1950s, designed for use with the emerging post-coordinate indexing systems of that time (where individual search terms were combined at the stage of searching in order to retrieve items with more than one search term entered by the user), which needed simple terms with low pre-coordination, not provided by the then existing indexing languages. Simply speaking, a thesaurus is a list of permitted terms showing synonyms and hierarchical and other relationships and dependencies, the function of which is to provide a standard vocabulary for information storage and retrieval systems (Chowdhury, 1999, 125; Rowley and Farrow, 2000, 143). The major objective of a thesaurus is to exert terminology control in indexing, and to aid searching by allowing the searcher to select appropriate search terms. A thesaurus is used in an information retrieval system in order to:

- control the term used in indexing, providing a means of translating the natural language of authors, indexers and enquirers into the more constrained language used for indexing and retrieval
- ensure, through the provision of a controlled language, consistent practice between different indexers
- limit the number of terms that need to be assigned to a document
- serve as a search aid in retrieval.

A huge volume of literature exists describing design features and experiments with the use of thesauri in various types of information retrieval system. Furnas et al. (1987), for instance, have studied vocabulary problems in using computer applications and cited the large variability of word selection by different users as evidence for the need to develop systems that recognize a rich variety of vocabularies. Bates (1986, 1998) has discussed the importance of information retrieval system interfaces and vocabularies to support users in the selection of search terms. Her well-cited model of a vocabulary-enriched interface, which she termed the Front-end System Mind (FSM), provides end-users with a wide range of search terms, displays of alternative terms and various approaches to term selection. She refers to the concept of an end-user thesaurus in order to highlight the importance of providing end-users with a large number of alternative terms. She elaborates on this concept by noting that users will be able to perform powerful searches if an initial term or topic submitted by a user results in a screen full of term possibilities, related subjects or classifications from which they can make a selection. Milstead (1997) states that thesauri are underused by searchers because of the fact that database providers do not make them readily available; some are available only in paper form while those provided online often have little or no user support in the interface. Shiri, Chowdhury and Revie (2002a, 2002b) review the thesaurus interfaces and search term selection processes in online databases. They note two major trends in modern information retrieval that justify additional research into thesaurus-assisted search term selection and query expansion by end-users. First, end-user searching is widely becoming universal because of developments associated with the internet and the web. To provide better information access systems, research focusing on the behaviour and attitudes of different types of end-user is needed. Second, a growing number of commercial retrieval systems have recently incorporated thesauri into their search interfaces to encourage users to enhance their queries. This development opens avenues for more research into the usefulness and usability of these systems and the extent to which they do in fact assist end-users in selecting search terms and expanding queries.

Alternative information retrieval models

In addition to the three classic models discussed above, various alternative models of information retrieval have been proposed that aim to tackle the problems of textual information retrieval differently. Two such models, the natural language processing model and the hypertext model, are discussed in the following subsections.

The natural language processing model

The fundamental difference between this model and others is that, unlike them, it aims to consider not only query and document terms, but sentences and discourse. In other words, natural language processing models process and match the query and document sentences, keeping in view the context or the domain, resulting in more relevant information retrieval. Natural language processing is an area of research and application that explores how natural language text entered into a computer system can be manipulated and transformed into a form that is suitable for further processing (Chowdhury, 1999, 333). Building systems that can process natural language texts and queries involves three levels of processing:

- *Syntactic analysis*, which is required to understand the structure of a given sentence. It generally involves a lexicon containing words with associated information, such as parts of speech, categories and syntactic markers or grammars, etc.

- *Semantic analysis*, which deals with the meaning of the words and sentence. Semantic knowledge, which is usually stored in a knowledge base (see Chowdhury, 1999, Chapter 18, for details), is used to derive meaning and resolve ambiguities that cannot be resolved by only structural considerations.
- *Pragmatic analysis*, which takes into consideration the specific domain and the context. Pragmatic knowledge – knowledge about a specific situation – allows the system to eliminate ambiguities and complete semantic interpretations.

While natural language processing systems propose alternative approaches to information retrieval, they require huge processing power and system resources; hence their use in commercial information retrieval has been rather limited. However, with recent improvements in computer storage and processing power, natural language processing systems are beginning to be popular in certain areas of information processing and retrieval. Recent developments and trends in natural language processing have been discussed in the *Annual review of information science and technology* by Haas (1996) and Chowdhury (2003).

The hypertext model

Conventional documents are written in a linear fashion, and users are expected to read the text sequentially from beginning to end. While this convention for preparing documents has been followed for centuries, it has an inherent problem. It does not make provision for navigation within and among a collection of documents. The hypertext model allows users to navigate within the different parts of a text, and among different texts in a collection. The term hypertext is used to describe a computer program that allows a person to browse a document by deliberately jumping from one text block to another (Rada, 1991). A hypertext model is an interactive navigational structure that allows users to browse text non-sequentially; it consists of nodes that are correlated by direct links in a graph structure (Baeza-Yates and Ribeiro-Neto, 1999, 67).

While the hypertext model provides great flexibility over the linear model, the flow of navigation of a user is controlled by the intended design of the hypertext by the creator. Hence, the design of a hypertext is an important task, and it should take into account the domain as well as the nature of the text and intended users. The hypertext model can be extended to allow users to navigate within and among multimedia documents. Hypertext provided the basis for the conceptual design of HTML (Hypertext Markup Language) and HTTP

(Hypertext Transfer Protocol), the technology that controls the world wide web and digital libraries.

Multimedia information retrieval

While the above models have been proposed for text information retrieval, different approaches are needed to deal with multimedia information. Borgman (2000b, 147) comments that 'It is possible to search for words in textual documents, even with minimal indexing. The same cannot be said for sounds or images.' Designing true multimedia searching capabilities is one of the major design challenges for digital libraries (Croft, 1995).

Images may be still or moving. Art images and documentary images such as photographs form a significant part of a digital library's collection. Art images have attributes such as author and title, and these can be used for cataloguing purposes. However, often descriptors are also added to describe the nature and content of art images. Getty's Art and Architecture Thesaurus (Getty Research Institute, 2000) may be used for this purpose. Documentary images such as photographs may be catalogued with various keys such as the name of the photographer, event describing the photograph or date. Often users search for photographs by using some keywords that describe the content, such as the name, or a certain property of the object, or event; for example 'show me all the pictures where Tony Blair appeared before becoming prime minister', or 'show me all those butterflies that have shades of purple on the wing'. Handling these kinds of queries requires the matching of images rather than text.

Moving images, such as film and video, can be catalogued according to the rules prescribed in the catalogue codes like AACR2 (*Anglo-American Cataloguing Rules*, 2002). Eakins and Graham (1999) provide a state-of-the-art report on content-based image retrieval (CBIR), a technique for retrieving images on the basis of automatically derived features such as colour, texture and shape. They report that 'Three commercial CBIR systems are now available – IBM's QBIC, Virage's VIR Image Engine, and Excalibur's Image RetrievalWare. In addition, demonstration versions of numerous experimental systems can be viewed on the web, including MIT's Photobook, Columbia University's WebSEEk, and Carnegie Mellon University's Informedia.'

Many digital libraries provide access to image resources. The British Library provides access to still images. The UC Berkeley digital library (see Table 3.4) allows for image retrieval by image content. DIGILIB (www.architect.uq.edu.au/digilib) at the University of Queensland, Australia, also provides access to architectural images. SETIS (Scholarly Electronic Text and Image Service; http://setis.library. usyd.edu.au/ozlit/) at the University of Sydney, Australia, provides access to images. The Greenstone Digital Library (www.nzdl.org/cgi-bin/ library) provides access to various image databases. Informedia digital video library (www.informedia.cs.cmu.edu/), a digital library research project at Carnegie Mellon University, has developed new approaches for automated video and audio indexing, navigation, visualization and multilingual search and retrieval.

Audio information resources have long formed part of a library's collection, and this will continue to be the case with digital libraries. Audio information may include sound, music and speech. Traditionally libraries have catalogued audio information resources quite similarly to bibliographic items; specific guidelines for cataloguing audio information resources are available in AACR2 (*Anglo-American Cataloguing Rules*, 2002). Lesk (1997, 80) suggests that 'there are two common levels of formatting for audio, a high-quality standard for music and a low-quality one for voice'.

Although audio information, especially music, forms a significant part of the collection of web and digital libraries, and although the first published work on music information retrieval appeared long ago (Kassler, 1966, 1970), very little research has so far been done on music information retrieval. In a recent article (2002) Byrd and Crawford (2002) have reviewed research on music information retrieval, and comment that music information retrieval is still a very immature field. Interest in this area has become prominent only very recently as is evident from the literature (Bainbridge et al., 1999; Downie and Nelson, 2000; Lemstrom, Laine and Perttu, 1999; Tseng, 1999; Uitdenbogerd and Zobel, 1998; Wiseman, Rusbridge and Griffin, 1999).

A piece of music may be monophonic, where only one note sounds at a time; or polyphonic, where multiple notes sound at a time. Several researchers (for example, Crawford, Iliopoulos and Raman, 1998; Smith, McNab and Witten, 1998) suggest that partial matching is the solution for music information retrieval. Specialized string matching techniques have been used by researchers (for example, Downie and Nelson, 2000) for the successful retrieval of monophonic music. Sequential searching, though useful for monophonic music, is not suitable for polyphonic music. Research reported by Lee and Chen (2000) on signature-based music information retrieval methods is promising. Some digital libraries provide access to digital music. One prominent example is the Greenstone Digital Library.

Basic information search techniques

A text search can be conducted by entering a single search term or a phrase comprising more than one term. Keyword search is the simplest form of search facility offered by a digital library retrieval system. The search term can be entered through the keyboard and more than one keyword can be used to formulate a query using Boolean or proximity operators (discussed below). Usually users are provided with a search box where the search terms or phrase have to be entered. The advanced search interfaces of digital libraries provide facilities to make a search statement more specific. Usually a phrase is entered within quotes or an appropriate option, such as 'search as a phrase', is to be chosen.

Boolean search

This is a very common search technique that combines search terms according to Boolean logic. Three types of Boolean search are possible: AND search, OR search and NOT search.

The AND search allows users to combine two or more search terms in order to retrieve those items that contain all the constituent terms. For example, the search expression 'internet and e-commerce' will retrieve all those records where both the terms occur. Boolean AND search adds more restrictions to a search expression by adding more search terms. The more search terms are ANDed, the more restricted, or specific, will be the search, and as a result the smaller will be the search output. Sometimes if too many search terms are ANDed a search may not produce any results.

The OR search allows users to combine two or more search terms in order to retrieve all those items that contain either one or all of the constituent terms. Thus, the search expression 'internet or e-commerce' will retrieve all those records (1) where the term internet occurs, (2) where the term e-commerce occurs, and (3) where both the terms occur. Note that this is contrary to the use of the term 'or' in normal English. The OR search broadens rather than restricts a search expression, because the search is conducted for occurrences of each single ORed term irrespective of whether the other term(s) occur in the same record or not. Consequently, the output of OR searches will be greater than that for AND searches or for single terms When too many search terms are ORed, the search output may be too big to handle.

The NOT search allows users to specify those terms that they do not want to occur in the retrieved records. For example, the search expression 'search engines NOT AltaVista' will retrieve all the records on search engines except those where the term AltaVista occurs. Boolean NOT searches restrict a search by forcing the search system to discard those items containing the NOT word(s). Hence the search output will decrease as the number of NOT words increases.

Different approaches to conducting Boolean searches are taken in digital libraries. The Boolean operators vary, but so do other operators and syntaxes. In the digital libraries of the ACM and IEEE (called IEL), Boolean searches can be conducted using the Boolean AND, OR and NOT, and terms and operators can be combined using parentheses. Many digital libraries use the plus and minus sign for Boolean AND and NOT searches. The operator '+' placed before a word or phrase means that all returned records should contain that search term. Similarly the minus operator '−' can be placed before a word or phrase to exclude all documents containing that search term, as in the Boolean NOT search. In many digital libraries, users are required to choose between options such as: all the words, any of the words, must contain, must not contain, and so on. For example, in the advanced search interface of the Virginia Tech. ETD (Electronic Library of Theses and Dissertations) users can choose the option 'must contain' to imply a Boolean AND search, or 'must not contain' to imply a Boolean NOT search.

Truncation

Truncation is a search facility that enables a search to be conducted for all the different forms of a word having the same common root. As an example, the truncated word Librar* will retrieve items containing Library, Libraries, Librarian, and so on. A number of different options are available for truncation: right-hand truncation, left-hand truncation and the masking of letters in the middle of a word. Left-hand truncation retrieves all words with the same characters at the end, e.g. '*hyl' will retrieve words like 'me*thyl*' and 'et*hyl*'. Similarly, middle truncation retrieves all words with the same characters at the beginning and end. For example, the middle-truncated search term 'colo*r' will retrieve the terms 'colour' and 'color'. A 'wild card' is used to allow any letter to appear in a specific location within a word.

Because left-hand truncation is more technically difficult, right-hand truncation and character masking or wild cards are the most common truncation search facilities available in most information retrieval systems. However, the search operators and their applications vary among search engines. For example, in the ACM digital library '*' is used for any number of characters, and '?'

is used for only one character. In some digital libraries, for example in the Greenstone Digital Library, users can activate stemming (which works like truncation in the sense that variant forms of the search term with the same root are searched) by choosing the appropriate option for the purpose.

Proximity search

This search facility allows users to specify the distance between two search terms in the retrieved results. A proximity search is similar, in principle, to the Boolean AND search, except that it makes the search more restricted. Specifying the distance between two search terms imposes the restriction. Therefore, proximity searches are likely to produce more specific results than a simple Boolean AND search. Digital libraries that support proximity search vary significantly in terms of the operators they support and their implementation. For example, in the ACM digital library the NEAR operator finds records matching specified search terms within close proximity to each other; the closer the search terms are to each other, the higher the document appears in the ranked results list.

Field or meta tag search

A searcher may sometimes want to restrict a search to a specific field with a view to obtaining more precise results. Searchers can specify the field tag by selecting an appropriate option, or by typing the field name before the search term(s). In the search engine terminology this is called a meta tag search since the fields in the web pages are specified by meta tags. Some examples of field search option in digital libraries follow:

- In the ACM digital library, the operator 'contains' can be used in a field search, for example *title CONTAINS e-commerce* will retrieve all those records where the term 'e-commerce' occurs in the title of the records.
- In the advanced search screen of the Virginia Tech ETD, users can select, from a drop-down box, the field where a search term or phrase should be looked for. The options are: 'in the entire document', 'in the title of the document', 'in the author's name', 'in the assigned keywords', and so on.

Limiting searches

Sometimes users may want to limit a given search by using certain criteria, such as language, year of publication, type of information sources, and so on. These are called limiting searches. This is particularly useful in the web environment where a simple search produces millions of hits. Criteria that can be used in a limiting search depend on the chosen information retrieval system. For example:

- In the advanced search screen of the Virginia Tech ETD, users can limit a search by specifying the date (of submission or examination) of a thesis.
- In the ACM digital library, users can limit a search by the date of publication, type of publication, etc.

Most digital libraries provide the options in boxes or as radio buttons from which searchers select the appropriate limiting criteria.

Information retrieval features of various resources accessible through digital libraries

As discussed in Chapter 5, digital libraries may contain different types of information sources in a variety of formats. For example, a digital library may contain simple metadata or catalogues of information resources, like OPACs, or may contain the full text of documents, images, audio and video materials. The information resources may be available in different formats, and they may have been produced using different types of hardware and software. For example, the text may be in MS Word or PDF or HTML format; images may be available in GIF or JPEG file formats. These information resources may reside on a number of different servers – local as well as remote – and they may have been indexed differently. All these issues make the information retrieval process very complex. Today, users of a digital library may have access to a variety of textual information resources. The following list represents the common choices that a user may have:

- electronic databases
  - — online search services
  - — CD-ROM databases
- OPACs
- e-journals
- other digital libraries, local and remote
- web resources.

Each information system mentioned above has its own characteristics. Since a user can get access to all or many of the above information systems through a digital library, it is necessary to have a basic idea of the characteristic features of each. Users may select any of these and get the appropriate user interface to interact – search, browse, and so on – with it. However, as discussed later in this chapter, some libraries, for example the California Digital Library, allow users to conduct a search across a range of information resources and services. In such cases, users need not move from one service to another, and consequently from one interface to another, in order to conduct a search. The system conducts a search across all the different services, and provides the results to the user.

Online search services

Traditional online information search systems, which began over three decades ago, were designed to provide access to remote databases, often through a database vendor or service provider such as Dialog or Ovid. These systems were expensive to use. They were not quite suitable for direct use by end-users, and in most cases were used by information intermediaries on behalf of, or in co-operation with, end-users. The major characteristics of this type of online information retrieval system are as follows:

- Users get access to remote databases that are often many in number and large in size.
- Many databases can be searched using a single search interface.
- Database records mainly contain bibliographic details of records with abstracts, and sometimes additional information, such as citations, etc.; only some databases contain full-text information.
- Service providers have their own search interface with good search and retrieval capabilities.
- Users need to register with the service providers.
- Users are charged for searching as well as for the content.
- Modern online service providers have web interfaces with good search features and hyperlinked records and information.

Although each online search service provider has its own proprietary retrieval engine and user interface, the commonly available search and retrieval features are as follows (Chowdhury and Chowdhury, 2001a, Chapter 7):

- Users can select one or more databases to search.
- Novice and expert search modes are available.

- A search can be conducted using one or more keywords or phrases.
- Common search facilities include Boolean search, truncation (some systems also allow users to search for the variant forms of a word), proximity search and field search (the number of fields that can be searched depends on the chosen database).
- Searches can be limited by applying certain restrictions, such as language, date, type of material, etc.
- A search can be conducted for a range of time as well as a single year (date of publication, for example).
- Some systems show the frequency of occurrence of the search terms in the output.
- Dialog provides a unique facility of searching through a common index file that allows users to select databases appropriate for a search topic.
- Some systems provide access to thesauri through the search interfaces.
- Search results can be sorted and sometimes ranked by selected criteria.

OPACs

Online public access catalogues (OPACs) are quite different from online databases in terms of content and structure, and also provide access to remote databases. OPACs form an important part of many digital libraries' collections. Their features have been discussed by several researchers (for example, Chowdhury and Chowdhury, 2001a; Hildreth, 1997, 1998; Rasmussen, 1999) and can be summarized as follows:

- OPACs allow users to search for the bibliographic records contained within a library's collection.
- Nowadays, some OPACs also provide access to electronic resources and databases, in addition to the traditional bibliographic records.
- Searches take place on the metadata of the records in the library's collection.
- Sometimes users can search more than one collection (within the same library or in different libraries).
- They have a relatively simple search interface.
- OPACs are nowadays available through the web.

Although each OPAC has a search interface and retrieval engine that is proprietary to the company providing the software for the purpose, the following information retrieval features are commonly available:

- browse and search facilities
- keyword and phrase search facilities
- subject headings assigned to the records by using a subject heading list like LCSH (Library of Congress Subject Headings); users can search by these assigned headings
- Boolean searching, usually limited to the keyword search option; in other words only keywords can be combined with Boolean operators
- proximity searching, also limited to the keyword search option
- unranked search results
- the ability to search records through selected keys such as author, title, ISBN or call number; these are searched as phrases, and are usually automatically right-hand truncated.
- the ability to limit searches by date, collection, language, etc.

e-journals

Electronic journals, or e-journals, form a very important part of the collection of today's libraries. Nowadays there are two major categories of e-journals: those that have their printed counterparts, for example the *Journal of Documentation*, and those that are available only in electronic format, for example, *D-Lib Magazine*. Access to electronic journals is provided either by publishers themselves or by aggregators. The benefits of getting access to an individual publisher's journals are value-added features and the lack of intermediaries. Aggregators, on the other hand, have the advantage of conglomerating the journals of several publishers under one interface and search system.

Each publisher and aggregator of e-journals has a proprietary retrieval engine and search interface that can be used to search one or more e-journals. Common information retrieval features of e-journals are:

- Users can browse each issue or search the entire collection.
- There are usually novice and expert search modes.
- Word and phrase search facilities are available.
- Common search facilities include Boolean search, truncation, field search, limiting search and range search.
- Searches can be conducted on metadata (author, title, etc.) or on the full text.
- Output is available in one or more formats such as HTML or PDF.

Web search engines

Search engines are the most commonly used tools for finding information on the web and digital libraries usually provide links to one or more search engines to allow users to search for web information resources. A search engine allows the user to enter search terms – keywords or phrases – that are run against a database containing information on the web pages collected automatically by programs called spiders. At the end of a search session, the search engine retrieves web pages from its database that match the search terms entered by the searcher. There are three main components of a search engine: (1) the spider – the program that automatically collects information about the millions of pages on the web, (2) the index, which stores information collected by the spider on the various web pages, and (3) the search engine software and interface with which the users interact to conduct a web search (Chowdhury and Chowdhury, 2001b, Chapter 3).

Search engines can be categorized in a number of ways. Two broad categories are search engines and meta search engines, the latter category referring to tools that allow users to conduct concurrent searches on more than one search engine. Some people also group search engines according to their indexing characteristics. For example, Nicholson (1998) categorizes search engines as full-text search tools, extracting search tools, subject-specific search tools and meta search tools. Searchenginewatch.com sorts search engines as follows.

- the major search engines, e.g. AltaVista, AOL Search, Google, HotBot
- children's search engines, e.g. KidsClick, Yahooligans
- news search engines, e.g. AltaVista News, Ananova, Yahoo News
- speciality search engines, e.g. Allexperts.com, AskJeeves, CNETDownload.com
- multimedia search engines, e.g. AltaVista Photofinder, Ditto, FAST Multimedia Search, Gnutella, Napster
- search utilities, e.g. Copernic, LexiBot, SearchWolf, Subject Search Spider
- paid listings search engines, e.g. Espotting.com, FindWhat.com, Google AdWords
- metacrawlers (meta search engines that conduct simultaneous searches across a range of search engines), e.g. InfoGrid, Kartoo, Query Server, Profusion
- regional search engines, e.g. Indiainfo.com, Mosaique.

Each search engine has proprietary software for all its information storage and retrieval operations. Consequently each has a specific set of search and retrieval features. The following are the common information retrieval facilities provided by most search engines:

- word, phrase and natural language search options
- simple and advanced search options
- special options for image, audio and video search
- a number of categories for browsing
- multilingual search
- Boolean search: AND, OR and NOT; + and – signs are used to indicate whether the search term that follows must or must not appear; parentheses can be used for nested Boolean searches; in the advanced search mode there may be options like Must Have, Good to Have and Must Not Have
- advanced search facilities such as proximity search, truncation, meta tag search (field search)
- the ability to constrain searches by different criteria, for example, by language, date of publication, collection type, etc.
- the ability to rank the search output according to various different criteria set by the search engine software.

In addition, some of the advanced search facilities include the following:

- *Link*. The keyword 'link' followed by a domain name or a complete URL returns every web page that has a hypertext link to a particular site, directory, or page (available in AltaVista).
- *Translate*. The automatic translation of web pages from selected languages. Some search engines also allow users to enter text in a given language which can be instantly translated into another language.
- *Family Filter*. Can be turned off or on to allow or avoid the retrieval of unwanted materials.

Information retrieval features of selected digital libraries

Information retrieval services are at the heart of digital libraries (Fox and Sornil, 1999; Fox and Urs, 2002). Since a hybrid library can provide access to one or more of the information resources mentioned above, users may search each system separately using the search interface of each respective system. Alternatively, there may be a single search interface to allow users to conduct searches across all the systems with just one query.

In the following sections we shall consider the basic information retrieval facilities provided by some digital libraries. In order to facilitate our discussions, we have selected one digital library representing each of the following loosely defined groups.

- Type 1. A fully fledged digital library may contain a variety of information distributed among a number of systems and platforms. However, ideally a user would like to use only one interface and would like to get results from all the different systems by submitting only one query. Although this poses a major challenge, some digital libraries provide such cross-database search facilities; the California Digital Library (CDL) is a prominent example.
- Type 2: digital libraries that provide access to some specific type of data, for example the Alexandria Digital Library, which provides access to spatial data.
- Type 3: digital libraries that provide access to a variety of information resources through different interfaces, e.g. the Greenstone Digital Library.
- Type 4: digital libraries that provide access to only one type of material, but allow a single- or a multiple-site (federated) search, e.g. the Networked Digital Library of Theses and Dissertations (NDLTD).
- Type 5: digital libraries that provide access to all the different types of publications from a given publisher, e.g. the ACM digital library.

Type 1: California Digital Library

From the main web page of CDL (www.cdlib.org), users can click on the 'Select a QuickLink' option, whereby they'll get a list of the various collections of CDL. The options 'Browse the CDL directory' or 'Search the CDL directory' can be chosen to browse or search for a specific collection, such as electronic journals, databases or reference texts. The following steps may be followed to browse the directory collections:

1 Select a broad topic.
2 Select a format (electronic journal, database, etc.).
3 Select a campus of interest (or no limit by campus).
4 Browse by title or narrower topic(s).

Table 9.1 shows the search and retrieval features of CDL. Search results are presented under various categories: books, journal indexes, electronic journals, e-texts and documents, reference resources and web directories. On the output page, users can:

- link directly to a given resource by clicking on the 'Go to it now' button under a given entry
- view a page with more information by clicking on the 'More information' link under a given entry for more complete information such as creator or publisher, dates of coverage, and links to tutorials where available
- examine and change the browse or search conditions.

Table 9.1 *Search and retrieval features of CDL*

Features	Explanation
Browse by selecting a topic	Users can select a topic to browse (or can select 'All the topics', which is the default) from a list of topics, such as General Interest and References, History, and Social Science. Browsing can be limited by format, e.g. electronic journal, database, reference text, and by library holdings.
Search options: 'Search collections' and 'Search'	Users can search the CDL directory or can choose the SearchLight option. In the CDL directory search option, a search can be conducted by keyword or by 'the exact beginning of the title'. A search can be limited to a specific format, and/or to a specific library collection. In the SearchLight option users have first to select a collection – Science and Engineering or Social Sciences and Humanities – and can then enter search terms in the search box.
Boolean search	Boolean OR and NOT operators are not supported by SearchLight; AND is implied between each word. Phrase search is also not supported by SearchLight.
Proximity search	Not supported by SearchLight
Truncation	Not available in SearchLight.
Limiting search by: format and the library holdings	Users can check one or more formats, and can select a particular library (the default is all the libraries) in the UC system. Users can search by the exact beginning of a title if they know it.
Other features: Query refinement	Users can go to the bottom of the search results page and revise a search by entering a new term(s) and/or changing the selected subject categories.

continued

Table 9.1 *continued*

Output size specification; result sorting; output format selection	SearchLight results are categorized according to the source (databases, journals, e-texts, etc.). Output is ranked by the number of hits under each category. Each record contains brief details of the document concerned and two options: more information and a hyperlink. The 'more info' option shows the details of the record with metadata information. By clicking on the number of hits, the user can get to another output window containing brief information on each output record with a hyperlink to the full document or the summary in PDF or HTML. The source hyperlink takes users to the particular collection where they can enter a search expression in the search interface of the source. The search can be modified by choosing the appropriate options on the same output screen.

Type 2: Alexandria Digital Library (ADL)

The Alexandria Digital Library has a collection of geographically referenced materials such as maps, images and texts and datasets in multimedia form in earth and social sciences. The ADL catalogue provides geospatial data and metadata in digital and hardcopy form. Users can enter a place name for a quick search or can browse through the ADL Gazetteer, the ADL catalogue (containing cartographic works, maps, photographs, aerial photographs and remote-sensing images), or ESSW AVHRR (Earth System Science Workbench: AVHRR imagery). Table 9.2 shows the various search and retrieval features of the ADL search interface. Users can follow the following steps:

1   Select a collection to search from those that are available.
2   Choose a geographic location either by orienting the Map Browser or typing in co-ordinates.
3   Enter search words or phrases.
4   Select the specific types of material that they want to find.
5   Select the specific formats that they want to find.
6   Choose between the available methods of ranking the results.
7   Specify the maximum number of hits.
8   Start search.

Table 9.2 *Search and retrieval features of ADL*

Features	Explanation
Map Browser	Allows users to pan and zoom a two-dimensional map of the world to locate their area(s) of interest and select an area to query.
Search options	Allows users to search by geographic names, latitude and longitude, resource types (maps, photographs, etc.) and formats (online, offline, paper, etc.).
Search options: by originators, assigned terms, identifiers, geographical locations; also free-text	Users can search by originator (e.g. author, publisher), assigned terms (subject headings and index terms assigned by the indexers), or free-text search (title, abstract, theme and place name in the metadata). Selection of 'Search on geographical locations' shows the the geographical location (the latitude, longitude, etc.) of the place in the query box. 'Identifier search' can be searched by URL, ISBN, ADL Control Number, etc.
Boolean search	The 'Any of the above words' option finds items with one or more of the words in the box (equivalent to the Boolean OR operator); 'All of the above words' will find items with all the words (equivalent to the Boolean AND operator); 'Exact phrase' will look for the exact phrase entered.
Thesaurus	For the ADL catalogue, there is the Object Type Thesaurus; for the ADL Gazetteer, there is the ADL Feature Type Thesaurus.
Search results	Results of a query are displayed in the lower right hand frame. Each item is represented by a short descriptive entry containing title (or name), type, format, date and collection ID. For each result, users can select the following options: • the 'Highlight in map' option will display the location (footprint) of the item in the Map Browser • the 'Complete description' option will display the full metadata record of the item in the same frame • the 'Access/Download' option will display the access and download information in the same frame. For online items, hyperlinks are included for accessing the data; for offline items, contact information is provided. At the end of each listing of results, a report is included describing the query, the date, and the time it took the system to return the results.

Type 3: The Greenstone Digital Library

The Greenstone Digital Library (GDL) software, which is available for free from the GDL team, is used to provide search and browsing facilities to all the collections. Users need to select a specific collection; each collection has a different set of searching and browsing facilities. Table 9.3 shows the search and retrieval features available in GDL.

Table 9.3 *Search and retrieval features of GDL*

Features	Explanation
Browsing	Each collection has a different set of criteria for browsing, e.g. the computer science reports collection can be browsed from a list of FTP sites; the women's history collection can be browsed by title, and so on.
Search options: different for each collection	For each collection, there is a different set of search options, which vary from keyword search to using the 'Melody Index' search. Depending on the search collection, users can limit a search by title, full text, photo, interview, section, paragraph, and so on. Users can click on a bookshelf icon for books on a given subject. There is a choice between a simple and advanced search option.
Boolean search	In the advanced search mode, search terms can be combined using Boolean AND, OR and NOT operators, and parentheses. Alternatively, one can choose the 'All the words' or 'Some words' option.
Truncation	The 'Preferences' button on top of the page may be chosen to set an option for stemming.
Other features: changing preferences	Users can change the preferences by clicking on the 'Preferences' button. The search parameters, including the language and interface format, can be changed by the user.
Ranked output	If the user specifies only one term, documents will be ordered by its frequency of occurrence.

GDL provides two facilities for searching for music. The first is a melody indexing service that allows users to search a database of tunes by melody. The second option is an optical music recognition service, which is available in demonstration mode only. In addition to the melody indexing, the text-based indexing service provides access to a collection of MIDI files of over 100,000 tunes including pop, rock, jazz and classical music.

Type 4: NDLTD

Users accessing the NDLTD website can search theses and dissertations available in any participating institution by checking the NDLTD Union Catalog. The Union Catalog serves as a repository of theses contributed by a number of member institutions from around the world. Users can search for words or exact phrases anywhere in the theses and dissertation catalogue record, or can specify a field such as author, title, subject, or name of thesis committee member to narrow the search. The Expert search function allows the use of Boolean operators in command mode.

The option 'Browse through collections at members' sites' can be chosen from the NDLTD web page to get the list of ETD sites of the participating members, including the Virginia Tech site. There is also an option for a federated search to retrieve information on theses and dissertations from all the participating institutions. The thesis collection in the Virginia Tech ETD collection can be browsed by authors or can be searched through the Infoseek search engine. Users can browse the collection by author by going through an alphabetical list of authors and titles of their theses. There are two search interfaces for ETD – simple and advanced. Table 9.4 shows the various search and retrieval features. While searching, users can select a specific collection or conduct searches across all the collections. However, when all the collections are chosen, the number of hits may be quite high. The search interface for each of the ETD digital libraries of the participating institutions varies.

Table 9.4 *Search and retrieval features of ETD (Virginia Tech)*

Features	Explanation
A particular DL can be selected to search, or a federated search can be conducted	Once the user selects a particular site, say Virginia Tech., the collection can be browsed or searched.
Search options: Specific collection or federated search Simple and advanced search	The InfoSeek search engine can be used to search the ETD site. Users can select a collection: Electronic Journals, Virginia Tech Spectrum, Special Collections, VT ETD Collection and WDBJ7 Script Archives.

continued

Table 9.4 *continued*

Features	Explanation

Field search
Search with
  InfoSeek or
  browse by author
	In the simple search mode, users need to enter words and phrases (within double quotes); a search can be restricted to the title field only.
	Users have to select a field from a list of fields.
	In the Virginia Tech collection, users have the choice between conducting a search with InfoSeek or browsing by author.

Boolean search	Users can use '+' to indicate that a search term must occur, and '−' to indicate that a search term must not occur in the result(s). In the advanced search mode, there are 'should contain', 'must contain' and 'must not contain' options. Users can select one of the two options to specify whether the output 'should' or 'must' contain the search terms/phrase.
Proximity search	No special operator; users can enter a phrase within quotes.
Limiting search: by time	Users can limit their search by the date of approval; the limiting options are days, weeks, months, year.

Other features:
  Phrase and name
  search
	Users can select to search for a word, a phrase or a name.

Output is ranked;
  number of hits and
  output format can be
  specified; output can
  be sorted.
	Users can specify the number of records to be retrieved, and also the nature of output, i.e. results with or without the summary. Output can be sorted by relevance, date or title. Each output record contains title and brief information. Once a title is chosen, another page appears giving the details of the thesis such as author, department, abstract, etc., as well as information on the files (number and format of the files) and availability information, e.g. access restrictions.

Type 5: ACM Portal: the ACM digital library

ACM Portal (http://portal.acm.org) is the digital library of the Association of Computing Machinery containing bibliographic information, abstracts, reviews, and the full text of articles published in ACM periodicals and proceedings since its foundation in 1947, together with selected works published by affiliated organizations.

From the main page of the ACM portal, users can select a particular collection, such as journals, magazines, transactions, proceedings, newsletters, publications by affiliated organizations, or special interest groups (SIGs). Upon selection of a particular collection, users get a simple search screen that allows them to browse the various titles or issues of the chosen publication type, or to conduct a simple search on the entire collection. From this screen users can also choose the advanced search option, which allows them to formulate a complex search. The different information retrieval features of the ACM digital library are shown in Table 9.5.

Table 9.5 *Search and retrieval features of the ACM digital library*

Features	Explanation
Browsing	Users can browse the collection by journal, magazine, transaction, proceeding, newsletter, etc.
Simple and advanced search options	Users can enter a search term or a phrase in the search box and conduct a simple search. Alternatively the advanced search option may be chosen.
Boolean search	All words are automatically ANDed. Other Boolean operators can be used: users can choose one of the three options 'must have all', 'must have any' or 'must have none', to indicate how the entered search terms or phrases are to be treated by the retrieval engine.
Proximity search	The NEAR operator finds pages matching specified search terms within close proximity to each other. The closer the search terms are to each other, the higher the document appears in the ranked results list. The SENTENCE and PARAGRAPH operators are used to specify a search within a sentence and paragraph.
Truncation	Search terms can be truncated with '*' (for any number of characters) or '?' (for specified number of characters; each '?' represents one character).
Field search	A search can be restricted to a field such as author, title, abstract or ISBN.
Limiting search: by time	Users can limit their search by the publication date, conference date, etc.
Phrase search	Phrases are entered in double quotes.

continued

Table 9.5 *Search and retrieval features of the ACM digital library (continued)*

Features	Explanation
Subject search	Subject searches can be conducted by the CCS subject code, subject descriptors or keywords
Output is ranked; output format can be specified; output can be sorted.	Results are ranked and a '%' sign shows their relevance. ranking. Users can choose the short or the long display format. Results can be sorted by title, publication type or publication date.

Common information retrieval features in digital libraries

Meyyappan, Chowdhury and Foo (2000) reviewed the general features, and Chowdhury and Chowdhury (2000) reviewed the information retrieval features of some selected digital libraries. Their major observations were as follows:

- Users can access the collections of a digital library by either browsing or searching.
- While most digital libraries allow users to search the local digital library collections, some digital libraries, e.g. NDLTD, provide facilities for a federated search or search across a number of digital libraries.
- Boolean, proximity and truncation search facilities are commonly available search options in digital libraries, though the operators vary. Some digital libraries provide options like 'also must contain', 'or may contain', 'but not contain', 'should contain', or 'must contain' to activate a Boolean search.
- Keyword and phrase search are common facilities of digital libraries, though the techniques for conducting a phrase search differs. In some cases, for example in BUILDER, users can enter a phrase in a special phrase search box, while in others, for example, in DIGILIB (at the University of Queensland) and NCSTRL (Networked Computer Science Technical Reference Library), a search phrase has to be entered within double quotes.
- Right-hand truncation and wild card search facilities are common in many digital libraries, and a variety of operators, such as '%', '*', '@' and '?' are used for the purpose. However, some digital libraries provide specific truncation search facilities. For example, in THOMAS and American Memory the 'Include word variants' option is used for truncation.
- Many digital libraries support proximity search, but the operators vary, e.g. 'NEAR', 'NEARBY', 'SENTENCE', 'PARAGRAPH', and so on.

- Most of the selected digital libraries allow users to conduct searches on specific fields.
- While most digital libraries allow users to specify the maximum number of hits, the output is not always ranked, except for a few like NDLTD.
- In some cases, for example in the ACM digital library, users can sort the results using some chosen keys.
- Usually the system comes up with a brief output that can lead to the full records. However, in many cases, an output format can be chosen by the user.

Special information retrieval features in digital libraries

In addition to the common features mentioned above, some digital libraries have some special information retrieval features (Chowdhury and Chowdhury, 2000). For example:

- The ACM digital library allows stem expansion, fuzzy expansion (spelled like), and 'sounds like' searching.
- DeLiver (the outcome of a DLI 1 project at the University of Illinois) allows users to search and view specific parts of an article, such as the figures or references. Thus the user can 'fine tune' a search and get more relevant results.
- iGEMS (the digital library of Nanyang Technological University, Singapore; launched as GEMS) allows users to set up their own profile for future searches and for obtaining SDI services. It also allows the instant opening of a CD-ROM and provides access to online journals and databases.
- HeadLine (a hybrid library project in the UK) is unique in two respects:
  — it automatically creates an information page, called the Subject Page, on the user's subject of interest; the necessary information is gathered from the user's log-in screen
  — it allows users to customize the Subject Page to create their own subject page.
- IEL (the digital library of the IEEE's publications) allows users to choose options to match similar subjects, or to search for the latest additions to the library. The search interface allows browsing and the selection of search terms from a displayed list. Superscript, subscript and special characters can be searched.
- The Greenstone Digital Library has developed digital library software, which is freely available.

- NDLTD uses the InfoSeek search engine, and therefore a number of good search features are available. Users can search a specific site or conduct a federated search across the digital libraries that are members of the NDLTD Federation.
- THOMAS uses a probabilistic information retrieval system called InQuery.
- The UC Berkeley Digital Library uses Cha-Cha and Chesire II search systems and has two unique features:
  — natural language search facilities
  — image retrieval by image content.
- The Universal Library (at Carnegie Mellon University) has a unique feature called the hyperbolic tree that has a unique visualization effect and can be used for searching the collection.

Problems and prospects

Information retrieval in digital libraries involves a number of challenges. There are a number of issues that need to be taken into consideration in order to develop efficient information retrieval systems for digital libraries.

Some issues that influence information retrieval have been discussed in other chapters in this book. These include:

- infrastructure and interoperability issues (discussed in Chapter 4)
- users and user interface issues (discussed in Chapter 8)
- information organization, metadata, and so on (discussed in Chapter 7)
- standards (discussed in Chapter 4).

In the following sections, we shall discuss some other information retrieval issues, and shall point out some research activities that aim to resolve them.

The integration of OPACs

One specific practical question highlighted by the hybrid library projects, the eLib Phase 3 research projects, is the relationship between the OPAC and the other elements of the electronic library (Pinfield, 2001b). Many libraries have developed their websites to be gateways with direct links to e-journals, CD-ROMs and quality web resources. Many have developed databases behind their website to provide access to these kinds of sources (Gardner and Pinfield, 2001), and the library website has become a search tool in its own right. Pinfield (2001a, 2001b) comments that websites and web OPAC interfaces have increasingly been given a similar 'look and feel' so that the distinction between the library website and the OPAC has become blurred.

Large databases

Digital libraries have to deal with a number of databases that are huge in size. Blair (2002a) argues that the scaling problem is central to document retrieval, and performance decreases rapidly as the size of the document databases is multiplied. He further argues that the success of a text retrieval system is strongly influenced by three factors: (1) the size of the document collection, (2) the type of search – exhaustive search, where the user wants everything, or almost everything available, or sample search, where the user does not need all of the useful items in the collection, and (3) the determinacy of document representation – how accurately the documents are represented (indexed) in the collection. Blair (2002b) proposes a two-stage search process based on the use of identifiable partitions of large document collections. Sornil and Fox (2001) propose an inverted index partitioning scheme to support searching for information in a large-scale digital library. They report some encouraging results based on some simulation experiments on a terabyte of text in the Hybrid Partitioned Inverted Index.

Cross-database searching

Designing systems to support cross-database searching is a major challenge. ANSI Z39.50 is a protocol designed for the exchange of bibliographic data. It is often seen as the most likely solution to the problem of integration. The standard specifies an abstract information system with a rich set of facilities for searching, retrieving records, browsing term lists, and so on. The essential power of this standard is that it allows diverse information resources to look and act in the same way to the individual user; it also allows each information system to have a different interface to suit user needs (Hammer and Favaro, 1996). The eLib Phase 3 'Clumps' projects were designed to 'kick start' the use of Z39.50 in the UK higher education sector and it was noted that the major problems of Z39.50 implementation stem from the inconsistencies of MARC implementation in library OPACs (Pinfield, 2001b). Many local variations are made by libraries at their local sites, which lead to inconsistencies in the exchange of data.

Metadata is used heavily in building software for cross-database searching among various text databases. However, the use of various metadata formats such as MARC (for libraries), ISADG (for archives) and Dublin Core (for websites) makes the task of interoperability difficult. Hence, searching descriptions of collections of material may be a useful preliminary to searching at the item level (Pinfield, 2001b). The Collection Development Focus (www.ukoln. ac.uk/cd-focus/) studies under UKOLN and the Research Support Libraries Programme (www.rslp.ac.uk/) are working towards this end.

A number of information retrieval software packages have been developed recently that support cross-database searching in digital libraries. These include Ex Libris's SFX (www.sfxit.com/) and MetaLib (www.exlibris.co.il/), WebExpress/iPort from OCLC (www.oclc.org/webexpress) and Fretwell Downing's VDX/Agora product (www.fdgroup.com/fdi/vdx). The last of these is partly based on work carried out on eLib projects, particularly the Agora hybrid library project (http://hosted.ukoln.ac.uk/agora/). The SearchLight software, developed by the California Digital Library team, uses the Z39.50 protocol for cross-database searching among the University of California OPACs and various online databases. Researchers at Virginia Tech are working on software for federated searching across a range of *ETD* (*Electronic Theses and Dissertations*) sites (Fox et al., 2001a, 2001b). Myaeng et al. (2001) report research done in Korea that makes heavy use of metadata for federated searching and retrieval. Their approach is based on a relatively simple mechanism by which various metadata are collected and passed on to the integrator. In exchanging the metadata, including queries and search results, the system requires that XML be used so that the metadata exchange format can be described by a DTD (Document Type Definition) and can be extended if necessary (Myaeng et al., 2001).

While many of these software packages are proprietary, for example SearchLight, some are available for free distribution among the digital library research community, the prominent example being the Greenstone Digital Library software developed in the course of the New Zealand Digital Library Project (Witten, Bainbridge and Boddie, 2001a, 2001b). Digital library researchers can download and use the Greenstone software for their research and development activities.

One interesting alternative to cross-database searching that has recently emerged is the Open Archives Initiative (OAI) protocol (www.openarchives. org). Rather than dynamically searching across different databases in response to a command from a user, the OAI protocol allows metadata to be harvested from OAI-compliant databases that can subsequently be collected into a single searchable database. Pinfield (2001a) comments that it is difficult to predict at this stage how widely this technology will be adopted but it has potential; adoption may partly depend on whether a formal metadata schema for OAI-compliant datasets can be worked out in detail.

Multilingual information retrieval

Borgman (1997) argues that digital libraries should support searching and display in multiple languages. She illustrates the multi-language challenge of digital libraries with examples drawn from the research library community, which typically handles collections of materials in about 400 different languages. She further suggests that a fundamental challenge of building a global digital library system is to provide access to the collections regardless of the language of the content and the language of the information seeker (Borgman, 2000a). The importance of multilingual information retrieval in the web and digital library environment has also been emphasized by other researchers (for example, Large and Moukdad, 2000). Even if a digital library contains materials in only one language, the content needs to be searchable and displayable on computers in countries speaking other languages. We also need to exchange data between digital libraries, whether in a single language or in multiple languages. Hence multilingual search and display in digital libraries should be a critical area of research.

Multilingual information retrieval in digital libraries involves two major issues: the recognition, manipulation and display of multiple languages; and cross-language information search and retrieval (Peters and Picchi, 1997). The first set of issues relates to the enabling technology that will allow users to access information in whatever language it is stored; the second set implies permitting users to specify their information needs in their preferred language while retrieving information in whatever language it is stored. Text translation can take place at two levels: translation of the full text from one language to another for the purpose of search and retrieval; and translation of queries from one language to one or more different languages. The first option is feasible for small collections or for specific applications, as in meteorological reports (Oudet, 1997). The translation of queries is a more practicable approach, however, and promising results have been reported in the literature. Oard (1997) comments that seeking information from a digital library could benefit from the ability to query large collections once using a single language.

Furthermore, if the retrieved information is not available in a language that the user can read, some form of translation will be needed at this stage too.

Multilingual thesauri such as EUROVOC help to address this challenge by facilitating controlled vocabulary searching using terms from several languages. Services such as INSPEC produce English abstracts for documents in other languages (Oard, 1997). However, as Oard mentions, fully automatic machine translation is presently neither sufficiently fast nor sufficiently accurate to support interactive cross-language information seeking on the web and in digital libraries adequately. Fortunately, an active and rapidly growing research community has coalesced around these and other related issues, applying techniques drawn from several fields – notably information retrieval and natural language processing – to provide access to large multilingual collections.

Ruiz and Srinivasan (1998) investigate an automatic method for cross-language information retrieval (CLIR) that uses the multilingual Unified Medical Language System (UMLS) Metathesaurus to translate Spanish natural language queries into English. They conclude that this method is at least equivalent to, if not better than, multilingual-dictionary-based approaches. Two Telematics Application Program projects in the Telematics for Libraries sector, TRANSLIB and CANAL/LS, were active between 1995 and 1997 (Oard, 1997). Both these projects investigated cross-language searching in library catalogues, and each included English, Spanish and at least one other language: CANAL/LS added German and French, while TRANSLIB added Greek. MULINEX (http://mulinex.dfki.de/), another European project, is concerned with the efficient use of multilingual online information. The project aims to process multilingual information and present it to the user in a way that facilitates finding and evaluating the desired information quickly and accurately. TwentyOne (http://twentyone.tpd.tno.nl/twentyone/), which started in 1996, is an EU-funded project with the target of developing a tool for the efficient dissemination of multimedia information in sustainable development. Details of these and CLIR research projects in the USA and other parts of the world have been reviewed by Oard and Diekama (1998). Sugimoto (2001) reports on a number of research projects for multilingual information access in digital libraries that are being carried out in Japan.

Fox and Powell (1998) describe a federated search system, called SearchDB-ML Lite, for searching heterogeneous multilingual theses and dissertations collections through NDLTD. A markup language called SearchDB was developed for describing the characteristics of a search engine and its interface, and a protocol was built for requesting word translations between languages. A review of the results generated from querying over 50 sites simultaneously revealed that in some cases more sophisticated query mapping is necessary to retrieve results sets that truly correspond to the original query.

Design integration

In order to design an effective and efficient information retrieval system for digital libraries, several layers of information system design need to be properly integrated. In short, the information retrieval system in a digital library aims to match the user requirements with the contents using the appropriate computer and networking technologies. However, different layers of work involving the organization and processing of information, user interfaces, networking, standards and protocols are involved in the process. All these different layers need to be properly integrated in order to develop a successful global digital library. Bates (2002, 396) warns that:

> all layers of the system for accessing and displaying digital library information should be simultaneously designed with knowledge of what is going forward in the other layers. It takes only one wrongly placed layer to thwart all the clever work done at every other layer. For effective information retrieval to occur, all layers of a system must be designed to work together, and the people doing the designing must genuinely communicate.

Interactive question-answering systems

Most information retrieval systems of today retrieve documents or parts of one or more documents in response to a user query. However, ideally users would like to have specific answers to their questions. Building digital libraries that are capable of providing answers in an interactive question-answering mode is a challenge. It needs expertise from a number of fields including information retrieval, natural language processing, human–computer interactions, expert systems, and so on.

A number of experimental question-answering systems are now being developed that aim to provide answers to natural language questions, as opposed to documents containing information related to the question. Such systems often use a variety of information extraction and retrieval operations using natural language processing tools and techniques to get the correct answer from the source texts. Breck et al. (1999) report on a question-answering system that uses techniques from knowledge representation, information retrieval and natural language processing. The authors claim that this combination enables domain independence and robustness in the face of text variability, both in the question and in the raw text documents used as knowledge sources. Research reported in the Question Answering (QA) track of TREC (Text Retrieval Conferences; http://trec.nist.gov) shows some interesting results. At the moment the experimental systems can provide answers to simple 'who' questions like 'Who is the prime minister of Japan?', and 'when' questions like 'When did the Jurassic period end?'. The experimental systems work well as long as the query types recognized by the system have broad coverage, and the system can classify questions reasonably accurately (Voorhees, 1999). In TREC-8, the first QA track of TREC, the most accurate QA systems could answer more than two-thirds of the questions correctly. In the second QA track (TREC-9), the best performing QA system, the Falcon system from Southern Methodist University, was able to answer 65% of the questions (Voorhees, 2000). These results are impressive in a domain-independent question-answering environment. However, the questions were still simple in the first two QA tracks. In the future more complex questions requiring answers to be obtained from more than one document will be handled by QA track researchers.

Summary

Information retrieval in digital libraries is a fascinating and challenging subject to study. Research in text information retrieval has been carried out over many years. With digital information retrieval, many of the same issues are involved. However, there are further factors to take into account, such as the much larger volume, variety and number of formats and languages of digital information resources, coupled with the problems of the widely varying nature and requirements of users, and of information producers. In this chapter we have discussed theoretical issues of information retrieval ranging from the basic functions of an information retrieval system to various information retrieval issues and models. Users of digital libraries should be familiar with the basics of information search techniques as well as with the information retrieval features of those systems that are accessible in modern digital libraries. A number of working digital libraries provide reasonably good information retrieval features, especially for textual information retrieval. Results of experimental studies in multimedia and multilingual information retrieval are promising, and one can expect to see their influence in information retrieval systmes in digital libraries of the future.

Chapter 10
Digital archiving and preservation

Outline

Digital information needs to be archived and preserved for future use. This chapter discusses various technical issues related to doing so. A number of research projects have been undertaken in different parts of the world in order to resolve related problems and develop standards and best practice. Some of them are briefly discussed here. This chapter aims to give an overview of the issues, problems and possible solutions related to digital preservation.

Introduction

> The Gutenberg printing revolution led Europe out of the Dark Ages – the loss of knowledge of the learning of the ancient Greeks and Romans. The digital revolution may land us in an age even darker if urgent action is not taken.
> (Deegan and Tanner, 2002a, 42)

> As we move into the electronic era of digital objects it is important to know that there are new barbarians at the gate and that we are moving into an era where much of what we know today, much of what is coded and written electronically, will be lost forever. (Kuny, 1998)

On January 20, 2001, Inauguration Day in the United States. When George Bush took over the presidency, he also took possession of the White House web site, www.whitehouse.gov. All of the previous content of that site, and its companion searchable document archive, www.pub.whitehouse.gov, were completely wiped clean, replaced with a skeleton site for the new administration. The result was a massive example of 'link rot' in one of the most popular sites on the web. AltaVista reported 170,000 links to the site – many of them 'deep links' (i.e. deep within the hierarchy of a web site) – that were suddenly broken. It is impossible to know how many thousands or millions of personal bookmarks were similarly trashed.

(Wiggins, 2001)

The above statements are terrifying (though information from the former whitehouse.gov site is not lost: the National Archives and Records Administration (NARA) has undertaken to preserve materials from whitehouse.gov across the Clinton years (Wiggins, 2001)). The message is that, as we are getting more and more used to new ways of generating and using information, we often tend to forget that there is a need for archiving and preserving the vast amount of digital information that we create. We often forget this because apparently we do not see the problems that could be caused by not preserving digital information; perhaps we are still tuned to the printed world where the responsibilities of preservation rest with libraries and archives. Results of some recent studies corroborate the fears expressed in the above statements. In a survey, Gould and Ebdon (1999) noted that half the libraries they had surveyed that were involved in digitization did not have a proper policy for preservation.

Many of us have experienced the frustration of having failed to locate a digital document – a letter, memo, e-mail message, report, paper, and so on – created some time ago, or of discovering with dismay that none of the current technology allows us to access information that was created some time ago using seemingly poor technology. If this continues then we will live in a society that cannot access past records, and this 'past' will not be very far from the present, thanks to the fast developments in ICT, especially the web and digital libraries.

A digital library deals with data that are born digital as well as those that have been digitized from their analogue form. Over 93% of new information produced is born digital (Wiggins, 2001). Digital data that we generate in our everyday life – through e-mail communications, memos, letters, web pages, for example – need to be archived; in the same way that we need to archive important electronic publications and documents, such as journal and conference papers, theses, reports, images, audio and video.

There are two sets of issues here, and both are equally important for making the data available and accessible in the future. While digital data need to be archived so that we can carry out retrospective searching or browsing, proper care has to be taken in order to preserve the data as well. Since digital data cannot be stored and seen physically, one needs to store and organize them in such a way that we can easily get access to them. The fundamental problem with digital information is that one cannot read it with the naked eye; special equipment – hardware, software and communication infrastructure – and skills are needed to be able to use them.

In this chapter we shall look at some research projects that focus on digital archiving and preservation. While some of these projects are undertaken outside the remit of digital libraries, they will have a tremendous impact on digital libraries since their main goal is to find ways and means of preserving information for posterity.

Digital preservation

Simply speaking, preservation is a response to the threat of destruction (Bennett, 1997). Archiving and preserving digital information resources are complex and resource-intensive processes. This applies to both born-digital and digitized information. The massive number of information resources available on the web often change their content from one version to another, move from one location to another, or even sometimes just disappear. The case cited at the beginning of this chapter shows just one example of the loss of digital information, in this case as a result of the changing of the political guard. However, digital information may be lost for many other reasons, for example:

- changes in an organization
- content reorganization
- cessation of sponsorship
- technology obsolescence
- content format obsolescence
- hacking and sabotage
- disaster, whether natural or man-made.

Digital information produced by institutions, for example unpublished documents or web pages, may also get lost after some time unless it is archived properly. An investigation into the digital preservation needs of universities and research funders, commissioned by the Digital Achiving Working Group and carried out by staff of the UK Data Archive, noted that the electronic materials being produced by researchers constitute a valuable resource and steps should be taken to preserve them in order to make the best use of those resources for the purposes of secondary analysis, evaluation and replication of past research, and the investigation of scientific misconduct (*An investigation*, accessed September 2002). This study found the following justifications for digital preservation:

- The expense of data collection makes the re-use of resources important.
- Uncompleted or unpublished research should be available to be built upon and extended or completed.
- Methods and results should be capable of being replicated to ensure scientific accountability.
- The output of research units that are closed or whose projects come to an end should not be lost.
- Data should be available for historical research in due course.

Issues related to digital preservation

Over the years, information management professionals have developed a number of approaches to preserving information, such as conversion and migration, and persistent digital archives (G. S. Hunter, 2002). However, as Stephens (2000a, 2000b) comments, archivists, records managers and other information management specialists throughout the world are now facing the biggest challenge the records and information community has yet confronted, and are trying to reinvent their professional practices to ensure the permanent or long-term preservation of digital information.

The basic concepts and issues of digital preservation have been discussed in a number of publications (for example, Beagrie and Greenstein, 1998; CPA/RLG, 1996; Lesk, 1999c; Sitts, 2000; Waters and Garrett, 1996). Day (2001b) noted that the following related areas are worth considering:

- *Preservation strategies*. Strategies concerned with digital preservation need to be involved at the beginning of the digital life cycle.
- *Data creators and publishers*. It is vital that there is good communication between those who create and publish digital information and those who are responsible for its preservation.

- *Intellectual property rights (IPR)*. Negotiating specific rights for preservation may need to be part of licence negotiations between publishers and library consortia.
- *Collection management*. Collection management policies for digital information will have to find a balance between keeping everything and keeping the minimum amount of information possible in order to maintain the possibility of future serendipity.
- *Metadata*. Appropriate standards and policies on metadata for digital preservation will be essential.
- *Web archiving*. Research is necessary to address the importance of preserving parts of the world wide web.
- *Staff expertise*. Education and training should focus on the staff skills required for digital preservation, especially the creation of technical metadata.
- *Collaboration*. The development of groups like the UK Digital Preservation Coalition will help foster international collaboration and co-operation.

Digital preservation strategy

Sitts (2000) comments that in the digital world preservation is the creation of digital products worth maintaining over time. An obvious question related to digital preservation is: what and how much should be preserved? This is a very important question since digital preservation is a resource-intensive process, and the rate of growth of information is very, very high.

> The world's total yearly production of print, film, optical, and magnetic content would require roughly 1.5 billion gigabytes of storage. This is the equivalent of 250 megabytes per person for each man, woman, and child on earth.
>
> (*How much information*, 2000)

Preservation of digital objects in a cost-effective manner requires stable technologies and standard formats (Kuny, 1998). However, Arms (2000b, 198) warns that the best methods for long-term preservation are often poor for access, and therefore preservation strategies should be balanced with access considerations. Hedstrom (1998) proposes that a preservation strategy should be based on (1) the nature of the materials, (2) known and expected use of the materials, and (3) institutional technical capabilities. Waugh et al. (2000) discuss another matter: whether it is possible to preserve digital information forever.

Tennant (2000) comments that most guidelines for the selection of materials for digital preservation agree on some key issues, for example:

- Do we have the legal right to preserve an item?
- Does the material have intrinsic value that will make it popular with the target clientele?
- Is there potential to add value to the material by increasing access to it, associating it with related materials, etc.?
- Is it unique?
- Is preservation possible (in terms of adequate institutional support, technical feasibility, etc.)?

The research programmes funded by the UK Joint Information Systems Committee of the Higher Education Funding Councils, called The Preservation of Electronic Materials: a Programme of Studies, proposed a number of areas of investigation related to digital preservation (Kuny, 1998):

- developing a topology of major data types and formats and identifying issues affecting the preservation of each category of material
- investigating the attitudes of originators and rights owners to the responsibilities of digital preservation
- examining costing models for the long-term preservation of digital materials
- examining the three main methods of digital preservation: technology preservation, technology emulation, information migration
- investigating the digital preservation needs of universities and research funders
- investigating progress towards permissive guidelines for digital preservation
- reporting on sampling methods and techniques for collecting materials, on the nature and extent of institutional electronic archives, and on the relevance of current archival practice to digital preservation
- investigating post hoc rescue of high-value digital material which cannot be accessed because the required IT environment is no longer available.

There are three possible approaches to digital preservation (Day, 1998):

1   *Technology preservation*. This proposes that digital data should be preserved on a stable medium and associated with preserved copies of the original

application software, operating system and the relevant hardware platform. In other words, this approach suggests that the material as well as the technology need to be preserved, which may eventually lead to the creation of what Cook (1995) calls a 'cybernetic museum'.

2 *Emulation*. This relies on the preservation of the original data in its original format, and proposes to build emulator programs that would mimic the behaviour of obsolete hardware platforms and emulate the relevant operating system. This strategy may be useful where the look and feel of an original digital resource is of importance but it is not worth investing in expensive technology preservation.

3 *Migration*. This involves the periodic transfer of digital materials from one hardware or software configuration to another, or from one generation of computer technology to a subsequent generation so as to preserve the integrity of digital objects and to retain the ability for users to retrieve, display and otherwise use them in the face of constantly changing technology. This approach requires continuous investment in the data in order to maintain access, but the advantages are obvious – the information will be available with faster and newer technologies.

One of the major problems with digital information is that it can be altered easily with little effort and few costs. Hence, it becomes important to ensure that the authenticity and originality of the information are maintained. Information may be lost or the original may change in the course of digitization, conversion or migration. Rothenberg (2001) proposes a number of strategies that may be considered to ensure the authenticity of digital information:

- *originality strategy*: to assess whether the information has altered from its original state
- *intrinsic properties strategy:* to identify certain properties of an informational entity that define authenticity, regardless of whether they imply the originality of the entity
- *suitability strategy*: to define authenticity in terms of whether an informational entity is suitable for some purpose.

Ensuring the authenticity of digital information sources is a complex and resource-intensive process. Common technologies include watermarking and digital signature (discussed in Chapter 12).

Research projects on digital archiving and preservation

Deciding on a specific strategy for preservation involves a number of factors. One of these is the complexity of the objects to be preserved. It is not clear whether migration is at all useful for the preservation of complex digital objects or whether emulation is always a better strategy in these cases. Lawrence et al. (2000) discuss the risks involved in the migration strategy. Wheatley (2001) comments that both the migration and emulation strategies will play an important role in the long-term preservation of digital materials: while migration will be crucial for the preservation of more simple data objects, emulation will be essential for preserving complex objects that incorporate software elements.

A number of studies related to the technical aspects of digital archiving and preservation have been undertaken at Stanford (for example, Cooper, Crespo and Garcia-Molina, 2000; Crespo and Garcia-Molina, 1998, 2000). Stephens (2000b) summarizes the major research activities in the UK related to digital preservation. The following sample studies constitute valuable source materials for anyone contemplating long-term preservation of digital objects:

- Bennett (1997) reports a framework of data types and formats appropriate for supporting the long-term retention of digital data.
- Hendley (1998) reports a comparison of preservation methodologies and costing models as a basis for determining the most appropriate method of long-term data preservation.
- Haynes et al. (1997) recommend that a publicly funded national body be established to support digital preservation efforts nationwide.
- Beagrie and Greenstein (1998) address digital preservation in the context of the life cycle of data.
- Ross and Gow (1999) address the issues of recovery of digital data when its integrity is imperilled because of abandonment or rapid hardware and software obsolescence.

CEDARS (www.leeds.ac.uk/cedars/)

As part of the UK Electronic Libraries programme (eLib), the CEDARS project began in April 1998 with the objective of exploring issues and practical exemplars for the long-term preservation of digital materials (Russell and Sergeant, 1999). CEDARS stands for CURL Exemplars in Digital Archives, and is led by the universities of Oxford, Cambridge and Leeds. The UK Office of Library Networking is also a partner in the project with a particular focus on metadata issues for long-term preservation. CEDARS intends to build a model that will conform to the OAIS (Open Archival Information System), which provides a useful framework including concepts and vocabulary to facilitate clear and meaningful discussions and the implementation of archival repositories (Holdsworth and Sergeant, 2000; Russell and Sergeant, 1999). The CEDARS architecture can be seen as a framework to underpin an archive based on the OAIS model (Holdsworth, 2001).

CAMiLEON (www.si.umich.edu/CAMILEON/)

CAMiLEON is a research project that is investigating emulation as a digital preservation strategy. It is a collaborative project between the University of Michigan and the University of Leeds and is funded by the National Science Foundation (USA) and the Joint Information Systems Committee (UK). CAMiLEON stands for Creative Archiving at Michigan and Leeds: Emulating the Old on the New, and was set up to achieve three main objectives:

- to explore the options for the long-term retention of the original functionality and 'look and feel' of digital objects
- to investigate technology emulation as a strategy for the long-term preservation of and access to digital objects
- to consider where and how emulation fits into a suite of digital preservation strategies.

As we have seen, migration is the process of transferring data from a platform that is in danger of becoming obsolete to a current platform. While it has many advantages, the notable danger of migration is that of data loss, or in some cases the loss of original functionality or the 'look and feel' of the original platform. For these reasons, the CAMiLEON project was designed to test the suitability of the emulation stategy. The essential idea behind emulation is to be able to access or run original data or software on a new/current platform by running software on the new or current platform that emulates the original platform (Granger, 2000). In order to assess the suitability of the emulation strategy for digital preservation, the CAMiLEON project will (*CAMiLEON*, n.d.; Granger, 2000):

- evaluate publicly available emulators
- explore emulator development

- conduct test cases from technical and user perspectives
- conduct user trials comparing original systems with emulation of those systems
- undertake cost–benefit analysis of emulation vs other digital preservation strategies.

The ICSTI study

In an effort to advance the state of the art and practice of digital archiving, the International Council for Scientific and Technical Information (ICSTI), a community of scientific and technical information organizations that includes national libraries, research institutes, publishers and bibliographic database producers, sponsored a study in March 1999 (Hodge 1999, 2000). This study aimed to identify new best practices that satisfy the requirements and are practical for the various stakeholders of digital preservation. The study selected 18 projects that involved a number of countries – Australia, Canada, Finland, Sweden, UK and USA – and four international organizations, and came from a variety of sectors including government scientific and technical programs, national archives, national libraries, publishers and research institutes. The project managers from the selected projects emphasized the importance of considering best practice for archiving at all stages of the information management life cycle – creation, acquisition, cataloguing or identification, storage, preservation and access. Several important points were noted, which can be summarized as follows (Hodge, 2000):

- Standards for creating digital objects and metadata description that specifically address archiving issues are being developed at organization and discipline levels.
- Regardless of whether acquisition is carried out by human selectors or software, there is a growing body of guidelines to support the question of what to select, the extent of the digital work, the archiving of related links and refreshing the contents of sites.
- Standards for cataloguing and unique identification are important in order to make the material known to the archive administration.
- A variety of metadata formats, content rules and identification schemes are currently in use, with an emphasis on crosswalks to support interoperability, while at the same time standardizing as much as possible.

- The migration strategy followed by the projects are arduous and expensive, and they may be eliminated if emulation strategies are developed among standards groups and hardware and software manufacturers.
- There are concerns about rights management, security and version control at the access and re-use stage of the life cycle.

The Mellon–CLIR Initiative (www.diglib.org/preserve/ejp.htm)

The Mellon Foundation invited a number of research libraries to apply for one-year planning grants to develop projects to create and operate experimental e-journal archives, based on a framework developed by the Council on Library and Information Resources (CLIR). Six planning grants were awarded in December 2000, and a seventh grant was given for a related technical development. The planning grants took three different approaches (Flecker, 2001).

- Three projects were publisher-oriented:
  —Harvard University proposed working with John Wiley and Sons, Blackwell Publishing and the University of Chicago Press.
  —The University of Pennsylvania proposed working with Oxford University Press and Cambridge University Press.
  —Yale University proposed working with Elsevier Science.
- Two projects were subject-oriented:
  —Cornell University in agriculture
  —The New York Public Library in performing arts.
- The Massachusetts Institute of Technology proposed investigating the challenging area of 'dynamic e-journals'.

The seventh grant was made to Stanford University to fund the further development and beta testing of LOCKSS (Lots Of Copies Keep Stuff Safe), a tool designed for libraries to use to ensure their community's continued access to web-published scientific journals (Reich and Rosenthal, 2001) and intended to support the large-scale replication of e-journal content automatically.

It is expected that the Mellon–CLIR Initiative will be able to address a number of issues related to the preservation of e-journals, such as (Flecker, 2001):

- the rights and responsibilities of archives and publishers
- the nature of the licence under which an archive has access to a publisher's content, including the key issues of who can access archived content and

under what circumstances
- technical issues concerning the form and format of archival submissions
- the technical architecture of an archive and the magnitude of development effort required to build one
- organizational models, operating characteristics and ongoing expenses of an archive.

The Internet Archive (www.archive.org/)

Anyone surfing the web has noticed that the content of websites changes very frequently, and it is extremely difficult to track a website that has since changed its address. The Internet Archive is a free archive of internet resources that helps users in this respect. Founded in 1996, the Internet Archive contains (as of October 2001) over 110 terabytes of internet resources. One of the excellent features of the Internet Archive is the Wayback Machine that makes it possible to surf pages stored in the Internet Archive's web archive. When users enter a URL they are given pointers to various archives of that URL created at different times since 1996. This is a valuable source for archives of various web resources.

E-print archives

Of late, the concept of the e-print archive has become very popular. The successes of the arXiv e-print server based at Los Alamos National Laboratory (LANL) and other e-print services are cited as exemplars of how authors' distribution of e-prints can start a revolution in scholarly and scientific communication. Following the establishment of the PubMed Central service that provides free online access to published materials in the biomedical sciences, some researchers have stepped up their campaign for the creation of services that give free access to all published papers. However, Day (2001a, 2001b) warns that digital preservation raises several issues that need to be considered by the proponents of e-print services, for example:

- who should be responsible for preserving the record of scholarly and scientific research – authors, libraries, publishers, or any other institutions
- how to ensure the quality and authenticity of the information.

While it may be ideal to build a comprehensive archive of national intellectual output, analogue as well as digital, at the moment it is not clear whether it is technically and economically feasible and affordable.

Summary

Archiving and preservation are significant subjects in digital libraries. Several projects have been undertaken at national and international level to examine the various issues, strategies and best practice involved. Any particular approach and methodology for digital preservation will not be suitable for all types of digital information and all types of digital library. For example, migration can be used effectively for some digital materials, but it is problematic when applied to large heterogeneous collections (Muir, 2001a). In addition to the technical issues, digital preservation involves a number of managerial and organizational factors such as management workflows, staffing, standardization, economic issues, and so on.

In December 2000, the US Congress passed legislation establishing the National Digital Information Infrastructure and Preservation Program (NDI-IPP) in the Library of Congress (LC). The legislation allocates US$100 million for the program, to be released in stages, and calls for the LC to lead a national planning effort for the long-term preservation of digital content and to work collaboratively with representatives of other federal, research, library and business organizations with a view to answering many technical, organizational and management concerns, such as (Friedlander, 2002):

- What does it mean to have a national strategy for digital collections?
- What are the roles and responsibilities?
- Should the LC partner all libraries, research libraries, cultural institutions and federal agencies with information management missions?
- What are we preserving for whom and for how long?
- In a fast-moving technological environment, how can the architecture accommodate future changes, and how far ahead should the programme plan – five, ten, 100 years?
- Finally, where to begin: should the LC (or any would-be digital archive) experiment with small focused projects in which much would be learned, or should it initiate an operational role immediately, intervening to capture important materials that are in danger of being lost?

In summary, there is no shortage of issues related to digital preservation and, as G. S. Hunter (2002) points out, information professionals owe it to their institutions to confront the digital preservation questions head-on. They may prove to be some of the most difficult professional challenges over the next few decades.

Chapter 11

Digital library services

Outline

Reference and information services are integral to traditional library services. Although digital library research and development so far has not concentrated on them, reference services should also form an important part of digital library services. A number of new free and fee-based reference and information services are now available through the web, and many of them are offered by non-library organizations. This chapter briefly discusses the features of these digital reference and information services. It also discusses the features of some digital reference services offered by libraries. Current research in this area is then discussed. Overall, this chapter will enable readers to understand and appreciate the current state of digital reference services and give them an insight into future developments in this area.

Introduction

A quick look at the current state of digital libraries (as discussed in Chapters 2 and 3) reveals that till now most digital libraries have focused mainly on providing access to diverse digital information resources. The expectation is that users will conduct a search or browse the collections in order to get access to the required information. However, providing access to information is just one among many different services provided by libraries and information systems. Traditional libraries have been engaged in providing different types of reactive and proactive information services to their users.

Reference services, sometimes referred to as reference and information services, provide personal assistance to users in the pursuit of information (Bunge, 1999). The provision of such personalized information services has remained one of the important characteristics of the library and information profession. The importance of these services has grown over time with the introduction of new technologies and services in libraries. Reference services may be categorized into three broad groups (Bunge, 1999):

- information services that involve either finding the required information on behalf of users, or assisting users in finding information themselves
- instruction in the use of library resources and services (broadly defined as information literacy skills)
- user guidance in which users are guided in selecting the most appropriate information sources and services.

Reference questions can range from the simple fact-finding type to complex queries requiring the consultation, and often analysis, of one or more information sources (Chowdhury and Chowdhury, 2001b). An important part of a reference service is the reference interview, which involves a personal discussion between a user and reference librarian. Through the interview the reference librarian not only tries to understand the specific information need(s) of the user but also collects information about him or her, such as the person's subject knowledge and the reason for looking for the information, and so on. Using the reference interview, the reference librarian is often able to filter the retrieved information in order to pick up the most appropriate source(s) for the user.

While reference services are largely reactive – the assistance or service is provided when asked for by the users – libraries have also played a key role in providing information services that anticipate user needs. Such proactive services include various forms of current awareness and selective dissemination of information services. This type of service, which aims to keep users abreast of the latest developments in their areas of interest, has not been provided by libraries only, however; online search services like Dialog and institutions like ISI (the Institute of Scientific Information) also provide such services, for example Dialog Alerts and Current Contents.

Reference work in today's libraries has been influenced by a host of related technical and economic factors, the chief among them being the increasing use of technology (Curry, 2001). Recent developments in the internet and in web technologies have brought significant changes in the notion of traditional reference services, and a number of web-based 'expert services' are now offered by many non-library organizations. This chapter briefly reviews some currently available web-based reference and information services. Although these services are not necessarily offered by libraries and they have different names, for example 'expert services', they are well used, and they do not require a visit to the library to get answers to the questions. While they do not form part of the currently available digital libraries, they will have a tremendous impact on the role and functions of the digital libraries of the future.

Personalized services: definitions of digital libraries revisited

It is evident from the discussions in Chapter 1 that a number of digital library researchers focus on access to and retrieval of digital information, and thereby neglect the personalized service aspects that have for a long time remained one of the primary goals of library and information services. Sloan (1998) laments, 'Human interaction in the digital library is discussed far less frequently. One would almost get the impression that the service tradition of the physical library will be unnecessary and redundant in the digital library environment.' He emphasizes the point that 'technology and information resources, on their own, cannot make up an effective digital library'. Stressing the need for personalized services in digital libraries, Lombardi (2000) argues that 'helping clients find resources in a digitally chaotic world is the first priority'. In a Delphi study of digital libraries, it was revealed that 'the primary roles librarians play in digital libraries include organization (cataloguing and indexing), selection and acquisition and acting as gateways to the provision of services involving information' (Kochtanek and Hein, 1999). This study also revealed that 'the best reasons for developing a digital library include: increasing access to information, serving end users' needs and bringing organization to the unstructured universe of electronically available information'. Note here the importance of 'serving end users' needs', and the role of the librarians acting as 'gateways to the provision of services involving information' in a digital library. Downs and Friedman (1999) also point out that there is a demand for end-user instruction on the use of digital libraries. Covi (1999) points out that digital librarians who are subject specialists should help users formulate disciplinary search strategies and provide assistance in developing new resources.

Arms (2000a), while trying to decide 'whether or not we need reference librarians in a digital library', points out that automatic tools are steadily reducing the need for reference librarians in fields like medicine, which used to require a significant amount of intermediation in information searching. The essence of Arms's argument is that computers can perform most of the traditional jobs of reference librarians, whose skills may be required only in the case of complex information searches.

Perhaps the most comprehensive view of the need for, and the nature of, personalized services in a digital library has been outlined by Marchionini and Fox in their editorial of the special issue of *Information Processing and Management* (1999) on digital libraries (see Chapter 1).

Reference and information services on the web

A number of web-based reference and information services are now available and many of these services are provided by non-library organizations. Not all the currently available services are free. A number of publications discuss the features of these services (for example, Chowdhury and Chowdhury, 2001a, 2001b; Lankes, Collins and Kasowitz, 2000; Sherman, 2000). McKiernan (2001) maintains a site that provides a categorized listing of libraries that offer real-time reference services using chat software, live interactive communication tools, call centre management software, bulletin board services and other internet technologies. Most of these services are designed for registered users of the libraries concerned.

Hodgkin (2002) proposes that the aggregation approach, whereby more than one reference sources is made accessible digitally, is more practicable in terms of visibility and profitability than a single reference source. According to Hodgkin, the advantages of the aggregated approach are:

- By providing access to several reference works through one URL, the reference service becomes much better known to potential users and thus easier to find.
- By tackling a number of reference works at a time, the publisher can achieve economies of scale in production and development.
- The user's search session is likely to be much more powerful and fruitful than if it was a conventional search, since a collection of reference resources 'behind' a common interface can be meta-searched.

These advantages are very important because they are all scaleable. Infoplease (www.Infoplease.com) and Bartleby (www.bartleby.com) are the two pioneers of the aggregation approach. Subsequently, some reference publishers have established frameworks within which they can deliver all their reference works online. The Gale Group and H. W. Wilson were early pioneers of this approach, and Oxford University Press has launched Oxford Reference Online.

However, a problem associated with the publisher-aggregated reference services is that they depend on what is available from a given publisher, and thus may not always meet the needs of all the different types of users. An alternative approach would be to aggregate works from a variety of publishers around a market focus. Hodgkin (2002) suggests that an early and innovative example is the KnowUK service established by Chadwyck-Healey, now part of the Proquest group (www.knowuk.co.uk/).

Chowdhury and Chowdhury (2001a) categorize online reference and information services into three broad groups:

- reference and information services from publishers, database search services and specialized institutions
- reference services provided by libraries and/or experts through the internet
- reference and information services where users need to conduct a search and find information through the web.

Several online information services that belong to the first category have been discussed by Chowdhury and Chowdhury (2001b). They have listed various current awareness and SDI services, for example:

- contents page services from commercial publishers, such as Elsevier's Contents Direct Service and IDEAL Alert from Academic Press
- information on new books available for free from publishers and vendors, such as Wiley Book Notification Service from Wiley, and Amazon.com
- SDI services from online search service providers, such as Dialog (Dialog Alerts)
- *Current Contents* and *ISI Alerting Services* from ISI, and so on.

Some of these services, particularly the contents page services from publishers of journals, are free, while for others, such as Dialog Alerts, or Current Contents from ISI, users need to register and pay for the services.

Table 11.1 provides a quick overview of some online reference and information services. This is not an exhaustive list, but shows the different types of services and some of their characteristics. The table provides the following facts about the web-based reference services listed there:

- The listed web-based reference services are offered by dot.com companies.
- These services use the web only for communication between the user and the system, while the information service is provided by a human expert.
- While most services are free, some charge as much as US$250 per question.
- In many cases services are provided by (self-proclaimed?) volunteer experts.
- There are some services offered in specific subject fields.

Table 11.1 *Characteristics of some web-based reference services*

Service	AllExperts
Subject	All
Payment	Free
Organization	Allexperts.com
Service providers	Volunteer experts
Question input	Select a sub-category and enter query through a web-based query form
Mode of delivery	e-mail
Service	Askme
Subject	All
Payment	Free
Organization	Askme.com
Service providers	Volunteer experts
Question input	Select a sub-category and enter query through a web-based query form
Mode of delivery	e-mail
Service	Find/SVP
Subject	Business
Payment	Fee-based (users can choose a cost band)
Organization	Findsvp.com
Service providers	Business experts
Question input	Enter query through a web-based query form
Mode of delivery	e-mail, phone, fax, courier
Service	LiveAdvice.com
Subject	All
Payment	Fee-based (each adviser sets a per-minute rate for phone and recorded advice)
Organization	Liveadvice.com
Service providers	Registered experts
Question input	Select a sub-category and enter query through a web-based query form
Mode of delivery	e-mail

continued

Table 11.1 *continued*

Service	Professional City
Subject	Law, Accounting, Marketing
Payment	Fee-based
Organization	ProfessionalCity.com
Service providers	LIS professionals
Question input	Enter query through a web-based query form
Mode of delivery	e-mail

In addition to those mentioned in Table 11.1, there are also some web-based reference services where users need to conduct a search in order to answer their reference query. Such services provide free access to various online reference sources, and allow users to either select a specific source or conduct a search on a range, or all, of the sources. Examples of such services include the following:

- the Internet Public Library (www.ipl.org)
- Information Please (www.infoplease.com)
- Britannica (www.britannica.com)
- Bartleby Reference (www.bartleby.com/reference)
- the Internet Library for Librarians (www.itcompany.com/inforetriever/)
- the Electric Library (http://ask.elibrary.com/refdesk.asp)
- Mediaeater Reference Desk (www.mediaeater.com/easy-access/ref.html)
- ReferenceDesk (www.referencedesk.org/)
- Xrefer (www.xrefer.com/).

While most of these web-based reference services are available free of charge, some charge a small fee. For example, the Electric Library charges an annual subscription fee.

Janes, Hill and Rolfe (2001) report on a study of 20 web-based 'expert services'. Having asked 240 questions to 20 selected expert services, they noted that the sites gave verifiable answers to 69% of factual questions. One interesting observation of this study was that the kind of reference interview that takes place in traditional reference service environments is non-existent in web-based reference services. In fact, the sites did not come back for any discussion or clarification after receiving the initial queries. As a justification, the authors suggest that the web-based information services have been built mainly to answer factual questions, and therefore the experts do not need to go through the reference interview process. Nevertheless, the high rate of success for factual questions shows that more and more end-users will move towards these expert services rather than to libraries for answers to simple (ready-reference) type questions.

Search engine services

Although Ask Jeeves (www.AskJeeves.co.uk) is basically a search engine, many researchers also see it as a web-based information service for two reasons:

- Unlike in other search and metasearch engines, users can ask a question in Ask Jeeves and in many cases get an answer right away
- Users can ask a question on a given topic and Ask Jeeves comes up with a list of questions on the same or similar topics; the user can select any of the those predefined questions, and then Ask Jeeves provides further answers.

This is an interesting service and may be considered a useful model for reference and information services in digital libraries. The Ask Jeeves site maintains that:

> Ask Jeeves combines a unique natural language engine with a proprietary knowledgebase. Taken together, this mechanism processes the meaning and grammar of real questions in plain English; provides intelligent responses for user confirmation; links directly to relevant, high-quality answers; and, perhaps most exciting of all, becomes more intelligent as its knowledgebase expands with each question asked and each answer delivered.

The site further says that Ask Jeeves processes each query syntactically (to analyse the grammar) and semantically (to determine meaning), and then Ask Jeeves's answer-processing engine provides the question template response (the list of questions that users see after they ask a question). When the user clicks on a response, the answer-processing engine retrieves the answer template that contains links to the answer locations. Thus, Ask Jeeves helps users select a query from a pre-defined set of queries on a given topic. However, there is a debate as to whether the kind of service provided by Ask Jeeves matches the reference services provided by libraries. Kresh (2000) reports an interesting finding:

> One consortial system in northern California conducted an informal test of Ask Jeeves by sending it 12 questions which were answered by the member libraries.

> There were no trick questions, none were arcane, just questions typically received by those libraries. However, Ask Jeeves was unable to answer any of the questions.

Nevertheless, the techniques and technology used by Ask Jeeves may be very useful for introducing reference services in digital libraries. Webhelp.com (www.webhelp.com) is another service that claims to offer 'real-time search assistance with a real live expert – any time, day or night'. About.com (www.about.com) is a service that shows a number of pre-defined categories related to a search topic given by the user. For example, a simple search on 'e-commerce' not only produces a list of sites, but also provides a set of topics related to e-commerce, such as e-commerce definition, e-commerce security, the advantages and disadvantages of e-commerce, e-commerce statistics, and so on.

Sherman (2000) made a comparative study of three web-based reference services, Ask Jeeves, the Electric Library, and Information Please, and noted that:

- Ask Jeeves is useful for complex questions, and is a good choice for searchers who lack Boolean or other searching skills, because of its strong natural language parser and question-and-answer template structure.
- The Electric Library is an excellent choice for a serious researcher in need of timely content from a wide array of otherwise unavailable sources.
- Information Please is a suitable tool for students and other researchers, as an authoritative source of facts and pointers for further investigation.

Digital reference services and libraries

Several libraries have now begun to offer web-based reference services and a number of recent studies report on current practice. The following section provides a quick overview of some services that are currently available.

Digital reference services for the general public

Ask A Librarian (www.earl.org.uk/ask/) is a web-based reference service, primarily designed for UK residents, provided by a network of public libraries in the UK. Users state their query on an enquiry page; it is automatically routed to one of the participating libraries which receives it as an e-mail message. Within two days the library sends an e-mail message to the user with their response.

The British Library provides special reference services for business, patent, scientific, technical, medical and environmental information. These services range from answering simple queries to complex questions involving online database searches. While some of these services are free, for others users need to pay. As an example of a free service, users can ask simple business questions using a form, and can expect an answer within ten working days. Similarly, users can send an e-mail with simple environmental queries and can expect an answer within ten working days. A typical answer in such a case may include (*The British Library STM Search*, n.d.):

- a list of bibliographies from a British Library Catalogue literature search
- a list of organizations to contact for more detailed information
- information retrieved from the internet.

However, for complex queries users need to pay. For example, the British Library provides an STM (Science Technology Medicine) search service for which users need to pay at the following rate (www.bl.uk/services/current/stm-search.html):

- £84 per hour of staff time divided into 15-minute periods, plus
- the costs of online searching, plus
- VAT (Value Added Tax).

As stated on the website, most searches take at least 30 minutes and therefore cost £42 for staff time plus the costs for online searching plus VAT. The site mentions that the average list of references costs £80 for medical subjects, and between £100 and £150 for others. Users are also charged a fee if the results are to be faxed. In order to use the STM search service, users have to fill in a form that has three parts. In the first part they fill in their personal details; in the second part the query, and in the third part they specify their chosen mode of delivery, mode of payment, etc. Boolean operators can be used in the query, and it can be limited by such factors as date and language.

Digital reference services for users of academic libraries

Academic libraries have also begun to offer web-based reference services. Wasik and Lankes (1999) discuss the value of digital reference and AskA services in the K-12 educational environment. They describe how AskA services are built and maintained, and also explain how the service works in the classroom. Archer and Cast (1999) emphasize the importance of the personal touch in reference services and discuss how web technology and the personal element of reference services can be combined to provide web-based services. Tenopir (2001) and Tenopir and Ennis (2001) report on a survey of the current practices of digital library services in 70 academic libraries in the USA. These studies noted that university libraries allow their patrons to pose reference questions in a variety of ways: 99% offer e-mail reference, 96% offer reference services by appointment, while 29% of the libraries offer real-time virtual reference. Breeding (2001) briefly describes the various CRM (customer relationship management) software packages, such as eGain (www.egain.com), LivePerson (www.liveperson. com) and WebLine (www.webline.com/prod ucts/web.htm), that are used by libraries for providing web-based reference services. He also suggests that while CRM software offers a great deal of sophistication to the virtual reference environment, it is more complex and expensive than chat-based utilities which allow a managed two-way text conversation between the reference provider and the remote library user, and thus replace the need for face-to-face communication.

(B. Smith, 2001) discusses current technologies, such as chat and videoconferencing software, used by libraries for providing digital reference services. Richardson et al. (2000) examine the information technology aspects and key organizational issues involved in establishing an electronic reference desk service in a library. They also review the usefulness of some electronic reference services. Stemper and Butler (2001) discuss the model for a digital reference service. Breeding (2001) provides an overview of some methodologies and collaborations currently in use to help users learn to use virtual resources and find the information they need for themselves.

Digital library services and co-operative library systems

In order to deal with the rising cost of reference sources and staff, and also the huge initial investment required for introducing new services in libraries, many have gone for a co-operative model of digital reference services. Oder and Weissman (2001) describe the 24/7 Reference Project at Metropolitan Co-operative Library System, a consortium around Los Angeles, and the Bay Area Libraries Project at San Francisco, which are co-operative projects for providing web-based reference services to customers. Scardellato (2001) discusses the features of Virtual Reference Library (VRL), a web-based reference service at Toronto Public Library.

One advantage of web-based reference services is that users can ask for such services from a remote location at any time of the day. However, Rogers (2001) presents an interesting report of a study analysing the web-based reference services in academic libraries in Illinois. This study shows a usage pattern that is similar to that of traditional reference services in libraries; for example, 80% of all use occurred between 8 a.m. and 10 p.m.; evening use was higher than morning use, and the busiest hour was between 2 and 3 p.m.

Current digital library research on personalized services

Meyyappan, Chowdhury and Foo (2000) and Chowdhury and Chowdhury (2000) have recently reviewed the status of some digital libraries from around the globe. These reviews reveal that while the digital libraries have very good information access and retrieval mechanisms in place, there is almost no provision for quality reference and information services. However, these studies also show that there is a trend towards the personalization of digital library service, as in the case of HeadLine (an eLib Phase 3 hybrid library project) and iGEMS (formerly GEMS, a digital library developed at Nanyang Technological University in Singapore).

A number of research projects aiming at the personalization of digital libraries have been discussed in Chapter 3. The major objective of these projects has been to allow users to personalize their interfaces for access to digital libraries so that they can view their most rewarding resources; hence information is automatically filtered. These projects aim automatically to select a subset of the digital library collection based on the nature and characteristics of the user. The user then can add new resources to, or delete recommended resources from, their page. The DWE (digital work environment) project (Meyyappan, Chowdhury and Foo, 2001a, 2001b, 2001c) is somewhat different from others in the sense that its main objective is to provide filtered access (based on the chosen task of a given user) to the local and remote digital library collections as well as to the traditional libraries and, most importantly, to the vast information resources available on the university intranet. The system also allows users to create their own personal workspace to store selected information resources for future use.

Current digital library projects on digital reference services

Some research projects aimed at providing reference and information services as part of the digital library services have recently begun. The most prominent among these is the Collaborative Digital Reference Service (CDRS) project launched by the Library of Congress. Other projects are funded by the US Digital Library Initiative Phase 2. These projects are briefly discussed in the following sections.

CDRS (www.loc.gov/rr/digiref/)

Rudner (2000) comments that 'by applying the best of what libraries and librarians have to offer (structure and organization, in-depth subject expertise and analog collections) to the labyrinthine universe of unstructured and unverified information on the internet, we can begin to bridge the gulf that exists between providers and users of information'. With this end in view, the Library of Congress has launched the Collaborative Digital Reference Service (CDRS), whose mission is to provide 'professional reference service to users, anywhere anytime, through an international, digital network of libraries' (*Collaborative Digital Reference Service*, n.d.). It is a 'library to library' network for asking and answering reference questions and has three main components:

* *Member Profiles*: containing information on member strengths and features
* *Request Manager*: software for entering, routing and answering reference questions
* *Knowledge Base*: a searchable database of question and answer sets.

The system is designed to work in a very simple manner. A participating library sends a question to the system on behalf of a user. The system looks into the knowledge base for a match. If the answer is found, a response is sent to the relevant library through e-mail. If the question (and the corresponding answer) is not found in the knowledge base, then it is passed on to the Request Manager. This part of the system, using the profiles of the participating libraries and their collection, expertise, etc., passes on the query to an appropriate library. This library receives the query, finds an answer and sends back the response to the Results Store, which then sends the response back to the asking library, and stores the query and the answer in the knowledge base. Hence, the strength of the system lies in the knowledge base and the Request Manager. From June

2000 CDRS was a 'working' pilot with a total of 220 active members to route real questions and answers. *QuestionPoint*, the next generation of CDRS, co-developed by the Library of Congress and OCLC, was launched in June 2002 (Kresh, 2000, 2001; Grotke, 2002). It integrates local and global e-reference networks.

Automatic Reference Librarians for the World Wide Web (www.fastlane.nsf.gov/servlet/showaward?award=9874759)

Etzioni and Weld (2001) report on Automatic Reference Librarians for the World Wide Web, a DLI-2-funded project at the University of Washington. The central objective of this project, according to them, 'is to create software agents that possess reference intelligence – a limited understanding of complex technical topics, but a very sophisticated understanding of how and where to find high-quality information on the World Wide Web'. Etzioni and Weld report on the basic principles of the proposed system, which works on a wrapper technology. The basic steps involved are:

- The user asks a question.
- The Query Router assigns a topic to the query.
- The topic maps to a number of relevant wrappers.
- The parallel web search module sends requests via wrappers to the sites.
- Responses from the sites are obtained and sent to the fusion engine for collation.
- The user gets the response.

The success of this system depends on the wrappers. Simply speaking, a wrapper is data that precedes or frames the main data or a program that sets up another program so that it can run successfully. In the project the Automatic Reference Librarian program explores web directories such as Yahoo! to find searchable sites. It queries each searchable site and obtains responses from them. The responses and other information about a given site are used to assign topics to that site. Thus, each searchable site gets a wrapper containing some assigned topics that are used for matching with the topics of user queries.

SIFTER (http://sifter.indiana.edu/)

SIFTER is an interdisciplinary research collaboration between faculty and students in the Computer and Information Science Department and the School of

Library and Information Science at Indiana University. The broad aim of the project is to develop information agents to perform a number of functions such as culling information from complex resources residing in diverse locations, and conducting analysis, synthesis and customization according to the requirements of the user.

The specific objectives are:

- dealing with heterogeneous information sources that may change over time
- handling shifting requirements and user interests with minimal human involvement
- creating a robust agent architecture for reactive, proactive and collaborative filtering
- supporting agent collaboration based on natural or artificial economic frameworks for multi-agent tasks.

The Virtual Reference Desk (www.vrd.org/)

The Virtual Reference Desk (VRD) is a project sponsored by the US Department of Education whose objective is 'the advancement of digital reference and the successful creation and operation of human-mediated, internet-based information services' (*The Virtual Reference Desk*, n.d.). VRD defines digital reference services as internet-based question-and-answer services that connect users with experts. The basic idea of VRD is that when a given user (a K-12 student, a teacher or a parent) asks a question that cannot be answered by a participating centre, it is forwarded to the VRD network for assistance. VRD services include the following:

- *Collaborative AskA Service*: a network of AskA services and volunteer information professionals
- *The Learning Center*: a website for the K-12 community with curriculum-related websites, frequently asked questions and other previously asked questions.
- *AskA + Locator*: a searchable database of high-quality K-12 AskA services.

VRD also supports research on interoperability standards, metadata and other aspects of digital reference services.

Tracking Footprints through an Information Space: Leveraging the Document Selections of Expert Problem Solvers (www.cse.ogi.edu/dot/research/footprints/)

This is a DLI 2 project at the Oregon Health Sciences University and Oregon Graduate Institute. The goals of this project are 'to understand how experts select information in a large and complex information space and to develop tools that assist them in this process' (Gorman et al., 2000). The project aims to capture the trace of information used by experts in the health field, for example medical doctors. The basic idea is that as medical experts traverse the large and diverse collection of documents available, they make explicit choices about which information resources to examine more carefully and which ones to ignore. These choices create a subset of documents relevant to a given problem and this subset of documents may be of interest to other users concerned with the same or similar problems. Thus, by capturing this information that is inherent in the selection of appropriate information resources for problem solving, this project aims to come up with models that may be useful for other users. The project proposes to develop:

- a trace that describes the path taken by an expert in solving the user's problem by using the available information resources
- a precis of information about each document, its content, and the history of its use by experts
- navigation tools to assist subsequent problem solvers using the collection by exploiting the knowledge inherent in the existing traces.

Though the project specifically deals with medical experts and looks into their problem-solving processes, the project team expects that the resulting technology will be scaleable, because the value of a set of precis and bundles within a collection should increase as the document collection grows and as more experts use the collection.

The evaluation of digital library services

Evaluation data for digital library services are not yet widely available. In fact, very few evaluation studies of digital library services have taken place so far. The most prominent papers reporting digital library evaluation experiments appear in the special issue of *Library Trends* (2000). Whitlatch (2001) comments that standards and criteria related to economic considerations, the reference process and service outcomes are to be developed for the evaluation of digital reference services. Evaluation of the reference questions handled by the Internet Public Library revealed that users seem to have difficulties in assigning subject categories to their questions, and also in determining whether they are factual or require a detailed information search (Carter and Janes, 2000).

Diamond and Pease (2001) report on the evaluation over a two-year period of a digital reference service in a medium-sized academic library. The results of this study showed that the digital reference service could handle the simple to complex questions typically asked at a physical reference desk. The study also suggested that strategies should be developed to answer complex reference questions in the digital environment.

Davies (2001) describes the creation of the Suffolk Libraries and Heritage virtual reference library in the UK. This was an interesting pilot experiment in four small rural libraries, which, for a period of three months, had their reference books removed to test whether they could indeed become virtually resourced. This project shows that in the absence of the printed reference sources users of the selected public libraries were able to get the information they required from subscription services like Ebsco and KnowUK as well as from the web.

For more on evaluation in general see Chapter 13.

Summary

The discussions in this chapter reveal some interesting facts that may be very useful in shaping the nature of personalized services in the second-generation digital libraries. The discussions on the current state of web-based reference and information services show that in most cases the web is used only as a medium of communication, for example for sending questions and answers.

Janes, Hill and Rolfe (2001) noted that web-based 'expert services' were reasonably successful in providing answers to factual questions. Their conclusion has been that 'the skills and knowledge of trained information service professionals may be better suited to detailed and source dependent questions in any event, and that the digital domain provides an environment rich with the potential for reference services to be greatly enhanced'.

Current research on personalized services in digital libraries reveals two different trends:

- the creation of personalized work space for users where they can store information that they find useful

- the automatic filtering of information based on user categories, user task, etc.

Janes (2002), reporting on the results of a survey of reference librarians in public and academic libraries of various sizes in the USA, notes that the best questions for digital reference include: ready-reference questions; those from regular users; and those in popular culture and entertainment; while the worst questions are: those that are of a personal or private nature; those that come from children; and research questions.

Coffman and Saxton (1999) found that networked reference services based on the call centre model could reduce the reference staff cost significantly. However, they caution that though the call centre model has been moderately successful in answering customer questions in the business environment, it may not be appropriate for answering reference questions since they may come from anyone on any topic asked in any form. Other researchers also oppose use of the call centre model for digital reference services. For example, Dilevko (2001, 241) comments that:

> The spectre of deprofessionalization of the reference function looms ominously. An increasing percentage of reference questions are being offloaded to paraprofessionals working in call centres notorious for low pay, high turn over, lack of advancement opportunities, and stressful working conditions. As reference functions become more and more automated through call-centre interactive voice-response systems and automated call distribution systems, the intellectual component traditionally associated with reference librarianship becomes increasingly etiolated.

Our brief review of some digital library research projects focusing on the digital reference and information services reveals that:

- Some projects aim to use agent technology for the identification, filtering and categorization of information.
- Collaboration among libraries and various institutions has been considered as a measure to cut costs and achieve higher performance levels.
- One project is trying to track expert users' information problem-solving techniques so as to create some generalized models to be useful for other users.

Lankes, Collins and Kasowitz (2000) have pointed out that 'the reference librarian in the new millennium will need the ability to read the situation a user is in and find the right information for that situation'. In consideration of this view and also to keep pace with the rapid developments of web-based reference and information services provided by non-library organizations, many library and information science professionals have now turned their attention to the provision of e-reference services. Oder and Weissman (2001) state, 'The year 2000 brought the advent of live reference. Several libraries, especially academic ones, have used or adapted chat or commercial call center software to communicate with surfers in real time and send web resources to their browser.'

Indeed this is a time when digital library researchers should think of the best ways and means to make optimum use of the technology and experience and expertise of human intermediaries in improving digital libraries from being mere access centres to being information service providers. Many recent projects have taken the approach of building software agents to do much of the work of reference librarians. While this is a useful approach, and such programs will reduce the workload of human experts, it is doubtful whether digital libraries can totally replace human experts and personalized services. So far as the information filtering aspect of personalized services is concerned, the personal digital library approach of automatic filtering based on user nature, and the DWE approach (Meyyappan, Chowdhury and Foo, 2001a, 2001b, 2001c) of information filtering based on user categories and tasks, seem to be promising.

Chapter 12
Social, economic and legal issues

Outline

The development and use of digital libraries involves social, economic and legal issues. This chapter highlights some of these issues and briefly discusses recent studies that aim to resolve some of the problems. It then considers the digital divide, created by inequality in access to and use of the internet and the web, and points out some recent developments in the digital library world that may help to bridge the gap. Economic issues related to the creation and use of digital information are examined. Authenticity and access control are then discussed, as are other legal issues, especially those of copyright, and the security and privacy of users in the digital library environment. This chapter will help readers develop an overall idea of the social, economic and legal issues connected with digital libraries and will provide references to some relevant research activities in these areas.

Introduction

The development and use of digital libraries involves a number of social, cultural and behavioural, economic and legal issues. The fast growth of ICT (information and communication technologies) and the internet is causing a major social problem called digital divide – the inequality caused by differences in access to the appropriate ICT, especially the internet, among people. The development and use of digital libraries will be significantly influenced by the digital divide in the developing as well as the developed world.

Digital libraries are designed to bring major changes in the habits of the population in terms of information seeking, information access and information use. Users are expected to interact with libraries through computer terminals, be able to express their information needs through user interfaces, and get access to and use information online. Thus users need to be able to read and write, and also to acquire a reasonable degree of information literacy coupled with a basic knowledge and understanding of ICT. Again, since digital libraries are supposed to provide access to digital information resources available anywhere in the world in any language, there has to be a mechanism for breaking down linguistic and cultural barriers.

A number of economic considerations are also involved. First, there is the cost issue. Digital library research and development require significant amounts of investment. Second, recent developments in ICT and the growing use of the internet and the web have brought significant changes in the economic models and practices followed in the information industry. This will be more prominent with the growth and development of digital libraries. Alternative models of information services are being developed, and libraries have to change their business plans to cope with them. Some services that had to be paid for in the past are now available free of charge, or at a much-reduced cost. Many companies provide free or fee-based reference services on the internet. Different models of access to e-journals and e-books are coming up, and many digital libraries are now providing free access to vast amounts of useful information resources.

Improved facilities for access to information through digital libraries also raise many legal issues. Access control and management form an important part of digital library management. A number of issues related to intellectual property rights as well as to authenticity are involved. The successful development and use of digital libraries will depend on how the new regulations for intellectual property rights are formulated and observed in the digital library world.

This chapter addresses these important issues for digital libraries. Some recent research studies and projects are also discussed.

Social issues

Libraries are social institutions, and they have evolved over many centuries by adapting themselves to the changing contexts, characteristics and demands of society. Borgman (2000b, 192) raises the following questions, which cut across a range of political, economic and social issues for digital libraries:

- What resources and services are needed, and whose needs are they?
- Which resources and services are essential, and which are desirable?
- What infrastructure is needed to support digital library services?
- Who should provide these infrastructures and facilities?

Bishop and Star (1996) raise a number of issues related to the social context of digital libraries, such as:

- How do the creators, librarians and users collaborate in the creation, searching and use of digital library documents?
- How does the introduction of digital libraries change the workplace and home?
- How do digital documents influence social interactions?
- How do organizations make their digital libraries usable for their members?

Assuming the appropriate mechanisms and systems are put in place, digital libraries will be able to play a significant role in diminishing the linguistic barriers in the information world. A number of technical matters, such as the issues of design and interoperability, information retrieval and metadata and user interfaces, are involved. Some of them have been discussed earlier in this book.

The digital divide

The socio-economic background of users will have a tremendous influence on the use and non-use of digital libraries. While ICT in general, and the internet and the web in particular, have made life easier by facilitating communication with virtually everyone, and providing access to information located virtually anywhere in the world, they have also widened the gap between the rich and the poor, the 'haves' and the 'have nots'. These new technologies, while improving our life in many ways, have created what is called the 'digital divide'. Digital libraries use ICT and the web as their foundation to provide access to local as well as remote digital information sources and services. Therefore, access to basic ICT and the internet are prerequisites to the development and use of digital libraries.

The *Digital divide basics fact sheet* (Digital Divide Network, 2002a) shows that there are an estimated 429 million people – 6% of the world's entire population – online globally, with the following distribution:

- 41% of the global online population is in the USA and Canada.
- 27% of the online population lives in Europe, the Middle East and Africa.
- 20% of the online population logs on from Asia Pacific.
- 4% of the world's online population live in South America.

Digital divide is not necessarily a developing country phenomenon. In the UK, it is estimated that more than 60% of the richest 10% of the population have household access to the internet, while only about 6% of the poorest 10% have this (Cronin, 2002). In autumn 2000, the US Department of Commerce found that only 41.5% of all US homes had internet access (Digital Divide Network, 2002a).

However, the disparities in the least-developed countries are mind-boggling; most people there don't even have a phone, let alone an online connection, either at work or at home. According to the BBC (1999), 'more than 80% of people in the world have never even heard a dial tone, let alone surfed the Web'. United Nations Secretary-General Kofi Annan recently said that the internet is used only by 5% of the world's population (Conhaim, 2001).

Library development has not been a top priority of governments in many countries, especially where they struggle to meet basic human needs like food, water, health, electricity, sanitation and transportation. Consequently, libraries have long been suffering from financial and other crises such as lack of appropriate technology, trained manpower, and so on. Libraries have also been affected by a number of social problems, the primary one being the illiteracy of the population. While governments are struggling to improve literacy rates, libraries struggle with another level of literacy – information literacy – which is absolutely necessary for citizens to become good information users. Because of the lack of suitable technologies and trained staff, and above all the lack of financial resources, most libraries in developing countries do not even have fully developed and up-to-date OPACs, let alone fully fledged automated library management systems. Thus, compared with the developed world, libraries in developing countries have already been left behind by at least one generation. The digital divide, and lack of resources for digital library research and development, may increase the gap significantly between library and information services in developed and developing countries.

The following are some of the major stumbling blocks for digital library research and development in developing countries:

- a shrinking library budget that forces the library management to struggle to maintain a minimum standard of services, leaving no room for new ventures and developments
- lack of separate financial support for digital library research and development
- the absence of fully developed and up-to-date OPACs and access to online information resources, such as online databases and e-journals
- lack of available technology – computers and networks
- poor facilities for internet access
- stringent government and institutional policies on internet access
- lack of trained manpower
- a poor information literacy rate that causes a lack of appreciation for modern information services and their use.

The list could go on and on. However, it is true that in countries where citizens still struggle for reliable sources of food, water, medical care and educational opportunity, bridging the digital divide may seem like a lofty goal, and digital library development is probably way down the list of priorities of governments and institutions.

While developing countries are threatened by the growing digital divide, and their information professionals and users feel that they are lagging behind the digital library revolution because of the high cost of digital library research and development, many new ventures are taking place that may reverse the situation if they are handled properly. In fact, over the past few years new services have been introduced that can be used by anyone and are free at the point of use. Many of these are the consequence of digital library research, while others are the result of new economic models in the information industry, and some are the result of humanitarian gestures.

Information from governmental, regional and international organizations

One of the direct impacts of the internet on governments and regional and international organizations has been that they are now trying to make as much information available on the net as possible. As a result, end-users can get access to up-to-date (as much as possible) information for which they used to have to wait a long time and go through a number of difficulties. Digital library services may provide access to all of these, or preferably to those selected as the most appropriate for their users, by creating a simple web page providing links to relevant resources. Alternatively, a better and more useful approach might be to organize the resources into various categories according to their content or the user requirements, and let users go through the organized structure.

Information through subject gateways and virtual libraries

One of the most prominent and useful, especially from the end-user perspective, outcomes of recent digital library research in the UK and Europe has been the development of a number of subject gateways. These gateways select and organize valuable subject-specific information available on the web, and let users access those resources through a custom-built interface. Several examples of subject gateways are discussed in this book, and a detailed list appears in Chowdhury and Chowdhury (2001a, 73–9).

At relatively minimal cost, digital library services can make one or more of these subject gateways accessible to their users by pointing to the appropriate service websites from their own web page. Alternatively, they may point users to a general subject gateway like BUBL, which will allow users to browse or search web information resources by subject.

Access to digital reference and information services

As discussed in Chapter 11, a number of free and fee-based reference and information services are now available on the web. Library and information professionals may tap into them to provide services to their users. This is particularly true for the developing countries where end-users may not have access to the internet from their home or office, and where access is expensive. LIS professionals could select one or more web-based reference services according to the nature and needs of their users, and either use those services on behalf of their users or let users use them on their own.

Access to electronic texts

One of the most valuable services digital libraries can offer is to provide online access to books, journals and other publications such as conference proceedings and theses. Indeed many digital libraries and other services have been set up that provide free access to a number of such resources.

While most e-journals are accessible only through payment, many e-journals and books are also available for free. Some publishers and associations or organizations are now making journals available free to the readers in some countries. For example:

- Blackwells (www.blackwells.co.uk) is making all 600 of its journals freely available to institutions within the Russian Federation (G. Smith, 2001).
- The World Health Organization (WHO) is spearheading an initiative to enable 100 of the world's poorest countries to access 1000 of their top biomedical journals, while Academic Press's Ideal service (www.idealibrary.com) is making 300 STM (science, technology and medicine) journals available to research centres across Senegal in West Africa.
- PubMed Central (www.pubmedcentral.nih.gov/is), a digital archive of life sciences journal literature managed by the National Center for Biotechnology Information (NCBI) at the US National Library of Medicine (NLM), is free for use from anywhere in the world.

A number of free e-journals are now coming up in different subjects. For example, in information science some very good online journals include *D-Lib Magazine*, *Ariadne* and *Information Research*. Fosmire and Yu (2000) comment that several high-quality, productive, free scholarly electronic journals exist currently. They conducted a survey of 1209 e-journals and noted that 213 scholarly ones (18%) were free. They further noted that these journals contain a reasonable number of articles and scored very well in impact factor (the total number of quotations during a year of the two immediately preceding years' issues) and in their immediacy index (the average number of times a specific article is cited during its year of publication).

Although electronic books are not yet as common as e-journals, the e-book service provided by netLibrary (www.netlibrary.org) is becoming popular. While netLibrary requires payment before use, many electronic books are now available for free. Some examples are given below:

- The Dictionary.com (www.dictionary.com/) site provides access to a number of dictionaries, thesauri, writing resources and other tools including the automatic web page translation services.
- The eLibrary reference desk (http://ask.elibrary.com/refsearch.asp) provides access to a number of dictionaries, encyclopedias and almanacs.
- The Classic Book Shop (www.classicbookshelf.com/SiteMap.htm) provides access to a number of classic books available in electronic format.
- The web books.com site (www.web-books.com/cool/ebooks/Library.htm) provides access to over 2200 electronic books on different subjects.

E-print archives and the Open Archives Initiative

E-prints are seen as a means of fighting the high costs of scholarly publications from publishers and they may play a key role in bridging the digital divide. The idea is that the fastest and cheapest way for authors to make their papers available is to store the electronic copies of their papers on e-print servers (Day, 2001a). The success and rapid growth of the arXiv e-print server (www.arxiv.org) has given birth to many new e-print services, such as CogPrints (the Cognitive Sciences Eprint Archive; http://cogprints.soton.ac.uk/), mathematics arXiv (http://front.math.ucdavis.edu/) and WoPeC (Working Papers in Economics; http://netec.mcc.ac.uk/WoPEc.html).

Theses, dissertations, etc.

The two most prominent digital libraries that provide access to electronic theses, dissertations and scholarly publications are NDLTD (the Networked Digital Library of Theses and Dissertations; www.NDLTD.org) and NCSTRL (the Networked Computer Science Technical Reference Library; www.ncstrl.org). One of the main objectives of NDLTD is to increase the availability of student research to scholars and to preserve the theses and dissertations electronically. The service has grown dramatically in its first few years and is becoming a global access point for electronic theses and dissertations. As of May 2002, the site provides access to the theses and dissertations from 138 members – 122 universities from around the world and 16 internationally renowned institutions.

Other free digital libraries

Many digital libraries provide free access to users from anywhere. The Greenstone Digital Library in New Zealand (www.nzdl.org/cgi-bin/library/) is a free digital library service that may be particularly valuable for users in developing countries. Witten et al. (2002) list five specific areas where digital libraries can promote development in the developing countries:

* the dissemination of humanitarian information
* disaster relief
* the preservation and propagation of indigenous culture
* building collections of locally produced information
* creating new opportunities to enter the global marketplace.

To this we can add another important point: digital libraries can facilitate life-long learning, which is the key to success in this fast-changing world.

Discussing the collection and services of the Greenstone Digital Library, and arguing how the digital library can meet many of the above objectives in developing countries, Witten et al. (2002) comment that digital libraries provide a golden opportunity to reverse the negative impact of ICT on developing countries.

Economic issues

Libraries and publishing are big businesses (Arms, 2000b, 100). The following extracts from the *US Business Reporter* (n.d.) will provide an idea of the size of the publishing business:

- In the USA total book sales reached US$24 billion in 1999 and US$25.32 billion in 2000.
- In 2001, the total revenue earned by some leading publishers was as follows:
  — Gannett Company US$6222 million
  — McGraw-Hill US$4280.9 million
  — Knight Ridder US$2900 million
  — Dow Jones US$2202 million.

A number of economic issues are involved with the design, development and management of digital libraries. The first and the major concern is the impact on the multi-billion dollar publishing industry. Printed books, journals, etc. have relied on the mechanism of payment per copy of the item sold – whether to an individual or to a library. The revenue is shared among the various stakeholders such as author, publisher and distributor. Recent developments in ICT have brought significant changes in the methods of creation, distribution and use of information. Majka (2000) comments that current ICT can offer unprecedented opportunities for cost savings, while at the same time producing significant improvements in staff and patron productivity. However, the economic models used by publishers, libraries and end-users in the printed world need to be changed for the digital. Indeed alternative economic models for access to remote online information have long been developed and practised. Models based on pay per use have been developed for electronic information accessible through online search service providers. For example, when searching Dialog, charges incurred include output and search time costs, as well as telecommunications charges. A unique unit, called a DialUnit, is used to calculate costs. Prices for DialUnits vary among databases, based on the relative value of the content (Dialog, 2002).

Every stage in the design, creation, management and use of digital libraries is expensive. As mentioned in Chapter 3, millions of dollars have been spent on digital library research around the globe over the past few years. However, the major challenge for digital library collection and service management is posed by several alternative economic models that are now available for access to electronic journals, electronic books, databases and online search services. Borgman (2000b, 183) describes the economic trade-offs between printed and electronic information resources as complex and evolving. The electronic models include annual fees, fee per use, fee based on the size of the user population, and a host of others. While part of the collections of a digital library will be born digital, a significant portion may need to be digitized from other forms of material. However, as discussed in Chapter 6, digitization is a complex and expensive affair. Deegan and Tanner (2002b, 87) suggest that realization of the benefits of digital implementation may require a long gestation period, and a radical strategy is not easily supported by every stakeholder.

Many digital library services came into being as a result of research projects, for example the information gateways that evolved in the course of the eLib programme. These services, although free at the point of use, require a considerable amount of money for their day-to-day operations, and they need sustainable support to run.

As discussed in Chapter 11, and also earlier in this chapter, many commercial companies now provide digital reference and information services that are free at the point of use. Digital libraries may be able to make use of these services for their users, while focusing more, and spending their scarce resources on, specific services. The study reported by Janes, Hill and Rolfe (2001) concludes that the skills and knowledge of trained information professionals in digital libraries may be better suited to detailed and source-dependent questions, and that the digital domain provides an environment that has the potential for reference services to be greatly enhanced.

A number of research projects have been undertaken to assess the economic impact of digital library development and management. Many researchers discuss the economic aspects of electronic journals (for example, Halliday and Oppenheim, 2000a, 2000b, 2001a, 2001b, 2001c; Oppenheim, 1996; Sairamesh et al., 1996; Varian, 1996). The Economic Models for the Digital Library project at Loughborough University, funded by JISC in the UK, came up with four models of electronic journal production and delivery, a model of a resource discovery network consisting of a centre and a number of hubs, and a model of a national electronic reserve service. The study revealed that non-commercial electronic journals recovering full costs (including an overhead on staff costs of 120%) and making a profit of 10% can be sold at a reasonable subscription price provided that they have at least 500 subscribers, the annual subscription price being calculated as £148.43 when the number of subscribers is 500, and £74.22 when the number of subscription is 1000.

Another project at Loughborough, called Pelic@n (Pricing Experiment Library Information Co-operative Network), was intended to develop an understanding of charging mechanisms for distributing commercially published electronic texts to students. The findings of the project were intended to help the relevant stakeholders to develop appropriate business plans so as to ensure the long-term viability of any systems developed for this purpose (*Pelic@n*, n.d.). The project noted that pricing is the biggest issue in the provision of digitized text, and it came up with three models:

- Pricing Model 1 involves a basic administrative system of purchasing units against a subscription fee.
- Pricing Model 2 is a mixed model that takes account of the different ways texts are used.
- Pricing Model 3 is value based. The same basic subscription system as Model 1 is adopted, but in this model, value factors are assigned to each text.

On 18 September 2001, the Pelic@n project team hosted a conference, which noted that:

- Currently, no stakeholders are satisfied with the pricing of digitized text for the higher education community.
- The results of the Pelic@n project are one step closer to addressing all stakeholders' concerns and to satisfying needs concerning pricing.
- Many believe that the service providing the texts is more important than the goods delivered.
- Pricing models will adapt according to the market, and multiple models will emerge.

Legal issues

The legal issues related to digital libraries are complex. By definition, a digital library can be accessed from anywhere in the world, and should be able to provide access to information residing on a computer anywhere in the world. This universal nature of digital libraries creates the major legal problem. Each country in the world has its own legal system, and practices that are acceptable or common in one country may be illegal in another. Hence, certain issues related to the management and use of digital libraries may be acceptable in one country but illegal in another, or even illegal in another state in the same country. Here is an interesting example of the differences in laws between different states in the USA: 'People who mounted sexual material on a server in California, where it is legal, were prosecuted in Louisiana, where it is deemed obscene' (Arms 2000b, 111–12).

There are many legal issues related to digital libraries, the most prominent one being intellectual property. Librarians, publishers, lawyers and governments have over the years formulated regulations that control the intellectual property rights of the owners of information in the printed world. These regulations protect the interests not only of author and publishers, but also of readers. Regulations governing the intellectual property rights of the creators or owners of various types of information sources, such as printed books and CD-ROMs, music, film and software, are observed by traditional libraries. However, since the bulk of the information in digital libraries is in digital form, new sets of regulations and guidelines are required for ensuring the authenticity of information resources as well as protecting the rights of their creators and owners. This is not an easy task since, compared with their printed counterparts, digital information resources can be easily changed, manipulated, re-created and communicated. Identifying the ownership of digital information and ensuring the rights of the creator and owner is not easy either, and there is plenty of room for argument and debate. There is a very strong group of creators and users of information who feel that information should be freely accessible to everyone and that therefore the question of protecting the economic interests of the creators and owners does not arise. While this might make life easier for the managers and users of digital libraries, it would probably be against the interests of many creators of information, and would certainly be against the interests of the multi-million-dollar publishing industry.

Mechanisms for assuring the authenticity of digital information resources and regulations on intellectual property rights are not yet available. Because of the lack of specific regulations, several legal battles have taken place where publishers have sought the legal protection of their rights over some form of digital information. In the following sections we shall look at the complexities of the legal issues of digital libraries, and briefly discuss some cases and studies that may give us some clues about resolving the legal problems.

Intellectual property rights

A number of legal issues are associated with the intellectual property rights of digital information. The various issues are (Petersen, 1999):

- questions related to whether or not a digital document is in the public domain
- how to secure permission or obtain a licence to use a particular source
- how to determine the legal owner of a piece of digital information
- how to exercise a statutory exception, for example 'fair use', which allows users to copy and use portions of documents for use in non-profit making activities, such as for academic and research purposes.

A number of researchers discuss several legal issues in the digital world. Oppenheim (1997) argues that 'fair dealing', which is a defence against a copyright infringement action and which was designed specifically for the printed world, is very much applicable to electronic data as far as UK law is concerned. Many digital libraries create hyperlinks among various digital information resources, including e-journals. Oppenheim (1997) cautions that one should be very careful in creating such links as they may involve questions of copyright and moral rights. A very general guideline for digital libraries is that there should be a strategy for copyright clearance for any third-party material; this process always takes more time and money than one would expect (Oppenheim, 1997). Ang (2001) examines legal issues in relation to the digitization of media, particularly the nature of digitization and its implications for copyright and libraries.

The development of an effective electronic copyright management systems (ECMSs) can pose many problems (Ramsden, 1997):

- A complex system requiring registration and passwords, linked to pay-per-use charging mechanisms, may deter use; however, increasing user training and awareness may improve the situation.

- A considerable overhead may be involved in implementing an ECMS, and hence digital libraries should be careful in selecting materials to come under it.
- A system may track and report to libraries and copyright owners on an individual user's reading and printing habits. There has to be a mechanism to store and use this information while ensuring that each individual user's identity remains anonymous.

There are several other factors that fuel the current debate and efforts to establish new policies, for example how to exercise control over the intellectual property developed by the faculty of a university that offers distance education. Many research projects are now aiming to provide resources and assistance to anyone who seeks to understand the issues, and corresponding policy alternatives for establishing copyright in the digital world. One such effort is a research project conducted by the University of Maryland and the Association of Research Libraries (ARL). The results of this ongoing research, including links to a number of university policies and associated resources, are available on a website called copyown[sm] (www.umd.edu/copyown)). The Computer Science and Telecommunications Board (CSTB) of the US National Academies appointed a committee in late 1997 to study the impacts of the emerging digital information infrastructure on intellectual property rights originating in the US Constitution. In November 1999, the committee released its report entitled *The digital dilemma: intellectual property in the information age* on the web. The report made several recommendations, some of which have been discussed by Gladney (1999) as follows:

- In contrast with the printed world, works published in digital form are not necessarily public, irrevocable or fixed. Therefore although the tradition of providing limited access to published materials established for physical materials must be continued in the digital context, the mechanisms for the access and the definition of 'limited' will need to evolve in the context of the digital world.
- The distinction between publication and private distribution is blurred in the digital world; hence the concept of 'publication' needs to be re-evaluated.
- The increasing use of 'licence to use' rather than 'owning' information may have a positive as well as negative impact on public access to information.

It is therefore necessary that representatives from government, rights holders, publishers, libraries and other cultural heritage institutions, the public and technology providers engage themselves in developing models for improved public access to information that are acceptable to all the stakeholders.

- There is a widespread and incorrect belief that copying for private use is almost always lawful. This calls for increased public awareness about the legal, ethical and economic implications of private copying. There should be widespread public education explaining why people should respect copyright and how it is beneficial for society as a whole.
- Fair use and other exceptions to copyright should continue to play a role in the digital environment though the appropriate scope of fair use may be reduced by the development of new licensing regimes.
- Research should be conducted to assess the economic impacts of copyright. Such research might consider the impact of networks on information industries and should assess the social and economic impacts of illegal commercial copying and how they interact with those of copying for personal use.
- Digital repositories pose difficult questions about authorship, ownership and the boundaries between protected works. Hence research should be undertaken on the status of temporary reproductions and derivative work rights to inform the process of adapting copyright law to the digital environment. This would assist policy makers and judges in their deliberations.

HERON (Higher Education Resource ON-demand), a Phase 3 eLib project, among other things looked into the copyright issues related to digital library services. The project began in August 1998 with the following major goals (*HERON*, n.d.):

- to develop a national database and resource bank of electronic texts in order to widen access to course materials throughout higher education in the UK
- to collaborate with copyright holders and representative bodies to remove blockages in copyright clearance and to determine appropriate fee levels and conditions for the digital age
- to offer opportunities to universities and colleges to market their own learning resources.

The HERON test service began in June 1999, with five universities actively participating. By the end of July 2000, membership had increased to 17 universities, and by the start of the academic year 2001/2002, HERON had over 40 members. HERON provides access to electronic course materials in a wide range of subjects such as literature, popular music, business studies, nursing and medicine, sociology and politics. Although HERON's remit is specifically related to the provision of digitized material, it can provide copyright clearance for paper course packs as well. HERON services will be made available by Ingenta in the future.

The ACORN (Access to Course Reading via Networks) project (August 1996 to June 1998) was based at Loughborough University's Pilkington Library, which provided the project's management and co-ordination. It explored the potential of ICT to deliver high demand materials to students via networks across the campus. This project looked at several issues including digitization and copyright clearance.

Authenticity

While intellectual property rights form the central part of the legal issues for digital libraries, there are other considerations too. Digital information is easy to manipulate and even forge. Ensuring the authenticity of digital information is often a major challenge.

Concern about authenticity in sources is an integral part of scholarly studies and research. By authenticity of digital information we mean (1) that it is unaltered from the original, (2) that it is what it purports to be, and (3) that its representation is transparent – the rules are stated (Bearman and Trant, 1998). Traditionally, when scholars encountered original sources – artefacts, documents or works of art – many physical clues assisted scholars in establishing their authenticity. If sources are studied in the surrogate such as in photographs, microfilm or other reprographic forms, questions concerning the authenticity of the original are overlaid with questions about the methods of representation. With the ubiquity of digital representations and the proliferation of source information on the internet, these issues are further complicated (Bearman and Trant, 1998).

Forgeries and fakes are not new, but they are much more easily made in the digital world. Forging printed documents, including painting and artworks, is very time consuming and complex because of the technical barriers, such as the need for the appropriate printing machinery, the ink or the paint, the materials, and so on. The other main problem is the difficulty of making the forged items enter into the authoritative information stream. These problems can be easily overcome in the digital world. Not only can digital information be altered relatively simply, but multiple copies of digital works can be produced and distributed very easily.

Ensuring the authenticity of digital information sources is a complex and resource-intensive process. Three distinct technical and social strategies for asserting authenticity can be identified (Bearman and Trant, 1998):

- *Public methods for asserting authenticity of sources*:
    — the creation of copyright deposit 'collections of record'
    — certified deposits of original sources combined with record certification services
    — the registration of unique document identifiers
    — the publication of 'key' data about documents which, when hashed, or otherwise calculated in a publicly available way, should match that of the document in hand
    — defining metadata structures to carry document authentication declarations or proofs.
- *Secret methods of asserting authenticity of sources*:
    — digital watermarking
    — stegonography
    — digital signatures.
- *Functionally dependent methods of asserting authenticity of sources*:
    — object encapsulation (whether physical or logical)
    — cryptolopes
    — encryption
    — embedded active agents.

Watermarking and digital signature are the common technologies used to ensure authenticity. Watermarking provides a mechanism to mark all copies of a data object with the owner's mark to assert ownership and copyright properties. Digital signature is a mechanism employed in public-key cryptosystems (PKCS) which enables the originator of an information object to generate a signature, by encipherment (using a private key) of a compressed string derived from the object. This technology can provide a recipient with proof of the authenticity of the object's originator. While these technologies do not provide foolproof protection, they make forgery more difficult.

A series of articles in the Safeguarding Series in *D-Lib Magazine* and a host of other articles discuss the technology and various issues of authenticity, access control and management, and so on. Gladney (1997, 1998), Gladney and Lotspiech (1997), and Gladney, Mintzer and Schiattarella (1997) discuss various issues of authenticity, rights protection and privacy of digital information along with giving reviews of the available technologies. Mintzer, Braudaway and Bell (1998) and Mintzer, Lotspiech and Morimoto (1997) discuss digital watermarking technology in the context of digital libraries. Since its inception in 1988, the Case Western Reserve University (CWRU) digital library project has pursued research in the area of intellectual property (IP) management (Alrashid et al., 1998). In the course of the project several IP management system architecture alternatives were developed and evaluated. After considering various options, the research team selected an end-to-end content management approach based on the client–server model for the rights management system (RMS) development efforts (Alrashid et al., 1998). Herzberg (1998) reports on charging mechanisms, especially micropayments – charging for small amounts. The work on which he reports, carried out at the IBM research laboratory, considered two credit-card-charging mechanisms using the most common protocol – the SSL protocol – and the SET standard for charge card payments, and recommended the MiniPay micropayment mechanism – a payment mechanism developed by IBM – for charging small amounts 'per click'.

InterPARES (International Research on Permanent Authentic Records in Electronic Systems) is a multidisciplinary collaborative archival research project organized into national, multinational and industry-based research teams and is based in the School of Library, Archival and Information Studies at the University of British Columbia. There are research teams in Canada, the USA, Italy, Northern Europe (France, Ireland, the Netherlands, Sweden and the UK), Australia and Asia (China and Hong Kong), as well as a global industry group that includes CENSA (the Collaborative Electronic Notebook Systems Association) (*InterPARES*, n.d.). The theoretical underpinning of InterPARES is based on contemporary archival diplomatics, a technique first developed in Europe in the 18th century as an analytical approach to the identification of the authenticity of medieval ecclesiastical documents. The technique studies the genesis, forms and transmission of archival documents, their relation to the facts represented in them, and their relation to their creator, in order to evaluate and communicate their true nature (Gilliland-Swetland and Eppard, 2000). The

InterPARES project has developed a template that allows for the analysis of authenticity, working on the hypothesis that all records have certain necessary and certain sufficient elements. The template is a model of an ideal record that, based upon prior archival knowledge of record types, contains all the possible known elements that a record may contain. It provides indicators that might allow archivists to identify when and how specific types of records have changed or are being re-invented, or where totally new forms are emerging (Gilliland-Swetland and Eppard, 2000). The Social Sciences and Humanities Research Council of Canada (SSHRC) has granted funding for a second phase of the InterPARES Project. InterPARES 2: Experiential, Interactive and Dynamic Records began on 1 January 2002 and will continue until 31 December 2006.

Privacy and security

Privacy and security are the two other legal issues related to digital libraries. Since one of the objectives of a digital library is to build a mechanism to facilitate the creation as well as the use of digital information resources online by anyone from anywhere, the issue of the security of the information becomes a major challenge. Digital library managers need to decide which user should have access to what digital information and how access can be secured. Many digital library services, especially the digital current awareness services and digital reference services, and the user-centred or task-based digital library interfaces, may need to store information about users and also to keep track of their usage patterns. While such information is collected and stored for the purpose of providing improved services, this may often encroach on the privacy of users. Users may not like others to know about the kind of information sources they use or about the track they follow to find and use information. Again there are no specific regulations that one can follow in this respect, and this may create problems for library managers as well as for the users.

Digital technologies can very easily keep track of users and their usage patterns. Sturges, Teng and Iliffe (2001) comment that internet use at public terminals in libraries is vulnerable to intrusion. Anyone who has used the Amazon.com service for purchasing books will know how easily a user's personal information, and even the user's browsing patterns for locating new books, CDs, etc., is captured by the system, and is used later. In this case, the information is used for providing services to the user, for example for automatically identifying them, for providing recommended titles, and so on, but this is nevertheless an example of how, if desired, users' personal information and information use patterns, can be gathered and used secretly. Bonita Wilson, managing editor of *D-Lib Magazine* comments that, unfortunately, there does not yet seem to be a 'legal, moral and cultural agreement' regarding online personal information, and 'Until and unless privacy legislation and the associated culture catch up with technology, the term "Internet privacy" may remain an oxymoron' (B. Wilson, 2001).

Safeguarding the economic, quality and confidentiality interests of copyright holders and end-users is an essential digital library service (Gladney and Lotspiech, 1997). The Legal and Policy Research Group at Loughborough University's Department of Information Science is working on a substantial investigation, funded by Resource: the Council for Museums, Archives and Libraries; www.resource.gov.uk/), into the issue of user privacy in the digital library environment. Guidelines on privacy matters for information professionals are being developed on the basis of the investigation (Sturges, Teng and Iliffe, 2001).

Legal deposit

One of the major difficulties of the digital world, compared with the printed information world, is that there is no legal deposit law to force the creators of digital information to submit a copy of every work to one or more designated institutions. The aim of legal deposit is to ensure the preservation of and access to a nation's intellectual and cultural heritage over time (Muir, 2001b). US law does not at present include any requirement for the deposit of works that exist solely in the form of web pages, and this may be the case with most countries in the world. In the absence of such a law, nations and national libraries may in future find themselves missing a significant and unrecoverable portion of their cultural heritage (Seadle, 2001).

Summary

The design, development and management of effective and efficient digital libraries involve a number of social issues. First, there are the broad social and economic factors that have created an inequality in access to the internet and digital libraries. Many countries do not have an infrastructure adequate to support the development of digital libraries. This, coupled with lack of staff resources and economic issues, especially financial crises, force many countries to stay away from digital library research and development activities. However, the picture is not all gloomy. As discussed above, many recent developments, broadly in the context of digital library services, make it easy for library and information professionals to provide some digital library services to their users almost without cost. There are also wider economic issues related to digital libraries that have an impact on the publishing industry and its various stakeholders, such as distributors and aggregates. New economic models are now being developed to support the businesses of publishers and libraries, while at the same time protecting the interests of the creators and users of information. The netLibrary model, discussed earlier in this book (Chapter 5), is a typical example.

Many legal issues are associated with the development and use of digital libraries. Intellectual property rights are a major concern; others are the authenticity of information sources, and privacy and security of users and institutions. Researchers have studied these areas and, again, produced supportive models.

Many people suggest that legal deposit laws should be extended to digital information resources in order to maintain comprehensive collections of the national intellectual output. However, there are some problems with this proposal. Muir (2001b) comments that including digital publications in legal deposit regulations is not enough to ensure the long-term preservation of these publications because at the moment mechanisms for identifying, selecting and depositing digital material either do not exist or are inappropriate for some kinds of digital publications. Fortunately a great deal of work is now underway and national and other deposit libraries, often in partnership with other libraries, publishers and technology vendors, are at the forefront of research and development in this area.

Chapter 13
Digital library evaluation

Outline

Digital libraries are designed and developed to provide better information accessibility and services to users. Evaluation studies of digital libraries aim to assess how far they meet their stated objectives, and provide insights for further improvements. However, the evaluation of digital libraries is a complex task because several factors are involved, and standard and best practice guidelines are not yet available. This chapter outlines some of the issues related to the evaluation of digital libraries and gives a set of guidelines on how to evaluate them. Some evaluation studies are also discussed briefly, and references are given so the interested reader may find out more. Overall this chapter will help readers understand the issues and complexities of digital library evaluation.

Introduction

An evaluation is basically a judgement of worth. We evaluate a system in order to ascertain the level of its performance or its value (Chowdhury, 1999, 200). Although there have been tremendous technological developments over the last two decades, information systems continue to be difficult to learn and use for the lay person. Special training is required and special skills need to be acquired to be able to use information systems effectively.

As discussed in Chapters 2 and 3, a tremendous amount of resources and research effort has gone into the research and development of digital libraries. However, as Saracevic (2000) comments, evaluation has not so far been a part of the digital library research efforts. One of the major reasons for this is perhaps the fact that digital libraries are still at the experimental stage, and it may be premature to evaluate them. The other impediments for digital library evaluation are that we hardly know what and how to evaluate.

Digital libraries have been defined differently by researchers (see Chapter 1); they are designed and developed with the specializations of people from a number of fields, such as computer science, engineering and information science, and they involve a host of social, economic, legal and management issues. Thus defining the standards and parameters for evaluation is a very complex task. Nevertheless, researchers have proposed a number of guidelines and criteria, some of which are discussed in this chapter. Some evaluation studies focusing on digital libraries have also been discussed briefly.

Evaluation: the basic problems

Saracevic (2000) has identified the following possible reasons for there having been comparatively little research on digital library evaluation:

- Digital libraries are still at the stage of evolution, evaluation at this stage may be a bit premature and even dangerous.
- At this early stage of digital library development, informal and anecdotal ways of evaluation may be sufficient.
- Evaluation at a very basic technical level – to provide that an electronic collection is accessible – may be sufficient.
- The outcome of the performance measures of digital libraries at the early stage of development may not be very encouraging; such studies may discourage the funding bodies, which in turn slows down the pace of digital library research.

The best practice standards for digital library evaluation against which the performance levels are to be measured are yet to develop (Saracevic, 2000). In fact, establishing generalizable benchmarks for the usability of digital libraries remains problematic owing to the variety of applications and the diversity of user communities served. Usability is a relative concept, and must be judged on the basis of a digital library's intended goals. According to Greenstein (2000), one of the defining characteristics of digital libraries is that they facilitate access to collections that they do not own; because of this they should be evaluated on how best they disclose, provide access to and support the use of their virtual collections. Greenstein (2000, 294) emphasizes the need for benchmarking standards for evaluation and reminds us that 'digital libraries operate in a networked environment where they are both consumers and suppliers of digital collections and services'.

Seadle (2000) suggests that the people involved in a digital library project must be understood before the digital library itself can be assessed. He argues that anthropology can provide the initial understanding and intellectual basis for choosing the design methodology and criteria. According to Seadle, most people are blends of micro-cultures, which he defines as units of meaning as small as professions, departments and interest groups. Drawing examples from the National Gallery of the Spoken World (NGSW) project (a DLI 2 project), Seadle (2000, 384) shows that a given digital library project may consist of several micro-cultures and a useful evaluation of services needs to include 'an understanding of the nuances of the meaning and connotation, implementation and limitation, for a wide range of vocabulary across the many micro-cultures involved'. He further argues that 'the precursor to developing a survey instrument, or selecting a survey population, or choosing the members of a focus group should involve an analysis of the project itself' (p.384). Marchionini (2000) advocates that the ultimate goal of digital library evaluation is to assess the impact of digital libraries on their patrons' lives and the larger social milieu. He defines evaluation as 'a research process that aims to understand the meaning of some phenomenon situated in a context and the changes that take place as the phenomenon and the context interact' (p.311).

What to evaluate?

A digital library may be evaluated from a number of perspectives, such as system, access and usability, user interfaces, information retrieval, content and domain, services, cost, and the overall benefits and impact. Marchionini (2000) comments that evaluating digital libraries is a bit like judging the success of a marriage where much depends on how successful the partners are as individuals as well as the emergent conditions made possible by the union.

Saracevic (2000) provides a long list of elements for the evaluation of digital libraries, and suggests that an evaluation project may select from these, clearly indicating what is included, and what is excluded, in the evaluation project. The list of elements for evaluation includes the following:

- digital collections, resources
- selection, gathering, holdings, media
- distribution, collections, links
- organization, structure, storage
- interpretation, representation, metadata

- management
- preservation, persistence
- access
- physical networks
- distribution
- interfaces, interaction
- search, retrieval
- services
- availability
- range of available services, e.g. dissemination delivery
- assistance, referral
- use, users, communities
- security, privacy, policies, legal aspects, licences
- management, operations, staff
- costs, economics
- integration, co-operation with other resources, libraries or services.

Digital libraries are bringing a paradigm shift in the ways we ask for, use and create information, and as a result have different kinds of impact on different individuals, institutions and society. Borgman (2000b, 122–3) comments that the relationship between the content to be provided and the user community to be served forms the central question of effective digital library design. She further argues that the usability of digital libraries may be influenced by a number of characteristics of users, such as 'computer skills, domain knowledge, familiarity with the system, technical aptitudes and personality characteristics' (Borgman, 2000b, 126).

Saracevic (2000) proposes seven general classes or levels of evaluation, three of which are user centred and three system centred, while the seventh is an interface between. The user-centred levels of evaluation are:

- *Social level*. At this level the major objective of an evaluation might be to assess how well a digital library supports the needs, roles and practices of a society or a community.
- *Institutional level*. At this level the objective might be to assess how well a digital library supports its parent organization's mission and objectives.

- *Individual level.* At this level the objective of an evaluation might be to assess how well a digital library supports the information needs, tasks and activities of people as individual users or small groups.

The interface level that is in between the user- and system-centred levels of evaluation aims to assess how well a digital library interface provides and supports access, searching, navigation, browsing and interactions with the library.

The three levels of system-centred evaluation of digital libraries include the following:

- *Engineering level*: how well the hardware, networks and related technologies work.
- *Processing level*: how well the various procedures, techniques, algorithms, operations, etc., perform.
- *Content level*: how well the information resources are selected, represented, organized, structured and managed.

It may be noted that while evaluation measures at the system-centred levels are likely to produce more quantitative and generalizable data, user-centred evaluation results will be both quantitative and qualitative and will depend on a number of social and cognitive factors. Moreover, the different levels of evaluation identified here are not mutually exclusive, and indeed in many cases the results of the evaluation of one level may need to be looked at in the context of the results from another level of evaluation. Nevertheless, digital library evaluation should be based on both the user- and the system-centred approaches, and the challenge is how to make both approaches work together.

Evaluation stages

An evaluative project usually involves the following five stages (HyLife, 2002c):

- design of the evaluation
- drawing up an evaluation plan
- data gathering and recording
- data analysis and interpretation of results
- presentation of findings.

Each of these stages involves a number of tasks, which may be complex depending on what is being evaluated, the objectives, methodology, and so on.

Evaluation criteria

Simply speaking, digital libraries can be judged by their effectiveness in retrieving relevant results, and by the time, effort and cost required to achieve those results. Factors used to measure the performance of physical libraries such as circulation, collection size and growth, patron visits, reference questions handled, user satisfaction and financial stability, may be equally useful for evaluating digital libraries. At the same time, factors used to assess information and communication technologies, such as storage capacity, accessibility, response rate and cost per transaction, are also useful. In addition, it is also necessary to measure the overall impact of digital libraries on users and society.

Criteria for the evaluation of libraries and information systems, information retrieval systems and user interfaces have been discussed in the literature. Lancaster's seminal work (1993) provides a detailed list of evaluation criteria for libraries and Saracevic and Kantor (1997a, 1997b) provide a number of evaluation criteria for library and information systems. Several publications discuss evaluation criteria for information retrieval systems (for example, Baeza-Yates and Ribeiro-Neto, 1999, Chapter 3; Chowdhury, 1999, Chapter 10; Harter and Hert, 1997; Voorhees, 2002). Evaluation criteria for user interfaces have been discussed by Marchionini (1992), Marchionini and Komlodi (1998) and Shneiderman (1998b).

Usability testing is an often-studied evaluation method that focuses on the effects obtained when individuals use an information system to accomplish tasks. The factors used in usability testing include time to completion, accuracy, satisfaction and number of errors (Marchionini, 2000). In addition to information retrieval and usability, system-related factors, such as hardware, software and networking issues, data formats, access and transfer time, mean time between failures and development and maintenance costs are also used in evaluating information systems. Dillon (1999) proposes an evaluation methodology called TIME that offers a framework to address key human factors in digital library design. In Dillon's words (1999, 173), 'TIME is a qualitative framework and is proposed for use as an advanced organizer for design, as a guide for expert usability evaluation, and as a means of generating scientific conjectures about the usability of any electronic text.' The framework identifies four key factors for consideration:

- T: a Task that reflects the reader's needs and uses for the material
- I: an Information model that consists of the user's mental representation of the information space
- M: the Manipulation facilities that support physical use of the materials
- E: the Ergonomic variables influencing the perceptual processing of words and images.

The EQUINOX evaluation criteria

A set of criteria for measuring the performance of digital libraries was developed under EQUINOX, a two-year project (27 November 1998–26 November 2000) funded under the Telematics for Libraries Programme of the European Commission. EQUINOX was designed to address the need of all libraries to develop and use methods for measuring performance in the new networked, electronic environment, alongside traditional performance measurement. The project had two main objectives: (1) to further develop existing international agreement on performance measures for libraries, by expanding these to include performance measures for the electronic library environment, and (2) to develop and test an integrated quality management and performance measurement tool for library managers. The project identified the following list of performance indicators for digital libraries (Brophy et al., 2000):

- percentage of the population reached by electronic library services
- number of sessions on each electronic library service per member of the target population
- number of remote sessions on electronic library services per member of the population to be served
- number of documents and entries (records) viewed per session for each electronic library service
- cost per session for each electronic library service
- cost per document or entry (record) viewed for each electronic library service
- percentage of information requests submitted electronically
- library computer workstation use rate
- number of library computer workstation hours available per member of the population to be served
- rejected sessions as a percentage of total attempted sessions
- percentage of total acquisitions expenditure spent on acquisition of electronic library services

- number of attendances at formal electronic library service training lessons per member of the population to be served
- number of library staff developing, managing and providing electronic library service and user training as a percentage of total library staff
- user satisfaction with electronic library services.

Saracevic's evaluation criteria

While the EQUINOX project identified general performance indicators, Saracevic (2000) provides a list of specific criteria for evaluation of digital libraries that are divided into three sets:

- traditional library criteria:
  — collection: purpose, subject, scope, coverage, authority, currency, audience, cost, format, treatment, preservation and persistence
  — information: accuracy, appropriateness, links, representation, uniqueness, compatibility, presentation, timeliness and ownership
  — use: accessibility, availability, searchability and usability
  — standards.
- traditional IR criteria:
  — relevance (recall, precision, etc.)
  — satisfaction
  — index, search, and output features
- traditional user interface criteria:
  — usability, functionality, effort
  — task appropriateness, failures
  — connectivity, reliability
  — design features
  — navigation, browsing
  — services, help.

The above list, though reasonably exhaustive, does not include criteria for measuring the overall impact of digital libraries on society. As Marchionini (2000) comments, assessing the impacts of digital libraries on the lives of patrons and the larger social milieu are the ultimate goals of digital library evaluation. While the general criteria for such measures have yet to be developed, some research projects (discussed below) have attempted to measure them.

Evaluation studies

Although not very many fully fledged evaluation studies of digital libraries have been reported, a few researchers have conducted evaluation studies to determine the design requirements, usability and overall impact of digital libraries on a specific set of users. These studies discuss the findings, methodologies and potential pitfalls of digital library evaluation. Some such studies are discussed briefly in the following sections.

Perseus

Perseus is one of the earliest digital libraries, having originated as an idea in 1985, and comprises a large hypertext collection of materials on the ancient Greek world. Evaluation has been an integral part of the project's development. The evaluation primarily focuses on educational evaluation – how electronic resources influence the educational context.

As early as 1987 Mylonas (1987) conducted a survey among 20 humanities professors to assess how Perseus might be used for instruction. The results of this survey suggested that it could be used both for reference and as a source for primary materials. Over the years, the Perseus digital library and related evaluation efforts have evolved guided by the central objective of understanding the effects of providing broad access to digital information in the humanities (Marchionini, 2000). The three high-level goals of Perseus were access to large volumes of multimedia information, freedom of self-directed access and use, and collaboration among learners and teachers. Four classes of evaluation objects were defined: learners, teachers, the technical system and the content. Five different types of observation process and interviews were used for data collection (Marchionini, 2000). Evaluation findings were summarized in four categories: amplification and augmentation of learning, physical infrastructure, conceptual infrastructure and systemic change to the field. Marchionini (2000) comments that such an ongoing evaluation serves many purposes, for example, to:

- produce valuable data and reports that may be used in making development and funding decisions
- inform the ongoing growth and development of the digital library
- involve staff and users in the work of the digital library, which may eventually improve use and support
- help the researchers or digital library managers explain the effects of the specific digital library and relate it the broader issues of digital library evolution.

Yang (2001) reports on another evaluation of Perseus using an interpretative and situated approach. The evaluation has identified the following interesting points that may help the designers develop the system in future:

- The Perseus Digital Library should at the same time acknowledge and satisfy experienced users while scaffolding learning in new areas.
- The design of the Perseus Digital Library should be integrated into the academic and classroom settings taking into account pedagogical and cultural issues.

ADEPT

An evaluation study within the Alexandria Digital Library project involved a series of user studies involving different user communities and concentrating on different design features as related to their usability and functionality (Hill et al., 2000). The results of this evaluation study helped the researchers specify a list of requirements for the new user interface for the Alexandria Digital Library.

Borgman et al. (2000) report an overview of the evaluation project related to the development and deployment of ADEPT (Alexandria Digital Earth Prototype), a DLI 2 project. ADEPT is an extension and enhancement of the Alexandria Digital Library. Its goal is to build a digital library that will make geospatial and georeferenced information resources useful in undergraduate instruction, leading to better learning outcomes than those achieved with the traditional modes of instruction. The evaluation study aimed to address a number of questions, such as:

- How can ADEPT modules support domain knowledge, work practices and reasoning models on multiple disciplines that use geospatial information?
- How can it accommodate users with different knowledge levels, skills, cognitive abilities and pedagogical styles?
- How can it help users view primary geographical evidence in answering science- or geography-related questions?
- How can it support the range of heterogeneous resources and their metadata necessary for learning applications?

The initial observations of the evaluation study suggest that digital libraries hold great potential for teaching and learning at the undergraduate level. However, it was noted that matching the content and capabilities of I-scapes (information landscapes, which are defined in the context of ADEPT as a means of expressing and visualizing geospatial concepts and processes for research, instruction and learning) to the range of instructors' approaches to teaching the same topic will be a major challenge (Borgman et al., 2000).

Tracking Footprints in a Medical Information Space

Gorman et al. (2000) report on an evaluation study that focuses on the information-seeking patterns of users in a digital library environment. They describe their observations based on the DLI 2 project Tracking Footprints in a Medical Information Space: Computer Scientists–Physician Collaborative Study of Expert Problem Solvers. This project is conducted by two teams – an observation team that aims to describe the information behaviour of expert clinicians, and a computer science team whose job is to investigate the application of information technology to help experts use information in the complex digital information spaces. This research suggests that experts create and use bundles – organized and highly selective collections of information – for solving problems. Gorman et al. (2000, 287) conclude that 'in the age of digital libraries computer-based tools for creating and managing bundles may be needed as the information in these settings is increasingly represented in digital collections which promise to be much larger, more complex, more diverse, and more difficult to explore and manipulate'.

The Internet Public Library

Peters (2000) comments that the provision and evaluation of public services, such as reference services, has received little attention over the first decade of digital library research. He suggests that for evaluation of online reference services it may be useful to concentrate on 'meta assessment', which he defines as the deliberate examination of the elements, basic conditions and needs of a thing – service, event, system, and so on – that transcend particular instantiations of that thing. He comments that we need to assess several variable components of online reference services, and that a combination of controlled-environment and real-life research projects will be needed.

Carter and Janes (2000) comment that providing a quality reference service without the involvement of human intermediaries is one of the greatest challenges of digital libraries. They report a study that analysed the log of over 3000 reference questions asked of the Internet Public Library (IPL), one of the most widely used reference services on the web. This study has identified different categories of reference questions, such as common questions, quick questions, regular questions and unanswered questions, which were handled by IPL. The findings of this research suggest that by carefully designing the question intake form, it is possible to explore a number of issues, such as user satisfaction, librarians' attitudes, performance level over a period of time, and comparisons with other online reference services.

DeLIver

Bishop (1998, 1999) reports on a user study on DeLIver – a testbed collection of journal articles across the University of Illinois campus – as part of the DLI 1 project at the University of Illinois. Bishop's findings corroborate the observations of the ELVYN project on the ease of use of digital information, which says that 'it is critical that barriers to use are minimal: if there is too much in the way of logging on, passwords, etc., people will not be bothered' (Rowland, McKnight and Meadows 1995, 89). In fact, Bishop's study (1998) noted that authentication and registration procedures presented an enormous and unexpected barrier to the use of DeLIver. The findings of this study have implications for user education and digital library system design (Bishop, 1999).

eVALUEd (www.cie.uce.ac.uk/evalued/)

eVALUEd is a project based at the University of Central England funded by the Higher Education Funding Council. It started in September 2001 and will run until February 2004. The project is expected to produce practical initiatives such as (Hartland-Fox and Dalton, 2002):

- a transferable model for the evaluation of digital library initiatives
- training workshops in aspects of evaluation (aimed at library managers in the higher education sector)
- a website for project dissemination and resource publication
- a final project report outlining the model of evaluation and other aspects of good practice in digital library evaluation.

HeadLine

HeadLine (Hybrid Electronic Access and Delivery in the Library Networked Environment) was one of the hybrid library projects funded under Phase 3 of the eLib programme. This three-year project began in January 1998 and its aims were to design and implement a working model of the hybrid library, specifically:

- a working model to provide consistent access to library materials regardless of physical form, transferable across broad subject disciplines and a range of different higher education environments
- a user-dependent dynamic web environment within which to manage individual access to the resource base
- mechanisms for incorporating user feedback and evaluation into the design, content and delivery of the service
- exploration of licensing and copyright issues involved in providing access to the broad range of hybrid library materials.

Throughout the course of the project, evaluation studies were conducted in order to assist with project design (Gambles, 2000, 2001). Phase 1 of the evaluation included a questionnaire survey that sought opinions from student users within the partner institutions. The majority of respondents (79%) were undergraduate students, while 11% were Masters students, 5% were academics and 5% were administrators. The project team was disappointed with the low rate of use of the PIE (personal information environment), but some important observations were made through the survey. For example, it was noted that:

- the demand for access to library resources from off-campus locations was strong
- personalized library portals, such as the HeadLine PIE, could help to facilitate resource access, with the ultimate aim of enabling seamless access to resources regardless of the user's location
- the PIE interface was not very easy to use by those who hadn't received training
- though the PIE was providing access to a broad range of resources, response time was low.

Phase 2 of the HeadLine evaluation included guests and more experienced users of the PIE. Guest access to the service was introduced in October 2000 and the additional feedback from the wider library community contributed to the final results. Feedback was in the form of completed online questionnaires and provided valuable information on users' experiences of the PIE. Results of the second phase of evaluation also pointed out that the response time needed improvement.

Overall, the results of the evaluation contributed towards improvements in design, content and delivery of the services. For example, it was noted that users would like to search for information with minimum distraction and inconvenience. In other words, the evaluation suggested that there was a need for more intuitive navigation and interface design, for the provision of holdings information within the search results and for document request facilities (Noble, 2001).

Agora case studies

Agora is one of the five hybrid library projects that began in January 1998 as part of the third phase of the eLib programme. It is a consortium-based project, led by the University of East Anglia; partners are UKOLN, Fretwell Downing Informatics and CERLIM (the Centre for Research in Library and Information Management). The evaluation study of Agora covered four major issues: the creation and use of information landscapes, the utility of collection-level descriptions as resource metadata, user reaction to, and use of, cross-domain searching, and the use of interlending as a document delivery mechanism within the system. The evaluation, conducted as case studies, produced a number of findings that are useful for digital library design. They include the following (Palmer and Robinson, 2001):

- Users approach their information requirements from a range of different perspectives, expectations and experiences, and the success of any future hybrid library management system (HLMS) system will depend on it being made understandable across the range of user types and user experiences.
- One way to manage this variety of users and expectations is by setting up a range of pre-defined interfaces offering different iterations of the HLMS specific to the needs of different groups. It was envisaged that this would help to simplify the perceived complexity of landscapes by offering simple default landscapes for the more naive user and the full power of the functionality for the more expert.
- Users clearly identified additional resources, such as internet search engines and commercial booksellers, that they would like to see incorporated in any future iteration of the hybrid library.

The KISTI ETD system

The Korea Institute of Science and Technology Information (KISTI) has been developing a digital library for ETDs (electronic theses and dissertations) since 1998, and as of early September 2001 the KISTI ETD collection had 23,368

ETDs with a wide range of subject areas from nine major participating universities in South Korea (Zhang, Lee and You, 2001; Zhang and Lee, 2001).

KISTI ETD project staff have kept a record of transaction logs which were analysed to find answers to the following questions:

- What is the pattern of usage volume over the period of two years?
- How frequently do users visit the KISTI ETD website?
- What are the characteristics of users' visits?
- What is the composition of users based on their geographic locations by country?
- What is the composition of organizations with which the users are affiliated?
- How are some of the system features used?

This study indicated that the majority of ETD users were from Korea and were affiliated with educational institutions. The variations in usage volume of the system echoed the academic calendar in South Korean universities. It was also noted that a very large number of users visited the site only once. Nevertheless, the system began to maintain a frequent user group in its second year in service, though the researchers felt that further study would be necessary to investigate why visitors left the system and how the system could be improved to keep visitors coming back.

The evaluation results have significant implications for the design of the ETD system. For example, it was noted that the search function was by far the most frequently used system function, and displaying bibliographic records was the second most frequently requested. The results revealed that the two unique features of the KISTI ETD system – displaying individual pages and tables of contents – proved to be very useful and effective in assisting users in selecting ETDs.

The VHI project

The Virginia Historical Inventory (VHI) project is a digital library of photographs, maps and detailed reports documenting the architectural, cultural and family histories of thousands of the 18th- and 19th-century buildings in communities across Virginia. A unique model for cost–benefit analyses of digital libraries based on the VHI project has been provided by Byrd et al. (2001). The evaluation study suggests that although the initial costs of digitization of images and texts and associated activities can be very high, the unit costs per use decreases drastically over time. The total cost of the VHI project was US$612,043.80, and an extensive unit cost analysis study suggests that the unit cost for the first-time transaction (first-time use after development including one four-page survey report, one photograph and one map) was US$415.14. This is indeed a high amount for a single transaction. However, the project team conducted a comparative study with the transaction data over a three-month period (consisting of 11,766 search transactions), and it was noted that the unit cost dropped from US$414.14 to US$0.035 per transaction. It was also estimated that through the digital library programme, the Library of Virginia was 'likely to save $244,321.00 over the cost to provide the materials to the on-site patron, and $327,833.00 over the cost to provide materials to the surface-mail patron' for 11,766 search transactions over the three months (Byrd et al., 2001).

Usability Study of ACM, IEEE-CS, NCSTRL and NDLTD

Kengeri et al. (1999) conducted an evaluation of the usability of four digital libraries: the ACM (Association of Computing Machinery) digital library, IEEE-CS (the Institute of Electrical and Electronic Engineers Computer Science) digital library, NCSTRL (Networked Computer Science Technical Reference Library) and NDLTD (Networked Digital Library of Theses and Dissertations). The objective of this study was to assess how the features of the digital libraries influenced the efforts of 48 chosen users to perform search and retrieval tasks. The study noted that a majority of the participants expected digital libraries to provide many of the features found in a traditional library, such as providing broad coverage of topics, easily readable online text and graphics, and full-text search. With regard to searching, varying opinions were noted: some found the search interfaces were too complex and distracting while others complained that there were not enough help facilities. Based on the observations of this evaluation, Kengeri et al. (1999) proposed a taxonomy of features that would be useful for the construction of an effective digital library. The features are:

- a clear overview
- simple and advanced search models, with clearly stated search criteria for each
- fast searching and retrieval

- example searches
- the ability to download a fraction of the article
- the ability to save queries for future refinement.

Summary

Digital libraries can be evaluated from a number of perspectives. However, since digital library research is at an early stage, and digital libraries themselves are still evolving, not many evaluation studies have taken place so far. Most evaluation studies conducted to date have focused on the usability aspects of digital libraries.

Several evaluation criteria and methodologies have been proposed by researchers. The evaluation criteria used to assess the performance of traditional libraries may also be applicable to digital libraries, alongside the criteria for the evaluation of information systems, user interfaces and information retrieval systems. The eVALUeD project discussed in this chapter is expected to build evaluation models.

There is also a variety of wider issues related to the overall impact of digital libraries on users and society. Consequently, an evaluation study has to focus on one or more specific areas for evaluation. Some evaluation measures have been applied and tested in the course of the few evaluation studies conducted so far. The variety of approaches taken in the evaluation projects discussed in this chapter shows the complexities involved in the task of evaluation. Saracevic (2000), comments that the ultimate goal for a digital library evaluation is to assess how digital libraries are transforming our education, research, learning and living. At this stage we do not have the parameters to answer these questions fully, but it is to be hoped that more digital library evaluation studies in the future will be able to produce appropriate answers.

Chapter 14
Digital libraries and the information profession

Outline

The design, development and management of digital libraries require a number of skills, and although many of the skills, tools and techniques required to manage traditional libraries are equally applicable to digital ones, they may need to be modified or sharpened to meet the requirements of the digital library world. New sets of skills, tools and techniques are also required. This chapter outlines the broad sets of skills required to design, develop and manage digital libraries.

Introduction

One of the defining characteristics of digital libraries is disintermediation: end-users are intended to interact directly with information resources and services without the direct involvement of human intermediaries. While most of the activities performed in traditional libraries take place behind the scenes, end-users come face to face with human intermediaries for reference and advisory services. 'Could we conceive of an automated digital library that disintermediates all the services that reference librarians now provide?' (Arms, 2000a). This is a very pertinent question for the future of digital libraries as well as for the library and information science profession. In fact the design, development and management of digital libraries require a range of skills and activities that are quite different from those required in traditional libraries. This does not mean that traditional library skills will no longer be required. In fact, most of them will be, perhaps with some changes, but many new skills will be required too.

In today's world, and perhaps more so in the world of the foreseeable future, we can see two different types of library services: (1) pure digital library services like NDLTD, NCSTRL, the Greenstone Digital Library and so on, where the physical library does not exist, and the information professionals deal with only digital information sources and services; and (2) hybrid library services where physical and digital libraries co-exist, and information professionals work with traditional as well as digital information sources and services. It is therefore a great challenge for the information and library studies programmes and educators to prepare the workforce to be able to deal with both types of system and service.

While best practice standards have yet to be developed, and exact job specifications for digital information professionals will emerge as digital library systems and services become more mature, some researchers have specified the changing roles and requirements of information professionals. This is the theme of this chapter. It aims to identify the basic skills required to develop and manage effective and efficient hybrid libraries.

Digital libraries: major activities and skills

Cronin (1998) comments that while the information world was once dominated by librarians whose primary concern was the management of book collections, today information workers operate in every sector of society and their charge is no longer just books, but a plethora of materials, many of which are dynamic and bibliographically unstable in character. Hastings and Tennant (1996) summarize the essential attributes of information professionals in the digital age, by saying that:

> Digital librarians must thrive on change. They should read constantly (but selectively) and experiment endlessly. They need to love learning, be able to self-teach, and be inclined to take risks. And they must have a keen sense of both the potentials and pitfalls of technology.

The design, development and management of digital library systems and services involves a number of activities calling for expertise from many different disciplines. Like printed collections, digital collections must be selected, acquired, organized, made accessible and preserved. Similarly, digital library services have to be planned, implemented and supported. While computers and the internet are the primary tools with which digital libraries are built, a variety of technological, computer and communication skills and information organization and retrieval skills are required of the people who manage them.

It is evident that past and present digital library research projects have attracted collaboration between people from many disciplines. Courses on digital libraries are now offered as part of most information and library studies programmes, and as part of some computer science programmes. However, digital and hybrid libraries involve a number of skills for their design, development, and day-to-day operations and management. Identification of these broad areas of activities may help educators and researchers identify the specific training required for producing suitable digital library professionals.

Pinfield (2001b) lists a number of skills required of a modern information professional, such as vision, professional skills, technical and IT skills, communication skills, presentation skills, negotiation skills, subject skills, project management skills, as well as a number of abilities, such as the ability to work with a variety of people, ability to work under pressure, ability to learn, and so on. These skills are required to manage any modern day library, not digital libraries in particular. Deegan and Tanner (2002b, p. 218) comment that information professionals in a digital world should be concerned mainly with resource discovery, resource provision, and resource delivery. This is not an exhaustive list of the essential skills for building and managing digital libraries. In fact, it is not easy to identify the essential skills required to manage a dynamic field like digital libraries. In the following sections, we have made an attempt to identify some essential skills that are specifically required to build and manage digital libraries. These skills may be categorized into four broad groups: ICT skills, information skills, management skills and research and project management skills.

ICT skills

Computers and the internet are the two major technologies that form the foundation of digital libraries. Hence, a basic understanding of these technologies is essential for any information professionals working in a digital library environment. However, in addition to an overall understanding of ICT, several specific skills are required for performing various digital library activities. In Chapter 6 we noted that a number of specific activities are involved in digitization, some of which are technologically quite demanding. Also, digital library professionals may often need to design web pages containing information about, and links to, various services. This requires web design skills. These skills may be required at varying levels depending on the nature of the web pages to be designed and the sophistication to be introduced. Often advanced web design skills, including the use of forms, scripting languages and interfacing with various active databases, may be required to make the web pages dynamic.

More technologically advanced information professionals may need to contribute to the architectural design of digital libraries, and to various other technologically demanding tasks involving metadata and interoperability issues, access control and management, security, and so on.

Digital libraries may also come up with novel product and service designs to be made available to the users through the digital library interfaces. The design and development of such products and services require advanced ICT skills. In some cases, digital information professionals may not actually do the design and development work themselves but would call on others, externally or internally. Nevertheless, an understanding of the required technology and skills will be useful to judge and appreciate the problems and to make optimum use of the resultant products and services.

Thus, the major ICT skills required by information professionals in a digital library environment include the following:

- digitization and document management skills
- basic networking skills
- web design and development skills
- skills for designing and evaluating digital library architecture, systems and software
- new digital library product and service design skills.

Information skills

A host of the information skills required to develop and manage traditional libraries may well be useful in a digital library environment. However, some of the traditional activities and the corresponding tools and techniques may have to be modified to suit the digital environment. Digital libraries also involve a number of new activities, tools and techniques for various operations and management purposes. Biddiscombe (2001) reports on a case study at Birmingham University that aimed to identify the ICT skills required for today's information professionals.

Chapter 5 discusses the various collection development issues and activities in a digital library environment. Digital libraries, and more typically hybrid libraries, deal with a variety of information resources – printed as well as electronic, coming from a variety of sources in a variety of formats. Information professionals need to be familiar with a whole new set of technical, financial, access and other management issues related to the development of printed as well as digital collections. While some of the digital library collections may be born digital, others may have to be digitized. Digital libraries call for a whole set of new skills to be acquired by the information professionals which range from digitization and document management (discussed in Chapter 6) to digital archiving and preservation (discussed in Chapter 10).

While the organization of traditional library resources calls for a specific set of skills with a specific set of tools and techniques (for classification, cataloguing, and so on), the organization of digital information resources require some new skills, tools and techniques. In a hybrid library environment, users are given access to the traditional library resources through OPACs, while access to the digital library sources and services is often provided through different access points in the library web pages. As discussed in Chapter 7, digital libraries often use specific tools and techniques for organizing their digital resources and services (see, for example, NDLTD and the Greenstone Digital Library in Chapter 7). Nevertheless, information professionals need to understand the basic technology and tools, including metadata and information organization using directories and subject gateways. Advanced information professionals may have sophisticated approaches to the organization of information resources using the user-centred approaches (as discussed in Chapter 7), or federated search and retrieval approaches (as discussed in Chapter 9).

Information retrieval and user interfaces are the two most prominent features of digital libraries that make them visible to the users. End-users cannot see, interact with, or measure a digital library except through its user interfaces. No matter how good the collection and organization of a digital library may be, a poor user interface or a bad information retrieval system may mar the whole project. As discussed in Chapters 8 and 9, a variety of skills are required to build good information retrieval systems and user interfaces, and a number of tools and techniques are used for the purpose. Information professionals should acquire these skills, and should be familiar with the various information retrieval tools and techniques in order to be able to build better digital libraries.

Reference and information services have long been an essential component of library services, and this will be the case in a digital library environment too. Chapter 11 discusses the current state of digital library services. This is an area that has changed significantly in a digital library environment – human interme-diaries have been replaced by e-mail or web-based reference question forms, and in many cases trained reference librarians have been replaced by subject experts. Some web-based reference services expect the end-users to find answers to their reference questions through search or browse interfaces. In any case, information professionals need to learn many new skills and techniques to be able to provide fast and efficient proactive and reactive digital information services.

Thus, the broad information skills required by information professionals in a digital library environment include the following:

- collection management skills
- information organization skills
- information retrieval skills
- digital reference and information service skills
- skills related to various types of user studies, user education, etc.
- skills for providing value-added information products and services.

Management skills

A number of management skills, including personnel and financial manage-ment, customer management and marketing, have been considered as essential for a successful library manager. While these skills are equally important in dig-ital libraries, many of them need to be modified in the context of the needs and characteristics of the digital environment. Web and digital libraries have brought significant changes in the business models of the publishing and infor-mation industry. Today there are many parallels between the publishing of printed and digital information resources and the resulting economies to be made. Many changes have also taken place in the online information industry – online search services are constantly changing their business model, while many new online services are evolving that provide free information search services with free access to the abstracts, and in some cases to the full texts. Many free online journals are being developed, and free digital library services are cropping up in areas where libraries and end-users had previously to spend a lot of money. A prominent example is NDLTD, which provides access to dig-ital theses and dissertations, a service for which end-users in the past had to pay and wait for quite some time to get the required documents.

Digital libraries need to adopt a business model where client service and sat-isfaction are the main goals, and in many cases they need to meet these goals while attaining self-sufficiency in a climate of ever more reduced budgets. This presents major challenges to information professionals, since building digital libraries, and maintaining and managing them, is a resource-intensive task, and in many cases users are not charged at the point of use. The marketing of digital information services will form a significant part of the work of digital information professionals. Other management issues and skills prevalent in the market economy, such as customer care and strategic decision making in a competitive environment, are also very useful for digital library managers.

Thus, the broad management skills required by information professionals in a digital library environment include the following:

- general management skills such as vision, leadership qualities, strategic decision-making qualities, interpersonal communication skills, etc.
- personnel and financial management skills
- marketing skills
- customer relations and management skills.

Research and project management skills

Digital libraries are still very much at the stage of evolution; there are many new areas need to be investigated and best practice standards to be developed. In addition, one of the major activities of many digital library managers in the future will be to embark on digitization projects. Other research areas for many digital libraries may centre on usability testing and evaluation. Raising funds for such projects may be a major challenge indeed, with the resultant goal of attaining improved levels of services to meet the break-even point as soon as possible. Digital library professionals thus need to acquire some research and project management skills in order to be able to undertake and successfully accomplish such projects.

Thus, the broad research skills required by information professionals in a digital library environment include the following:

- research design and management skills
- fundraising skills
- project management skills
- learning skills
- publication and reporting skills.

Summary

It is apparent from the above discussions that a great variety of skills are required for the design, development and management of digital library services. Saracevic (2002) comments that education for digital libraries has not received the same amount of attention as research, development and practical applications. He further adds that many institutions are teaching, or are beginning to teach, courses on digital libraries. In order to meet the growing demand for materials on digital library education and training, he has set up a website at Rutgers University, called D-Lib Edu, whose main purpose is to enhance the pursuit of excellence in education in digital libraries by providing a rich assortment of relevant resources accessible to all.

Websites like these can help; however, the skills necessary to run digital libraries will have to be acquired through the courses offered by library and information science programmes. At the moment most library school programmes offer an elective course on digital libraries. But a single course on digital libraries can only provide an overview of the various issues involved. Only a series of courses on digital libraries can provide a good balance of topics covering the technological, technical, management and social issues. Since most of the future information professionals will work in a digital or hybrid library environment, it is high time for library and information science schools all over the world to revise the curriculum to suit the needs of the changing profession. At the moment many of the required skills may be acquired piecemeal through parts of other courses offered by library and information science programmes. However, the best option would be to begin an entirely new programme on digital libraries that would cover all the general skills, with provision for specialization in other areas, such as the technical issues of information services – information organization and retrieval, metadata, and so on; technological issues, such as digitization and content management; policy issues, such as the legal and economic aspects of digital libraries; or more general sociological issues, such as the digital divide and social inclusion. Information professionals who are more interested in business and management applications might also concentrate on specific topics, such as the business implications of digital libraries, their role in knowledge management, and so on.

With rapid developments in information and communication technologies, especially the internet and the world wide web, end-users are becoming more demanding. In many cases, recent developments in the creation of and accessibility to digital information raise questions in the minds of end-users about the need for formal information systems and services. Furthermore, since information access is becoming more end-user oriented through use of the internet and digital libraries, the role of the information professional is becoming more vulnerable. It is high time that information managers, educators, researchers and planners concentrated on revising information science programmes in order to produce trained professionals who can shape and properly manage the world of digital libraries.

Chapter 15

Trends in digital library research and development

Outline

Research and development in digital library management is increasing. Consequently assessing the trends in such a huge and fast-growing field is a difficult task, albeit useful. In this chapter we point out the trends of research and development activity in digital library management, and identify some areas that need further attention.

Introduction

Analysing the trends of research in a huge interdisciplinary field like digital libraries is difficult. Digital library developments are taking place so fast that it may be a foolish idea to predict the future. Nevertheless, as an epilogue to this book, we have made an attempt to point out the research trends in certain areas of digital library research and development activities. In that process we have identified some areas that have not been addressed properly so far.

Digital libraries: growth and development

Thanks to the funding agencies who have poured millions of pounds into digital library research and development, and to the thousands of researchers who have spent enormous amounts of time and effort in making the dream of digital libraries a reality within a period of less than a decade, hundreds of digital libraries now exist, some small and some large. Most of today's big libraries have introduced digital library services side by side with their traditional library services, and thus may be called hybrid libraries. As a result of continued research and development activities, digital libraries in specialized areas, or dealing with specific types of information sources, like NCSTRL, NDLTD, Informedia and the Alexandria Digital Library, will grow rapidly, and many new digital libraries in niche areas will be set up. However, for the foreseeable future, the existing (traditional) libraries will continue to function as hybrid ones.

Digital library research and development activities have mainly focused on the academic and research sector, and thus, unlike the internet, have not so far been able to reach the general public. Today's digital libraries can benefit academics, researchers and the elite. Attention needs to be paid to building digital library environments that can benefit the ordinary person. Another important area that has hardly been covered by current digital library development is the provision of library and information services for users with special needs. Digital libraries have many interesting features; for example they can overcome the barriers of language and geographical distance, and even the economic disparities among users. Hence, they can be of great assistance to users with special needs. More research needs to be done in this area.

The impact of digital libraries

Digital libraries have the potential to make a tremendous impact on our everyday life. They will bring a paradigm shift in the ways we create, distribute, seek and use information, and thus will make significant impacts on the way we do our day-to-day work – study, research, jobs, problem solving, decision making, and so on. Digital libraries will also have a tremendous impact on the information industry, affecting the information generators, publishers and distributors, and information service providers. Some researchers have tried to address these problems, but detailed facts and figures have yet to be arrived at before conclusions can be drawn.

Very few studies have so far been conducted on the use and impact of digital libraries on specific sections of society. An exception is ADEPT, which aims to assess the impact of the Alexandria Digital Library on undergraduate students. However, similar studies need to be conducted in different areas to gather data on the usefulness and weaknesses of current digital libraries.

Assessing the impact of digital libraries on our day-to-day lives and activities will be a complex and resource-intensive undertaking. In addition to the technical and methodological issues involved, the classic problem of assessing the impact of information intensity – which may not be easy to measure in absolute terms – must be studied. Nevertheless, some basic parameters may be identified to assess how people use digital libraries in their everyday lives, and how information access and use have changed, compared with the traditional print library scenario.

Digital libraries to bridge the digital divide

As discussed in Chapter 12, the digital divide exists not only in developing countries, but is increasingly noticeable in developed countries too. Even if governments and institutions in the developed world are making significant efforts in making ICT and the internet easily available to the whole population, there is still a gap in terms of providing access to and making effective use of ICT. A recent survey by the US Department of Commerce shows that slightly less than half of the US population still do not use computers and the internet (US Department of Commerce, 2002). The scenario in other developed countries may be pretty much the same.

The first step towards bridging the digital divide is understanding the divide itself. This may involve several questions, such as: What is it? Why does it exist? How does it affect different communities over time? Digital divide research is an interdisciplinary field, bringing together experts in economics, population studies, political science, communications policy, education policy, and many other social sciences; no one area of study can provide all the answers (Digital Divide Network, 2002b). The digital divide, as Law puts it, 'has many faces, governed by geography, by class, by national circumstances and by technology' (Law, 2002, 11). While we can have some influence for change and can challenge the status quo, there will still be some issues that are too big and complex in magnitude to handle.

Digital libraries cannot solve all the problems facing society today, but Shimmon (2001a, 2001b) points out they can play a significant role in bridging the digital divide. Chowdhury (2002a) emphasizes how recent developments in digital libraries can help us do this. As a measure to bridge the divide by bringing everyone in the UK online by the year 2015, the People's Network (www.peoplesnetwork.gov.uk) project has been set up with the primary aim of connecting all public libraries to the internet. Through this network connectivity, public libraries will support the information needs of local businesses and community groups, and provide access to internet-based government services. Thus the People's Network, coupled with proper digital library development, will enable users to access and use:

- internet and e-mail facilities
- text and multimedia information related to studies, business, jobs, hobbies, leisure, etc.
- social and community – local and international – information
- reference and information services
- government information and services
- library, museum and archive objects and information
- a range of office software applications.

It will also enable users to scan documents or images. In short, the People's Network and digital libraries will offer opportunities to everyone, regardless of age or individual circumstances.

However, the People's Network and digital libraries alone cannot promise the optimum access to, and use of, information unless specific measures are taken, especially in the areas of information and digital literacy. Since ICT is changing very fast, and digital libraries require users to interact with the vast and rapidly growing world of information directly through the digital library interfaces without the intervention of human intermediaries, appropriate training in information literacy skills are needed for every user. Determining the content and delivery of such training may not be easy. Bawden (2001) comments that to deal with the complexities of the current information environment, a multifaceted and broad form of literacy is required that should subsume all the skill-based literacies, but should not be restricted to any particular technology or set of technologies.

To impart information literacy skills to every citizen in the country regularly is a major undertaking. However, since this is a prerequisite to the success of the People's Network and digital libraries, measures should be taken to incorporate information literacy training schemes as part of the regular academic and institutional staff training programmes. Only such concerted efforts can prepare citizens for making optimum use of ICT, the internet and digital libraries in future.

Users' information search behaviour

The success of digital libraries will largely depend upon how well they are equipped to meet the information needs and search behaviour of users. So far there have not been many studies on user search behaviour in digital libraries. Nevertheless, some recent studies on this topic in the web environment will provide some insight and guidelines for digital library researchers and managers.

Hoelscher (1998), while analysing about 16 million queries from the German search engine Fireball, noted that only 2.6% of queries used Boolean operators, and over 54% had only one search term. Gordon and Pathak (1999) compared the retrieval effectiveness of eight search engines: Yahoo!, Excite, Magellan, HotBot, AltaVista, Lycos, Infoseek and Open Text, and noted, among other things, that there were no statistical differences in the retrieval effectiveness among users for recall, though there were for precision. Although this study talks mainly about the performance of the selected search engines, some observations are very important as far as the general question of precision in digital library searching is concerned. It shows that in general web search engines lack precision and their performance varies significantly. This could be a good lesson for digital library designers, since precision is an important determining factor for the performance of digital libraries.

Jansen and Pooch (2001), and Jansen, Spink and Saracevic (2000, 2001) studied user search behaviour on the web. Overall their observations show the rather poor state of end-user searching skills. For example, on average users entered two terms per web search query, only 8% of search queries contained Boolean operators, 9% were advanced search queries and 54% of searches viewed ten or fewer retrieved items. The major findings of these studies, presented in Table 15.1, show some interesting searching behaviours of users across three different search systems.

Table 15.1 *User search patterns in different online search environments*

Issues	Web search systems	Traditional IR systems	OPAC search systems
No. of queries per user per session	1–2	7–16	2–5
No. of terms per query	2	6–9	1–2
No. of relevant documents viewed per session	10 or fewer	approx. 10	less than 50
No. of queries containing advanced options	9%	9%	8%
No. of queries containing Boolean operators	8%	37%	1%
No. of queries improperly formatted	10%	17%	7–9%

Similar observations have been made in a study conducted by Spink et al. (2001). They analysed over one million web queries to discern how the public searches the web and made some astonishing findings, which may be useful for digital library designers:

- The great majority of web queries are short, not much modified, and very simple in structure.
- Very few queries incorporate advanced search features, and half of those that do so contain mistakes.
- Despite gathering a large number of websites as answers to their queries, users do not view beyond the first or the second page of results.
- Web users are not much interested in relevance feedback.

Another study (Cooper, 2001) reveals some interesting findings that may offer good lessons for digital library researchers, particularly those who deal with information retrieval issues. Cooper analysed the usage of the Melvyl web catalogue at the University of California at Berkeley. During the 479-day study period users conducted about 2.5 million search sessions, during which about 7.4 million search statements were executed. The findings of this study reveal the following:

- The length of time some searchers spent at a session grew from six to ten minutes during the 16-month study period.
- During the study period, about 7.4 million database selections were made, out of which the catalogue database accounted for 32% (about 2.4 million uses), Medlars 22%, the magazine database 10%, periodicals database 8%, Inspec 4% and Current Contents 4%.
- The time users spent on each database also varied; it was about 3 minutes per search in the Medlars database and 2.2 minutes for the catalogue database.
- Users displayed roughly four or five citations for each search they performed.
- The length of time users spent displaying results was 30–40 seconds.

A joint research project between the University of Pennsylvania and University of Sheffield has revealed several interesting observations (Spink et al., 2002a, 2002b, 2002c, 2002d) that may be extremely useful for digital library designers. Ford, Miller and Moss (2001) conducted a study with the AltaVista web search engine to test the link between web search strategies and relevance judgements in order to discover whether Boolean and other advanced features are less effective than best match or combined Boolean and best match search strategies. They noted the following:

- Boolean-only searches were associated with poor retrieval.
- Boolean-only searches performed worse compared with the best match and combined searches.
- Combined searches performed worse than best match alone searches.
- There was no evidence that such results were due to errors on the user's part when using Boolean searching, such as wrong formulation of terms.

A major characteristic of digital libraries is that there are no human intermediaries playing a major role in online search services. Appropriate online support for query formulation and modification may improve digital library search results. Again, since most users do not look at more than a handful of records, appropriate mechanisms have to be developed for filtering retrieved output.

The evaluation studies reported above reveal the following:

- Users find it difficult to formulate their questions.
- In general, users spend very little time searching a given web search tool or database.
- In most cases users formulate very short and simple queries with one or two search terms and very few search operators.
- Users spend very little time looking at and deciding the usefulness or relevance of retrieved items.
- Very few queries contain advanced search features.

These findings may be used as guidelines while designing information retrieval systems for digital libraries. The findings also re-emphasize the need for training users and giving them assistance in online searching. This is in contrast to the view of Arms (2000a), discussed earlier, that information retrieval tasks can now be successfully performed by end-users without the assistance of reference librarians. User training or information literacy programmes should be conducted regularly; sophisticated online tutorial programmes using digital video technology may be developed to assist users.

Digital library services

In addition to providing improved mechanisms for access to distributed information sources, digital libraries should play a key role in providing specialized information services, both reactive and proactive. As mentioned in Chapter 2, some digital libraries provide proactive information services, like the selective dissemination of information whereby users are regularly informed about the recent information available in their field of interest. The current state of digital reference services has been discussed in Chapter 11, and by Chowdhury (2002a). However, so far little research has focused on reference and information services, except some that concentrated on the personalization of information services (discussed in Chapters 4 and 8).

Lessons learnt from currently available digital reference and information services on the web may be useful for the development of such services within digital libraries. For example, the approach taken by Ask Jeeves in the use of templates for storing queries, and the knowledge base for storing the queries and their answers, may be suitable for digital libraries. The strength of Ask Jeeves is the knowledge base, which according to the site 'contains links to more than 7 million answers, which contain information about the most frequently asked questions on the internet' (www.ask.co.uk). Library and information professionals are trained in organizing information, and new research could well be conducted to find the best ways to organize reference queries and answers on various topics. A facet analysis technique could be used in formulating different templates around a given search topic and they could be stored in a knowledge base. A knowledge base developed on such an approach will grow fast initially, but after a time the growth rate will be minimal, new growth only occurring when new aspects of a given topic appear in the research and literature (Chowdhury, 2002b).

Co-operation in providing ready-reference and subject-specific reference services may be a useful cost-cutting measure. Indeed the high cost of staff in libraries has been a major problem. However, since digital libraries can be accessed easily from remote locations, co-operative mechanisms based on subject specialization and other criteria could be considered.

Specialized search and other forms of assistance need not always have to be free. In fact, some reference services mentioned in Chapter 11 charge fees and this is perfectly reasonable, especially where specialized and reliable searches can save end-users' time. Payments for such services need not necessarily come from the end-users themselves. They could, for example, be recovered from research projects in an academic institution, or commercial projects in a business organization. Holmes-Wong (1999) suggests that by combining internet technology with electronic commerce, libraries may be able to offer customizable electronic reference services to users. Nevertheless, new research for testing e-commerce models for digital library reference services needs to be undertaken.

Discussions earlier in this book, especially in Chapter 11, re-emphasized the need for the provision of personalized information services in the next generation of digital libraries. The current research projects aiming at finding the best means of providing such services through digital libraries are trying a variety of techniques and technologies, including:

- information filtering mechanisms based on users' personal characteristics and tasks
- agent technology for automatic information discovery, organization, filtering and retrieval based on users' natures and needs
- co-operative models for sharing resources and specializations – both the content and staff
- internet technologies such as internet chat, call centre management software, video conferencing, etc.

These research projects will definitely give rise to some useful models and approaches that the second-generation digital libraries may adopt. Further research could be carried out in a number of areas including (Chowdhury, 2002b):

- building appropriate packages for end-user training, involving best practice for digital library use, suitable for specific user needs and characteristics
- testing the query template and knowledge-based approaches in a digital library environment (approaches somewhat similar to those of About.com and Ask Jeeves, for example)
- testing e-commerce models for handling the payment and cost management aspects of sophisticated and resource-intensive personalized services
- tracing the techniques of expert information problem-solving processes, and building models for other users in a given domain
- testing traditional library classification tools and facet analysis techniques for creating question templates and knowledge bases for storing answers in specific subject fields.

The economics of digital libraries

Library and information systems are usually funded publicly or by their parent organizations. Hence there is always an issue of accountability, though the direct impact or benefits of library and information services are difficult to measure. Building and managing digital libraries requires a huge amount of investment. Most digital libraries and related services have so far been funded by research projects or institutions as experiments. Very few of them have received funds for becoming a sustainable service. There is little evidence so far to prove that digital libraries save money, or are cheaper, than their print counterparts. In fact building and managing digital libraries appears to be more expensive than building and managing traditional libraries. More research needs to be done to find accurate cost–benefit data on digital libraries.

Halliday and Oppenheim have conducted some interesting studies on some specific economic aspects of digital library systems and services. A study on the economic aspects of the electronic reserve service provided to the students of higher education in the UK through the HERON services revealed that these services are extremely expensive and are inefficient overall (Halliday and Oppenheim, 2001a). In another study Halliday and Oppenheim (2001b) aimed to determine the level of sponsorship required for a resource discovery network (RDN) to be self-sustaining within a period of ten years. The results of their study suggest that, with a combination of sponsorship and subscriptions income, a RDN could succeed without grant funding within ten years of its launch. In another study on the economic models of e-journals, Halliday and Oppenheim (2000b) noted that staff and overhead costs are the substantial costs incurred when producing e-journals. They comment that scholarly journals can be produced and distributed for a modest fee as long as there are at least 55 subscribers.

As discussed in Chapter 6, many researchers have proposed models for the calculation of costs for digitization, and various electronic publications address this matter. The VHI project in the USA, discussed in Chapter 13, proposes a unique model for the cost–benefit analysis of digital libraries, especially digital image libraries. As far as archiving and preservation is concerned, it is not yet clear whether it is economically feasible to build an archive of the national intellectual output both in analogue and digital form.

While these research studies reveal interesting observations, other economic issues are involved in the design and management of digital libraries. Many alternative models now exist for getting access to digital information systems and services. At present the vendors or the service providers more or less dictate their terms, and there are no uniform practices. More research needs to be done to develop best practice models in this area. Moreover, concerted efforts are necessary to convince users as well as policy makers that the primary goal of digital libraries is not to save money but to provide better information services to the user community in real time.

Digital library education

The discussions in various chapters in this book clearly demonstrate that we need people with various technical as well as managerial skills to build and manage digital libraries. Unfortunately, as we have seen, very few library and information science programmes have courses that provide all-round theoretical and practical training on digital libraries. In most cases there is just one paper or course that aims to provide a general overview of digital library issues and problems. There is a need for fully developed courses on digital libraries to produce personnel trained in all the different areas mentioned in the course of this book.

One of the most significant recent research projects focusing on the need of information science education is KALIPER, the Kellogg-ALISE Information Professions and Education Renewal Project (ALISE, 2000). KALIPER was a two-year project (1998–2000) supported by the W. K. Kellogg Foundation and ALISE to analyse the nature and extent of major curricular changes in library and information science education. The report identified several new areas for concentration in LIS education. Several other studies have also been conducted to assess LIS education needs. For example, Baruchson-Arbib and Bronstein (2002) conducted a Delphi study to identify the future role of information professionals, and noted that while they will continue to play a key role in locating, filtering and evaluating information, they will also have an increasingly large part to play in user education and training.

Digital libraries and knowledge management

Predicting the future of a huge and fast-changing area like digital libraries is a difficult task. However, digital libraries will no doubt play a key role in creating a perfect information management environment or, as the new terminology has it, a knowledge management environment.

Knowledge management (KM) is the new buzzword, in corporate as well as government sectors. In KM terms, organizational knowledge may be divided into tacit knowledge, explicit knowledge and cultural knowledge (Choo, 1998a, 1998b, 2000). Implicit in this suggestion is the important idea that knowledge is not just an object or artefact, but also the outcome of people working together, sharing experiences and constructing meaning out of what they do. Digital libraries can play a significant role in achieving this goal.

Davenport, Delong and Beers (1998) studied a number of knowledge management projects and noted that the major objectives of such projects have been:

- to create knowledge repositories
- to improve access to knowledge
- to create a knowledge environment
- to manage knowledge as an asset.

Keeping these broad objectives in view, Rowley (1999) comments that knowledge management is concerned with the exploitation and development of the knowledge assets of an organization with a view to furthering the organization's objectives. The knowledge assets to be managed include explicit, documented knowledge and tacit, subjective knowledge.

Digital libraries, with the major objective of making digital information – local as well as remote on distributed servers – accessible to every user in the community, can play a key role in knowledge management in any organization. In future all organizations will need to have mechanisms for gaining easy access to local as well as global information. In order to create a knowledge-based environment, organizations should also build mechanisms for capturing information on local expertise. Figure 15.1 shows a general framework for knowledge management in any organization that makes optimum use of digital libraries, along with intranet and internet resources, through a task-based interface and user-driven information retrieval system.

Such a knowledge management environment should enable users to search for the required information, or get access to a set of information resources recommended automatically by the system based on user tasks and characteristics. In other words, the system should be able to personalize the environment for the user.

As discussed in Chapter 11, one of the major attributes of digital libraries of the future will be to provide reference services by providing answers to questions asked by the users. In a knowledge management environment, as shown in Figure 15.1, this could be accomplished by building a question–answer

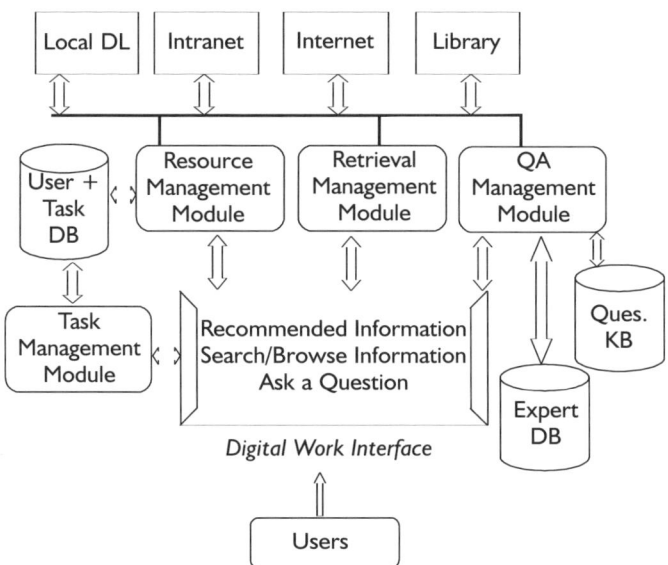

Fig. 15.1 *A simple KM environment*

management module that would use the appropriate technologies to find and filter answers from the global digital library system. Finally, again as shown in Figure 15.1, a knowledge management environment should be able to capture information on human expertise, and should be able to direct users to appropriate human experts or a knowledge base created from expert knowledge.

The future

Digital library development and use throughout the world will not only be influenced by the development of information and communication technologies (ICTs) but also by a myriad of social, economic and political matters. While researchers can handle some significant research issues and problems associated with digital libraries, nonetheless governments, businesses and users themselves have a major role to play in the fulfillment of the dream of providing distributed global digital libraries.

Recent developments in ICT no longer require users to sit before a computer terminal to be able to interact with a library. Library users in many countries like Japan and Singapore can now perform a number of basic OPAC-related activities, such as checking borrower details, renewal of items, and so on, by using mobile phones. Researchers are now working on the use of mobile phones for OPAC searches (Negishi, 2002). Further research in this area will facilitate more access to digital libraries by mobile phone, thereby exploiting the true benefits of digital libraries – providing access to information from anywhere at any time.

Although printed libraries will continue to exist for the foreseeable future, 'born digital' materials are growing at a very fast pace. Electronic journals, conferences, theses and many books are now coming out in digital format. These commercial efforts to create digital information resources are supplemented by institutional efforts in digitization. Several inter-governmental projects are also creating digital materials. A prominent example of this is the Million Books Project. The project began in 2001 at Carnegie Mellon University, in collaboration with six Chinese universities and ten research centres in India, with the aim of providing full-text searching of one million books, thus making them accessible to anyone, anywhere. It has received the support of the National Science Foundation (NSF) and the governments of India and China (Michalek, 2002). These digital information resources, coupled with the massive growth of web information resources, will make the collections of future digital libraries more rich and diverse.

Digital library research has brought together researchers and practitioners from a variety of disciplines, resulting in collaborative research activities at national, regional and international levels. Although many innovations have been implemented over the past few years, many more challenges remain to be met. First of all, digital library research has been undertaken by people from different backgrounds with varied levels of understanding of digital libraries and several different objectives. As a result, there is no unified theory of digital libraries. In order to get the best of these massive research efforts, it is very important to formulate universally agreed common principles and policy for the digital library field. Appropriate methods and standards must be developed to enable uniform growth and use of digital libraries. Proper guidelines have to be developed for the management of digital library services and appropriate methods, tools and techniques are needed for their evaluation. Evaluation methods and techniques such as those discussed in Chapter 13, some recently developed approaches such as the CAPM (Comprehensive Access to Printed Materials) project, developed at the John Hopkins University (Choudhury et al, 2002), or the quantitative approach to analysing the retrieval habits of users to assess the impact of digital libraries (Bollen and Luce, 2002) need to be widely applied and tested in order to develop best practice standards and benchmarks.

The success of digital libraries will largely depend on the skills of the people who build and manage them. At the moment there is hardly any proper education and training facility in digital libraries in the UK. Although there are some such courses in other parts of the world, especially in the USA, Saracevic and Dalbello (2001) noted that:

- Only 32% of such courses were independent, while 49% (23 courses) pursued an integrated approach where digital library content was integrated within another course.
- The digital library educational approach was predominantly information technology oriented.

Since digital library research and development involves experts from multiple disciplines, an interdisciplinary model for digital library education, as proposed by Coleman (2002), may be appropriate.

Digital libraries are not properly integrated at present. For example, one may have to use a number of digital libraries, one at a time, to obtain different types of information on a given topic. Digital library research and development activities must be properly integrated to meet user needs. For example, a local public library may be linked to a digital library interface that could enable users to obtain information from a variety of sources – libraries, museums, archives, government departments, local councils, and so on – all integrated behind the scenes. At the moment most of these systems work in isolation, thereby forcing users to employ each system separately. An integrated digital library service would facilitate the creation of a proper knowledge environment.

Digital library development and use will be influenced by a number of social, economic and political topics, the most prominent ones being intellectual property, privacy and security. Laws governing these issues vary from country to country. However, proper mechanisms should be built to ensure the rights, at national and international level, of creators and providers as well as users of digital libraries.

Finally, as discussed throughout this book, digital library research and development activities are progressing well with the active involvement of a large number of national and international organizations, universities, research institutions, and businesses. The pace at which these developments are taking place is very encouraging, and at this fast rate of research and development the creation of a global digital library system no longer seems to be merely a lofty but unachievable goal.

References

Abdulla, G., Liu, B. and Fox, E. (1998) Searching the world wide web: implications from studying different user behaviour. In *Proceedings of the WebNet98 Conference, Orlando, Florida*, available at www.aace.org/conf/webnet.

ACM Portal: the ACM digital library http://portal.ac.org.

Agora http://hosted.ukoln.ac.uk/agora/.

ALISE (2000) *Educating library and information professionals for a new century. KALIPER report executive summary*, available at www.alise.org/nondiscuss/kaliper_final.pdf.

Alrashid, T. et al. (1998) Safeguarding copyrighted contents: digital libraries and intellectual property management – CWRU's rights management system, *D-Lib Magazine*, **4** (4), available at www.dlib.org/dlib/april98/04barker.html.

American Memory: historical collections for the National Digital Library http://memory.loc.gov/.

Ang, S. (2001) Agenda for change: intellectual property rights and access management – a framework for discussion on the relationship between copyright and the role of libraries in the digital age, *Library Review*, **50** (7, 8), 382–94.

Anglo-American Cataloguing Rules (2002) 2nd edn, 2002 Revision, London, Facet Publishing.

Archer, S. and Cast, M. (1999) Going where the questions are: using media to maintain personalised contact in reference service in medium-sized academic libraries, *The Reference Librarian*, **66**, 39–50.

Arms, W. (2000a) Automated digital libraries: how effectively can computers

be used for the skilled tasks of professional librarianship?, *D-Lib Magazine*, **6** (7/8), available at
www.dlib.org/dlib/july00/arms/07arms.html.

Arms, W. (2000b) *Digital libraries*, Cambridge, MA, MIT Press.

Arms, W. Y. (1995) Key concepts in the architecture of the digital library, *D-Lib Magazine*, **1** (1), (July), available at
www.dlib.org/dlib/July95/07arms.html.

Arms, W. Y. et al. (2002) A spectrum of interoperability: the site for science prototype for the NSDL, *D-Lib Magazine*, **8** (1), available at
www.dlib.org/dlib/january02/arms/01arms.html.

Ask A Librarian
www.earl.org.uk/ask/.

Baeza-Yates, R. and Ribeiro-Neto, B. (1999) *Modern information retrieval*, New York, ACM Press.

Baeza-Yates, R. et al. (2002) Preface to the special topic issue: XML, *Journal of the American Society for Information Science and Technology*, **53** (6), 413–14.

Bainbridge, D. et al. (1999) Towards a digital library of popular music. In *Proceedings of Digital Libraries '99 Conference*, New York, ACM.

Baldonado, M. (2000) A user-centred interface for information exploration in a heterogeneous digital library, *Journal of the American Society for Information Science*, **51** (3), 297–310.

Baldonado, M. Q. W. and Winograd, T. (1996) *SenseMaker: an information exploration interface supporting the contextual evolution of a user's interests*, available at
http://dbpubs.stanford.edu/pub/1996-85.

Barry, W. and Barbara, R. (1999) Creating personal digital libraries. In *Proceedings of the Computers in Libraries Conference, Arlington, VA, USA, March 8–10*, Medford, NJ, Information Today, 191–8.

Baruchson-Arbib, S. and Bronstein, J. (2002) A view to the future of the library and information science profession: a Delphi study, *Journal of the American Society for Information Science and technology*, **53** (5), 397–408.

Bates, M. J. (1977) Factors affecting subject catalog search success, *Journal of the American Society for Information Science*, **28** (3), 161–9.

Bates, M. J. (1979) Information search tactics, *Journal of the American Society for Information Science*, **30** (4), 205–14.

Bates, M. J. (1981) Search techniques. In Williams, M. E. (ed.) *Annual review of information science and technology (ARIST)*, vol. 16, New York, Knowledge Industry for ASIS, 139–69.

Bates, M. J. (1984) The fallacy of the perfect thirty-item online search, *RQ*, **24** (1), 43–50.

Bates, M. J. (1986) Subject access in online catalogs: a design model, *Journal of the American Society for Information Science*, **37** (6), 357–76.

Bates, M. J. (1989) The design of browsing and berrypicking techniques for the online search interface, *Online Review*, **13** (5), 407–31.

Bates, M. J. (1998) Indexing and access for digital libraries and the internet: human, database, and domain factors, *Journal of the American Society for Information Science* **49** (13), 1185–205.

Bates, M. J. (2002) The cascade of interactions in the digital library interface, *Information Processing and Management*, **38** (3), 381–400.

Bawden, D. (2001) Information and digital literacies, *Journal of Documentation*, **57** (2), 218–59.

Bawden, D. and Rowlands, I. (1999) *Understanding digital libraries: towards a conceptual framework*, British Library Research and Innovation Report 170, London, British Library Research and Innovation Centre.

BBC (1999) *Information rich information poor*, BBC News, 14 October, available at
http://news.bbc.co.uk/hi/english/special_report/1999/10/99/
information_rich_information_poor/newsid_466000/466651.stm.

Beagrie, N. (2000) *Going digital: issues in digitisation for public libraries. An issue paper from the Networked Services Policy Taskgroup*, available at www.ukoln.ac.uk/public/earl/issuepapers/digitisation.htm.

Beagrie, N. and Greenstein, D. (1998) *Digital collections: a strategic policy framework for creating and preserving digital resources*, Arts and Humanities Data Service, available at
www.ahds.ac.uk /manage/framework.htm.

Bearman, D. and Trant, J. (1998) Authenticity of digital resources: towards a statement of requirements in the research process, *D-Lib Magazine*, June, available at
www.dlib.org/dlib/june98/06bearman.html.

Belkin, N. J. (1980) Anomalous states of knowledge as a basis for information retrieval, *Canadian Journal of Information Science*, **5**, 133–43.

Belkin, N. J., Oddy, R. N. and Brooks, H. M. (1982a) ASK for information retrieval. Part 1. Background and theory, *Journal of Documentation*, **38** (2), 61–71.

Belkin, N. J., Oddy, R. N. and Brooks, H. M. (1982b) ASK for information retrieval. Part 2. Results of a design study, *Journal of Documentation*, **38** (3), 145–164.

Bennett, J. C. (1997) *A framework of data types and formats, and issues affecting the long term preservation of digital material*, British Library Research and Innovation Report 50, London, The British Library, available at www.ukoln.ac.uk/services/papers/bl/jisc-npo50/bennet.html.

Biddiscombe, R. (2001) Case study: the development of information professionals' needs for internet and IT skills: experiences at the University of Birmingham, *Program*, **35** (2), 157–66.

BIOME
www.biome.ac.uk.

Bishop, A. P. (1998) Measuring access, use, and success in digital libraries, *Journal of Electronic Publishing*, **4** (2), available at www.press.umich.edu/jep/04-02/bishop.html.

Bishop, A. P. (1999) Document structures and digital libraries: how researchers mobilize information in journal articles, *Information Processing and Management*, **35** (3), 255–79.

Bishop, A. P. and Star, S. L. (1996) Social informatics for digital library use and infrastructure. In Williams, M. E. (ed.), *Annual review of information science and technology (ARIST)*, vol. 31, Medford, NJ, Information Today on behalf of ASIS, 301–401.

Blair, D. C. (2002a) The challenge of commercial document retrieval. Part I: major issues, and a framework based on search exhaustivity, determinacy of representation and document collection size, *Information Processing and Management*, **38** (2), 273–91.

Blair, D. C. (2002b) The challenge of commercial document retrieval. Part II: a strategy for document searching based on identifiable document partitions, *Information Processing and Management*, **38** (2), 293–304.

Boehm, K., Croft, W. B. and Schek, H. (eds) (2000) *Proceedings of the first DELOS Network of Excellence workshop on information seeking, searching and querying in digital libraries. Zurich. December 11–12*, ERCIM Workshop Proceedings No. 01/W001, European Research Consortium for Informatics and Mathematics, available at www.ercim.org/publication/ws-proceedings/DelNoe01/.

Bollen, J. and Luce, R. (2002) Evaluation of digital library impact and user communities by analysis of usage patterns, *D-Lib Magazine*, **8** (6), available at
www.dlib.org/dlib/june02/bollen/06bollen.html.

Borgman, C. (1993) National electronic library report. In Fox, E. A. (ed.), *Sourcebook on digital libraries: report for the National Science Foundation*, TR-93-35, Blacksburg, VA, VPI&SU Computer Science Department, 126–47.

Borgman, C. (1997) Multi-media, multi-cultural and multi-lingual digital libraries: or how do we exchange data in 400 languages, *D-Lib Magazine*, June, available at
www.dlib.org/dlib/june97/ 06borgman.html.

Borgman, C. (1999) What are digital libraries? Competing visions, *Information Processing and Management*, **35** (3), 227–43.

Borgman, C. (2000a) Digital libraries and the continuum of scholarly communication, *Journal of Documentation*, **56** (4), 412–30.

Borgman, C. (2000b) *From Gutenberg to the global information infrastructure: access to information in the networked world*, New York, ACM Press.

Borgman, C. et al. (2000) Evaluating digital libraries for teaching and learning in undergraduate education: a case study of the Alexandria Digital Earth Prototype (ADEPT), *Library Trends*, **49** (2), 228–50.

Börner, K. (2001) *Visual interfaces to digital libraries – the first international workshop at the First ACM+IEEE Joint Conference on Digital Libraries*, available at
www.dlib.org/dlib/july01/07inbrief.html.

Brack, E. V., Palmer, D. and Robinson, B. (2000) Collection level description – the RIDING and Agora experience, *D-Lib Magazine*, **6** (9), available at www.dlib.org/dlib/september00/brack/09brack.html.

Breck, E. et al. (1999) Question answering from large document collections. In *Question answering systems. Papers from the 1999 AAAI Fall symposium, North Falmouth, MA, 5–7 November*, Menlo Park, CA, AAAI Press, 26–31.

Breeding, M. (2001) Providing virtual reference service: libraries are finding ways to expand services to remote library users, *Information Today*, **18** (4), 42–3.

The British Library. Treasures of the British Library
www.bl.uk/about/treasures.html.

The British Library STM Search
www.bl.uk/services/stb/stmsearc/stmreqst.html.

Brophy, P. (2000) Towards a generic model of information and library services in the information, *Journal of Documentation*, **56** (2), 161–84.

Brophy, P. (2001) *The library in the twenty-first century*, London, Library Association Publishing.

Brophy, P. et al. (2000) *EQUINOX: library performance measurement and quality management system – performance indicators for electronic library services*, available at
http://equinox.dcu.ie/reports/pilist.html#pis.

Broughton, V. and Lane, H. (2000) Classification schemes revisited: applications to web indexing and searching. In Thomas, A. and Shearer, J. R. (eds), *Internet searching and indexing: the subject approach*, New York, Haworth Press, 143–55.

BUBL LINK / 5:15. Selected internet resources covering all academic subject areas
www.bubl.ac.uk/link/.

Bunge, C.A. (1999) Reference services, *The Reference Librarian*, **66**, 185–99.

Burnett, P. and Seuring, C. (2001) Organising access to free internet resources: an overview of selection and management issues in large academic and national libraries with a view to defining a policy at Oxford University, *Program*, **35** (1), 15–31.

Byrd, D. and Crawford, T. (2002) Problems of music information retrieval in the real world, *Information Processing and Management*, **38** (2), 249–72.

Byrd, S. et al. (2001) Cost/benefit analysis for digital library projects: the Virginia Historical Inventory project (VHI), *The Bottom Line: Managing Library Finances*, **14** (2), 65–75.

California Digital Library
www.cdlib.org.

CAMiLEON: creating creative archiving at Michigan and Leeds: emulating the old on the new
www.si.umich.edu/CAMILEON/.

Carter, D. S. and Janes, J. (2000) Unobtrusive data analysis of digital reference questions and service at the Internet Public Library: an exploratory study, *Library Trends*, **49** (2), 251–65.

CASA: A Cooperative Archive of Serials and Articles
http://decsite.cib.unito.it:1999/.

Case, D. O., Borgman, C. L. and Meadow, C. T. (1986) End-user information-
seeking in the energy field: implications for the end-user access to DOE
RECON databases, *Information Processing and Management*, **22** (4),
299–308.

CEDARS: CURL Exemplars in Digital Archives
www.leeds.ac.uk/cedars/.

Centre for Digital Library Research (2000)
http://cdlr.strath.ac.uk

Chapman, S. and Kenney, A. R. (1996) Digital conversion of research library
materials: a case for full informational capture, *D-Lib Magazine*, October,
available at
www.dlib.org/dlib/october96/cornell/10chapman.html.

Chen, C. (1999) NII, GII I2 and NGI and IT2 initiatives: implications to the
digital library development in the US. In Chen, C. (ed.), *IT and global
digital library development*, West Newton, MA, MicroUse Information,
49–64.

Chen, H. (2000) Introduction to the special topic issue: part 2. *Journal of the
American Society for Information Science*, **51** (4), 311–12.

Choo, C. W. (1998a) *Information management for the intelligent organization:
the art of scanning the environment*, 2nd edn, Medford, NJ, Information
Today.

Choo, C. W. (1998b) *The knowing organization: how organizations use information to construct meaning, create knowledge, and make decisions*, New York,
Oxford University Press.

Choo, C. W. (2000) Working with knowledge: how information professionals
help organisations manage what they know, *Library Management*, 21 (8),
395–403.

Choudhury, S. et al. (2002) A framework for evaluating digital library services,
D-Lib Magazine, **8** (7/8), available at
www.dlib.org/dlib/july02/choudhury/07choudhury.html.

Chowdhury, G. G. (1999) *Introduction to modern information retrieval*, London, Library Association Publishing.

Chowdhury, G. G. (2002a) Digital divide: how the digital libraries can bridge
the gap, 5th International Conference on Asian Digital Libraries, Singapore, December 11–14, 2002, Springer, forthcoming.

Chowdhury, G. G. (2002b) Digital libraries and reference services: present and future, *Journal of Documentation*, **58** (3), 258–83.

Chowdhury, G. G. (2003) Natural language processing. In Cronin, B. (ed.) *Annual review of information science and technology (ARIST)*, vol. 37, Medford, NJ, Information Today Inc. on behalf of ASIS, forthcoming.

Chowdhury, G. G. and Chowdhury, S. (1999) Digital library research: major issues and trends, *Journal of Documentation*, **55** (4), 409–48.

Chowdhury, G. G. and Chowdhury, S. (2000) An overview of the information retrieval features of twenty digital libraries, *Program*, **34** (4), 341–73.

Chowdhury, G. G. and Chowdhury, S. (2001a) *CD-ROM and online information sources and searching*, London, Library Association Publishing.

Chowdhury, G. G. and Chowdhury, S. (2001b) *Information sources and searching on the world wide web*, London, Library Association Publishing.

Chudnov, D. (1999) Towards seamlessness with XML. In Stern, D. (ed.) *Digital libraries: philosophies, technical design considerations, and example scenarios*, New York, Haworth Press, 121–30.

Clayton, P. and Gorman, M. (2001) *Managing information resources in libraries: collection management in theory and practice*, London, Library Association Publishing.

Cliff, P. (2002) Building ResourceFinder, *Ariadne*, **30**, available at www.ariadne.ac.uk/issue30/rdn-oai/.

Coffman, S. and Saxton, M. L. (1999) Staffing the reference desk in the largely-digital library, *The Reference Librarian*, **66**, 141–61.

Cohen, S. et al. (2000) MyLibrary: Personalized Electronic Services in the Cornell University Library, *D-Lib Magazine*, **6** (4), available at www.dlib.org/dlib/pril00/mistlebauer 04mistlebauer.html.

Coleman, A. (2002) Interdisciplinarity: the road ahead for education in digital libraries, *D-Lib Magazine*, **8** (7/8), available at www.dlib.org/dlib/july02/coleman/07coleman.html.

Colet, L. S. (2000) *Research Libraries Group and Digital Library Federation. Guides to quality in visual resource imaging.1. Planning an imaging project*, available at www.rlg.org/visguides/visguide1.html.

Collaborative Digital Reference Service: delivering answers to your desktop now, when you need them www.loc.gov/rr/digiref/.

Computer Science and Telecommunications Board. Commission on Physical Sciences, Mathematics, and Applications. National Research Council (1997) *Toward an every-citizen interface to the nation's Information Infra-*

structure Steering Committee, Washington, DC, National Academy Press, available at
www.nap.edu/readingroom/books/screen/.

Computer Science and Telecommunications Board. National Research Council (1998) Design and evaluation: a review of the state-of-the-art, *D-Lib Magazine*, July, available at
www.dlib.org/dlib/july98/nrc/07nrc.html.

Conhaim, W. W. (2001) The global digital divide, *Information Today*, **18** (7), available at
http://proquest.umi.com.

Connaway, L. S. (2001) A web-based electronic book (e-book) library: the netLibrary model, *Library Hi Tech*, **19** (4), 340–9.

Cook, T. (1995) It's 10 o'clock: do you know where your data are? (electronic data loss), *Technology Review*, **98** (1), 48–53.

Cooper, B., Crespo, A. and Garcia-Molina, H. (2000) Implementing a reliable digital object archive. In *Proceedings of the Fourth European Conference on Research and Advanced Technology for Digital Libraries (ECDL), Lisbon, September 18–20*, available at
www.db.stanford.edu/pub/papers/arpaperext.ps.

Cooper, M. D. (2001) Usage patterns of a web-based library catalog, *Journal of the American Society for Information Science and Technology*, **52** (2), 137–48.

Copyown^{sm}*: a resource on copyright ownership for the higher education community*
www.umd.edu/copyown.

Cousins, S. et al. (1997) *The Digital Library Integrated Task Environment (DLITE)*, available at
http://dbpubs.stanford.edu/pub/1997-69.

Covi, L. M. (1999) Material mastery: situating digital library use in university research practices, *Information Processing and Management*, **35** (3), 293–316.

CPA/RLG (1996) *Preserving digital information: report of the Task Force on Archiving of Digital Information* Commission on Preservation and Access and The Research Libraries Group, Inc, available at
www.rlg.org/ArchTF/.

Crawford, T., Iliopoulos, C. and Raman, R. (1998) String-matching techniques for musical similarity and melodic recognition. In Hewlett, W. H. and Selfridge-Field, E. (eds), *Melodic similarity: concepts, procedures, and applications*,

Computing in Musicology vol. 11, Cambridge, MA, MIT Press.

Crespo, A. and Garcia-Molina, H. (1998) *Archival storage for digital libraries. Third ACM Conference on Digital Libraries. Pittsburgh, PA, USA, June 23–26*, available at http://dbpubs.stanford.edu:8090/pub/1998-49.

Crespo, A. and Garcia-Molina, H. (2000) Modeling archival repositories. In *Proceedings of the Fourth European Conference on Digital Libraries (ECDL) Lisbon, 18–20 September, 2000*, available at http://dbpubs.stanford.edu:8090/pub/1999-24.

Croft, W. B. (1995) What do people want from information retrieval? The top ten research issues for companies that use and sell IR systems, *D-Lib Magazine*, available at www.dlib.org/dlib/november95/11croft.html.

Cromwell-Kessler, W. (1998) Crosswalks, metadata mapping, and interoperability: what does it all mean? In Murtha, B. (ed.), *Introduction to metadata: pathways to digital information*, Los Angeles, CA, Getty Information Institute, 19–33.

Cronin, B. (1998) Information professionals in the digital age, *International Information and Library Review*, **30**, 37–50.

Cronin, B. (2002) The digital divide, *Library Journal*, **127** (3), 148.

Curry, E. (2001) Introduction to 'The Social Context of Reference Work', special issue of *Library Trends*, **50** (2), 165–7.

CyberDewey: the fast well organized internet directory www.anthus.com/CyberDewey/CyberDewey.html.

*CyberStacks*sm www.public.iastate.edu/~CYBERSTACKS/.

Davenport, T. H., Delong, D. W. and Beers, M. C. (1998) Successful knowledge management projects, *Sloan Management Review*, **39** (2), 43–57.

Davies, M. (2001) Creating a virtual reference library: experiences at Suffolk Libraries and Heritage, *Program*, **35** (1), 43–56.

Davis, J. R. and Lagoze, C. (2000) NCSTRL: design and deployment of a globally distributed digital library, *Journal of the American Society for Information Science*, **51** (3), 273–80.

Day, M. (1998) *Issues and approaches to preservation metadata. Joint RLG and NPO Preservation Conference on Guidelines for Digital Imaging, 28–30 September*, available at www.rlg.org/preserv/joint/day.html.

Day, M. (2001a) E-print services and long-term access to the record of scholarly and scientific research, *Ariadne*, **28**, available at www.ariadne.ac.uk/issue28/metadata/.

Day, M. (2001b) Preservation 2000, *Ariadne*, **26**, available at www.ariadne.ac.uk /issue26/metadata/intro.html.

DCDot: Dublin Core metadata editor www.ukoln.ac.uk/metadata/dcdot/.

Deegan, M. and Tanner, S. (2002a) The digital dark ages, *Update*, **1** (2), 42–3.

Deegan, M. and Tanner, S. (2002b) *Digital futures: strategies for the information age*, London, Library Association Publishing.

DELOS
    www.iei.pi.cnr.it/DELOS/DLW/dlw.htm.

Dempsey, L. (1996) ROADS to Desire: some UK and other European metadata and resource discovery projects, *D-Lib Magazine*, July, available at www.dlib.org/dlib/july96/07dempsey.html.

Dempsey, L. and Heery, R. (1997) *A review of metadata: a survey of the current resource description formats*, Work Package 3 of Telematics for Research project DESIRE (RE1004), available at www.ukoln.ac.uk/metadata/desire/overview.

Dempsey, L. and Heery, R. (1998) Metadata: a current view of practice and issues, *Journal of Documentation*, **54** (2), 145–72.

Dempsey, L. and Weibel, S. L. (1996) The Warwick Metadata Workshop: a framework for the deployment of resource description, *D-Lib Magazine*, July/August, available at www.dlib.org/dlib/july96/07weibel.html.

Dempsey, L. et al. (1998) *eLib standards guidelines version 2.0*, available at www.ukoln.ac.uk/services/elib/papers/other/standards/version2/.

Department of Special Collections. University of California, Santa Barbara. Cylinder Digitization and Preservation pilot project www.library.ucsb.edu/speccoll/pa/cylinders.html.

Dervin, B. (1977) Useful theory for librarianship: communication, not information, *Drexel Library Quarterly*, **13** (3), 16–32.

DESIRE
    www.desire.org.

DESIRE (n.d.) *Information Gateways handbook*, available at www.desire.org/handbook/.

Dialog (2002) *Dialog pricing information*, available at http://products.dialog.com/products/dialog/dial_pricing.html.

Diamond, W. and Pease, B. (2001) Digital reference: a case study of question types in an academic library, *Reference Services Review*, 29 (3), 210–19.

DIGILIB
www.architect.uq.edu.au/Digilib/info.html.

Digital Divide Network (2002a) *Digital divide basics fact sheet*, available at www.digitaldividenetwork.org/content/stories/index.cfm?key=168.

Digital Divide Network (2002b) *Knowledge to help everyone succeed in the digital age*, available at
www.digitaldividenetwork.org/.

Digital Libraries Initiatives (2002) *DLI2: Digital Libraries Initiative Phase 2*, available at
www.dli2.nsf.gov/projects.html.

Dilevko, J. (2001) An ideological analysis of digital reference service models, *Library Trends*, **50** (2), 218–44.

Dillon, A. (1999) Evaluating on TIME: a framework for the expert evaluation of digital library interface usability, *International Journal on Digital Libraries*, **2** (2/3), 170–7.

Document Object Model (DOM)
www.w3.org/DOM/.

Downie, J. S. and Nelson, M. (2000) Evaluation of a simple and effective music information retrieval system. In *Proceedings of ACM SIGIR Conference on Research and Development in Information Retrieval*, New York, ACM.

Downs, R. R. and Friedman, E. A. (1999) Digital library support for scholarly research, *Information Processing and Management*, **35** (3), 281–91.

Duval, E. et al. (2002) Metadata principles and practicalities, *D-Lib Magazine*, **8** (4), available at
www.dlib.org/dlib/april02/weibel/04weibel.html.

Eakins, J. and Graham, M. (1999) *Content-based image retrieval :a report to the JISC Technology Applications Programme*, available at
www.unn.ac.uk/iidr/report.html.

EBONI
http://ebooks.strath.ac.uk/eboni/overview.html.

EEVL: the internet guide to engineering, mathematics and computing
www.eevl.ac.uk.

eLib: Electronic Libraries programme
www.ukoln.ac.uk/services/elib/.

eLib (1998) *The eLib Phase 3 programme: hybrid libraries and large scale resource discovery and digital preservation*, available at www.ukoln.ac.uk/services/elib/background/pressreleases/summary2.html.

Ellis, D. (1989) A behavioural model for information retrieval system design, *Journal of Information Science*, **15**, 237–47.

Ellis, D. and Vasconcelos, A. (2000) The relevance of facet analysis for world wide web subject organization and searching. In Thomas, A. and Shearer, J. R. (eds), *Internet searching and indexing: the subject approach*, New York, Haworth Press, 97–114.

Engineering E-Library, Sweden: the Swedish Universities of Technology Libraries http://eels.lub.lu.se/.

Etzioni, O. and Weld, D. (2001) Automatic reference librarians for the world wide web, available at www.cs.odu.edu/~dlibuser/nsf/dlib2/dli23/.

The Extensible Stylesheet Language (XSL) www.w3.org/Style/XSL/.

Flecker, D. (2001) Preserving scholarly e-journals, *D-Lib Magazine*, **7** (9), available at www.dlib.org/dlib/september01/flecker/09flecker.html.

Ford, N. (1999) Information retrieval and creativity: towards support for the original thinker, *Journal of Documentation*, **55** (5), 528–42.

Ford, N., Miller, D. and Moss, N. (2001) The role of individual differences in Internet searching: an empirical study, *Journal of the American Society for Information Science and Technology*, **52** (12), 1049–66.

Fosmire., M. and Yu, S. (2000) Free scholarly electronic journals: how good are they?, *Issues in Science and Technology Librarianship*, (Summer), available at www.library.ucsb.edu/istl/00-summer/refereed.html.

Fox, E. A. (1999) Digital Libraries Initiative (DLI) projects 1994–1999. American Society for Information Science, *Bulletin of the American Society for Information Science*, **26** (1), 7–11.

Fox, E. A. and Powell, J. (1998) Multilingual federated searching across heterogeneous collections, *D-Lib Magazine*, September, available at www.dlib.org/dlib/september98/powell/09powell.html.

Fox, E. and Sornil, O. (1999) Digital libraries. In Baeza-Yates, R. and Ribeiro-Neto, B. (eds) (1999) *Modern information retrieval*, New York, ACM Press, 415–32.

Fox, E. A. and Urs, S. (2002) Digital libraries. In Cronin, B. (ed.) *Annual review of information science and technology (ARIST)*, vol. 36, Medford, NJ, Information Today Inc. on behalf of ASIST, 503–89.

Fox, E. A. et al. (2001a) Networked Digital Library of Theses and Dissertations: bridging the gaps for global access. Part 1, Mission and progress, *D-Lib Magazine*, **7** (9), available at www.dlib.org/dlib/september01/suleman/09suleman-pt1.html.

Fox, E. A. et al. (2001b) Networked Digital Library of Theses and Dissertations: bridging the gaps for global access. Part 2, Services and research, *D-Lib Magazine*, **7** (9), available at www.dlib.org/dlib/september01/suleman/09suleman-pt2.html.

Friedlander, A. (2002) The National Digital Information Infrastructure Preservation Program: expectations, realities, choices and progress to date, *D-Lib Magazine*, **8** (4), available at www.dlib.org/dlib/april02/friedlander/04friedlander.html.

Furnas, G. W. et al. (1987) The vocabulary problem in human-system communication, *Communications of ACM*, **30** (11), 964–71.

Gambles, A. (2000) Put yourself in the PIE – the HeadLine personal information environment, *D-Lib Magazine*, **6** (4), available at www.dlib.org/dlib/april00/04inbrief.html.

Gambles, A. (2001) The HeadLine personal information environment: evaluation Phase One, *D-Lib Magazine*, **7** (3), available at www.dlib.org/dlib/march01/gambles/03gambles.html.

Gardner, M. and Pinfield, S. (2001) Database-backed library web sites: a case study of the use of PHP and MySQL at the University of Nottingham, *Program*, **35** (1), 33–42.

Getty Research Institute (2000) *Art and architecture thesaurus browser*, available at www.getty.edu/research/tools/vocabulary/aat/index.html.

Gill, T. (1998) Metadata and the world wide web. In Baca, M. (ed.), *Introduction to metadata: pathways to digital information*, Los Angeles, CA, Getty Information Institute, 9–18.

Gilliland-Swetland, A. (1998) Defining metadata. In Baca, M. (ed.), *Introduction to metadata: pathways to digital information*, Los Angeles, CA, Getty Information Institute, 1–8.

Gilliland-Swetland, A. J. and Eppard, P. B. (2000) Preserving the authenticity of contingent digital objects: the InterPARES project, *D-Lib Magazine*, **6**

(7/8), available at www.dlib.org/dlib/july00/eppard/07eppard.html.

Gladney, H. M. (1997) Safeguarding digital library contents and users: document access control, *D-Lib Magazine*, June, available at www.dlib.org/dlib/june97/ibm/06gladney.html.

Gladney, H. M. (1998) Safeguarding digital library contents and users: interim retrospect and prospects, *D-Lib Magazine*, July, available at www.dlib.org/dlib/july98/gladney/07gladney.html.

Gladney, H. M. (1999) Digital dilemma: intellectual property: synopsis and views on the study by the National Academies' Committee on Intellectual Property Rights and the Emerging Information Infrastructure, *D-Lib Magazine*, **5** (12), available at www.dlib.org/dlib/december99/12gladney.html.

Gladney, H. M. and Lotspiech, J. B. (1997) Safeguarding digital library contents and users: assuring convenient security and data quality, *D-Lib Magazine*, May, available at www.dlib.org/dlib/may97/ibm/05gladney.html.

Gladney, H. M., Mintzer, F. C. and Schiattarella, F. (1997) Safeguarding digital library contents and users: digital images of treasured antiquities, *D-Lib Magazine*, July, available at www.dlib.org/dlib/july97/vatican/07gladney.html.

Gladney, H. M. et al. (1994) *Digital library: gross structure and requirements: report from a March 1994 workshop*, available at www.csdl.tamu.edu/DL94/paper/fox.html.

Gordon, M. and Pathak, P. (1999) Finding information on the world wide web: the retrieval effectiveness of web search engines, *Information Processing and Management*, **35** (2), 141–80.

Gorman, P. et al. (2000) Bundles in the wild: managing information to solve problems and maintain situation awareness, *Library Trends*, **49** (2), 266–89.

Gould, S. and Ebdon, R. (1999) *IFLA/UNESCO survey on digitisation and preservation*, IFLA.

Granger, S. (2000) Emulation as a digital preservation strategy, *D-Lib Magazine*, **6** (10), available at www.dlib.org/dlib/october00/granger/10granger.html.

Greenstein, D. (2000) Digital libraries and their challenges, *Library Trends*, **49** (2), 290–303.

Griffin, S. M. (1999) Digital Libraries Initiative – Phase 2: fiscal year 1999 awards, *D-Lib Magazine*, 5 (7/8), available at www.dlib.org/dlib/july999/07griffin.html.

Grotke, A. (2002) *CDRS*, personal communication, 31 January 2002.

Gutenberg http://gutenberg.hwg.org/.

Haas, S. W. (1996) Natural language processing: toward large-scale robust systems. In Williams, M. E. (ed.), *Annual review of information science and technology (ARIST)*, vol. 31, Medford, NJ: Learned Information Inc. for the American Society for Information Science, 83–119.

Halliday, L. and Oppenheim, C. (2000a) Comparison and evaluation of some economic models of digital-only journals, *Journal of Documentation*, **56** (6), 660–73.

Halliday, L. and Oppenheim, C. (2000b) Economic models of digital only journals, *Serials*, **13** (2), 59–65.

Halliday, L. and Oppenheim, C. (2001a) Economic aspects of a national electronic reserve service, *Journal of Documentation*, **57** (3), 434–43.

Halliday, L. and Oppenheim, C. (2001b) Economic aspects of a resource discovery network, *Journal of Documentation*, **57** (2), 296–302.

Halliday, L. and Oppenheim, C. (2001c) Developments in digital journals, *Journal of Documentation*, **57** (2), 260–83.

Hammer, S. and Favaro, J. (1996) Z39.50 and the world wide web, *D-Lib Magazine*, March, available at www.dlib.org/dlib/march96/briefings/03indexdata.html.

Hamson, A. (2001) Case study: practical experiences of digitisation in the BUILDER hybrid library project, *Program*, **35** (3), 263–75.

Hansen, P. (1999) 8th DELOS Workshop on User Interfaces in Digital Libraries, *ERCIM News*, 36, available at www.ercim.org/publication/Ercim_News/enw36/hansen.html.

Hansen, P. and Karlgren, J. (1999) *8th DELOS Workshop on User Interfaces in Digital Libraries*, **5** (1), January, available at www.dlib.org/dlib/january99/01clips.html.

Harter, S. and Hert, C. (1997) Evaluation of information retrieval systems: approaches, issues and methods. In Williams, M. E. (ed.), *Annual review of information science and technology (ARIST)*, vol. 32, Medford, NJ, Learned Information, 3–94.

Hartland-Fox, B. and Dalton, P. (2002) eVALUEd – an evaluation model for

e-library developments, *Ariadne*, 31, available at
www.ariadne.ac.uk /issue31/evalued/intro.html.

Harvard University (2002) *Library preservation at Harvard: digitization*, available at
http://preserve.harvard.edu/resources/digital.html.

Harvard University Library Digital Library Initiative (n.d.) *Image reformatting*, available at
http://hul.harvard.edu/ldi/html/reformatting_image.html.

Harvard University Library Digital Library Initiative (n.d.) *Text reformatting*, available at
http://hul.harvard.edu/ldi/html/reformatting_text.html.

Hastings, K. and Tennant, R. (1996) How to build a digital librarian, *D-Lib Magazine*, November, available at
www.dlib.org/dlib/november96/ucb/11hastings.html.

Hayes, S. (1990) Serving the professional staff in higher education, *College & Research Libraries News*, **51**, 1059–61.

Haynes, D. et al. (1997) *Responsibility for digital archiving and long-term access to digital data*, British Library Research and Innovation Report 67, London, The British Library.

HeadLine
www.headline.ac.uk.

Hearst, M. (1999) User interfaces and visualization. In Baeza-Yates, R. and Ribeiro-Neto, B. (eds), *Modern information retrieval*, New York, ACM Press, 257–323.

HEDS (n.d.(a)) *Costing a digitisation project*, available at
http://heds.herts.ac.uk/resources/costing.html.

HEDS (n.d. (b)) *The HEDS matrix of potential cost factors*, available at
http://heds.herts.ac.uk/resources/matrix.html.

Hedstrom, M. (1998) *Issues and approaches to digital archiving: guidance and practice. Joint RLG and NPO Preservation Conference on Guidelines for Digital Imaging, 28–30 September 1998*, available at
www.rlg.org/preserv/joint/hedstrom/hedstrom.html.

HEIR Alliance (1995) *evaluation guideline for institutional information resources*, available at
www.educause.edu/collab/heirapapers/hei2000.html.

Hendley, T. (1998) *Comparison of methods and costs of digital preservation*, British Library Research and Innovation Report 106, London, The British Library.

HERON www.heron.ac.uk/.

Herzberg, A. (1998) Charging for online content. *D-Lib Magazine*, January, available at www.dlib.org/dlib/january98/ibm/01herzberg.html.

Hildreth, C. (1997) The use and understanding of keyword searching in an university online catalog, *Information Technology and Libraries*, **16**, 52–62.

Hildreth, C. (1998) Online library catalogs as IR systems: what can we learn from research? In Yates-Mercer, P. A. (ed.), *Future trends in information science and technology*, London, Taylor Graham, 9–25.

Hill, L. et al. (1997) User evaluation: summary of the methodologies and results for the Alexandria Digital Library, University of California at Santa Barbara. In Schwartz, C. and Rorvig, M. (eds) *Proceedings of the 60th ASIS Annual Meeting*, vol. 34, 225–43, Silver Springs, MD, American Society for Information Science.

Hill, L. L. et al. (2000) Alexandria Digital Library: user evaluation studies and system design, *Journal of the American Society for Information Science*, **51** (3), 246–59.

Hodge, G. (1999) *Digital electronic archiving: the state of the art and the state of the practice*, available at www.icsti.org/99ga/digarch99_TOCP.pdf.

Hodge, G. (2000) Best practices for digital archiving: an information life cycle approach, *D-Lib Magazine*, **6** (1), available at www.dlib.org/dlib/january00/01hodge.html.

Hodgkin, A. (2002) Integrated and aggregated reference services: the automation of drudgery, *D-Lib Magazine*, **8** (4), available at www.dlib.org/dlib/april02/hodgkin/04hodgkin.html.

Hoelscher, C. (1998) *How internet experts search for information on the web*, paper presented at the World Conference of the World Wide Web, Internet and Intranet, Orlando, FL, Association for the Advancement of Computing in Education, available at www.aace.org/pubs.

Holdsworth, D. (2001) *Architecture of CEDARS demonstrator*, available at www.leeds.ac.uk/cedars/archive/architecture.html.

Holdsworth, D. and Sergeant, D. (2000) *A blueprint for representation information in the OAIS Model*, available at http://esdis-it.gsfc.nasa.gov/MSST/conf2000/PAPERS/D02PA.PDF.

Holmes-Wong, D. (1999) Richness vs. reach: using technology to overcome economic impediments to reference services, *The Reference Librarian*, **66**, 201–11.

How much information (2000) available at www.sims.berkeley.edu/research/projects/how-much-info/.

Hudson, L. and Windsor, L. (1998) Providing access to electronic journals: the Ohio University experience, *Against the Grain*, **10** (3), 16–18.

Hunter, E. (2002) Classification: are we underdoing it? M@ilbox, *Update*, **1** (2), 33.

Hunter, G. S. (2002) The digital future: a look ahead, *Information Management Journal*, **36** (1), 70–2.

HyLife (2002a) *The hybrid library toolkit. The hybrid library*, available at http://hylife.unn.ac.uk/toolkit/The_hybrid_library.html.

HyLife (2002b) *The hybrid library toolkit. Interoperability*, available at http://hylife.unn.ac.uk/toolkit/Interoperability.html.

HyLife (2002c) *The HyLife hybrid library toolkit. Evaluation*, available at http://hylife.unn.ac.uk/toolkit/evaluation.htm.

HyLife (2002d) *The HyLife hybrid library toolkit. Information landscapes*, available at http://hylife.unn.ac.uk/toolkit/infoland2.html.

Ianella, R. (1996) Australian digital library initiatives, *D-Lib Magazine*, December, available at www.dlib.org/dlib/december96/12ianella.html.

IEL www.ieee.org/products/onlinepubs/iel/iel.html.

The IMesh Toolkit: an architecture and toolkit for distributed subject gateways www.imesh.org/toolkit/.

INFOMINE http://infomine.ucr.edu.

Information Processing and Management (1999) Special issue. Progress toward digital libraries: augmentation through integration, **35**, 219–420.

The Internet Archive: building an internet library www.archive.org/.

InterPARES: International Research on Permanent Authentic Records in Electronic Systems
www.interpares.org.

InterPARES2 Project (2002) *InterPARES2: experimental, interactive and dynamic records*, available at
www.interpares.org/ip2_index.cfm.

International Organization for Standardization (1996) *ISO 2709: 1996. Information and documentation – Format for Information Exchange*, 3rd edn, Geneva, International Organization for Standardization.

International Standards Organization (1986) *ISO 8879: 1986. Information processing – text and office systems – Standard Generalised Markup Language (SGML)*, Geneva, International Standards Organization.

An investigation into the digital preservation needs of universities and research funders, available at
www.ukoln.ac.uk/services/papers/bl/blri109/datrep.html#Heading2.

Janes, J. (2002) Digital reference: reference librarians' experiences and attitudes, *Journal of the American Society for Information Science and Technology*, **53** (7), 549–66.

Janes, J., Hill, C. and Rolfe, A. (2001) Ask-an-expert services analysis, *Journal of the American Society for Information Science and Technology*, **52** (13), 1106–21.

Jansen, B. and Pooch, U. (2001) A review of web searching studies and a framework for future research, *Journal of the American Society for Information Science and Technology*, **52** (3), 235–46.

Jansen, B., Spink, A. and Saracevic, T. (2000) A study of user queries on the web, *Information Processing and Management*, **36** (2), 207–27.

Jansen, B., Spink, A. and Saracevic, T. (2001) Searching the web: the public and their queries, *Journal of the American Society for Information Science and Technology*, **52** (3), 226–34.

Jenkins, C. and Morley, M. (eds) (1999) *Collection management in academic libraries*, London, Gower.

JISC (1998) *JISC Circular 15/98*, available at
www.jisc.ac.uk/pub98/c15_98.html.

JISC (1999) *Adding value to the UK's learning, teaching and research resources: the Distributed National Electronic Resource (DNER)*, available at
http://hylife.unn.ac.uk/toolkit/.

JISC (2000) Report of the Joint Funding Councils' Libraries Review Group,

JISC (Joint Information Systems Committee), available at
www.jisc.ac.uk/.

JISC (2001) *JISC NSF International Digital Library Initiative: a collaboration between the Joint Information Systems Committee (JISC) and the US National Science Foundation (NSF)*, available at
www.jisc.ac.uk/nsf/proj_0010.html.

JISC Multimedia File Formats Database
http://mvc.man.ac.uk/SIMA/mmffdb.html.

Jones, D. (1999) Collection development in the digital library. In Stern, D. (ed.) *Digital libraries: philosophies, technical design considerations, and example scenarios*, New York, Haworth Press, 27–37.

Jones, S. (2002) Classification: are we overdoing it?, *Update*, **1** (1), 24.

Journal of the American Society for Information Science (2000a) Special topic issue: Digital libraries – Part 1, **51** (3), 213–310.

Journal of the American Society for Information Science (2000b) Special topic issue: Digital libraries – Part 2, **51** (4), 311–413.

Jul, E. (1995) *OCLC Internet Cataloging Project*, available at
www.dlib.org/dlib/december95/briefings/12oclc.html.

Kahle, B., Prelinger, R. and Jackson M. E. (2001) Public access to digital material, *D-Lib Magazine*, **7** (10), available at
www.dlib.org/dlib/october01/kahle/10kahle.html.

Kahn, R. and Wilensky, R. (1995) *A framework for distributed digital object services*, available at
www.CNRI.Reston.VA.US/home/cstr/arch/k-w.html.

Kakimoto, T. and Kambayashi, Y. (1999) Browsing functions in three-dimensional space for digital libraries, *International Journal on Digital Libraries*, **2** (2&3), 68–78.

Kassler, M. (1966) Toward musical information retrieval, *Perspectives of New Music*, **4** (2), 59–67.

Kassler, M. (1970) MIR – a simple programming language for musical information retrieval. In Lincoln, H. B. (ed.) *The computer and music*, Ithaca, NY, Cornell University Press, 299–327.

Kengeri, R. et al. (1999) Usability study of digital libraries: ACM, IEEE-CS, NCSTRL and NDLTD, *International Journal on Digital Libraries*, **2** (2/3), 157–169.

Kochtanek, T. R. and Hein, K. K. (1999) Delphi study of digital libraries, *Information Processing and Management*, **35** (3), 245–54.

Korfhage, R. (1997) *Information storage and retrieval*, New York, John Wiley.

Kovács, A. et al. (2000) AQUA (Advanced Query User Interface Architecture). In Borbinha, J. and Baker, T. (eds), *Proceedings of the 4th European Conference on Research and Advanced Technology for Digital Libraries (ECDL 2000), Lisbon, Portugal, 18–20 September 2000*, Berlin, Springer, 372–5.

Kresh, D. N. (2000) Offering high quality reference service on the web: the Collaborative Digital Reference Service (CDRS), *D-Lib Magazine*, **6** (6), available at www.dlib.org/dlib/june00/kresh/06kresh.html.

Kresh, D. N. (2001) Libraries meet the world wide web: the Collaborative Digital Reference Service, *ARL*, **219** (December), 1–3, available at www.arl.org/newsltr/219/cdrs.html.

Kuhlthau, C. (1988a) Developing a model of the library search process: cognitive and affective aspects, *RQ*, **28** (2), 232–42.

Kuhlthau, C. (1988b) Longitudinal case studies of the information search process of users in libraries, *Library and Information Science Research*, **10**, 257–304.

Kuhlthau, C. et al. (1990) Validating a model of the search process: a comparison of academic, public and school library users, *Library and Information Science Research*, **12**, 5–31.

Kuny, T. (1998) The digital dark ages? Challenges in the preservation of electronic information, *International Preservation News*, **17**, (May), available at www.ifla.org/VI/4/news/17-98.htm#2.

Lagoze, C. (1996) The Warwick Framework: a container architecture for diverse sets of metadata, *D-Lib Magazine*, July/August, available at www.dlib.org/dlib/july96/lagoze/07lagoze.html.

Lagoze, C. and Fielding, D. (1998) Defining collections in distributed digital libraries, *D-Lib Magazine*, November, available at www.dlib.org/dlib/november98/lagoze/11lagoze.html.

Lagoze, C. and Van de Sompel, H. (2001a) *The Open Archives Initiative Protocol for Metadata Harvesting*, Open Archives Initiative, available at www.openarchives.org/OAI/openarchivesprotocol.html.

Lagoze, C. and Van de Sompel, H. (2001b) *The Open Archives Initiative: building a low cost interoperability framework*, paper presented at the Joint Conference on Digital Libraries, Roanoke VA, June 2001, available at www.openarchives.org/documents/oai.pdf.

Lagoze, C. et al. (1995) *Dienst: implementation reference manual*, available at http://cs-tr.cs.cornell.edu/Dienst/UI/1.0/Display/ncstrl.cornell/TR95-1514.

Lancaster, F. W. (1986) *Vocabulary control for information retrieval*, 2nd edn,, Arlington, VA: Information Resources Press Inc.

Lancaster, F. W. (1993) *If you want to evaluate your library*, 2nd edn, Urbana-Champaign, University of Illinois.

Landoni, M., Wilson, R. and Gibb, F. (2000a) From the visual book to the WEB book: the importance of design, *The Electronic Library*, **18** (6), 2000.

Landoni, M., Wilson, R. and Gibb, F. (2000b) From the visual book to the WEB book: the importance of good design. In Borbinha, J. and Baker, T. (eds), *Proceedings of the 4th European Conference on Research and Advanced Technology for Digital Libraries (ECDL 2000), Lisbon, Portugal, September 2000*, Berlin, Springer, 3305–14.

Landoni, M., Wilson, R. and Gibb, F. (2001) Looking for guidelines for the production of electronic textbooks, *Online Information Review*, **25** (3), 181–95.

Lange, H. R. and Winkler, B. J. (1997) Taming the internet: metadata, a work in progress. In Godden, I. (ed.) *Advances in Librarianship*, vol. 21, San Diego, Academic Press, 47–72.

Lankes, D., Collins, J. W. and Kasowitz, A. S. (eds) (2000) *Digital reference service in the new millennium: planning, management, and evaluation*, Neal-Schuman.

Large, A. and Moukdad, H. (2000) Multilingual access to web resources: an overview, *Program*, **34** (1), 43–58.

Law, D. (2002) Presidential address. An apology of a life. *Scottish Libraries*, **17** (1), 7–11.

Lawrence, G. W. et al. (2000*) Risk management of digital information: a file format investigation*, Washington, DC, CLIR.

Lee, H. et al. (2000) Implementation and analysis of several keyframe-based browsing interfaces to digital video. In Borbinha, J. and Baker, T. (eds), *Proceedings of the 4th European Conference on Research and Advanced Technology for Digital Libraries (ECDL 2000), Lisbon, Portugal, September 2000*, Berlin, Springer.

Lee, S. and Morris, W. (2000) Making friends with e-journals, *The Library Association Record*, 102 (7), 392–3.

Lee, S. D. (2001) *Digital imaging: a practical handbook*, Library Association Publishing.

Lee, W. and Chen, A. L. P. (2000) Efficient multi-feature index structures for music data retrieval. In Yeung, M. M., Yeo, B-L. and Bouman, C. A. (eds) *Proceedings of SPIE conference on storage and retrieval for image and video database*, Bellingham, WA, International Society for Optical Engineering, 177–88.

Lemstrom, K., Laine, P. and Perttu, S. (1999) Using relative interval slope in music information retrieval. In *Proceedings of the International Computer Music Conference, 22–28 October, 1999, Beijing, China*, available at www.cs.helsinki.fi/u/klemstrom/icmc99.ps.

Lesk, M. (1997) *Practical digital libraries: books, bytes and bucks*, San Francisco, CA, Morgan Kaufmann.

Lesk, M. (1999a) Perspectives on DLI-2 – growing the field, *D-Lib Magazine*, **5** (7/8), available at www.dlib.org/dlib/july99/07lesk.html.

Lesk, M. (1999b) Perspectives on DLI-2 – growing the field, *Bulletin of the American Society for Information Science*, **26** (1), available at www.asis.org/Bulletin/Oct-99/lesk.html.

Lesk, M. (1999c) *Preserving digital objects: recurrent needs and challenges*, available at www.lesk.com/mlesk/auspres/aus.html.

The Library of Congress (n.d.) *About the library*, available at www.loc.gov/about/.

Library Trends (2000) Special issue. Assessing digital library services (edited by Thomas A. Peters), **49** (2).

Lombardi, J. V. (2000) Academic libraries in a digital age, *D-Lib Magazine*, **6** (10), available at www.dlib.org/dlib/october00/lombardi/10lombardi.html.

Luk, R. W. P. et al. (2002) A survey in indexing and searching XML documents, *Journal of the American Society for Information Science and Technology*, **53** (6), 415–37.

Luther, J. (1998) *Full text journal subscriptions: an evolutionary process*, available at www.arl.org:591/luther.html.

McClelland, M. et al. (2002) Challenges for service providers when importing metadata in digital libraries, *D-Lib Magazine*, **8** (4), available at www.dlib.org/dlib/april02/mcclelland/04mcclelland.html.

Machovec, G. (1997) *Electronic journal market overview – March 1997*, available at
www.coalliance.org/reports/ejournal.htm.

McKiernan, G. (1995) CyberStacks[sm]: a 'library-organized' virtual science and technology reference collection, *D-Lib Magazine*, December, available at www.dlib.org/dlib/december95/briefings/12cyber.html.

McKiernan, G. (2001) *LiveRef[sm]: a registry of real-time digital reference services*, available at
www.public.iastate.edu/~CYBERSTACKS/LiveRef.htm.

McLean, N. (2000) Matching people and information resources: authentication, authorisation and access management and experiences at Macquarie University, Sydney, *Program*, **34** (3), 239–55.

Majka, D. R. (2000) The 'great exchange': the economic promise and peril of the digital library, *The Bottom Line: Managing Library Finances*, **13** (2), 68–74.

Marchionini, G. (1992) Interfaces for end-user information seeking, *Journal of the American Society for Information Science*, **43** (2), 156–63.

Marchionini, G. (1995) Information seeking in electronic environments, Cambridge, Cambridge University Press.

Marchionini, G. (1998) Research and development on digital libraries. In *Encyclopedia of Information and Library Science*, vol. 63, New York, Marcel Dekker, 259–79.

Marchionini, G. (2000) Evaluating digital libraries: a longitudinal and multifaceted view, *Library Trends*, **49** (2), 304–33.

Marchionini, G. and Fox, E. A. (1999) Editorial: Progress toward digital libraries: augmentation through integration, *Information Processing and Management*, **35** (3), 219–25.

Marchionini, G. and Komlodi, A. (1998) Design of interfaces for information seeking. In Williams, M. E. (ed.), *Annual review of information science and technology (ARIST)*, vol. 33, Medford, NJ, Learned Information, 89–130.

Maron, M. E. and Kuhns, J. L. (1960) On relevance, probabilistic indexing and information retrieval, *Journal of the ACM*, **7**, 216–44.

Meadow, C. T., Boyce, B. R. and Kraft, D. H. (2000) *Text information retrieval systems*, 2nd edn, San Diego, Academic Press.

Meyyappan, N., Chowdhury, G. G. and Foo, S. (2000) A review of twenty digital libraries, *Journal of Information Science*, **26** (5), 331–48.

Meyyappan, N., Chowdhury, G. G. and Foo, S. (2001a) An architecture of a user-centred digital library for the academic community, In Chen, C. C. (ed.), *Global digital library development in the new millennium: fertile ground for distributed cross-disciplinary collaboration. NIT 2001 12th International Conference on New Information Technology, Tsinghua University in Beijing, China, May 29–31, 2001*, Beijing, Tsinghua University Press, 175–82.

Meyyappan, N., Chowdhury, G. G. and Foo, S. (2001b) Design and development of a user-centred digital library system: some basic guidelines. In Urs, S., Rajashekar, T. B. and Raghavan, K. S. (eds), *Digital libraries: dynamic landscape for knowledge creation, access and management: the 4th International Conference on Asian Digital Libraries, Bangalore, December 10–12, 2001*, Bangalore, University of Mysore, 135–48.

Meyyappan, N., Chowdhury, G. G. and Foo, S. (2001c) Use of a digital work environment (DWE) prototype to create a user-centred university digital library, *Journal of Information Science*, **27** (4), 249–64.

Michalek, G. (2002) The Universal Library and the Million Book project. *D-Lib Magazine*, **8** (6), available at www.dlib.org/dlib/june02/06inbrief.html#MICHALEK

Michelle, B. and Wang, Q. (2000) A user-centered interface for information exploration in a heterogeneous digital library, *Journal of the American Society for Information Science*, **51** (3), 297–310.

Miller, E. (1998) An introduction to the Resource Discovery Framework, *D-Lib Magazine*, May, available at www.dlib.org/dlib/may98/miller/05miller.html.

Milstead, J. L. (1997) Use of thesauri in the full-text environment. In Cochrane, P. A. and Johnson, E. H. (eds), *Visualizing subject access for 21st century information resources. Proceedings of the 34th Annual Clinic on Library Applications of Data Processing, Graduate School of Library and Information Science, University of Illinois, Illinois, March 1997*, Urbana-Champaign, IL, University of Illinois.

Mintzer, F., Braudaway, G. W. and Bell, A. E. (1998) Opportunities for watermarking Standards, *Communications of the ACM*, 41 (7), 56–65.

Mintzer, F., Lotspiech, J. and Morimoto, N. (1997) Safeguarding digital library contents and users: digital watermarking, *D-Lib Magazine*, December, available at www.dlib.org/dlib/december97/ibm/12lotspiech.html.

Mitchell, S. (1999) Interface design considerations in libraries. In Stern, D. (ed.) *Digital libraries: philosophies, technical design considerations, and example scenarios*, New York, Haworth Press, 131–81.

Mitchell, S. and Mooney, M. (1996) INFOMINE: a model web-base academic virtual library, *Information Technology and Libraries*, **15** (1), 20–5.

MODELS: MOving to Distributed Environments for Library Services www.ukoln.ac.uk/dlis/models/.

Muir, A. (2001a) Digital library research. In Scammell, A. (ed.), *Handbook of information management*, 8th edn, London, Aslib, 498–512.

Muir, A. (2001b) Legal deposit and preservation of digital publications: a review of research and development activity, *Journal of Documentation*, **57** (5), 652–82.

Myaeng, S. et al. (2001) A protocol-based architecture for federated searching in digital libraries. In Urs, S., Rajashekar, T. B. and Raghavan, K. S. (eds), *Digital libraries: dynamic landscapes for knowledge creation, access and management: the 4th International Conference on Asian Digital Libraries, Bangalore, December 10–12, 2001*, Bangalore, University of Mysore, 116–24.

MyLibrary@NCState (2001) http://my.lib.ncsu.edu/.

Mylonas, E. (1987) *Using Perseus in a variety of educational settings*, Perseus Working Papers 2, Cambridge, MA, unpublished.

National Library of Canada. *Digital Library of Canada* www.nlc-bnc.ca/index-e.html.

National Science Foundation (n.d.) *International digital libraries collaborative research and applications testbeds*, NSF-02-085, available at www.nsf.gov/pubs/2002/nsf02085/nsf02085.html.

Negishi, M. (2002) Mobile access to libraries: librarians and users experience for I-mode applications in libraries: paper presented at the 68th IFLA Conference, Glasgow, 18–24 August, not yet published.

Networked Digital Library of Theses and Dissertations www.ndltd.org.

Nicholas, D. (1996) *Assessing information needs*, London, Aslib.

Nicholas, D. and Dobrowolski, T. (2001) The information 'player': a new and timely term for the digital information user. In Scammell, A. (ed.), *Handbook of information management*, London, Aslib, 513–22.

Nichols, D. et al. (2000) DEBORA: developing an interface for support collaboration in a digital library. In Borbinha, J. and Baker, T. (eds), *Proceedings of the 4th European Conference on Research and Advanced Technology for Digital Libraries (ECDL 2000), Lisbon, Portugal, September 2000*, Berlin, Springer, 239–48.

Nicholson, S. (1998) A proposal for categorization and nomenclature for web search tools. In Iyer, H. (ed.), *Electronic resources: use and user behaviour*, Haworth Press, 9–28.

Noble, I. (ed.) (2001) *HeadLine evaluation report – PIE evaluation report: Phase Two*, available at www.headline.ac.uk/public/ph2guestreport.pdf.

Oard, D. W. (1997) Serving users in many languages: cross-language information retrieval for digital libraries, *D-Lib Magazine*, December, available at www.dlib.org/dlib/december97/oard/12oard.html.

Oard, D. W and Diekama, A. R. (1998) Cross-language information retrieval. In Williams, M. E. (ed.), *Annual review of information science and technology (ARIST)*, vol. 33, Medford, NJ, Learned Information Inc. for the American Society for Information Science, 223–56.

Oder, N. and Weissman, S. (2001) The shape of e-reference, *Library Journal*, **126** (2), 46–50.

Oliveira, J. L., Goncalves, M. A. and Medeiros, C. B. (1999) A framework for designing and implementing the user interface of a geographic digital library, *International Journal on Digital Libraries*, **2** (2/3), 190–206.

Open Archives Initiative www.openarchives.org/.

Oppenheim, C. (1996) Paying for scholarly communication – the future as a guide to the past, *Interlending and Document Supply*, **24**, 30.

Oppenheim, C. (1997) Copyright issues in projects funded by the Electronic Libraries programme, *Ariadne*, **7**, available at www.ariadne.ac.uk/issue7/copyright-corner/intro.html.

Oppenheim, C. and Smithson, D. (1999) What is the hybrid library?, *Journal of Information Science*, **25** (2), 97–112.

Oudet, B. (1997) Multilingualism on the internet, *Scientific American*, **276** (3), 77–8.

Palmer, D. and Robinson, B. (2001) Agora: the hybrid library from a users perspective, *Ariadne*, **26**, available at www.ariadne.ac.uk /issue26/case-studies/intro.htm.

Pan, R. and Higgins, R. (2001) Digitisation projects at Durham University Library – an overview, *Program*, **35** (4), 355–68.

Pelic@n
www.jisc.ac.uk/dner/development/projects/pelican/.

The People's Network
www.peoplesnetwork.gov.uk/.

Perseus
www.perseus.tufts.edu.

Peters, C. and Picchi, E. (1997) Across languages, across cultures: issues in multilinguality and digital libraries, *D-Lib Magazine*, May, available at www.dlib.org/dlib/may97/peters/05peters.html.

Peters, T. H. (2000) Introduction to the special issue on assessing digital library services, *Library Trends*, **49** (2), 221–27.

Petersen, R. J. (1999) Copyright ownership issues and higher education policies, *D-Lib Magazine*, available at www.dlib.org/dlib/june99/06clips.html.

Pinfield, S. (2001a) *Beyond eLib: lessons from Phase 3 of the Electronic Libraries programme*, available at www.ukoln.ac.uk/services/elib/papers/other/intro.html#elib-evaluation.

Pinfield, S. (2001b) Managing electronic library services: current issues in UK higher education institutions, *Ariadne,* **29**, available at www.ariadne.ac.uk/issue29/pinfield/.

Pinfield, S. et al. (1998) Realizing the hybrid library, *D-Lib Magazine*, October, available at www.dlib.org/dlib/october98/10pinfield.html.

Pitti, D. (1999) Encoded Archival Description: an introduction and overview, *D-Lib Magazine*, **5** (11), November, available at www.dlib.org/dlib/november99/11pitti.html.

Pollitt, A. (2002) Still the name of the game. M@ailbox, *Update*, **1** (2), 33.

Porteous, J. (1997) Plugging into electronic journals, *Nature*, **389**, 137–8.

Powell, J. and Fox, E. A. (1998) Multilingual federated searching across heterogeneous collections, *D-Lib Magazine*, September, available at www.dlib.org/dlib/september98/powell/09powell.html.

Puglia, S. (1999) The costs of digital imaging projects, *RLG Diginews*, **3** (5), available at www.rlg.ac.uk/preserv/diginews/diginews3-5.html#feature.

Rada, R. (1991) Focus on links: a holistic view of hypertext, *Knowledge Organization*, **18** (1), 13–18.

Ramsden, A. (1997) Copyright management technologies: the key to unlocking digital works?, *Ariadne*, **10**, available at www.ariadne.ac.uk/issue10/copyright/.

Ramsden, A. et al. (eds) (1998) *ELINOR Electronic Library Project*, London, Bowker-Saur.

Ranganathan, S. R. (1931) *Five laws of library science*, Madras, Madras Library Association.

Rao, R. et al. (1995) Rich interaction in the digital library, *Communications of the ACM*, **38** (4), 29–39.

Rasmussen, E. (1999) Libraries and bibliographic systems. In Baeza-Yates, R. and Ribeiro-Neto, B. (eds) *Modern information retrieval*, New York, ACM Press, 397–413.

RDN
www.rdn.ac.uk/about/.

Reich, V. and Rosenthal, D. S. H. (2001) LOCKSS: a permanent web publishing and access system, *D-Lib Magazine*, **7** (6), available at www.dlib.org/dlib/june01/reich/06reich.html.

Reich, V. and Winograd, T. (1995) *Working assumptions about the digital library*, available at http://dbpubs.stanford.edu:8090/pub/1995-52.

Reid, G. (2000) The digitisation of heritage material: arguing for an interpretative approach based on the experience of the Powys Digital History Project, *Program*, **34** (2), 143–58.

Renardus
www.renardus.org.

Research Libraries Group (RLG)
www.rlg.ac.uk.

Research Libraries Group and OCLC (2002) *Trusted digital repositories: attributes and responsibilities, an RLG–OCLC report*, available at www.rlg.org/longterm/repositories.pdf.

Richardson, J. et al. (2000) 'Ask a Librarian' electronic reference services: the importance of corporate culture, communication and service attitude, *LASIE (Library Automated Systems Information Exchange)*, **31** (4), 25–37.

The RIDING Gateway
www.riding.ac.uk/.

Rijsbergen, C. J. von (1979) *Information retrieval*, 2nd edn, London, Butterworth.

Roberts, S. A. (2001) Trends and developments in financial management of collections in academic and research libraries, *The Bottom Line: Managing Library Finances*, **14** (3), 152–64.

Robertson, G. G., Card, S. K. and Mackinlay, J. D. (1993) Information visualization using 3D interactive animation, *Communications of the ACM*, **36** (4), 57–71.

Robertson, S. E. and Sparck Jones, K. (1976) Relevance weighting of search terms, *Journal of the American Society for Information Science*, **27** (3), 129–46.

Rogers, M. (2001) Academic libraries test web-based reference, *Library Journal*, **126** (12), 25.

Ross, S. and Gow, A. (1999) *Digital archaeology: the recovery of digital materials at risk*, British Library Research and Innovation Report 108, London, The British Library.

Rothenberg, J. (2001) *Preserving authentic digital information*, available at www.clir.org/pubs/reports/pub92/rothenberg.html.

Rowland, F., McKnight, C. and Meadows, A. J. (eds) (1995) *Project ELVYN: an experiment in electronic journal delivery: facts, figures, and findings*, London, Bowker-Saur.

Rowlands, I. and Bawden, D. (1999) Building the digital library on solid research foundations, *Aslib Proceedings*, **51** (8), 275–82.

Rowley, J. (1999) What is knowledge management?, *Library Management*, **20** (8), 416–20.

Rowley, J. and Farrow, J. (2000) *Organizing knowledge: an introduction to managing access to information*, 3rd edn, Aldershot, Gower.

Rudner, L. (2000) Who is going to mine digital library resources? And how?, *D-Lib Magazine*, 6 (5), available at www.dlib.org/dlib/may00/rudner/05rudner.html.

Ruiz, M. E. and Srinivasan, P. (1998) Cross-language information retrieval: an analysis of errors. In Preston, C. M. (ed.), *Proceedings of the 61st ASIS Annual Meeting, Pittsburgh, PA, October 25–29*, Silver Spring, MD, American Society for Information Science and Technology, 153–65.

Rusbridge, C. (1995) The UK electronic libraries programmes: project briefings and updates, *D-Lib Magazine*, December, available at www.dlib.org/dlib/december95/briefings/12uk.html.

Rusbridge, C. (1998) Towards the hybrid library, *D-Lib Magazine*, July, available at
www.dlib.org/dlib/july98/rusbridge/07rusbridge.html.

Rusbridge, C. (2001) After eLib, *Ariadne*, **26**, available at
www.ariadne.ac.uk/issue26/chris/intro.htm.

Russell, K. and Sergeant, D. (1999) The CEDARS project: implementing a model for distributed digital archives, *RLG DigiNews*, **3** (3), available at www.rlg.ac.uk/preserv/diginews/diginews3-3.html.

Russell, R., Gardner, T. and Miller, P. (1999) *MIA requirements analysis study: hybrid information environments – overview and requirements*, available at www.ukoln.ac.uk/dlis/models/requirements/overview/.

Sairamesh, J. et al. (1996) Economic framework for pricing and charging in digital libraries, *D-Lib Magazine*, February, available at www.dlib.org/dlib/february96/forth/02sairamesh.html.

Salton, G. (1971) *The SMART retrieval system – experiments in automatic document processing*, New Jersey, Prentice Hall Inc.

Salton, G. (1989) *Automatic text processing: the transformation, analysis and retrieval of information by computer*, Reading, MA, Addison-Wesley.

Salton, G. and Buckley, C. (1988) Term-weighting approaches in automatic retrieval, *Information Processing and Management*, **24** (5), 513–23.

Salton, G. and McGill, M. J. (1983) *Introduction to modern information retrieval*, Auckland, McGraw-Hill Book Co., 1983.

Saracevic, T. (2000) Digital library evaluation: toward evolution of concepts, *Library Trends*, **49** (2), 350–69.

Saracevic, T. (2002) *D-Lib Edu: resources for education in digital libraries*, available at
www.scils.rutgers.edu/~tefko/D_LibEdu_home.htm.

Saracevic, T. and Dalbello, M. (2001) *A survey of digital library education: Libraries in the Digital Age* (LIDA, 2000), Dubrovnik, Croatia, 23–26 May 2001; also *Libraries in the Digital Age*, (LIDA, 2001) (to be presented at the 2001 Annual Meeting of the American Society for Information Science and Technology, Washington DC, 4–8 November 2001), available at www.ffzg.hr/infoz/lida/lida2001/present/saracevic_dalbello.doc.

Saracevic, T. and Kantor, P. (1997a) Studying the value of library and information services. I. Establishing a theoretical framework, *Journal of the American Society for Information Science*, **48** (6), 527–42.

Saracevic, T. and Kantor, P. (1997b) Studying the value of library and information services. II. Methodology and taxonomy, *Journal of the American Society for Information Science*, **48** (6), 543–63.

Savage-Knepshield, P. A. and Belkin, N. J. (1999) Interaction in information retrieval: trends over time, *Journal of the American Society for Information Science*, **50** (12), 1067–82.

Scardellato, K. (2001) Case study: experiences in developing and maintaining the Virtual Reference Library at Toronto Public Library, *Program*, **35** (2), 167–80.

Schoonbaert, D. (1998) Biomedical journals and the world wide web, *The Electronic Library*, **16** (2), 95–103.

Schwartz, C. (2001) *Sorting out the web: approaches to subject access*, Westport, Ablex Publishing.

SCONUL (1999) *Information skills in higher education*, SCONUL position paper, available at www.sconul.ac.uk/publications/99104Rev1.doc.

The Scorpion Project http://orc.rsch.oclc.org:6109/.

Scout Report Signpost (2000), available at www.ilrt.bris.ac.uk/mirrors/scout/addserv/signpost/help.html#01.

Seadle, M. (2000) Project ethnography: an anthropological approach to assessing digital library services, *Library Trends*, **49** (2), 370–85.

Seadle, M. (2001) Copyright in the networked world: digital legal deposit, *Library Hi Tech*, **19** (3), 299–303.

Shafer, K. (1997) *Scorpion helps catalog the web*, available at http://orc.rsch.oclc.org:6109/b-asis.html.

Sherman, C. (2000) *Reference resources on the web*, *Online*, **24** (1), 52–6.

Shimmon, R. (2001a) Can we bridge the digital divide?, *The Library Association Record*, **103** (11), 687–9.

Shimmon, R. (2001b) *From digital divide to digital opportunity*, available at www.unesco.org/webworld/points_of_view/shimmon.html.

Shiri, A., Chowdhury, G. and Revie, C. (2002a) Thesaurus-assisted search term selection and query expansion: a review of user-centred studies, *Knowledge Organization*, **29** (1), 1–19.

Shiri, A., Chowdhury, G. and Revie, C. (2002b) Thesaurus-enhanced search interfaces, *Journal of Information Science*, **28** (2), 111–22

Shneiderman, B. (1998a) Codex, memex. Genex: the pursuit of transformational technologies, *International Journal of Human–Computer Interaction*, **10** (2), 87–106.

Shneiderman, B. (1998b) *Designing the user interface: strategies for effective human–computer interaction*, 3rd edn, Reading, MA, Addison-Wesley.

Shneiderman, B. (1999) User interfaces for creativity support tools. In *Proceedings of the Third Conference on Creativity and Cognition, Loughborough*, New York, ACM Press, 15–22.

Shneiderman, B., Byrd, D. and Croft, W. B. (1997) Clarifying search: a user-interface framework for text searches, *D-Lib Magazine*, **3** (1), available at www.dlib.org/dlib/january97/retrieval/01shneiderman.html.

Shneiderman, B., Byrd, D. and Croft, W. B. (1998) Sorting out searching: a user-interface framework for text searches, *Communications of the ACM*, **41** (4), 95–8.

Sifter
http://sifter.indiana.edu/.

Simmons, P. and Hopkinson, A. (eds) (1992) *CCF/B: the common communication format for bibliographic information & CCF/F: the common communication format for factual information*, Paris, Unesco.

Sitts, M. A. (ed.) (2000) *Handbook for digital projects: a management tool for preservation and access*, Andover, MA, Northeast Document Conservation Center, available at www.nedcc.org/digital/dman.pdf.

Sloan, B. G. (1998) Service perspectives for the digital library remote reference services, *Library Trends*, **47** (1), 117–43.

Smith, A. (2002) *Evaluation of information resources*, available at www.ac.nz/~agsmith/evaln/evaln.htm.

Smith, B. (2001) Enhancing reference services through technology, *Legal Reference Services Quarterly*, **19** (1/2), 133–46.

Smith, G. (2001) Closing the digital divide, *Information World Review*, issue 172, available at http://proquest.umi.com.

Smith, L., McNab, R. and Witten, I. (1998) Sequence-based melodic comparison: a dynamic programming approach. In Hewlett, W. H. and Selfridge-Field, E. (eds), *Melodic similarity; concepts, procedures and applications*, Computing in Musicology vol. 11, Cambridge, MA, MIT Press, 101–17.

Smith, T. R. (1996) The meta-information environment of digital libraries, *D-Lib Magazine*, available at www.dlib.org/dlib/july96/new/07smith.html.

Social Science Information Gateway www.sosig.ac.uk.

Sornil, O. and Fox, E. A. (2001) Hybrid partitioned inverted indices for large-scale digital libraries. In Urs, S., Rajashekar, T. B. and Raghavan, K. S. (eds), *Digital libraries: dynamic landscapes for knowledge creation, access and management: the 4th International Conference on Asian Digital Libraries, Bangalore, December 10–12, 2001*, Bangalore, University of Mysore, 192–207.

Sparck Jones, K. and Willett, P. (eds) (1997) *Readings in information retrieval*, San Francisco, CA, Morgan Kaufmann Pub. Inc.

Spiller, D. (2000) *Providing materials for library users*, London, Library Association Publishing.

Spink, A. et al.. (2001) Searching the web: the public and their queries, *Journal of the American Society for Information Science and Technology*, **52** (3), 226–34.

Spink, A. et al. (2002a) Information seeking and mediated searching. Part 1. Theoretical framework and research design, *Journal of the American Society for Information Science and Technology*, **53** (9), 695–703.

Spink, A. et al. (2002b) Information seeking and mediated searching. Part 2. Uncertainty and its correlates, *Journal of the American Society for Information Science and Technology*, **53** (9), 704–15.

Spink, A. et al. (2002c) Information seeking and mediated searching. Part 3. Successive searching, *Journal of the American Society for Information Science and Technology*, **53** (9), 716–27.

Spink, A. et al. (2002d) Information seeking and mediated searching. Part 4. Cognitive style in information seeking, *Journal of the American Society for Information Science and Technology*, **53** (9), 728–35.

Sreenivasulu, V. (2000) The role of a digital librarian in the management of digital information systems (DIS), *The Electronic Library*, **18** (1), 12–20.

Stemper, J. A. and Butler, J. T. (2001) Developing a model to provide digital reference services, *Reference Services Review*, **29** (3), 172–88.

Stephens, D. O. (2000a) Digital preservation: a global information management problem, *Information Management*, **34** (3), 68.

Stephens, D. O. (2000b) Digital preservation in the United Kingdom, *Infor-*

mation Management Journal, **34** (4), 68–71.

Sturges, P., Teng, V. and Iliffe, V. (2001) User privacy in the digital library environment: a matter of concern for information professionals, *Library Management*, **22** (8, 9), 364–70.

Sugimoto, S. (2001) Helping information access across languages using simple tools: multilingual projects at ULIs and lessons learned. In Urs, S., Rajashekar, T. B. and Raghavan, K.S. (eds), *Digital libraries: dynamic landscapes for knowledge creation, access and management: the 4th International Conference on Asian Digital Libraries, Bangalore, December 10–12, 2001*, Bangalore, University of Mysore, 16–29.

Suleman, H. and Fox, E. A. (2001) A framework for building open digital libraries, *D-Lib Magazine*, **7** (12), available at www.dlib.org/dlib/december01/suleman/12suleman.html#OAI.

Sutcliffe, A. G. (1999) User-centred design for multimedia applications. In *Proceedings of the IEEE International Conference on Multimedia Computing and Systems, 1999*, available at http://dlib.computer.org/conferen/icmcs/0253/pdf/02539116.pdf.

Tanner, S. (2001) Librarians in the digital age: planning digitisation projects, *Program*, **35** (4), 327–37.

Tanner, S. and Smith, J. L. (1999) *Digitisation: how much does it really cost?*, paper for the digital resources for the humanities 1999 conference held at Kings College, London, 12–15 September 1999, available at http://heds.herts.ac.uk/resources/papers/drh99.pdf.

TASI (2001a) *File formats*, available at www.tasi.ac.uk/framework/capture/fileformat.html.

TASI (2001b) *Hardware and software*, available at www.tasi.ac.uk/framework/capture/hwandsw.html.

TASI (2001c) *Image handling and preparation*, available at www.tasi.ac.uk/framework/capture/imagehand.html.

TASI (2001d) *Welcome to the Technical Advisory Service for Images*, available at www.tasi.ac.uk.

Taylor, A. (1999) *The organization of information*, Englewood, CO, Libraries Unlimited Inc.

Tennant, R. (1999) Skills for the new millennium, *Library Journal*, **124** (1), 39.

Tennant, R. (2000) Selecting collections to digitise, *Library Journal*, **125** (19), 26.

Tenopir, C. (2001) Virtual reference services in a real world, *Library Journal*,

126 (12), 38–40.

Tenopir, C. and Ennis, L. A. (2001) Reference services in the new millennium, *Online*, **25** (4), 40–5.

Theng, Y. L. et al. (1999) Design guidelines and user-centred digital libraries. In Abiteboul, S. and Vercoustre, A. (eds), *Research and advanced technology for digital libraries: Proceedings of the 3rd European Conference on Digital Libraries (ECDL '99), Paris, France, September 22–24, 1999*, Berlin, Springer.

Thibadeau, R. (1996) Digital labels for digital libraries, *D-Lib Magazine*, October, available at
www.dlib.org/dlib/october96/cmu/10thibadeau.html.

THOMAS: legislative information on the internet
http://thomas.loc.gov/.

Tracking Footprints through an Information Space: leveraging the document selections of expert problem solvers
www.cse.ogi.edu/dot/research/footprints/.

Tseng, Y. H. (1999) Content-based retrieval for music collections. In *Proceedings of the 22nd Annual International ACM SIGIR Conference on Research and Development in Information Retrieval*, 1999, Berkeley, CA, New York, ACM Press, 176–82.

UC Berkeley Library (2001) *Critical evaluation of resources*, available at
www.lib.berkeley.edu/TeachingLib/Guides/Evaluation.html.

Uitdenbogerd, A. L. and Zobel, J. (1998) Manipulation of music for melody matching. In *Proceedings of the 6th ACM International Conference on Multimedia*, Bristol, UK, New York, ACM Press, 235–40.

UNIMARC manual: bibliographic format (1994) 2nd edn, London, K. G. Saur.

US Business Reporter
www.activemedia-guide.com/publishing_industry.htm.

US Department of Commerce. Economics and Statistics Administration. National Telecommunications and Information Administration (2002) *A nation online: how Americans are expanding their use of the internet*, Washington, DC, available at
www.ntia.doc.gov/ntiahome/dn/nationonline_020502.htm.

USA federally funded cooperative projects (n.d.) *D-Lib Magazine*, available at
www.dlib.org/projects.html#federal.

VADS: Visual Arts Data Service (2001) *Guides to good practice*, available at
http://vads.ahds.ac.uk/guides/index.html.

Varian, H. R. (1996) Pricing electronic journals, *D-Lib Magazine*, June, available at
www.dlib.org/dlib/june96/06varian.html.

Vellucci, S. L. (1998) Metadata. In Williams, M. E. (ed.) *Annual review of information science and technology (ARIST)*, vol. 33, Medford, NJ, Information Today Inc. on behalf of ASIS, 187–222.

The Virtual Reference Desk
www.vrd.org/about.shtml.

Voorhees, E. (1999) *The TREC-8 question answering track report*, available at http://trec.nist.gov/pubs/trec8/papers/qa-report.pdf.

Voorhees, E. (2000) *The TREC-9 question answering track report*, available at http://trec.nist.gov/pubs/trec9/papers/qa-report.pdf.

Voorhees, E. (2002) *Overview of TREC 2001*, available at http://trec.nist.gov/pubs/trec10/t10_proceedings.html.

VTLS Inc
www.vtls.com.

W3C Communications Team (2001) *XML in 10 points*, available at www.w3.org/XML/1999/XML-in-10-points.

Wade, M. (1998) HeadLine, *Ariadne*, **13**, available at www.ariadne.ac.uk/issue13/headline/.

Wasik, J. M. (2000) Asking the experts: digital reference and the virtual reference desk, *D-Lib Magazine*, **6** (5), available at www.dlib.org/dlib/may00/05inbrief.html#WASIK.

Wasik, J. M. and Lankes, R. D. (1999) The virtual reference desk: supporting education through a network of human expertise. In *Proceedings of the Internet Librarian Conference 1999, San Diego, CA, November 8, 1999*, Medford, NJ, Information Today, Inc., 198–202.

Waters, D. and Garrett, J. (1996) *Preserving digital information: report of the task force on archiving of digital information*, Washington, DC, CLIR.

Waters, D. J. (1998) What are digital libraries?, *CLIR Issues*, **4**, available at www.clir.org/pubs/issues/issues04.html#dlf.

Waugh, A. et al. (2000) Preserving digital information forever. In *Proceedings of the 5th ACM Conference on Digital Libraries, June 2–7, 2000, San Antonio, Texas*, New York, ACM Press, 175–84.

Weibel, S. (1995) Metadata: the foundations of resource description, *D-Lib Magazine*, July, available at www.dlib.org/dlib/July95/07weibel.html.

Weibel, S., Iannella, R. and Cathro, W. (1997) The 4th Dublin Core metadata workshop report. DC4, March 3–5, 1997, National Library of Australia, Canberra, *D-Lib Magazine*, June, available at www.dlib.org/dlib/june97/metadata/06weibel.html.

Weibel, S. et al. (1998) *Network Working Group Request for Comments: 2413*, available at www.ietf.org/rfc/rfc2413.txt.

Wheatley, P. (2001) Migration: a CAMiLEON discussion paper, *Ariadne*, **29**, available at www.ariadne.ac.uk/issue29/camileon/intro.html.

Whitelaw, A. and Joy, G. (2000a) *Summative evaluation of Phase 1 and 2 of the eLib initiative: overview*, Guildford: ESYS Consulting, available at www.ukoln.ac.uk/services/elib/info-projects/phase-1-and-2-evaluation/overview.pdf.

Whitelaw, A. and Joy, G. (2000b) *Summative evaluation of Phase 1 and 2 of the eLib initiative: final report*, Guildford: ESYS Consulting, available at www.ukoln.ac.uk/services/elib/info-projects/phase-1-and-2-evaluation/elib-fr-v1-2.pdf.

Whitelaw, A. and Joy, G. (2001) *Summative evaluation of phase 3 of the eLib initiative: final report*, available at www.ukoln.ac.uk/services/elib/papers/other/summative-phase-3/elib-eval-main.pdf.

Whitlatch, J. B. (2001) Evaluating reference services in the electronic age, *Library Trends*, **50** (2), 207–21.

Widharto [no forename] (2002) Challenges in accessing scientific and technological information in Indonesia during the economic crisis, *Bulletin of the American Society for Information Science and Technology*, **28** (4), 25–7.

Wiggins, R. (2001) Digital preservation: paradox and promise, *Library Journal*, 12–15.

Wilensky, R. (2000) Digital library resources as a basis for collaborative work, *Journal of the American Society for Information Science*, **51** (3), 228–45.

Wilson, B. (2001) Internet privacy: an oxymoron? Editorial, *D-Lib Magazine*, **7** (5), available at www.dlib.org/dlib/may01/05editorial.html.

Wilson, R. (2001) Evolution of portable electronic books, *Ariadne*, **29**, available at www.ariadne.ac.uk/issue29/wilson/.

Wilson, R. (2002) EBONI: designing effective electronic textbooks,

Library Hi Tech News, **19** (4), 41.

Wilson, R. and Landoni, M. (2001) Evaluating electronic textbooks: a methodology. In Constantopoulos, P. and Sølvberg, I. (eds), *5th European Conference on Research and Advanced Technology for Digital Libraries (ECDL 2001), Darmstadt, Germany, 4–9 September 2001*.

Wilson, T. (1981) On user studies and information needs, *Journal of Documentation*, **37** (1), 3–15.

Wilson, T. (1994) Information needs and uses: fifty years of progress? In Vickery, B. C. (ed.), *Fifty years of information progress: a Journal of Documentation review*, London, Aslib, 15–51.

Wilson, T. (1999) Models in information behaviour research, *Journal of Documentation*, **55** (3), 249–70.

Wiseman, N., Rusbridge, C. and Griffin, S. (1999) The Joint NSF/JISC International Digital Libraries Initiative, *D-Lib Magazine*, **5** (6), available at www.dlib.org/dlib/june99/06wiseman.html.

Witten, I. H. et al. (2002) The promise of digital libraries in developing countries, *The Electronic Library*, **20** (1), 7–13.

Witten, I. H., Bainbridge, D. and Boddie, Stefan J. (2001a) Greenstone: open-source digital library software, *D-Lib Magazine*, **7** (10), available at www.dlib.org/dlib/october01/witten/10witten.html.

Witten, I. H., Bainbridge, D. and Boddie, Stefan J. (2001b) Greenstone: open-source digital library software with end-user collection building, *Online Information Review*, **25** (5), 288–98.

Wondir (2002) *Welcome to Wondir Foundation*, available at wondir.org/index.html.

Woodyard, D. (2002) Digital preservation at the British Library, *Update*, **1** (2), 36–8.

Yang, S. C. (2001) An interpretative and situated approach to an evaluation of Perseus digital libraries, *Journal of the American Society for Information Science and Technology*, **52** (14), 1210–23.

Zhang, A. (1999) *Multimedia file formats on the internet: a beginner's guide for PC users*, available at www.lib.rochester.edu/multimed/contents.htm.

Zhang, Y. and Lee, K. (2001) Features and uses of a multilingual full-text electronic theses and dissertations (ETDs) system. In Williams, M. E. (ed.), The Global Conference and Exhibition on Electronic Information and Knowledge Management, *Proceedings of National Online Conference, May*

15–17, 2001, Medford, NJ, Information Today, 556–66.

Zhang, Y., Lee, K. and You, B.-J. (2001) Usage patterns of an electronic theses and dissertations system, *Online Information Review*, **25** (6), 370–7.

Zhao, D. (1998) The personal digital library. In Ramsden, A. (ed.) *ELINOR: electronic library project*, London, Bowker-Saur for The British Library, 97–103.

Zhao, D. G. and Ramsden, A. (1995) A. report on the ELINOR electronic library pilot (user aspect, system architecture, copyright management), *Information Services & Use*, **15** (3), 199–212.

Index

Introduction to Modern Information Retrieval

G. G. CHOWDHURY

An information retrieval system is designed to analyse, process and store sources of information and retrieve those that match a particular user's requirements. A bewildering range of techniques is now available to the information professional attempting to achieve this goal.

It is recognized that today's information professionals need to concentrate their efforts on learning the techniques of computerized information retrieval. However, it is this book's contention that it also benefits them to learn in depth the theory, techniques and tools that constitute the traditional approaches to the organization and processing of information. In fact much of this knowledge may still be applicable in the storage and retrieval of electronic information in digital library environments.

The text is one of the first to blend together the traditional and the new, and to give the student of information studies a comprehensive view of information retrieval. Unique in its scope, it covers the whole spectrum of information storage and retrieval, including:

- classification, cataloguing, subject indexing, abstracting and vocabulary control
- CD-ROM and online information retrieval, multimedia, hypertext and hypermedia
- expert systems and natural language processing techniques
- knowledge-based natural language text processing and user interface systems
- information retrieval in the context of the internet, the world wide web and the digital library environment.

Illustrated with many examples and comprehensively referenced for an international audience, this is an indispensable textbook for students of library and information studies undertaking courses in information retrieval, information organization, information use and knowledge-based systems at both undergraduate and postgraduate level. It is also an invaluable aid for information practitioners wishing to brush up on their skills and keep up to date with the latest techniques.

1999; 480pp; paperback; 1-85604-318-5; £39.95

Information Sources and Searching on the World Wide Web

G. G. CHOWDHURY AND SUDATTA CHOWDHURY

As the world wide web grows increasingly vast, more and more information sources are becoming available to information professionals: virtual libraries, e-journals, and bibliographic databases, to name but a few. Users of the web must not only be aware of what information is out there but also how they can find it quickly and retrieve the precise information they need. Learning about these sources and mastering information retrieval is essential for information professionals if they are to make the most of what the world wide web offers.

This comprehensive text aims to give students and information professionals a thorough overview of the various information sources and services available on the web and the corresponding tools and techniques required to search and retrieve the information effectively. It adopts an evaluative approach that assesses in detail both the usefulness and quality of these sources and search facilities, equipping the reader with the confidence and knowledge to make optimum use of the web. Topics covered include:

- an introduction to the web and its underlying technology
- search engines offering search and retrieval features
- directories
- web-based reference and information services
- electronic journal resources and e-books
- virtual library resources and subject gateways
- digital library collections
- search techniques
- issues and trends in the field of web information searching.

Full of examples and screenshots this is an invaluable text for students of library and information studies, as well as for any information practitioner wanting to learn how to use and get the best out of the wide variety of information sources and services available on the web.

2001; 192pp; paperback; 1-85604-394-0; £29.95

Searching CD-ROM and Online Information Sources

G.G. CHOWDHURY AND SUDATTA CHOWDHURY

Over the years most information sources have appeared in electronic form: on remote online databases; on CD-ROM; and most recently on the world wide web. Learning about these electronic sources and mastering the corresponding search and retrieval techniques is vital for information professionals faced with the mass of information available in the twenty-first century.

This timely and forward-looking text aims to alert information practitioners and students to the breadth of information available in CD-ROM and online format and provide them with the skills to make optimum use of these sources. The first part of the book discusses the basics of information searching and the information problem-solving process using OPACs, CD-ROMs and online search services. It evaluates different types of services, including reference and current awareness information services, and highlights the basic tools essential for effective searching. The second part describes the search features of selected subject-specific sources, including science and technology, social sciences and humanities, business, legal, patent, health and government electronic information sources. Topics covered include:

* basic information skills
* information services and subject study
* basic search techniques and tools
* common reference sources
* searching online public access catalogues, CD-ROM and online databases
* subject-specific information sources and searching
* trends in the electronic information sources and searching environment.

Useful appendices list selected CD-ROM and online information sources in a range of subject areas. Full of practical examples, screenshots and sample searches this is an indispensable text for all library and information practitioners wishing to become acquainted with the techniques of searching electronic information sources. It will also be invaluable to students of library and information studies undertaking courses in reference sources and information retrieval.

2001; 352pp; paperback; 1-85604-388-6; £39.95